HISTORY

OF THE

INTELLECTUAL DEVELOPMENT

OF

EUROPE.

By JOHN WILLIAM DRAPER, M.D., LL.D.,
Professor of Chemistry in the University of New York, Author of a "Treatise on Human Physiology," "Civil Policy of America," "History of the American Civil War," &c.

REVISED EDITION, IN TWO VOLUMES.

VOL. I.

NEW YORK:
HARPER & BROTHERS, PUBLISHERS,
FRANKLIN SQUARE.

PREFACE.

At the meeting of the British Association for the Advancement of Science, held at Oxford in 1860, I read an abstract of the physiological argument contained in this work respecting the mental progress of Europe, reserving the historical evidence for subsequent publication.

This work contains that evidence. It is intended as the completion of my treatise on Human Physiology, in which man was considered as an individual. In this he is considered in his social relation.

But the reader will also find, I think, that it is a history of the progress of ideas and opinions from a point of view heretofore almost entirely neglected. There are two methods of dealing with philosophical questions—the literary and the scientific. Many things which in a purely literary treatment of the subject remain in the background, spontaneously assume a more striking position when their scientific relations are considered. It is the latter method that I have used.

Social advancement is as completely under the control of natural law as is bodily growth. The life of an individual is a miniature of the life of a nation. These propositions it is the special object of this book to demonstrate.

No one, I believe, has hitherto undertaken the labour of arranging the evidence offered by the intellectual history of Europe in accordance with physiological principles, so as to illustrate the orderly progress of civilization, or collected the facts furnished by other branches of science with a view of enabling us to recognize clearly the conditions under which that progress takes place. This philosophical deficiency I have endeavoured in the following pages to supply.

Seen thus through the medium of physiology, history presents a new aspect to us. We gain a more just and thorough appreciation of the thoughts and motives of men in successive ages of the world.

In the Preface to the second edition of my Physiology, published in 1858, it was mentioned that this work was at that time written. The changes that have been since made in it have been chiefly with a view of condensing it. The discussion of several scientific questions, such as that of the origin of species, which have recently attracted public attention so strongly, has, however remained untouched, the principles offered being the same as presented in the former work in 1856.

New York, 1861.

PREFACE TO THE REVISED EDITION.

MANY reprints of this work having been issued, and translations published in various foreign languages, French, German, Russian, Polish, Servian, &c., I have been induced to revise it carefully, and to make additions wherever they seemed to be desirable. I therefore hope that it will commend itself to the continued approval of the public.

November, 1875.

CONTENTS.

CHAPTER I.

ON THE GOVERNMENT OF NATURE BY LAW.

The subject of this Work proposed.—Its difficulty.

Gradual Acquisition of the Idea of Natural Government by Law.—Eventually sustained by Astronomical, Meteorological, and Physiological Discoveries.—Illustrations from Kepler's Laws, the Trade-winds, Migrations of Birds, Balancing of Vegetable and Animal Life, Variation of Species and their Permanence.

Individual Man is an Emblem of Communities, Nations, and Universal Humanity.—They exhibit Epochs of Life like his, and, like him, are under the Control of Physical Conditions, and therefore of Law.

Plan of this Work.—The Intellectual History of Greece.—Its Five characteristic Ages.—European Intellectual History.

Grandeur of the Doctrine that the World is governed by Law . Page 1

CHAPTER II.

OF EUROPE: ITS TOPOGRAPHY AND ETHNOLOGY.

ITS PRIMITIVE MODES OF THOUGHT, AND THEIR PROGRESSIVE VARIATIONS, MANIFESTED IN THE GREEK AGE OF CREDULITY.

Description of Europe: its Topography, Meteorology, and secular Geological Movements.—Their Effect on its Inhabitants.

Its Ethnology determined through its Vocabularies.

Comparative Theology of Greece; the Stage of Sorcery, the Anthropocentric Stage.—Becomes connected with false Geography and Astronomy.—Heaven, the Earth, the Under World.—Origin, continuous Variation and Progress of Greek Theology.—It introduces Ionic Philosophy.

Decline of Greek Theology, occasioned by the Advance of Geography and Philosophical Criticism.—Secession of Poets, Philosophers, Historians.—Abortive public Attempts to sustain it.—Duration of its Decline.—Its Fall . . . . Page 23

CHAPTER III.

DIGRESSION ON HINDU THEOLOGY AND EGYPTIAN CIVILIZATION.

Comparative Theology of India; its Phase of Sorcery; its Anthropocentric Phase.

VEDAISM *the Contemplation of Matter, or Adoration of Nature, set forth in the Vedas and Institutes of Menu.—The Universe is God.—Transmutation of the World.—Doctrine of Emanation.—Transmigration.—Absorption.—Penitential Services.—Happiness in Absolute Quietude.*

BUDDHISM *the Contemplation of Force—The supreme impersonal Power.—Nature of the World—of Man.—The Passage of every thing to Nonentity.—Development of Buddhism into a vast monastic System marked by intense Selfishness.—Its practical Godlessness.*

EGYPT *a mysterious Country to the old Europeans.—Its History, great public Works, and foreign Relations.—Antiquity of its Civilization and Art.—Its Philosophy, hieroglyphic Literature, and peculiar Agriculture.*

Rise of Civilization in rainless Countries.—Geography, Geology, and Topography of Egypt.—The Inundations of the Nile lead to Astronomy.

Comparative Theology of Egypt.—Animal Worship, Star Worship.—Impersonation of Divine Attributes—Pantheism.—The Trinities of Egypt.—Incarnation.—Redemption.—Future Judgment.—Trial of the Dead.—Rituals and Ceremonies 56

CHAPTER IV.

GREEK AGE OF INQUIRY.

RISE AND DECLINE OF PHYSICAL SPECULATION.

IONIAN PHILOSOPHY, *commencing from Egyptian Ideas, identifies in Water, or Air, or Fire, the First Principle.—Emerging from the Stage of Sorcery, it founds Psychology, Biology, Cosmogony, Astronomy, and ends in doubting whether there is any Criterion of Truth.*

ITALIAN PHILOSOPHY *depends on Numbers and Harmonies.—It reproduces the Egyptian and Hindu Doctrine of Transmigration.*

ELEATIC PHILOSOPHY *presents a great Advance, indicating a rapid Approach to Oriental Ideas.—It assumes a Pantheistic Aspect.*

RISE OF PHILOSOPHY IN EUROPEAN GREECE.—*Relations and Influence of the Mediterranean Commercial and Colonial System.—Athens attains to commercial Supremacy.—Her vast Progress in Intelligence and Art.—Her Demoralization.—She becomes the Intellectual Centre of the Mediterranean.*

Commencement of the Athenian higher Analysis.—It is conducted by THE SOPHISTS, *who reject Philosophy, Religion, and even Morality, and end in Atheism.*

Political Dangers of the higher Analysis.—Illustration from the Middle Ages . . . . Page 94

CHAPTER V.

THE GREEK AGE OF FAITH.

RISE AND DECLINE OF ETHICAL PHILOSOPHY.

SOCRATES *rejects Physical and Mathematical Speculations, and asserts the Importance of Virtue and Morality, thereby inaugurating an Age of Faith.—His Life and Death.—The schools originating from his Movement teach the Pursuit of Pleasure and Gratification of Self.*

PLATO *founds the Academy.—His three primal Principles.—The Existence of a personal God.—Nature of the World and the Soul.—The ideal Theory, Generals or Types.—Reminiscence.—Transmigration.—Plato's political Institutions.—His Republic.—His Proofs of the Immortality of the Soul.—Criticism on his Doctrines.*

RISE OF THE SCEPTICS, *who conduct the higher Analysis of Ethical Philosophy.—Pyrrho demonstrates the Uncertainty of Knowledge.—Inevitable Passage into tranquil Indifference, Quietude, and Irreligion, as recommended by Epicurus.—Decomposition of the Socratic and Platonic Systems in the later Academies.—Their Errors and Duplicities.—End of the Greek Age of Faith* 143

CHAPTER VI.

THE GREEK AGE OF REASON.

RISE OF SCIENCE.

THE MACEDONIAN CAMPAIGN.—*Disastrous in its political Effects to Greece, but ushering in the Age of Reason.*

ARISTOTLE *founds the Inductive Philosophy.—His Method the Inverse of that of Plato.—Its great power.—In his own hands it fails for want of Knowledge, but is carried out by the Alexandrians.*

ZENO.—*His Philosophical Aim is the Cultivation of Virtue and Knowledge.—He is in the Ethical Branch the Counterpart of Aristotle in the Physical.*

FOUNDATION OF THE MUSEUM OF ALEXANDRIA.—*The great Libraries, Observatories, Botanical Gardens, Menageries, Dissecting Houses.—Its Effect on the rapid Development of exact Knowledge.—Influence of Euclid, Archimedes, Eratosthenes, Apollonius, Ptolemy, Hipparchus, on Geometry, Natural Philosophy, Astronomy, Chronology, Geography.*

Decline of the Greek Age of Reason . . . . Page 171

CHAPTER VII.

THE GREEK AGE OF INTELLECTUAL DECREPITUDE.

THE DEATH OF GREEK PHILOSOPHY.

Decline of Greek Philosophy: it becomes Retrospective, and in Philo the Jew and Apollonius of Tyana leans on Inspiration, Mysticism, Miracles.

NEO-PLATONISM *founded by Ammonius Saccas, followed by Plotinus, Porphyry, Iamblicus, Proclus.—The Alexandrian Trinity.—Ecstasy.—Alliance with Magic, Necromancy.*

The Emperor Justinian closes the philosophical Schools.

Summary of Greek Philosophy.—Its four Problems: 1. Origin of the World; 2. Nature of the Soul; 3. Existence of God; 4. Criterion of Truth.—Solution of these Problems in the Age of Inquiry—in that of Faith—in that of Reason—in that of Decrepitude.

Determination of the Law of Variation of Greek Opinion.—The Development of National Intellect is the same as that of Individual.

Determination of the final Conclusions of Greek Philosophy as to God, the World, the Soul, the Criterion of Truth.—Illustrations and Criticisms on each of these Points . . . . Page 207

CHAPTER VIII.

DIGRESSION ON THE HISTORY AND PHILOSOPHICAL INFLUENCES OF ROME.

PREPARATION FOR RESUMING THE EXAMINATION OF THE INTELLECTUAL PROGRESS OF EUROPE.

Religious Ideas of the primitive Europeans.—The Form of their Variations is determined by the Influence of Rome.—Necessity of Roman History in these Investigations.

Rise and Development of Roman Power, its successive Phases, territorial Acquisitions.—Becomes Supreme in the Mediterranean.—Consequent Demoralization of Italy.—Irresistible Concentration of Power.—Development of Imperialism.—Eventual Extinction of the true Roman Race.

Effect on the intellectual, religious, and social Condition of the Mediterranean Countries.—Produces homogeneous Thought.—Imperialism prepares the Way for Monotheism.—Momentous Transition of the Roman World in its religious Ideas.

Opinions of the Roman Philosophers.—Coalescence of the new and old Ideas.—Seizure of Power by the Illiterate, and consequent Debasement of Christianity in Rome 239

CHAPTER IX.

THE EUROPEAN AGE OF INQUIRY.

THE PROGRESSIVE VARIATION OF OPINIONS CLOSED BY THE INSTITUTION OF COUNCILS AND THE CONCENTRATION OF POWER IN A PONTIFF.

RISE, EARLY VARIATIONS, CONFLICTS, AND FINAL ESTABLISHMENT OF CHRISTIANITY.

Rise of Christianity.—Distinguished from ecclesiastical Organization.—It is demanded by the deplorable Condition of the Empire.—Its brief Conflict with Paganism.—Character of its first Organization.—Variations of Thought and Rise of Sects: their essential Difference in the East and West.—The three primitive Forms of Christianity: the Judaic Form, its End—the Gnostic Form, its End—the African Form, continues.

Spread of Christianity from Syria.—Its Antagonism to Imperialism, their Conflicts.—Position of Affairs under Diocletian.—The Policy of Constantine.—He avails himself of the Christian Party, and through it attains supreme Power.—His personal Relations to it.

The Trinitarian Controversy.—Story of Arius.—The Council of Nicea.

The Progress of the Bishop of Rome to Supremacy.—The Roman Church; its primitive subordinate Position.—Causes of its increasing Wealth, Influence, and Corruptions.—Stages of its Advancement through the Pelagian, Nestorian, and Eutychian Disputes.—Rivalry of the Bishops of Constantinople, Alexandria, and Rome.

Necessity of a Pontiff in the West and ecclesiastical Councils in the East.—Nature of those Councils and of pontifical Power.

The Period closes at the Capture and Sack of Rome by Alaric.—Defence of that Event by St. Augustine.—Criticism on his Writings.

Character of the Progress of Thought through this Period.—Destiny of the three great Bishops . . . . Page 266

CHAPTER X.

THE EUROPEAN AGE OF FAITH.

AGE OF FAITH IN THE EAST.

Consolidation of the Byzantine System, or the Union of Church and State.—The consequent Paganization of Religion and Persecution of Philosophy.

Political Necessity for the enforcement of Patristicism, or Science of the Fathers.—Its peculiar Doctrines.

Obliteration of the Vestiges of Greek Knowledge by Patristicism.—The Libraries and Serapion of Alexandria.—Destruction of the latter by Theodosius.—Death of Hypatia.—Extinction of Learning in the East by Cyril, his Associates and Successors 308

CHAPTER XI.

PREMATURE END OF THE AGE OF FAITH IN THE EAST.

THE THREE ATTACKS, VANDAL, PERSIAN, ARAB.

THE VANDAL ATTACK *leads to the Loss of Africa.—Recovery of that Province by Justinian after great Calamities.*

THE PERSIAN ATTACK *leads to the Loss of Syria and Fall of Jerusalem.—The true Cross carried away as a Trophy.—Moral Impression of these Attacks.*

THE ARAB ATTACK.—*Birth, Mission, and Doctrines of Mohammed.—Rapid Spread of his Faith in Asia and Africa.—Fall of Jerusalem.—Dreadful Losses of Christianity to Mohammedanism.—The Arabs become a learned Nation.*

Review of the Koran.—Reflexions on the Loss of Asia and Africa by Christendom . . . . Page 326

CHAPTER XII.

THE AGE OF FAITH IN THE WEST.

The Age of Faith in the West is marked by Paganism.—The Arabian military Attacks produce the Isolation and permit the Independence of the Bishop of Rome.

GREGORY THE GREAT *organizes the Ideas of his Age, materializes Faith, allies it to Art, rejects Science, and creates the Italian Form of Religion.*

An Alliance of the Papacy with France diffuses that Form.—Political History of the Agreement and Conspiracy of the Frankish Kings and the Pope.—The resulting Consolidation of the new Dynasty in France, and Diffusion of Roman Ideas.—Conversion of Europe.

The Value of the Italian Form of Religion determined from the papal Biography 349

CHAPTER XIII.

DIGRESSION ON THE PASSAGE OF THE ARABIANS TO THEIR AGE OF REASON.

INFLUENCE OF MEDICAL IDEAS THROUGH THE NESTORIANS AND JEWS.

The intellectual Development of the Arabians is guided by the Nestorians and the Jews, and is in the Medical Direction.—The Basis of this Alliance is theological.

Antagonism of the Byzantine System to Scientific Medicine.—Suppression of the Asclepions.—Their Replacement by Miracle-cure.—The resulting Superstition and Ignorance.

Affiliation of the Arabians with the Nestorians and Jews.

1st. *The Nestorians, their Persecutions, and the Diffusion of their Sectarian Ideas.—They inherit the old Greek Medicine.*

Sub-digression on Greek Medicine.—The Asclepions.—Philosophical Importance of Hippocrates, who separates Medicine from Religion.—The School of Cnidos.—Its Suppression by Constantine.

Sub-digression on Egyptian Medicine.—It is founded on Anatomy and Physiology.—Dissections and Vivisections.—The Great Alexandrian Physicians.

2nd. *The Jewish Physicians.—Their Emancipation from Superstition.—They found Colleges and promote Science and Letters.*

The contemporary Tendency to Magic, Necromancy, the Black Art.—The Philosopher's Stone, Elixir of Life, etc.

The Arabs originate scientific Chemistry.—Discover the strong Acids, Phosphorus, etc.—Their geological Ideas.—Apply Chemistry to the Practice of Medicine.—Approach of the Conflict between the Saracenic material and the European supernatural System . . . Page 383

CHAPTER XIV.

THE AGE OF FAITH IN THE WEST—(*Continued*).

IMAGE-WORSHIP AND THE MONKS.

Origin of IMAGE-WORSHIP.—*Inutility of Images discovered in Asia and Africa during the Saracen Wars.—Rise of Iconoclasm.*

The Emperors prohibit Image-worship.—The Monks, aided by court Females, sustain it.—Victory of the latter.

Image-worship in the West sustained by the Popes.—Quarrel between the Emperor and the Pope.—The Pope, aided by the Monks, revolts and allies himself with the Franks.

THE MONKS.—*History of the Rise and Development of Monasticism.—Hermits and Cœnobites.—Spread of Monasticism from Egypt over Europe.—Monk Miracles and Legends.—Humanization of the monastic Establishments.—They materialize Religion, and impress their Ideas on Europe* 413

THE INTELLECTUAL DEVELOPMENT OF EUROPE.

CHAPTER I.

ON THE GOVERNMENT OF NATURE BY LAW.

The subject of this Work proposed.—Its difficulty.
Gradual Acquisition of the Idea of Natural Government by Law.—Eventually sustained by Astronomical, Meteorological, and Physiological Discoveries.—Illustrations from Kepler's Laws, the Trade-winds, Migrations of Birds, Balancing of Vegetable and Animal Life, Variation of Species and their Permanence.
Individual Man is an Emblem of Communities, Nations, and Universal Humanity.—They exhibit Epochs of Life like his, and, like him, ar under the Control of Physical Conditions, and therefore of Law.
Plan of this Work.—The Intellectual History of Greece.—Its Five characteristic Ages.—European Intellectual History.
Grandeur of the Doctrine that the World is governed by Law.

I INTEND, in this work, to consider in what manner the advancement of Europe in civilization has taken place, to ascertain how far its progress has been fortuitous, and how far determined by primordial law. The subject proposed.

Does the procession of nations in time, like the erratic phantasm of a dream, go forward without reason or order? or, is there a predetermined, a solemn march, in which all must join, ever moving, ever resistlessly advancing, encountering and enduring an inevitable succession of events?

In a philosophical examination of the intellectual and political history of nations, an answer to these questions is to be found. But how difficult it is to master the mass of facts necessary to be collected, to handle so great an accumulation, to place it in the clearest point of view;

how difficult it is to select correctly the representative men, to produce them in the proper scenes, and to conduct successfully so grand and complicated a drama as that of European life! Though in one sense the subject offers itself as a scientific problem, and in that manner alone I have to deal with it; in another it swells into a noble epic—the life of humanity, its warfare and repose, its object and its end.

Its difficulty and grandeur.

Man is the archetype of society. Individual development is the model of social progress.

Some have asserted that human affairs are altogether determined by the voluntary action of men, some that the Providence of God directs us in every step, some that all events are fixed by Destiny. It is for us to ascertain how far each of these affirmations is true.

The life of individual man is of a mixed nature. In part he submits to the free-will impulses of himself and others, in part he is under the inexorable dominion of law. He insensibly changes his estimate of the relative power of each of these influences as he passes through successive stages. In the confidence of youth he imagines that very much is under his control, in the disappointment of old age very little. As time wears on, and the delusions of early imagination vanish away, he learns to correct his sanguine views, and prescribes a narrower boundary for the things he expects to obtain. The realities of life undeceive him at last, and there steals over the evening of his days an unwelcome conviction of the vanity of human hopes. The things he has secured are not the things he expected. He sees that a Supreme Power has been using him for unknown ends, that he was brought into the world without his own knowledge, and is departing from it against his own will.

Individual life of a mixed kind.

Whoever has made the physical and intellectual history of individual man his study, will be prepared to admit in what a surprising manner it foreshadows social history. The equilibrium and movement of humanity are altogether physiological phenomena. Yet not without hesitation may such an opinion be frankly avowed, since it is offensive to the pride, and to many of the prejudices and interests of our age. An author

It foreshadows social life.

who has been disposed to devote many years to the labour of illustrating this topic, has need of the earnest support of all who prize the truth; and, considering the extent and profundity of his subject, his work, at the best, must be very imperfect, requiring all the forbearance, and even the generosity of criticism.

First opinions of savage life.

In the intellectual infancy of a savage state, Man transfers to Nature his conceptions of himself, and, considering that every thing he does is determined by his own pleasure, regards all passing events as depending on the arbitrary volition of a superior but invisible power. He gives to the world a constitution like his own. His tendency is necessarily to superstition. Whatever is strange, or powerful, or vast, impresses his imagination with dread. Such objects are only the outward manifestations of an indwelling spirit, and therefore worthy of his veneration.

After Reason, aided by Experience, has led him forth from these delusions as respects surrounding things, he still clings to his original ideas as respects objects far removed. In the distance and irresistible motions of the stars he finds arguments for the supernatural, and gives to each of those shining bodies an abiding and controlling genius. The mental phase through which he is passing permits him to believe in the exercise of planetary influences on himself.

Fetichism displaced by star-worship.

But as reason led him forth from fetichism, so in due time it again leads him forth from star-worship. Perhaps not without regret does he abandon the mythological forms he has created; for, long after he has ascertained that the planets are nothing more than shining points, without any perceptible influence on him, he still venerates the genii once supposed to vivify them, perhaps even he exalts them into immortal gods.

Philosophically speaking, he is exchanging by ascending degrees his primitive doctrine of arbitrary volition for the doctrine of law. As the fall of a stone, the flowing of a river, the movement of a shadow, the rustling of a leaf, have been traced to physical causes, to like causes at last are traced the revolutions of the stars. In events and scenes continually increasing in greatness and grandeur, he is detecting the dominion of law. The goblins, and genii, and gods who successively extorted his fear and veneration, who determined events by their fitful passions or whims, are at last displaced by the noble conception of one Almighty Being, who rules the universe according to reason, and therefore according to law.

The idea of government by law.

In this manner the doctrine of government by law is extended, until at last it embraces all natural events. It was thus that, hardly two centuries ago, that doctrine gathered immense force from the discovery of Newton that Kepler's laws, under which the movements of the planetary bodies are executed, issue as a mathematical necessity from a very simple material condition, and that the complicated motions of the solar system cannot be other than they are. Few of those who read in the beautiful geometry of the 'Principia' the demonstration of this fact, saw the imposing philosophical consequences which must inevitably follow this scientific discovery. And now the investigation of the aspect of the skies in past ages, and all predictions of its future, rest essentially upon the principle that no arbitrary volition ever intervenes, the gigantic mechanism moving impassively in accordance with a mathematical law.

Its application to the solar system.

And so upon the earth, the more perfectly we understand the causes of present events, the more plainly are they seen to be the consequences of physical conditions, and therefore the results of law. To allude to one example out of many that might be considered, the winds, how proverbially inconstant, who can tell whence they come or whither they go! If any thing bears the fitful character of arbitrary volition, surely it is these. But we deceive ourselves in imagining that atmospheric events are fortuitous. Where shall a line be drawn between that eternal trade-wind, which, originating in well-understood physical causes, sweeps, like the breath of Destiny, slowly, and solemnly, and everlastingly over the Pacific Ocean, and the variable gusts into which it degenerates in more northerly and southerly regions—gusts which seem to come without any cause, and to pass

And to terrestrial events.

away without leaving any trace? In what latitude is it that the domain of the physical ends, and that of the supernatural begins?

All mundane events are the results of the operation of law. Every movement in the skies or upon the earth proclaims to us that the universe is under government.

But if we admit that this is the case, from the mote that floats in the sunbeam to multiple stars revolving round each other, are we willing to carry our principles to their consequences, and recognise a like operation of law among living as among lifeless things, in the organic as well as the inorganic world? What testimony does physiology offer on this point?

And to the organic world.

Physiology, in its progress, has passed through the same phases as physics. Living beings have been considered as beyond the power of external influences, and, conspicuously among them, Man has been affirmed to be independent of the forces that rule the world in which he lives. Besides that immaterial principle, the soul, which distinguishes him from all his animated companions, and makes him a moral and responsible being, he has been feigned, like them, to possess another immaterial principle, the vital agent, which, in a way of its own, carries forward all the various operations in his economy.

Especially to man.

But when it was discovered that the heart of man is constructed upon the recognised rules of hydraulics, and with its great tubes is furnished with common mechanical contrivances, valves; when it was discovered that the eye has been arranged on the most refined principles of optics, its cornea, and humours, and lens properly converging the rays to form an image—its iris, like the diaphragm of a telescope or microscope, shutting out stray light, and also regulating the quantity admitted; when it was discovered that the ear is furnished with the means of dealing with the three characteristics of sound—its tympanum for intensity, its cochlea for pitch, its semicircular canals for quality; when it was seen that the air brought into the great air-passages by the descent of the diaphragm, calling into play atmospheric pressure, is conveyed upon physical principles into the ultimate cells of the lungs, and thence into the blood, producing chemical changes throughout the system, disengaging heat, and permitting all the functions of organic life to go on; when these facts and very many others of a like kind were brought into prominence by modern physiology, it obviously became necessary to admit that animated beings do not constitute the exception once supposed, and that organic operations are the result of physical agencies.

If thus, in the recesses of the individual economy, these natural agents bear sway, must they not operate in the social economy too?

In social as well as individual life.

Has the great shadeless desert nothing to do with the habits of the nomade tribes who pitch their tents upon it—the fertile plain no connection with flocks and pastoral life—the mountain fastnesses with the courage that has so often defended them—the sea with habits of adventure? Indeed, do not all our expectations of the stability of social institutions rest upon our belief in the stability of surrounding physical conditions? From the time of Bodin, who nearly three hundred years ago published his work 'De Republica,' these principles have been well recognized: that the laws of Nature cannot be subordinated to the will of Man, and that government must be adapted to climate. It was these things which led him to the conclusion that force is best resorted to for northern nations, reason for the middle, and superstition for the southern.

Effects of the seasons on animals and plants.

In the month of March the sun crosses the equator, dispensing his rays more abundantly over our northern hemisphere. Following in his train, a wave of verdure expands towards the pole. The luxuriance is in proportion to the local brilliancy. The animal world is also affected. Pressed forward, or solicited onward by the warmth, the birds of passage commence their annual migration, keeping pace with the developing vegetation beneath. As summer declines, this orderly advance of light and life is followed by an orderly retreat, and in its turn the southern hemisphere presents the same glorious phenomenon. Once every year the life of the earth pulsates; now there is an abounding vitality, now a desolation. But what is the cause of all this? It is only mechanical. The earth's axis of rotation is inclined to the plane of her orbit of revolution round the sun.

Let that wonderful phenomenon and its explanation be a lesson to us; let it profoundly impress us with the importance of physical agents and physical laws. They intervene in the life and death of man personally and socially. External events become interwoven in our constitution; their periodicities create periodicities in us. Day and night are incorporated in our waking and sleeping; summer and winter compel us to exhibit cycles in our life.

Individual existence depends on physical conditions.

They who have paid attention to the subject have long ago ascertained that the possibility of human existence on the earth depends on conditions altogether of a material kind. Since it is only within a narrow range of temperature that life can be maintained, it is needful that our planet should be at a definite mean distance from the source of light and heat, the sun; and that the form of her orbit should be so little eccentric as to approach closely to a circle. If her mass were larger or less than it is, the weight of all living and lifeless things on her surface would no longer be the same; but absolute weight is one of the primary elements of organic construction. A change in the time of her diurnal rotation, as affecting the length of the day and night, must at once be followed by a corresponding modification of the periodicities of the nervous system of animals; a change in her orbitual translation round the sun, as determining the duration of the year, would, in like manner, give rise to a marked effect. If the year were shorter, we should live faster and die sooner.

Animal and vegetable life interbalanced by material conditions.

In the present economy of our globe, natural agents are relied upon as the means of regulation and of government. Through heat, the distribution and arrangement of the vegetable tribes are accomplished; through their mutual relations with the atmospheric air, plants and animals are interbalanced, and neither permitted to obtain a superiority. Considering the magnitude of this condition, and its necessity to general life, it might seem worthy of incessant Divine intervention, yet it is in fact accomplished automatically.

Of past organic history the same remark may be made. The condensation of carbon from the air, and its inclusion in the strata, constitute the chief epoch in the organic life of the earth, giving a possibility for the appearance of the hot-blooded and more intellectual animal tribes. That great event was occasioned by the influence of the rays of the sun. And as such influences have thus been connected with the appearance of organisms, so likewise have they been concerned in the removal. Of the myriads of species which have become extinct, doubtless every one has passed away through the advent of material conditions incompatible with its continuance. Even now, a fall of half-a-dozen degrees in the mean temperature of any latitude would occasion the vanishing of the forms of warmer climates, and the advent of those of the colder. An obscuration of the rays of the sun for a few years would compel a redistribution of plants and animals all over the earth; many would totally disappear, and everywhere new comers would be seen.

And also appearances and extinctions determined.

The permanence of organic forms is altogether dependent on the invariability of the material conditions under which they live. Any variation therein, no matter how insignificant it might be, would be forthwith followed by a corresponding variation in the form. The present invariability of the world of organization is the direct consequence of the physical equilibrium, and so it will continue as long as the mean temperature, the annual supply of light, the composition of the air, the distribution of water, oceanic and atmospheric currents, and other such agencies remain unaltered; but if any one of these, or of a hundred other incidents that might be mentioned, should suffer modification, in an instant the fanciful doctrine of the immutability of species would be brought to its true value. The organic world appears to be in repose, because natural influences have reached an equilibrium. A marble may remain for ever motionless upon a level table; but let the

Permanence of organisms due to immobility of external conditions.

surface be a little inclined, and the marble will quickly run off. What should we say of him, who, contemplating it in its state of rest, asserted that it was impossible for it ever to move?

They who can see no difference between the race-horse and the Shetland pony, the bantam and the Shanghai fowl, the greyhound and the poodle dog, who altogether deny that impressions can be made on species, and see in the long succession of extinct forms, the ancient existence of which they must acknowledge, the evidences of a continuous and creative intervention, forget that mundane effects observe definite sequences, event following event in the necessity of the case, and thus constituting a chain, each link of which hangs on a preceding, and holds a succeeding one. Physical influences thus following one another, and bearing to each other the inter-relation of cause and effect, stand in their totality to the whole organic world as causes, it representing the effect, and the order of succession existing among them is perpetuated or embodied in it. Thus, in those ancient times to which we have referred, the sun-light acting on the leaves of plants disturbed the chemical constitution of the atmosphere, gave rise to the accumulation of a more energetic element therein, diminished the mechanical pressure, and changed the rate of evaporation from the sea, a series of events following one another so necessarily that we foresee their order, and, in their turn, making an impression on the vegetable and animal economy. The natural influences, thus varying in an orderly way, controlled botanical events, and made them change correspondingly. The orderly procedure of the one must be imitated in the orderly procedure of the other. And the same holds good in the animal kingdom; the recognized variation in the material conditions is copied in the organic effects, in vigour of motion, energy of life, intellectual power.

Orderly sequence of conditions is followed by orderly organic changes.

When, therefore, we notice such orderly successions, we must not at once assign them to a direct intervention, the issue of wise predeterminations of a voluntary agent; we must first satisfy ourselves how far they are dependent on mundane or material conditions, occurring in a definite and necessary series, ever bearing in mind the important principle that an orderly sequence of inorganic events necessarily involves an orderly and corresponding progression of organic life.

To this doctrine of the control of physical agencies over organic forms I acknowledge no exception, not even in the case of man. The varied aspects he presents in different countries are the necessary consequences of those influences.

Universal control of physical agents over organisms.

He who advocates the doctrine of the unity of the human race is plainly forced to the admission of the absolute control of such agents over the organization of man, since the originally-created type has been brought to exhibit very different aspects in different parts of the world, apparently in accordance with the climate and other purely material circumstances. To those circumstances it is scarcely necessary to add manner of life, for that itself arises from them. The doctrine of unity demands as its essential postulate an admission of the paramount control of physical agents over the human aspect and organization, else how could it be that, proceeding from the same stock, all shades of complexion in the skin, and variety in the form of the skull, should have arisen? Experience assures us that these are changes assumed only by slow degrees, and not with abruptness; they come as a cumulative effect. They plainly enforce the doctrine that national type is not to be regarded as a definite or final thing, a seeming immobility in this particular being due to the attainment of a correspondence with the conditions to which the type is exposed. Let those conditions be changed, and it begins forthwith to change too. I repeat it, therefore, that he who receives the doctrine of the unity of the human race, must also accept, in view of the present state of humanity on various parts of the surface of our planet, its necessary postulate, the complete control of physical agents, whether natural, or arising artificially from the arts of civilization and the secular progress of nations toward a correspondence with the conditions to which they are exposed.

The case of man.

To the same conclusion also must he be brought who advocates the origin of different races from different centres. It comes to the same thing, whichever of those doctrines we adopt. Each brings us to the admission of the transitory nature of typical forms, to their transmutations and extinctions.

Human variations.

Variations in the aspect of men are best seen when an examination is made of nations arranged in a northerly and southerly direction; the result is such as would ensue to an emigrant passing slowly along a meridional track; but the case would be quite different if the movement were along a parallel of latitude. In this latter direction the variations of climate are far less marked, and depend much more on geographical than on astronomical causes. In emigrations of this kind there is never that rapid change of aspect, complexion, and intellectual power which must occur in the other. Thus, though the mean temperature of Europe increases from Poland to France, chiefly through the influence of the great Atlantic current transferring heat from the Gulf of Mexico and tropical ocean, that rise is far less than would be encountered on passing through the same distance to the south. By the arts of civilization man can much more easily avoid the difficulties arising from variations along a parallel of latitude than those upon a meridian, for the simple reason that in that case those variations are less.

Their political result.

But it is not only complexion, development of the brain, and, therefore, intellectual power, which are thus affected. With difference of climate there must be differences of manners and customs, that is, differences in the modes of civilization. These are facts which deserve our most serious attention, since such differences are inevitably connected with political results. If homogeneousness be an element of strength, an empire that lies east and west must be more powerful than one that lies north and south. I cannot but think that this was no inconsiderable cause of the greatness and permanence of Rome, and that it lightened the task of the emperors, often hard enough, in government. There is a natural tendency to homogeneousness in the east and west direction, a tendency to diversity and antagonism in the north and south, and hence it is that government under the latter circumstances will always demand the highest grade of statesmanship.

The transitional forms which an animal type is capable of producing on a passage north and south are much more numerous than those it can produce on a passage east and west. These, though they are truly transitional as respects the type from which they have proceeded, are permanent as regards the locality in which they occur, being, in fact, the incarnation of its physical influences. As long, therefore, as those influences remain without change the form that has been produced will last without any alteration. For such a permanent form in the case of man we may adopt the designation of an ethnical element.

Nature of transitional forms.

An ethnical element is therefore necessarily of a dependent nature; its durability arises from its perfect correspondence with its environment. Whatever can affect that correspondence will touch its life.

Conditions of change in an ethnical element.

Such considerations carry us from individual man to groups of men or nations. There is a progess for races of men as well marked as the progress of one man. There are thoughts and actions appertaining to specific periods in the one case as in the other. Without difficulty we affirm of a given act that it appertains to a given period. We recognize the noisy sports of boyhood, the business application of maturity, the feeble garrulity of old age. We express our surprise when we witness actions unsuitable to the epoch of life. As it is in this respect in the individual, so it is in the nation. The march of individual existence shadows forth the march of race-existence, being, indeed, its representative on a little scale.

Progress of nations like that of individuals.

Groups of men, or nations, are disturbed by the same accidents, or complete the same cycle as the individual. Some scarcely pass beyond infancy, some are destroyed on a sudden, some die of mere old age. In this confusion of events, it might seem altogether hopeless to disentangle the law which is guiding them all, and demonstrate it clearly. Of such groups, each may exhibit, at the same moment, an advance to a different stage, just as we see in the same family the young, the middle-aged, the old. It is thus

Communities, like families, exhibit members in different stages of advance.

that Europe shows in its different parts societies in very different states—here the restless civilization of France and England, there the contentment and inferiority of Lapland. This commingling might seem to render it difficult to ascertain the true movement of the whole continent, and still more so for distant and successive periods of time. In each nation, moreover, the contemporaneously different classes, the educated and illiterate, the idle and industrious, the rich and poor, the intelligent and superstitious, represent different contemporaneous stages of advancement. One may have made a great progress, another scarcely have advanced at all. How shall we ascertain the real state of the case? Which of these classes shall we regard as the truest and most perfect type?

Though difficult, this ascertainment is not impossible. The problem is to be dealt with in the same manner that we should estimate a family in which there are persons of every condition from infancy to old age. Each member of it tends to pursue a definite course, though some, cut off in an untimely manner, may not complete it. One may be enfeebled by accident, another by disease; but each, if his past and present circumstances be fully considered, will illustrate the nature of the general movement that all are making. To demonstrate that movement most satisfactorily, certain members of such a family suit our purpose better than others, because they more closely represent its type, or have advanced farthest in their career.

The intellectual class the true representative of a community.

So in a family of many nations, some are more mature, some less advanced, some die in early life, some are worn out by extreme old age; all show special peculiarities. There are distinctions among kinsmen, whether we consider them intellectually or corporeally. Every one, nevertheless, illustrates in his own degree the march that all are making, but some do it more, some less completely. The leading, the intellectual class, is hence always the true representative of a state. It has passed step by step through the lower stages, and has made the greatest advance.

In an individual, life is maintained only by the production and destruction of organic particles, no portion of the system being in a state of immobility, but each displaying incessant change. Death is, therefore, necessarily the condition of life, and the more energetic the function of a part—or, if we compare different animals with one another—the more active the mode of existence, correspondingly, the greater the waste and the more numerous the deaths of the interstitial constituents.

Interstitial change and death the condition of individual life.

To the death of particles in the individual answers the death of persons in the nation, of which they are the integral constituents. In both cases, in a period of time quite inconsiderable, a total change is accomplished without the entire system, which is the sum of these separate parts, losing its identity. Each particle or each person comes into existence, discharges an appropriate duty, and then passes away, perhaps unnoticed. The production, continuance, and death of an organic molecule in the person answers to the production, continuance, and death of a person in the nation. Nutrition and decay in one case are equivalent to well-being and transformation in the other.

Particles in the individual answer to persons in the state.

In the same manner that the individual is liable to changes through the action of external agencies, and offers no resistance thereto, nor any indication of the possession of a physiological inertia, but submits at once to any impression, so likewise it is with aggregates of men constituting nations. A national type pursues its way physically and intellectually through changes and developments answering to those of the individual, and being represented by Infancy, Childhood, Youth, Manhood, Old Age, and Death respectively.

Epochs in national the same as in individual life.

But this orderly process may be disturbed exteriorly or interiorly. If from its original seats a whole nation were transposed to some new abode, in which the climate, the seasons, the aspect of nature were altogether different, it would appear spontaneously in all its parts to commence a movement to come into harmony with the new conditions—a movement of a secular nature, and implying the consumption of many generations for its accomplishment. During such a period

Disturbance through emigration.

of transmutation there would, of course, be an increased waste of life, a risk, indeed, of total disappearance or national death; but the change once completed, the requisite correspondence once attained, things would go forward again in an orderly manner on the basis of the new modification that had been assumed. When the change to be accomplished is very profound, involving extensive anatomical alterations not merely in the appearance of the skin, but even in the structure of the skull, long periods of time are undoubtedly required, and many generations of individuals are consumed.

And through blood admixture.

Or, by interior disturbance, particularly by blood admixture, with more rapidity may a national type be affected, the result plainly depending on the extent to which admixture has taken place. This is a disturbance capable of mathematical computation. If the blood admixture be only of limited amount, and transient in its application, its effect will sensibly disappear in no very great period of time, though never, perhaps, in absolute reality. This accords with the observation of philosophical historians, who agree in the conclusion that a small tribe intermingling with a larger one will only disturb it in a temporary manner, and, after the course of a few years, the effect will cease to be perceptible. Nevertheless, the influence must really continue much longer than is outwardly apparent; and the result is the same as when, in a liquid, a drop of some other kind is placed, and additional quantities of the first liquid then successively added. Though it might have been possible at first to detect the adulteration without trouble, it becomes every moment less and less possible to do so, and before long it cannot be done at all. But the drop is as much present at last as it was at first: it is merely masked; its properties overpowered.

Considering in this manner the contamination of a numerous nation, a trifling amount of foreign blood admixture would appear to be indelible, and the disturbance, at any moment, capable of computation by the ascertained degree of dilution that has taken place. But it must not be forgotten that there is another agency at work, energetically tending to bring about homogeneity: it is the influence of external physical conditions. The intrusive adulterating element possesses in itself no physiological inertia, but as quickly as may be is brought into correspondence with the new circumstances to which it is exposed, herein running in the same course as the element with which it had mingled had itself antecedently gone over.

National homogeneity is thus obviously secured by the operation of two distinct agencies: the first, gradual but inevitable dilution; the second, motion to come into harmony with the external natural state. The two conspire in their effects.

Secular variations of nations.

We must therefore no longer regard nations or groups of men as offering a permanent picture. Human affairs must be looked upon as in continuous movement, not wandering in an arbitrary manner here and there, but proceeding in a perfectly definite course. Whatever may be the present state, it is altogether transient. All systems of civil life are therefore necessarily ephemeral. Time brings new external conditions; the manner of thought is modified; with thought, action. Institutions of all kinds must hence participate in this fleeting nature, and, though they may have allied themselves to political power, and gathered therefrom the means of coercion, their permanency is but little improved thereby; for, sooner or later, the population on whom they have been imposed, following the external variations, spontaneously outgrows them, and their ruin, though it may have been delayed, is none the less certain. For the permanency of any such system it is essentially necessary that it should include within its own organization a law of change, and not of change only, but change in the right direction—the direction in which the society interested is about to pass. It is in an oversight of this last essential condition that we find an explanation of the failure of so many such institutions. Too commonly do we believe that the affairs of men are determined by a spontaneous action or free will; we keep that overpowering influence which really controls them in the background. In individual life we also accept a like deception,

Their institutions must correspondingly change.

living in the belief that every thing we do is determined by the volition of ourselves or of those around us; nor is it until the close of our days that we discern how great is the illusion, and that we have been swimming—playing and struggling—in a stream which, in spite of all our voluntary motions, has silently and resistlessly borne us to a predetermined shore.

In the foregoing pages I have been tracing analogies between the life of individuals and that of nations. There is yet one point more.

Nations, like individuals, die. Their birth presents an ethnical element; their death, which is the most solemn event that we can contemplate, may arise from interior or from external causes. Empires are only sand-hills in the hour-glass of Time; they crumble spontaneously away by the process of their own growth.

The death of nations.

A nation, like a man, hides from itself the contemplation of its final day. It occupies itself with expedients for prolonging its present state. It frames laws and constitutions under the delusion that they will last, forgetting that the condition of life is change. Very able modern statesmen consider it to be the grand object of their art to keep things as they are, or rather as they were. But the human race is not at rest; and bands with which, for a moment, it may be restrained, break all the more violently the longer they hold. No man can stop the march of destiny.

Time, to the nation as to the individual, is nothing absolute; its duration depends on the rate of thought and feeling. For the same reason that to the child the year is actually longer than to the adult, the life of a nation may be said to be no longer than the life of a person, considering the manner in which its affairs are moving. There is a variable velocity of existence, though the lapses of time may be equable.

There is nothing absolute in time.

The origin, existence, and death of nations depend thus on physical influences, which are themselves the result of immutable laws. Nations are only transitional forms of humanity. They must undergo obliteration as do the transitional forms offered by the animal series. There is no more an immortality

Nations are only transitional forms.

for them than there is an immobility for an embryo in any one of the manifold forms passed through in its progress of development.

The life of a nation thus flows in a regular sequence, determined by invariable law, and hence, in estimating different nations, we must not be deceived by the casual aspect they present. The philosophical comparison is made by considering their entire manner of career or cycle of progress, and not their momentary or transitory state. Though they may encounter disaster, their absolute course can never be retrograde; it is always onward, even if tending to dissolution. It is as with the individual, who is equally advancing in infancy, in maturity, in old age. Pascal was more than justified in his assertion that "the entire succession of men, through the whole course of ages, must be regarded as one man, always living and incessantly learning." In both cases, the manner of advance, though it may sometimes be unexpected, can never be abrupt. At each stage events and ideas emerge which not only necessarily owe their origin to preceding events and ideas, but extend far into the future and influence it. As these are crowded together, or occur more widely apart, national life, like individual, shows a variable rapidity, depending upon the intensity of thought and action. But, no matter how great that energy may be, or with what rapidity modifications may take place—since events are emerging as consequences of preceding events, and ideas from preceding ideas — in the midst of the most violent intellectual oscillations, a discerning observer will never fail to detect that there exists a law of continuous variation of human opinions.

Their course is ever advancing, never retrograde.

Variable rapidity of national life.

In the examination of the progress of Europe on which we now enter, it is, of course, to intellectual phenomena that we must, for the most part, refer; material aggrandisement and political power offering us less important though still valuable indications, and serving our purpose rather in a corroborative way. There are five intellectual manifestations to which we may resort—philosophy, science, literature, religion, govern-

Plan of this work.

ment. Our obvious course is, first, to study the progress of that member of the European family, the eldest in point of advancement, and to endeavour to ascertain the characteristics of its mental unfolding. We may reasonably expect that the younger members of the family, more or less distinctly, will offer us illustrations of the same mode of advancement that we shall thus find for Greece; and that the whole continent, which is the sum of these different parts, will, in its secular progress, comport itself in like manner.

Selection among European communities.

Of the early condition of Europe, since we have to consider it in its prehistoric times, our information must necessarily be imperfect. Perhaps, however, we may be disposed to accept that imperfection as a sufficient token of its true nature. Since history can offer us no aid, our guiding lights must be comparative theology and comparative philology. Proceeding from those times, we shall, in detail, examine the intellectual or philosophical movement first exhibited in Greece, endeavouring to ascertain its character at successive epochs, and thereby to judge of its complete nature. Fortunately for our purpose, the information is here sufficient, both in amount and distinctness. It then remains to show that the mental movement of the whole continent is essentially of the same kind, though, as must necessarily be the case, it is spread over far longer periods of time. Our conclusions will constantly be found to gather incidental support and distinctness from illustrations presented by the aged populations of Asia, and the aborigines of Africa and America.

Our investigation limited to the intellectual, and commencing with Greece.

From thence we pass to the examination of all Europe

The intellectual progress of Europe being of a nature answering to that observed in the case of Greece, and this, in its turn, being like that of an individual, we may conveniently separate it into arbitrary periods, sufficiently distinct from one another, though imperceptibly merging into each other. To these successive periods I shall give the titles of—1, the Age of Credulity; 2, the Age of Inquiry; 3, the Age of Faith; 4, the Age of Reason; 5, the Age of Decrepitude; and

The five ages of European life.

shall use these designations in the division of my subject in its several chapters.

From the possibility of thus regarding the progress of a continent in definite and successive stages, answering respectively to the periods of individual life—infancy, childhood, youth, maturity, old age—we may gather an instructive lesson. It is the same that we have learned from inquiries respecting the origin, maintenance, distribution, and extinction of animals and plants, their balancing against each other; from the variations of aspect and form of an individual man as determined by climate; from his social state, whether in repose or motion; from the secular variations of his opinions, and the gradual dominion of reason over society: this lesson is, that the government of the world is accomplished by immutable law.

The world is ruled by law.

Such a conception commends itself to the intellect of man by its majestic grandeur. It makes him discern the eternal in the vanishing of present events and through the shadows of time. From the life, the pleasures, the sufferings of humanity, it points to the impassive; from our wishes, wants, and woes, to the inexorable. Leaving the individual beneath the eye of Providence, it shows society under the finger of law. And the laws of Nature never vary; in their application they never hesitate nor are wanting.

But in thus ascending to primordial laws, and asserting their immutability, universality, and paramount control in the government of this world, there is nothing inconsistent with the free action of man. The appearance of things depends altogether on the point of view we occupy. He who is immersed in the turmoil of a crowded city sees nothing but the acts of men, and, if he formed his opinion from his experience alone, must conclude that the course of events altogether depends on the uncertainties of human volition. But he who ascends to a sufficient elevation loses sight of the passing conflicts, and no longer hears the contentions. He discovers that the importance of individual action is diminishing, as the panorama beneath him is extending.

And yet there is free-will for man.

And if he could attain to the truly philosophical, the general point of view, disengaging himself from all terrestrial influences and entanglements, rising high enough to see the whole globe at a glance, his acutest vision would fail to discover the slightest indication of man, his free-will, or his works. In her resistless, onward sweep, in the clock-like precision of her daily and nightly revolution, in the well-known pictured forms of her continents and seas, now no longer dark and and doubtful, but shedding forth a planetary light, well might he ask what had become of all the aspirations and anxieties, the pleasures and agony of life. As the voluntary vanished from his sight, and the irresistible remained, and each moment became more and more distinct, well might he incline to disbelieve his own experience, and to question whether the seat of so much undying glory could be the place of so much human uncertainty, whether beneath the vastness, energy, and immutable course of a moving world, there lay concealed the feebleness and imbecility of man. Yet it is none the less true that these contradictory conditions co-exist—Free-will and Fate, Uncertainty and Destiny. It is only the point of view that has changed, but on that how much has depended! A little nearer we gather the successive ascertainments of human inquiry, a little further off we realize the panoramic vision of the Deity. A Hindu philosopher has truly remarked, that he who stands by the banks of a flowing stream sees, in their order, the various parts as they successively glide by, but he who is placed on an exalted station views, at a glance, the whole as a motionless silvery thread among the fields. To the one there is the accumulating experience and knowledge of man in time, to the other there is the instantaneous the unsuccessive knowledge of God.

Changeability of forms and unchangeability of law.

Is there an object presented to us which does not bear the mark of ephemeral duration? As respects the tribes of life, they are scarcely worth a moment's thought, for the term of the great majority of them is so brief that we may say they are born and die before our eyes. If we examine them, not as individuals, but as races, the same conclusion holds good, only the scale is enlarged from a few days to a few centuries. If from living we turn to lifeless nature, we encounter again the evidence of brief continuance. The sea is unceasingly remoulding its shores; hard as they are, the mountains are constantly yielding to frost and to rain; here an extensive tract of country is elevated, there depressed. We fail to find any thing that is not undergoing change.

Then forms are in their nature transitory, law is everlasting. If from visible forms we turn to directing law how vast is the difference. We pass from the finite, the momentary, the incidental, the conditioned—to the illimitable, the eternal, the necessary, the unshackled.

The object of this book is to assert the control of law in human affairs.

It is of law that I am to speak in this book. In a world composed of vanishing forms I am to vindicate the imperishability, the majesty of law, and to show how man proceeds, in his social march, in obedience to it. I am to lead my reader, perhaps in a reluctant path, from the outward phantasmagorial illusions which surround us, and so ostentatiously obtrude themselves on our attention, to something that lies in silence and strength behind. I am to draw his thoughts from the tangible to the invisible, from the limited to the universal, from the changeable to the invariable, from the transitory to the eternal; from the expedients and volitions so largely amusing the life of man, to the predestined and resistless issuing from the fiat of God.

CHAPTER II.

OF EUROPE: ITS TOPOGRAPHY AND ETHNOLOGY.

ITS PRIMITIVE MODES OF THOUGHT, AND THEIR PROGRESSIVE VARIATIONS, MANIFESTED IN THE GREEK AGE OF CREDULITY.

Description of Europe: its Topography, Meteorology, and secular Geological Movements.—Their Effect on its Inhabitants.

Its Ethnology determined through its Vocabularies.

Comparative Theology of Greece; the Stage of Sorcery, the Anthropocentric Stage.—Becomes connected with false Geography and Astronomy.—Heaven, the Earth, the Under World.—Origin, continuous Variation and Progress of Greek Theology.—It introduces Ionic Philosophy.

Decline of Greek Theology, occasioned by the Advance of Geography and Philosophical Criticism.—Secession of Poets, Philosophers, Historians. —Abortive public Attempts to sustain it.—Duration of its Decline.—Its Fall.

Europe is geographically a peninsula, and historically a dependency of Asia.

Description of Europe.

It is constructed on the western third of a vast mountain axis, which reaches in a broken and irregular course from the Sea of Japan to the Bay of Biscay. On the flanks of this range, peninsular slopes are directed toward the south, and extensive plateaus to the north. The culminating point in Europe is Mont Blanc, 16,000 feet above the level of the sea. The axis of elevation is not the axis of figure; the incline to the south is much shorter and steeper than that to the north. The boundless plains of Asia are prolonged through Germany and Holland. An army may pass from the Pacific to the Atlantic Ocean, a distance of more than six thousand miles, without encountering any elevation of more than a few hundred feet. The descent from Asia into Europe is indicated in a general manner by the mean elevation of the two continents above the level of the sea; that for Asia being 1132 feet, that for Europe 671. Through the avenue thus open to them, the Oriental hordes have again and again precipitated themselves on the West. With an abundance of springs and head-waters, but without any stream capable of offering a serious obstacle, this tract has a temperature well suited to military movements. It coincides generally with the annual isothermal line of 50°, skirting the northern boundary beyond which the vine ceases to grow, and the limiting region beyond which the wild boar does not pass.

The great path-zone.

Constructed thus, Europe is not only easily accessible from Asia, a fact of no little moment in its ancient history, but it is also singularly accessible interiorly, or from one of its parts to another. Still more, its sea-line is so broken, it has so many intrusive gulfs and bays, that, its surface considered, its maritime coast is greater than that of any other continent. In this respect it contrasts strikingly with Africa. Europe has one mile of coast-line for every 156 square miles of surface, Africa has only one for every 623. This extensive maritime contact adds, of course, greatly to its interior as well as exterior accessibility.

Exterior and interior accessibility.

The mean annual temperature of the European countries on the southern slope of the mountain axis is from 60° to 70° F., but of those to the north the heat gradually declines, until, at the extreme limit on the shores of Zembla, the ground is perpetually frozen. As on other parts of the globe, the climate does not correspond to the latitude, but is disturbed by several causes, among which may be distinguished the great Atlantic current—the Gulf Stream coming from America—and the Sahara Desert. The latter gives to the south of Europe an unduly high heat, and the former to Ireland, England, and the entire west a genial temperature. Together they press into higher latitudes the annual isothermal lines. If in Europe there are no deserts, there are none of those impenetrable forests seen in tropical countries. From the westerly shores of

Distribution of heat in Europe.

Portugal, France, and Ireland, the humidity diminishes as we pass to the east, and, indeed, if we advance into Asia, it disappears in the desert of Gobi. There are no vast homogeneous areas as in Asia, and therefore there is no widespread uniformity in the races of men.

But not only is the temperature of the European continent elevated by the Gulf Stream and the south-west wind, its luxuriance of vegetation depends on them; for luxuriance of vegetation is determined, among other things, by the supply of rain. A profusion of water gives to South America its amazing forests; a want inflicts on Australia its shadeless trees, with their shrunken and pointed leaves. With the diminished moisture the green gardens of France are replaced in Gobi by ligneous plants covered with a gray down. Physical circumstances control the vegetable as well as the animal world.

And the quantity of rain.

The westerly regions of Europe, through the influence of the south-west wind, the Gulf Stream, and their mountain ranges, are supplied with abundant rains, and have a favourable mean annual temperature; but as we pass to the eastern confines the number of rainy days diminishes, the absolute annual quantity of rain and snow is less, and the mean annual temperature is lower. On the Atlantic face of the mountains of Norway it is perpetually raining: the annual depth of water is there 82 inches; but on the opposite side of those mountains is only 21 inches. For similar reasons, Ireland is moist and green, and in Cornwall the laurel and camellia will bear a winter exposure.

There are six maximum points of rain—Norway, Scotland, South-western Ireland and England, Portugal, North-eastern Spain, Lombardy. They respectively correspond to mountains. In general, the amount of rain diminishes from the equator toward the poles; but it is greatly controlled by the disturbing influence of elevated ridges, which in many instances far more than compensate for the effects of latitude. The Alps exercise an influence over the meteorology of all Europe.

Not only do mountains thus determine the absolute quantity of rain, they also affect the number of rainy days in a year. The occurrence of a rainy season depends on the amount of moisture existing in the air; and hence its frequency is greater at the Atlantic sea-board than in the interior, where the wind arrives in a drier state, much of its moisture having been precipitated by the mountains forcing it to a great elevation. Thus, on the eastern coast of Ireland it rains 208 days in a year; in England, about 150; at Kazan, 90; and in Siberia only 60 days.

The number of rainy days;

When the atmospheric temperature is sufficiently low, the condensed water descends under the form of snow. In general, the annual depth of snow and the number of snowy days increase toward the north. In Rome the snowy days are 1½; in Venice, 5½; in Paris, 12; in St. Petersburgh, 171. Whatever causes interfere with the distribution of heat must influence the precipitation of snow; among such are the Gulf Stream and local altitude. Hence, on the coast of Portugal, snow is of infrequent occurrence; in Lisbon it never snowed from 1806 to 1811.

and of snowy days.

Such facts teach us how many meteorological contrasts Europe presents, how many climates it contains. Necessarily it is full of modified men.

If we examine the maps of monthly isothermals, we observe how strikingly those lines change, becoming convex to the north as summer approaches, and concave as winter. They by no means observe a parallelism to the mean, but change their flexures, assuming new sinuosities. In their absolute transfer they move with a variable velocity, and through spaces far from insignificant. The line of 50° F., which in January passes through Lisbon and the south of the Morea, in July has travelled to the north shore of Lapland, and incloses the White Sea. As in some grand musical instrument, the strings of which vibrate, the isothermal lines of Europe and Asia beat to and fro, but it takes a year for them to accomplish one pulsation.

Vibrations of the isothermal lines.

All over the world physical circumstances control the human race. They make the Australian a savage; incapacitate the negro, who can never invent an alphabet or an arithmetic, and whose theology never passes beyond the stage of sorcery. They cause the Tartars to delight in a diet of milk, and the American Indian to abominate it. They make the dwarfish races of Europe instinctive miners and metallurgists. An artificial control over temperature by dwellings, warm for the winter and cool for the summer; variations of clothing to suit the season of the year, and especially the management of fire, have enabled man to maintain himself in all climates. The invention of artificial light has extended the available term of his life; by giving the night to his use, it has, by the social intercourse it encourages, polished his manners and refined his tastes, perhaps as much as any thing else has aided in his intellectual progress. Indeed, these are among the primary conditions that have occasioned his civilization. Variety of natural conditions gives rise to different national types, artificial inventions occasion renewed modifications. Where there are many climates there will be many forms of men. Herein, as we shall in due season discover, lies the explanation of the energy of European life, and the development of its civilization.

Europe is full of meteorological contrasts, and therefore of modified men.

Would any one deny the influence of rainy days on our industrial habits and on our mental condition even in a civilized state? With how much more force, then, must such meteorological incidents have acted on the ill-protected, ill-clad, and ill-housed barbarian! Would any one deny the increasing difficulty with which life is maintained as we pass from the southern peninsulas to the more rigorous climates of the north? There is a relationship between the mean annual heat of a locality and the instincts of its inhabitants for food. The Sicilian is satisfied with a light farinaceous repast and a few fruits; the Norwegian requires a strong diet of flesh; to the Laplander it is none the less acceptable if grease of the bear, or train oil, or the blubber of whales be added. Meteorology to no little extent influences the morals; the instinctive propensity to drunkenness is a function of the latitude. Food, houses, clothing, bear a certain relation to the isothermal lines.

For similar reasons, the inhabitants of Europe each year tend to more complete homogeneity. Climate and meteorological differences are more and more perfectly equalized by artificial inventions; nor is it alone a similarity of habits, a similarity of physiological constitution also ensues. The effect of such inventions is to equalize the influences to which men are exposed; they are brought more closely to the mean typical standard, and—especially is it to be remembered—with this closer approach to each other in conformation, comes a closer approach in feelings and habits, and even in the manner of thinking.

But, through artificial inventions, it tends to homogeneousness in modern times.

On the southern slope of the mountain axis project the historic peninsulas, Greece, Italy, Spain. To the former we trace unmistakably the commencement of European civilization. The first Greeks patriotically affirmed that their own climate was the best suited for man; beyond the mountains to the north there reigned a Cimmerian darkness, an everlasting winter. It was the realm of Boreas, the shivering tyrant. In the early ages man recognized cold as his mortal enemy. Physical inventions have enabled him to overcome it, and now he maintains a more difficult and doubtful struggle with heat.

The Mediterranean peninsulas.

Beyond these peninsulas, and bounding the continent on the south, is the Mediterranean, nearly two thousand miles in length, isolating Europe from Africa socially, but uniting them commercially. The Black Sea and that of Azof are dependencies of it. It has, conjointly with them, a shore-line of 13,000 miles, and exposes a surface of nearly a million and a quarter of square miles. It is subdivided into two basins, the eastern and western, the former being of high interest historically, since it is the scene of the dawn of European intelligence; the western is bounded by the Italian peninsula, Sicily, and the African promontory of Cape Bon on one side, and at the other has as its portal the Straits of Gibraltar. The temperature is ten or twelve degrees higher than the Atlantic, and, since much of the water is removed by evaporation, it is necessarily more saline than that ocean. Its colour is green where shallow, blue where deep.

The Mediterranean Sea.

For countless centuries Asia has experienced a slow upward movement, not only affecting her own topography, but likewise that of her European dependency. There was a time when the great sandy desert of Gobi was the bed of a sea which communicated through the Caspian with the Baltic, as may be proved not only by existing geographical facts, but also from geological considerations. It is only necessary, for this purpose, to inspect the imperfect maps that have been published of the silurian and even tertiary periods. The vertical displacement of Europe, during and since the latter period, has indisputably been more than 2000 feet in many places. The effects of such movements on the flora and fauna of a region must, in the course of time, be very important, for an elevation of 350 feet is equal to one degree of cold in the mean annual temperature, or to sixty miles on the surface northward. Nor has this slow disturbance ended. Again and again, in historic times, have its results operated fearfully on Europe, by forcibly precipitating the Asiatic nomades along the great path-zone; again and again, through such changes of level, have they been rendered waterless, and thus driven into a forced emigration. Some of their rivers, as the Oxus and Jaxartes, have, within the records of history, been dry for several years. To these topographical changes, rather than to political influences, we must impute many of the most celebrated tribal invasions. It has been the custom to refer these events to an excessive overpopulation periodically occurring in Central Asia, or to the ambition of warlike chieftains. Doubtless those regions are well adapted to human life, and hence liable to overpopulation, considering the pursuits man there follows, and doubtless there have been occasions on which those nations have been put in motion by their princes: but the modern historian cannot too carefully bear in mind the laws which regulate the production of men, and also the body of evidence which proves that the crust of the earth is not motionless, but rising in one place and sinking in another. The grand invasions of Europe by Asiatic hordes have been much more violent and abrupt than would answer to a steady pressure resulting from overpopulation, and too extensive for mere warlike incitement; they answer more completely to the experience of some irresistible necessity arising from an insuperable physical cause, which could

Secular geological movement of Europe and Asia, and its social consequences.

drive in hopeless despair from their homes the young and the old, the vigorous and feeble, with their cattle, and waggons, and flocks. Such a cause is the shifting of the soil and disturbance of the courses of water. The tribes compelled to migrate were forced along the path-zone, their track being, therefore, on a parallel of latitude, and not on a meridian; and hence, for the reasons set forth in the preceding chapter, their movements and journey of easier accomplishment.

Rate and extent of these movements.

These geological changes then enter as an element in human history, not only for Asia, of which the great inland sea has dwindled away to the Caspian, and lost its connection with the Baltic, but for Europe also. The traditions of ancient deluges, which are the primitive facts of Greek history, refer to such movements; perhaps the opening of the Thracian Bosphorus was one of them. In much later times we are perpetually meeting with incidents depending on geological disturbances; the caravan trade of Asia Minor was destroyed by changes of level and the accumulation of sands blown from the encroaching deserts; the Cimbri were impelled into Italy by the invasion of the sea on their possessions. There is not a shore in Europe which does not give similar evidence; the mouths of the Rhine, as they were in the Roman times, are obliterated; the eastern coast of England has been cut away for miles. In the Mediterranean the shore-line is altogether changed; towns, once on the coast, are far away inland; others have sunk beneath the sea. Islands, like Rhodes, have risen from the bottom. The North Adriatic, once a deep gulf, has now become shallow; there are leaning towers and inclining temples that have sunk with the settling of the earth. On the opposite extremity of Europe, the Scandinavian peninsula furnishes an instance of slow secular motion, the northern part rising gradually above the sea at the rate of about four feet in a century. This elevation is observed through a space of many hundred miles, increasing toward the north. The southern extremity, on the contrary, experiences a slow depression.

These slow movements are nothing more than a continuation of what has been going on for numberless ages.

Since the tertiary period two-thirds of Europe have been lifted above the sea. The Norway coast has been elevated 600 feet, the Alps have been upheaved 2000 or 3000, the Apennines 1000 to 2000 feet. The country between Mont Blanc and Vienna has been thus elevated since the adjacent seas were peopled with existing animals. Since the Neolithic age, the British Islands have undergone a great change of level, and, indeed, have been separated from the continent through the sinking of England and the rising of Scotland.

At the earliest period Europe presents us with a double population. An Indo-Germanic column had entered it from the east, and had separated into two portions the occupants it had encountered, driving one to the north, the other to the south-west. These primitive tribes betray, physiologically, a Mongolian origin; and there are indications of considerable weight that they themselves had been, in ancient times, intruders, who, issuing from their seats in Asia, had invaded and dislocated the proper autochthons of Europe. In the Pleistocene age there existed in Central Europe a rude race of hunters and fishers, closely allied to the Esquimaux. Man was contemporary with the cave bear, the cave lion, the amphibious hippopotamus, the mammoth. Caves that have been examined in France or elsewhere have furnished for the stone age, axes, knives, lance and arrow points, scrapers, hammers. The change from what has been termed the chipped, to the polished stone period, was very gradual. It coincides with the domestication of the dog, an epoch in hunting life. The appearance of arrow heads indicates the invention of the bow, and the rise of man from a defensive to an offensive mode of life. The introduction of barbed arrows shows how inventive talent was displaying itself; bone and horn tips, that the huntsman was including smaller animals, and perhaps birds, in his chase; bone whistles, his companionship with other huntsmen, or with his dog. The scraping knives of flint, indicate the use of skin for clothing, and rude bodkins and needles, its manufacture. Shells perforated for bracelets and necklaces, prove how soon a taste for personal adornment was acquired; the implements necessary for the

Early inhabitants of Europe.

preparation of pigments suggest the painting of the body, and perhaps, tattooing; and batons of rank bear witness to the beginning of a social organization.

We have thus as our starting-point a barbarian population, believers in sorcery, and, in some places, undoubtedly cannibals, maintaining, in the central and northern parts of Europe, their existence with difficulty by reason of the severity of the climate. In the southern, more congenial conditions permitted a form of civilization to commence, of which the rude Cyclopean structures here and there met with, such as the ruins of Orchomenos, the lion gate of Mycenæ, the tunnel of Lake Copais, are perhaps the vestiges.

At what period this intrusive Indo-Germanic column made its attack cannot be ascertained. The national vocabularies of Europe, to which we must resort for evidence, might lead us to infer that the condition of civilization of the conquering people was not very advanced. They were acquainted with the use of domestic animals, farming implements, carts, and yokes; they were also possessed of boats, the rudder, oars, but were unacquainted with the movement of vessels by sails. These conclusions seem to be established by the facts that words equivalent to boat, rudder, oar, are common to the languages of the offshoots of the stock, though located very widely asunder; but those for mast and sails are of special invention, and differ in adjacent nations.

Their social condition.

In nearly all the Indo-Germanic tongues, the family names, father, mother, brother, sister, daughter, are the same respectively. A similar equivalence may be observed in a great many familiar objects, house, door, town, path. It has been remarked, that while this holds good for terms of a peaceful nature, many of those connected with warfare and the chase are different in different languages. Such facts appear to prove that the Asiatic invaders followed a nomadic and pastoral life. Many of the terms connected with such an avocation are widely diffused. This is the case with ploughing, grinding, weaving, cooking, baking, sewing, spinning; with such objects as corn,

Their civil state deduced from their vocabularies.

flesh, meat, vestment; with wild animals common to Europe and Asia, as the bear and the wolf. So, too, of words connected with social organization, despot, rex, queen. The numerals from 1 to 100 coincide in Sanscrit, Greek, Latin, Lithuanian, Gothic; but this is not the case with 1000, a fact which has led comparative philologists to the conclusion that, though at the time of the emigration a sufficient intellectual advance had been made to invent the decimal system, perhaps from counting upon the fingers, yet that it was very far from perfection. To the inhabitants of Central Asia the sea was altogether unknown; hence the branches of the emigrating column, as they diverged north and south, gave it different names. But, though unacquainted with the sea, they were familiar with salt, as is proved by the recurrence of its name. Nor is it in the vocabularies alone that these resemblances are remarked; the same is to be said of the grammar. M. Max Müller shows that in Sanscrit, Zend, Lithuanian, Doric, Slavonic, Latin, Gothic, the forms of the auxiliary verb *to be* are all varieties of one common type, and that "the coincidences between the language of the Veda and the dialect spoken at the present day by the Lithuanian recruits at Berlin are greater by far than between French and Italian, and that the essential forms of grammar had been fully framed and established before the first separation of the Aryan family took place."

But it should not be overlooked that such interesting deductions founded on language, its vocabularies and grammar, must not be pressed too closely. The state of civilization of the Indo-Germanic column, as thus ascertained, must needs have been inferior to that of the centre from which it issued forth. Such we observe to be the case in all migratory movements. It is not the more intellectual or civilized portions of a community which voluntarily participate therein, but those in whom the physical and animal character predominates. There may be a very rough offshoot from a very polished stock. Of course, the movement we are here considering must have taken place at a period chronologically remote, yet not so remote as might seem to be indicated by the state of civilization of the invaders, used as an indication of the state of civilization of the country from which they had come. In Asia, social advancement, as far back as we can discover, has ever been very slow; but, at the first moment that we encounter the Hindu race historically or philologically, it is dealing with philosophical and theological questions of the highest order, and settling, to its own satisfaction, problems requiring a cultivated intellect even so much as to propose. All this implies that in its social advancement there must have already been consumed a very long period of time.

But what chiefly interests us is the relation which must have been necessarily maintained between the intrusive people and those whom they thus displaced, the commingling of the ideas of the one with those of the other, arising from their commingling of blood. It is because of this that we find coexisting in the pre-Hellenic times the sorcery of the Celt and the polytheism of the Hindu. There can be no doubt that many of the philosophical lineaments displayed by the early European mythology are not due to indigenous thought, but were derived from an Asiatic source.

Commingling of blood and of ideas.

Moreover, at the earliest historic times, notwithstanding the disturbance which must have lasted long after the successful and perhaps slow advance of the Asiatic column, things had come to a state of equilibrium or repose, not alone socially, but also physiologically. It takes a long time for the conqueror and conquered to settle together, without farther disturbance or question, into their relative positions; it takes a long time for the recollection of conflicts to die away. But far longer does it take for a race of invaders to come into unison with the climate of the countries they have seized, the system of man accommodating itself only through successive generations, and therefore very slowly, to new physical conditions. It takes long before the skin assumes its determinate hue, and the skull its destined form. A period amply sufficient for all such changes to be accomplished in Europe had transpired at the very dawn of history, and strands of population in conformity with meteorological and geographical influences, though of such origin as has been described, were already

Climate-modification of Asiatic intruders.

distributed upon it. A condition of ethnical equilibrium had been reached. Along each isothermal or climatic band were its correspondingly modified men, spending their lives in avocations dictated by their environment. These strands of population were destined to be dislocated, and some of them to become extinct, by inventing or originating among themselves new and unsuitable artificial physical conditions.

Already Europe was preparing a repetition of those events of which Asia from time immemorial has been the scene. Already among the nations bordering on the Mediterranean, inhabitants of a pleasant climate, in which life could be easily maintained—where the isothermal of January is 41° F., and of July 73½° F.—civilization was commencing. There was an improving agriculture, an increasing commerce, and, the necessary consequence thereof, germs of art, the accumulation of wealth. The southern peninsulas were offering to the warlike chieftains of middle Europe a tempting prize.

First gleams of civilization

Under such influences Europe may be considered as emerging from the barbarian state. It had lost all recollection of its ancient relations with India, which have only been disclosed to us by a study of the vocabularies and grammar of its diverse tongues. Upon its indigenous sorcery an Oriental star-worship had been ingrafted, the legends of which had lost their significance. What had at first been feigned of the heavenly bodies had now assumed an air of personality, and had become attributed to heroes and gods.

and first religious opinions.

The negro under the equinoctial line, the dwarfish Laplander beyond the Arctic Circle—man everywhere, in his barbarous state, is a believer in sorcery, witchcraft, enchantments; he is fascinated by the incomprehensible. Any unexpected sound or sudden motion he refers to invisible beings. Sleep and dreams, in which one-third of his life is spent, assure him that there is a spiritual world. He multiplies these unrealities; he gives to every grotto a genius; to every tree, spring, river, mountain, a divinity.

Comparative theology, which depends on the law of continuous variation of human thought, and is indeed one of its expressions, universally proves that the moment man adopts the idea of an existence of invisible beings, he recognizes the necessity of places for their residence, all nations assigning them habitations beyond the boundaries of the earth. A local heaven and a local hell are found in every mythology. In Greece, as to heaven, there was a universal agreement that it was situated above the blue sky; but as to hell, much difference of opinion prevailed. There were many who thought that it was a deep abyss in the interior of the earth, to which certain passages, such as the Acherusian cave in Bithynia, led. But those who with Anaximenes considered the earth to be like a broad leaf floating in the air, and who accepted the doctrine that hell was divided into a Tartarus, or region of night on the left, and an Elysium, or region of dawn on the right, and that it was equally distant from all parts of the upper surface, were nearer to the original conception, which doubtless placed it on the under or shadowy side of the earth. The portals of descent were thus in the west, where the sun and stars set, though here and there were passages leading through the ground to the other side, such as those by which Hercules and Ulysses had gone. The place of ascent was in the east, and the morning twilight a reflection from the Elysian Fields.

Localization of the invisible.

The picture of Nature thus interpreted has for its centre the earth; for its most prominent object, man. Whatever there is has been made for his pleasure, or to minister to his use. To this belief that every thing is of a subordinate value compared with himself, he clings with tenacity even in his most advanced mental state.

The anthropocentric stage of thought.

Not without surprise do we trace the progress of the human mind. The barbarian, as a believer in sorcery, lives in incessant dread. All Nature seems to be at enmity with him and conspiring for his hurt. Out of the darkness he cannot tell what alarming spectre may emerge; he may, with reason, fear that injury is concealed in every stone, and hidden behind every leaf. How wide is the interval from this terror-stricken condition to that state in which man persuades himself of the human destiny of the universe! Yet, wonderful to be said, he passes that interval at a single step.

In the infancy of the human race, geographical and astronomical ideas are the same all over the world, for they are the interpretation of things according to outward appearances, the accepting of phenomena as they are presented, without any of the corrections that reason may offer. This universality and homogeneity is nothing more than a manifestation of the uniform mode of action of human organization.

From homogeneous ideas the comparative sciences emerge.

But such homogeneous conclusions, such similar pictures, are strictly peculiar to the infancy of humanity. The reasoning faculty at length inevitably makes itself felt, and diversities of interpretation ensue. Comparative geography, comparative astronomy, comparative theology thus arise, homogeneous at first, but soon exhibiting variations.

Introduction of personified forms.

To that tendency for personification which marks the early life of man are due many of the mythologic conceptions. It was thus that the Hours, the Dawn, and Night with her black mantle bespangled with stars, received their forms. Many of the most beautiful legends were thus of a personified astronomical origin; many were derived from terrestrial or familiar phenomena, The clouds were thus made to be animated things; a moving spirit was given to the storm, the dew, the wind. The sun setting in the glowing clouds of the west became Hercules in the fiery pile; the morning dawn extinguished by the rising sun was embodied in the story of Orpheus and Eurydice. These legends still survive in India.

The gradual and affiliated advance of Greek theological ideas.

But it must not be supposed that all Greek mythology can be thus explained. It is enough for us to examine the circumstances under which, for many ages, the European communities had been placed, to understand that they had forgotten much that their ancestors had brought from Asia. Much that was new had also spontaneously arisen. The well-known variations of their theogony are not merely similar legends of different localities, they are more frequently the successive improvements of one place. The general theme upon which they are based requires the admission of a primitive chaotic disturbance of incomprehensible gigantic powers, brought into subjection by Divine agency, that agency dividing and regulating the empire it had thus acquired in a harmonious way. To this general conception was added a multitude of adventitious ornaments, some of which were of a rude astronomical, some of a moral, some, doubtless, of a historical kind. The primitive chaotic conflicts appear under the form of the war of the Titans; their end is the confinement of those giants in Tartarus; whose compulsory subjection is the commencement of order: thus Atlas, the son of Iapetos, is made to sustain the vault of heaven in its western verge. The regulation of empire is shadowed forth in the subdivision of the universe between Zeus and his brothers, he taking the heavens, Poseidon the sea, and Hades the under world, all having the earth as their common theatre of action. The moral is prefigured by such myths as those of Prometheus and Epimetheus, the fore-thinker and the after-thinker; the historical in the deluge of Deucalion, the sieges of Thebes and of Troy. A harmony with human nature is established through the birth and marriage of the gods, and likewise by their sufferings, passions, and labours. The supernatural is gratified by Centaurs, Gorgons, Harpies, and Cyclops.

The composite nature of the resulting mythology.

It would be in vain to attempt the reduction of such a patchwork system to any single principle, astronomical or moral, as some have tried to do—a system originating from no single point as to country or to time. The gradual growth of many ages, its diversities are due to many local circumstances. Like the romances of a later period, it will not bear an application of the ordinary rules of life. It recommended itself to a people who found pleasure in accepting without any question statements no matter how marvellous, impostures no matter how preposterous. Gods, heroes, monsters, and men might figure together without any outrage to probability when there was no astronomy, no geography, no rule of evidence, no standard of belief. But the downfall of such a system was inevitable as soon as men began to deal with facts; as soon as history commenced to record, and philosophy to discuss.

Yet not without reluctance was the faith of so many centuries given up. The extinction of a religion is not the abrupt movement of a day, it is a secular process of many well-marked stages—the rise of doubt among the candid; the disapprobation of the conservative; the defence of ideas fast becoming obsolete by the well-meaning, who hope that allegory and new interpretations may give renewed probability to what is almost incredible. But dissent ends in denial at last.

Before we enter upon the history of that intellectual movement which thus occasioned the ruin of the ancient system, we must bring to ourselves the ideas of the Greek of the eighth century before Christ, who thought that the blue sky is the floor of heaven, the habitation of the Olympian gods; that the earth, man's proper abode, is flat and circularly extended like a plate beneath the starry canopy. On its rim is the circumfluous ocean, the source of the rivers, which all flow to the Mediterranean, appropriately in after ages so called, since it is in the midst, in the centre of the expanse of the land. "The sea-girt disk of the earth supports the vault of heaven." Impelled by a celestial energy, the sun and stars, issuing forth from the east, ascend with difficulty the crystalline dome, but down its descent they more readily hasten to their setting. No one can tell what they encounter in the land of shadows beneath, nor what are the dangers of the way. In the morning the dawn mysteriously appears in the east, and swiftly spreads over the confines of the horizon; in the evening the twilight fades gradually away. Besides the celestial bodies, the clouds are continually moving over the sky, for ever changing their colours and their shape. No one can tell whence the wind comes or whither it goes; perhaps it is the breath of that invisible divinity who launches the lightning, or of him who rests his bow against the cloud. Not without delight men contemplated the emerald plane, the sapphire dome, the border of silvery water, ever tranquil and ever flowing. Then, in the interior of the solid earth, or perhaps on the other side of its plane—under world, as it was well termed—is the realm of Hades or Pluto,

Primitive astronomy and geography.

The under world and its spectres.

the region of Night. From the midst of his dominion, that divinity, crowned with a diadem of ebony, and seated on a throne framed out of massive darkness, looks into the infinite abyss beyond, invisible himself to mortal eyes, but made known by the nocturnal thunder which is his weapon. The under world is also the realm to which spirits retire after death. At its portals, beneath the setting sun, is stationed a numerous tribe of spectres—Care, Sorrow, Disease, Age, Want, Fear, Famine, War, Toil, Death and her half-brother Sleep—Death, to whom it is useless for man to offer either prayers or sacrifice. In that land of forgetfulness and shadows there is the unnavigable lake Avernus, Acheron, Styx, the groaning Cocytus, and Phlegethon, with its waves of fire. There are all kinds of monsters and forms of fearful import: Cerberus, with his triple head; Charon, freighting his boat with the shades of the dead; the Fates, in their garments of ermine bordered with purple; the avenging Erinnys; Rhadamanthus, before whom every Asiatic must render his account; Æacus, before whom every European; and Minos, the dread arbiter of the judgment-seat. There, too, are to be seen those great criminals whose history is a warning to us: the giants, with dragons' feet extended in the burning gulf for many a mile; Phlegyas, in perpetual terror of the stone suspended over him, which never falls; Ixion chained to his wheel; the daughters of Danaus still vainly trying to fill their sieve; Tantalus, immersed in water to his chin, yet tormented with unquenchable thirst; Sisyphus despairingly labouring at his ever-descending stone. Warned by such examples, we may learn not to contemn the gods. Beyond these sad scenes, extending far to the right, are the plains of pleasure, the Elysian Fields; and Lethe, the river of oblivion, of which whoever tastes, though he should ascend to the eastern boundary of the earth, and return again to life and day, forgets whatever he has seen.

If the interior or the under side of the earth is thus occupied by phantoms and half-animated shades of the dead, its upper surface, inhabited by man, has also its wonders. In its centre is the Mediterranean Sea, as we have said, round which are placed all the known countries, each full of its own mysteries and marvels. Of these how many we might recount if we followed the wanderings of Odysseus, or the voyage of Jason and his heroic comrades in the ship *Argo*, when they went to seize the golden fleece of the speaking ram. We might tell of the Harpies, flying women-birds of obscene form; of the blind prophet; of the Symplegades, self-shutting rocks, between which, as if by miracle, the Argonauts passed, the cliffs almost entrapping the stern of their vessel, but destined by fate from that portentous moment never to close again; of the country of the Amazons, and of Prometheus groaning on the rock to which he was nailed, of the avenging eagle for ever hovering and for ever devouring; of the land of Æêtes, and of the bulls with brazen feet and flaming breath, and how Jason yoked and made them plough; of the enchantress Medea, and the unguent she concocted from herbs that grew where the blood of Prometheus had dripped; of the field sown with dragons' teeth, and the mail-clad men that leaped out of the furrows; of the magical stone that divided them into two parties, and impelled them to fight each other; of the scaly dragon that guarded the golden fleece, and how he was lulled with a charmed potion, and the treasure carried away; of the River Phasis, through whose windings the *Argo* sailed into the circumfluous sea; of the circumnavigation round that tranquil stream to the sources of the Nile; of the Argonauts carrying their sentient, self-speaking ship on their shoulders through the sweltering Libyan deserts; of the island of Circe, the enchantress; of the rock, with its grateful haven, which in the height of a tempest rose out of the sea to receive them; of the arrow shot by Apollo from his golden bow; of the brazen man, the work of Hephæstos, who stood on the shore of Crete, and hurled at them as they passed vast fragments of stone; of their combat with him and their safe return to Iolcos; and of the translation of the ship *Argo* by the goddess Athene to heaven.

The Argonautic voyage.

Such were some of the incidents of that celebrated voyage, the story of which enchanted all Greece before the Odyssey was written. I have not space to tell of the wonders that served to decorate the geography of those times. On the north there was the delicious country of the Hyperboreans, beyond the reach of winter; in the west the garden of the Hesperides, in which grew apples of gold; in the east the groves and dancing-ground of the sun; in the south the country of the blameless Ethiopians, whither the gods were wont to resort. In the Mediterranean itself the Sirens beguiled the passers-by with their songs near where Naples now stands; adjoining were Scylla and Charybdis; in Sicily were the one-eyed Cyclops and cannibal Læstrygons. In the island of Erytheia the three-headed giant Geryon tended his oxen with a double-headed dog. I need not speak of the lotus-eaters, whose food made one forget his native country; of the floating island of Æolus; of the happy fields in which the horses of the sun were grazing; of bulls and dogs of immortal breed; of hydras, gorgons, and chimeras; of the flying man Dædalus, and the brazen chamber in which Danae was kept. There was no river, no grotto that had not its genius; no island, no promontory without its legend.

Union of the geographical and the marvellous.

It is impossible to recall these antique myths without being satisfied that they are, for the most part, truly indigenous, truly of European growth. The seed may have been brought, as comparative philologists assert, from Asia, but it had luxuriantly germinated and developed under the sky of Europe. Of the legends, many are far from answering to their reputed Oriental source; their barbarism and indelicacy represent the state of Europe. The outrage of Kronos on his father Uranos speaks of the savagism of the times; the story of Dionysos tells of man-stealing and piracy; the rapes of Europa and Helen, of the abduction of women. The dinner at which Itys was served up assures us that cannibalism was practised; the threat of Laomedon that he would sell Poseidon and Apollo for slaves shows how compulsory labour might be obtained. The polygamy of many heroes often appears in its worst form under the practice of sister-marriage, a crime indulged in from the King of Olympus downward. Upon the whole, then, we must admit that Greek mythology indicates a barbarian social state, man-stealing,

Earliest Greek theological ideas indicate a savage state.

piracy, human sacrifice, polygamy, cannibalism, and crimes of revenge that are unmentionable. A personal interpretation, such as man in his infancy resorts to, is embodied in circumstances suitable to a savage time. It was not until a later period that allegorical phantasms, such as Death, and Sleep, and Dreams were introduced, and still later when the whole system was affected by Lydian, Phrygian, Assyrian, and Egyptian ideas.

Their gradual improvement in the historic times.

Not only thus from their intrinsic nature, but also from their recorded gradual development, are we warranted in imputing to the greater part of the myths an indigenous origin. The theogony of Homer is extended by Hesiod in many essential points. He prefixes the dynasty of Uranos, and differs in minor conceptions, as in the character of the Cyclops. The Orphic theogony is again another advance, having new fictions and new personages, as in the case of Zagreus, the horned child of Jupiter by his own daughter Persephone. Indeed, there is hardly one of the great and venerable gods of Olympus whose character does not change with his age, and, seen from this point of view, the origin of the Ionic philosophy becomes a necessary step in the advance. That philosophy, as we shall soon find, was due not only to the expansion of the Greek intellect and the necessary improvement of Greek morals; an extraneous cause, the sudden opening of the Egyptian ports, 670 B.C., accelerated it. European religion became more mysterious and more solemn. European philosophy learned the error of its chronology, and the necessity of applying a more strict and correct standard of evidence for ancient events.

The inevitable tendency is to the Ionic philosophy.

It was an ominous circumstance that the Ionian Greeks, who first began to philosophize, commenced their labours by depersonifying the elements, and treating not of Zeus, Poseidon, and Hades, but of Air, Water, Fire. The destruction of theological conceptions led irresistibly to the destruction of religious practices. To divinities whose existence he denied, the philosopher ceased to pray. Of what use were sacrificial offerings and entreaties directed to phantasms of the imagination? but advantages might accrue from the physical study of the impersonal elements.

Greek religion contained within itself the principles of its own destruction. It is for the sake of thoroughly appreciating this that I have been led into a detail of what some of my readers may be disposed to regard as idle and useless myths. Two circumstances of inevitable occurrence insured the eventual overthrow of the whole system; they were geographical discovery and the rise of philosophical criticism. Our attention is riveted by the fact that, two thousand years later, the same thing again occurred on a greater scale.

Inevitable destruction of Greek religious ideas

As to the geographical discovery, how was it possible that all the marvels of the Mediterranean and Black Seas, the sorcerers, enchanters, giants, and monsters of the deep, should survive when those seas were daily crossed in all directions? How was it possible that the notion of a flat earth, bounded by the horizon and bordered by the circumfluous ocean, could maintain itself when colonies were being founded in Gaul, and the Phœnicians were bringing tin from beyond the Pillars of Hercules? Moreover, it so happened that many of the most astounding prodigies were affirmed to be in the track which circumstances had now made the chief pathway of commerce. Not only was there a certainty of the destruction of mythical geography as thus presented on the plane of the earth looking upward to day; there was also an imminent risk, as many pious persons foresaw and dreaded, that what had been asserted as respects the interior, or the other face looking downward into night, would be involved in the ruin too. Well, therefore, might they make the struggle they did for the support of the ancient doctrine, taking the only course possible to them, of converting what had been affirmed to be actual events into allegories, under which, they said, the wisdom of ancient times had concealed many sacred and mysterious things. But it is apparent that a system forced to this necessity is fast hastening to its end.

by geographical discovery.

Nor was it maritime discovery only that thus removed fabulous prodigies and gave rise to new ideas. In due course of time the Macedonian expedition opened a new world to the Greeks and presented them with real wonders; climates in marvellous diversity, vast deserts, mountains covered with eternal snow, salt seas far from the ocean, colossal animals, and men of every shade of colour and every form of religion. The numerous Greek colonies founded all over Asia gave rise to an incessant locomotion, and caused these natural objects to make a profound and permanent impression on the Hellenic mind. If through the Bactrian empire European ideas were transmitted to the far East, through that and other similar channels Asiatic ideas found their way to Europe.

Fictitious marvels replaced by grand actualities.

At the dawn of trustworthy history, the Phœnicians were masters of the Mediterranean Sea. Europe was altogether barbarous. On the very verge of Asiatic civilization the Thracians scalped their enemies and tattooed themselves; at the other end of the continent the Britons daubed their bodies with ochre and woad. Contemporaneous Egyptian sculptures show the Europeans dressed in skins like savages. It was the instinct of the Phœnicians everywhere to establish themselves on islands and coasts, and thus, for a long time, they maintained a maritime supremacy. By degrees a spirit of adventure was engendered among the Greeks. In 1250 B.C. they sailed round the Euxine, giving rise to the myth of the Argonautic voyage, and creating a profitable traffic in gold, dried fish, and corn. They had also become infamous for their freebooting practices. From every coast they stole men, women, and children, thereby maintaining a considerable slave-trade, the relic of which endures to our time in the traffic for Circassian women. Minos, King of Crete, tried to suppress these piracies. His attempts to obtain the dominion of the Mediterranean were imitated in succession by the Lydians, Thracians, Rhodians, the latter being the inventors of the first maritime code, subsequently incorporated into Roman law. The manner in which these and the inhabitants of other towns and islands supplanted one another shows on what trifling circumstances the dominion of the eastern basin depended. Meantime Tyrian seamen stealthily

Development of Mediterranean commerce.

sailed beyond the Pillars of Hercules, visiting the Canaries and Azores, and bringing tin from the British Islands. They used every precaution to keep their secret to themselves. The adventurous Greeks followed those mysterious navigators step by step; but in the time of Homer they were so restricted to the eastern basin that Italy may be said to have been to them an unknown land. The Phocæans first explored the western basin; one of their colonies built Marseilles. At length Coleus of Samos passed through the frowning gateway of Hercules into the circumfluous sea, the Atlantic Ocean. No little interest attaches to the first colonial cities; they dotted the shores from Sinope to Saguntum, and were at once trading depôts and foci of wealth. In the earliest times the merchant was his own captain, and sold his commodities by auction at the place to which he came. The primitive and profitable commerce of the Mediterranean was peculiar—it was for slaves, mineral products, and articles of manufacture; for, running coincident with parallels of latitude, its agricultural products were not very varied, and the wants of its populations the same. But tin was brought from the Cassiterides, amber from the Baltic, and dyed goods and worked metals from Syria. Wherever these trades centred, the germs of taste and intelligence were developed; thus the Etruscans, in whose hands was the amber trade across Germany, have left many relics of their love of art. Though a mysterious, they were hardly a gloomy race, as a great modern author has supposed, if we may judge from their beautiful remains.

Effect of philosophical criticism.

Added to the effect of geographical discovery was the development of philosophical criticism. It is observed that soon after the first Olympiad the Greek intellect very rapidly expanded. Whenever man reaches a certain point in his mental progress, he will not be satisfied with less than an application of existing rules to ancient events. Experience has taught him that the course of the world to-day is the same as it was yesterday; he unhesitatingly believes that this will also hold good for to-morrow. He will not bear to contemplate any break in the mechanism of history; he will not be satisfied with a mere uninquiring faith, but insists upon having the same voucher for an old fact that he requires for one that is new. Before the face of History Mythology cannot stand.

Secession of literary men from the public faith.

The operation of this principle is seen in all directions throughout Greek literature after the date that has been mentioned, and this the more strikingly as the time is later. The national intellect became more and more ashamed of the fables it had believed in its infancy. Of the legends, some are allegorized, some are modified, some are repudiated. The great tragedians accept the myths in the aggregate, but decline them in particulars; some of the poets transform or allegorize them; some use them ornamentally, as graceful decorations. It is evident that between the educated and the vulgar classes a divergence is taking place, that the best men of the times see the necessity of either totally abandoning these cherished fictions to the lower orders, or of gradually replacing them with something more suitable. Such a frittering away of sacred things was, however, very far from meeting with public approbation in Athens itself, although so many people in that city had reached that state of mental development in which it was impossible for them to continue to accept the national faith. They tried to force themselves to believe that there must be something true in that which had been believed by so many great and pious men of old, which had approved itself by lasting so many centuries, and of which it was by the common people asserted that absolute demonstration could be given. But it was in vain; intellect had outgrown faith. They had come into that condition to which all men are liable—aware of the fallacy of their opinions, yet angry that another should remind them thereof. When the social state no longer permitted them to take the life of a philosophical offender, they found means to put upon him such an invisible pressure as to present him the choice of orthodoxy or beggary. Thus they disapproved of Euripides permitting his characters to indulge in any sceptical reflections, and discountenanced the impiety so obvious in the 'Prometheus Bound' of Æschylus. It was by appealing to this sentiment that Aristophanes added no little to the excitement against

Socrates. They who are doubting themselves are often loudest in public denunciations of a similar state in others.

If thus the poets, submitting to common sense, had so rapidly fallen away from the national belief, the philosophers pursued the same course. It soon became the universal impression that there was an intrinsic opposition between philosophy and religion, and herein public opinion was not mistaken; the fact that polytheism furnished a religious explanation for every natural event made it essentially antagonistic to science. It was the uncontrollable advance of knowledge that overthrew Greek religion. Socrates himself never hesitated to denounce physics for that tendency; and the Athenians extended his principles to his own pursuits, their strong common sense telling them that the philosophical cultivation of ethics must be equally bad. He was not loyal to science, but sought to support his own views by exciting a theological odium against his competitors—a crime that educated men ought never to forgive. In the tragedy that ensued the Athenians only paid him in his own coin. The immoralities imputed to the gods were doubtless strongly calculated to draw the attention of reflecting men, but the essential nature of the pursuit in which the Ionian and Italian schools were engaged bore directly on the doctrine of a providential government of the world. It not only turned into a fiction the time-honoured dogma of the omnipresence of the Olympian divinities—it even struck at their very existence, by leaving them nothing to do. For those personifications it introduced impersonal nature or the elements. Instead of uniting scientific interpretations to ancient traditions, it modified and moulded the old traditions to suit the apparent requirements of science. We shall subsequently see what was the necessary issue of this—the Divinity became excluded from the world he had made, the supernatural merged in natural agency; Zeus was superseded by the air, Poseidon by the water; and, while some of the philosophers received in silence the popular legends, as was the case with Socrates, or, like Plato, regarded it as a patriotic duty to accept the public faith, others, like Xenophanes, denounced the whole as

Secession of the philosophers.

an ancient blunder, converted by time into a national imposture.

As I shall have occasion to speak of Greek philosophy in a detailed manner, it is unnecessary to enter into other particulars here. For the present purpose it is enough to understand that it was radically opposed to the national faith in all countries and at all times, from its origin with Thales down to the latest critic of the Alexandrian school.

Antagonism of science and polytheism.

As it was with philosophers, so it was with historians; the rise of true history brought the same result as the rise of true philosophy. In this instance there was added a special circumstance which gave to the movement no little force. Whatever might be the feigned facts of the Grecian foretime, they were altogether outdone in antiquity and wonder by the actual history of Egypt. What was a pious man like Herodotus to think when he found that, at the very period he had supposed a superhuman state of things in his native country, the ordinary passage of affairs was taking place on the banks of the Nile? And so indeed it had been for untold ages. To every one engaged in recording recent events, it must have been obvious that a chronology applied where the actors are superhuman is altogether without basis, and that it is a delusion to transfer the motives and thoughts of men to those who are not men. Under such circumstances there is a strong inducement to decline traditions altogether; for no philosophical mind will ever be satisfied with different tests for the present and the past, but will insist that actions and their sequences were the same in the foretime as now.

Secession of historians.

Thus for many ages stood affairs. One after another, historians, philosophers, critics, poets, had given up the national faith, and lived under a pressure perpetually laid upon them by the public, adopting generally, as their most convenient course, an outward compliance with the religious requirements of the state. Herodotus cannot reconcile the inconsistencies of the Trojan War with his knowledge of human actions; Thucydides does not dare to express his disbelief of it; Eratosthenes sees contradictions between the voyage of

Universal disbelief of the learned.

Odysseus and the truths of geography; Anaxagoras is condemned to death for impiety, and only through the exertions of the chief of the state is his sentence mercifully commuted to banishment. Plato, seeing things from a very general point of view, thinks it expedient, upon the whole, to prohibit the cultivation of the higher branches of physics. Euripides tries to free himself from the imputation of heresy as best he may. Æschylus is condemned to be stoned to death for blasphemy, and is only saved by his brother Aminias raising his mutilated arm—he had lost his hand in the battle of Salamis. Socrates stands his trial, and has to drink hemlock. Even great statesmen like Pericles had become entangled in the obnoxious opinions. No one has anything to say in explanation of the marvellous disappearance of demigods and heroes, why miracles are ended, or why human actions alone are now to be seen in the world. An ignorant public demands the instant punishment of every suspected man. In their estimation, to distrust the traditions of the past is to be guilty of treason to the present.

Attempts at a reformation.

But all this confusion and dissent did not arise without an attempt among well-meaning men at a reformation. Some, and they were, perhaps, the most advanced intellectually, wished that the priests should abstain from working any more miracles; that relics should be as little used as was consistent with the psychical demands of the vulgar, and should be gradually abandoned; that philosophy should no longer be outraged with the blasphemous anthropomorphisms of the Olympian deities. Some, less advanced, were disposed to reconcile all difficulties by regarding the myths as allegorical; some wished to transform them so as to bring them into harmony with the existing social state; some would give them altogether new interpretations. With one, though the fact of a Trojan War is not to be denied, it was only the eidolon of Helen whom Paris carried away; with another expressions, perhaps once intended to represent actual events, are dwindled into mere forms of speech. Unwilling to reject the attributes of the Olympian divinities, their human passions and actions, another asserts that they must once have all existed as men. While one denounces the impudent atheists who find fault with the myths of the Iliad, ignorant of its allegorical meaning, another resolves all its heroes into the elements; and still another, hoping to reconcile to the improved moral sense of the times the indecencies and wickednesses of the gods, imputes them all to demons; an idea which found much favour at first, but became singularly fatal to polytheism in the end.

Inveterate superstition of the vulgar.

In apparent inconsistency with this declining state of belief in the higher classes, the multitude, without concern, indulged in the most surprising superstitions. With them it was an age of relics, of weeping statues, and winking pictures. The tools with which the Trojan horse was made might still be seen at Metapontum, the sceptre of Pelops was still preserved at Chæroncia, the spear of Achilles at Phaselis, the sword of Memnon at Nicomedia; the Tegeates could still show the hide of the Calydonian boar, very many cities boasted their possession of the true palladium from Troy. There were statues of Athene that could brandish spears, paintings that could blush, images that could sweat, and numberless shrines and sanctuaries at which miracle-cures were performed. Into the hole through which the deluge of Deucalion receded the Athenians still poured a customary sacrifice of honey and meal. He would have been an adventurous man who risked any observation as to its inadequate size. And though the sky had been proved to be only space and stars, and not the firm floor of Olympus, he who had occasion to refer to the flight of the gods from mountain tops into heaven would find it to his advantage to make no astronomical remark. No adverse allusions to the poems of Homer, Arctinus, or Lesches were tolerated; he who perpetrated the blasphemy of depersonifying the sun went in peril of death. It was not permitted that natural phenomena should be substituted for Zeus and Poseidon; whoever was suspected of believing that Helios and Selene were not gods, would do well to purge himself to public satisfaction. The people vindicated their superstition in spite of all geographical and physical difficulties, and, far from concerning themselves

Their jealous intolerance of doubts.

with the contradictions which had exerted such an influence on the thinking classes, practically asserted the needlessness of any historical evidence.

Slowness of the decline and fall of Polytheism.

It is altogether erroneous to suppose that polytheism mantained its ground as a living force until the period of Constantine and Julian. Its downfall commenced at the time of the opening of the Egyptian ports. Nearly a thousand years were required for its consummation. The change first occurred among the higher classes, and made its way slowly through the middle ranks of society. For many centuries the two agencies—geographical discovery, arising from increasing commerce and the Macedonian expedition, and philosophical criticism—silently continued their incessant work, and yet it does not appear that they could ever produce a change in the lowest and most numerous division of the social grade. In process of time, a third influence was added to the preceding two, enabling them to address themselves even to the humblest rank of life; this influence was the rise of the Roman power. It produced a wonderful activity all over the Mediterranean Sea and throughout the adjoining countries. It insured perpetual movements in all directions. Where there had been only a single traveller there were now a thousand legionaries, merchants, government officials, with their long retinues of dependents and slaves. Where formerly it was only the historian or philosopher in his retirement who compared or contrasted the laws and creeds, habits and customs of different nations incorrectly reported, now the same things were vividly brought under the personal observation of multitudes. The crowd of gods and goddesses congregated in Rome served only to bring one another into disrepute and ridicule.

The secondary causes of its downfall.

Long, therefore, previous to the triumph of Christianity, paganism must be considered as having been irretrievably ruined. Doubtless it was the dreadful social prospect before them—the apparent impossibility of preventing the whole world from falling into a totally godless state, that not only reconciled so many great men to give their support to the ancient system,

The alarm of good and religious men.

but even to look without disapprobation on that physical violence to which the uneducated multitude, incapable of judging, were so often willing to resort. They never anticipated that any new system could be introduced which should take the place of the old, worn-out one; they had no idea that relief in this respect was so close at hand; unless, perhaps, it might have been Plato, who, profoundly recognizing that, though it is a hard and tedious process to change radically the ideas of common men, yet that it is easy to persuade them to accept new names if they are permitted to retain old things, proposed that a regenerated system should be introduced, with ideas and forms suited to the existing social state, prophetically asserting that the world would very soon become accustomed to it, and give to it an implicit adhesion.

Plato's remedy for the evil.

In this description of the origin and decline of Greek religion I have endeavoured to bring its essential features into strong relief. Its fall was not sudden, as many have supposed, neither was it accomplished by extraneous violence. There was a slow, and, it must be emphatically added, a spontaneous decline. But, if the affairs of men pass in recurring cycles—if the course of events with one individual has a resemblance to the course of events with another—if there be analogies in the progress of nations, and circumstances reappear after due periods of time, the succession of events thus displayed before us in the intellectual history of Greece may perhaps be recognised again in grander proportions on the theatre of all Europe. If there is for the human mind a predetermined order of development, may we not reasonably expect that the phenomena we have thus been noticing on a small scale in a single nation will reappear on the great scale in a continent; that the philosophical study of this history of the past will not only serve as an interpretation of many circumstances in the history of Europe in the Dark and Middle Ages, but will also be a guide to us in pointing out future events as respects all mankind? For, though it is true that the Greek intellectual movement was anticipated, as respects its completion, by being enveloped

The Greek movement has been repeated on a greater scale by all Europe.

and swallowed up in the slower but more gigantic movements of the southern European mind, just as a little expanding circle upon the sea may be obliterated and borne away by more imposing and impetuous waves, so even the movement of a continent may be lost in the movement of a world. It was criticism and physical discovery, and intellectual activity, arising from political concentration, that so profoundly affected the modes of Grecian thought, and criticism and discovery have within the last four hundred years done the same in all Europe. To one who forms his expectations of the future from the history of the past—who recalls the effect produced by the establishment of the Roman empire, in permitting free personal intercommunication among all the Mediterranean nations, and thereby not only destroying the ancient forms of thought which for centuries had resisted all other means of attack, but also replacing them by a homogeneous idea—it must be apparent that the wonderfully increased facilities for locomotion, the inventions of our own age, are the ominous precursors of a vast philosophical revolution.

The organization of hypocrisy.

Between that period during which a nation has been governed by its imagination and that in which it submits to reason, there is a melancholy interval. The constitution of man is such that, for a long time after he has discovered the incorrectness of the ideas prevailing around him, he shrinks from openly emancipating himself from their dominion, and, constrained by the force of circumstances, he becomes a hypocrite, publicly applauding what his private judgment condemns. Where a nation is making this passage, so universal do these practices become that it may be truly said hypocrisy is organized. It is possible that whole communities might be found living in this deplorable state. Such, I conceive, must have been the case in many parts of the Roman empire just before the introduction of Christianity. Even after ideas have given way in public opinion, their political power may outlive their intellectual vigour, and produce the disgraceful effect we here consider.

It is not to be concealed, however, that, to some extent,

this evil is incident to the position of things. Indeed, it would be unfortunate if national hypocrisy could not find a better excuse for itself than in that of the individual. In civilized life, society is ever under the imperious necessity of moving onward in legal forms, nor can such forms be avoided without the most serious disasters ensuing. To absolve communities too abruptly from the restraints of ancient ideas is not to give them liberty, but to throw them into political vagabondism, and hence it is that great statesmen will authorize and even compel observances the essential significance of which has disappeared, and the intellectual basis of which has been undermined. Truth reaches her full action by degrees, and not at once; she first operates upon the reason, the influence being purely intellectual and individual; she then extends her sphere, exerting a moral control, particularly through public opinion; at last she gathers for herself physical and political force. It is in the time consumed in this gradual passage that organized hypocrisy prevails. To bring nations to surrender themselves to new ideas is not the affair of a day.

CHAPTER III.

DIGRESSION ON HINDU THEOLOGY AND EGYPTIAN CIVILIZATION.

Comparative Theology of India; its Phase of Sorcery; its Anthropocentric Phase.

VEDAISM *the Contemplation of Matter, or Adoration of Nature, set forth in the Vedas and Institutes of Menu.—The Universe is God.—Transmutation of the World.—Doctrine of Emanation.—Transmigration.—Absorption.—Penitential Services.—Happiness in Absolute Quietude.*

BUDDHISM *the Contemplation of Force.—The supreme impersonal Power.—Nature of the World—of Man.—The Passage of every thing to Nonentity.—Development of Buddhism into a vast monastic System marked by intense Selfishness.—Its practical Godlessness.*

EGYPT *a mysterious Country to the old Europeans.—Its History, great public Works, and foreign Relations.—Antiquity of its Civilization and Art.—Its Philosophy, hieroglyphic Literature, and peculiar Agriculture.*

Rise of Civilization in rainless Countries.—Geography, Geology, and Topography of Egypt.—The Inundations of the Nile lead to Astronomy.

Comparative Theology of Egypt.—Animal Worship, Star Worship.—Impersonation of Divine Attributes—Pantheism.—The Trinities of Egypt.—Incarnation.—Redemption.—Future Judgment.—Trial of the Dead.—Rituals and Ceremonies.

AT this stage of our examination of European intellectual development, it will be proper to consider briefly two foreign influences—Indian and Egyptian—which affected it.

Of Hindu philosophy.

From the relations existing between the Hindu and European families, as described in the preceding chapter, a comparison of their intellectual progress presents no little interest. The movement of the elder branch indicates the path through which the younger is travelling, and the goal to which it tends. In the advanced condition under which we live we notice Oriental ideas perpetually emerging in a fragmentary way from the obscurities of modern metaphysics—they are the indications of an intellectual phase through which the Indo-European mind must pass. And when we consider the ready manner in which these ideas have been adopted throughout China and the entire East, we may, perhaps, extend our conclusion from the Indo-European family to the entire human race. From this we may also infer how unphilosophical and vain is the expectation of those who would attempt to restore the aged populations of Asia to our state. Their intellectual condition has passed onward, never more to return. It remains for them only to advance as far as they may in their own line and to die, leaving their place to others of a different constitution and of a renovated blood. In life there is no going back; the morose old man can never resume the genial confidence of maturity; the youth can never return to the idle and useless occupations, the frivolous amusements of boyhood; even the boy is parted by a long step from the innocent credulity of the nursery.

The phase of sorcery, and anthropocentric phase.

The earlier stages of the comparative theology of India are now inaccessible. At a time so remote as to be altogether prehistoric the phase of sorcery had been passed through. In the most ancient records remaining the Hindu mind is dealing with anthropocentric conceptions, not, however, so much of the physical as of the moral kind. Man had come to the conclusion that his chief concern is with himself. "Thou wast alone at the time of thy birth, thou wilt be alone in the moment of death; alone thou must answer at the bar of the inexorable Judge."

Comparative theology advances in two directions—Matter, Force.

From this point there are two well-marked steps of advance. The first reaches the consideration of material nature; the second, which is very grandly and severely philosophical, contemplates the universe under the conceptions of space and force alone. The former is exemplified in the Vedas and Institutes of Menu, the latter in Buddhism. In neither of these stages do the ideas lie idle as mere abstractions; they introduce a moral plan, and display a constructive power not equalled even by the Italian papal system. They take charge not only of the individual, but regulate society, and show their influence in accomplishing political organizations, commanding our attention from their prodigious extent, and venerable for their antiquity.

Vedaism contemplates matter, Buddhism force.

I shall, therefore, briefly refer, first, to the older, Vedaism, and then to its successor, Buddhism.

Among a people possessing many varieties of climate, and familiar with some of the grandest aspects of Nature —mountains the highest upon earth, noble rivers, a vegetation incomparably luxuriant, periodical rains, tempestuous monsoons, it is not surprising that there should have been an admiration for the material, and a tendency to the worship of Nature. These spectacles leave an indelible impression on the thoughts of man, and, the more cultivated the mind, the more profoundly are they appreciated.

Vedaism is the adoration of Nature.

The Vedas, which are the Hindu Scriptures, and of which there are four, the Rig, Yagust, Saman and Atharvan, are asserted to have been revealed by Brahma. The fourth is, however, rejected by some authorities and bears internal evidence of a later composition, at a time when hierarchical power had become greatly consolidated. These works are written in an obsolete Sanscrit, the parent of the more recent idiom. They constitute the basis of an extensive literature, Upavedas, Angas, &c., of connected works and commentaries. For the most part they consist of hymns suitable for public and private occasions, prayers, precepts, legends, and dogmas. The Rig, which is the oldest, is composed chiefly of hymns, the other three of liturgical formulas. They are of different periods and of various authorship, internal evidence seeming to indicate that if the later were composed by priests, the earlier were the production of military chieftains. They answer to a state of society advanced from the nomad to the municipal condition. They are based upon an acknowledgment of a universal Spirit pervading all things. Of this God they therefore necessarily acknowledge the unity: "There is in truth but one Deity, the Supreme Spirit, the

The Vedas and their doctrines.

The Veda doctrine of God,

Lord of the universe, whose work is the universe." "The God above all gods, who created the earth, the heavens, the waters." The world, thus considered as an emanation of God, is therefore a part of him; it is kept in a visible state by his energy, and would instantly disappear if that energy were for a moment withdrawn. Even as it is, it is undergoing unceasing transformations, every thing being in a transitory condition. The moment a given phase is reached, it is departed from, or ceases. In these perpetual movements the present can scarcely be said to have any existence, for as the Past is ending the Future has begun.

and of the world.

In such a never-ceasing career all material things are urged, their forms continually changing, and returning, as it were, through revolving cycles to similar states. For this reason it is that we may regard our earth, and the various celestial bodies, as having had a moment of birth, as having a time of continuance, in which they are passing onward to an inevitable destruction, and that after the lapse of countless ages similar progresses will be made, and similar series of events will occur again and again.

Its transformation.

But in this doctrine of universal transformation there is something more than appears at first. The theology of India is underlaid with Pantheism. "God is One because he is All." The Vedas, in speaking of the relation of nature to God, make use of the expression that he is the Material as well as the Cause of the universe, "the Clay as well as the Potter." They convey the idea that while there is a pervading spirit existing everywhere of the same nature as the soul of man, though differing from it infinitely in degree, visible nature is essentially and inseparably connected therewith; that as in man the body is perpetually undergoing changes, perpetually decaying and being renewed, or, as in the case of the whole human species, nations come into existence and pass away, yet still there continues to exist what may be termed the universal human mind, so for ever associated and for ever connected are the material and the spiritual. And under this aspect we must contemplate the Supreme Being, not merely as a presiding intellect, but as illustrated

It is the visisemblance of God.

by the parallel case of man, whose mental principle shows no tokens except through its connexion with the body; so matter, or nature, or the visible universe, is to be looked upon as the corporeal manifestation of God.

The nature of mundane changes.

Secular changes taking place in visible objects, especially those of an astronomical kind, thus stand as the gigantic counterparts both as to space and time of the microscopic changes which we recognize as occurring in the body of man. However, in adopting these views of the relations of material nature and spirit, we must continually bear in mind that matter "has no essence independent of mental perception; that existence and perceptibility are convertible terms; that external appearances and sensations are illusory, and would vanish into nothing if the divine energy which alone sustains them were suspended but for a moment."

Of the soul of man.

As to the relation between the Supreme Being and man, the soul is a portion or particle of that all-pervading principle, the Universal Intellect or Soul of the World, detached for a while from its primitive source, and placed in connexion with the bodily frame, but destined by an inevitable necessity sooner or later to be restored and rejoined—as inevitably as rivers run back to be lost in the ocean from which they arose. "That Spirit," says Varuna to his son, "from which all created beings proceed, in which, having proceeded, they live, toward which they tend, and in which they are at last absorbed, that Spirit study to know: it is the Great One."

Its final absorption in God.

Since a multitude of moral considerations assure us of the existence of evil in the world, and since it is not possible for so holy a thing as the spirit of man to be exposed thereto without undergoing contamination, it comes to pass that an unfitness may be contracted for its rejoining the infinitely pure essence from which it was derived, and hence arises the necessity of its undergoing a course of purification.

Of purifying penances.

And as the life of man is often too short to afford the needful opportunity, and, indeed, its events, in many instances, tend rather to increase than to diminish the stain, the season of purification is prolonged by perpetuating a connexion of the sinful spirit with other forms, and permitting its transmigration to other bodies, in which, by the penance it undergoes, and the trials to which it is exposed, its iniquity may be washed away, and satisfactory preparation be made for its absorption in the ocean of infinite purity. Considering thus the relation in which all animated nature stands to us, being a mechanism for purification, this doctrine of the transmigration of the soul leads necessarily to other doctrines of a moral kind, more particularly to a profound respect for life under every form, human, animal, or insect.

and transmigration of souls.

The forms of animal life, therefore, furnish a grand penitential mechanism for man. Such, on these principles, is their teleological explanation. In European philosophy there is no equivalent or counterpart of this view. With us animal life is purposeless. Hereafter we shall find that in Egypt, though the doctrine of transmigration must of course have tended to similar suggestions, it became disturbed in its practical application by the base fetich notions of the indigenous African population. Hence the doctrine was cherished by the learned for philosophical reasons, and by the multitude for the harmony of its results with their idolatries.

The religious use of animal life.

From such theological dogmas a religious system obviously springs having for its object to hasten the purification of the soul, that it may the more quickly enter on absolute happiness, which is only to be found in absolute rest. The methods of shortening its wanderings and bringing it to repose are the exercises of a pious life, penance, and prayer, and more especially a profound contemplation of the existence and attributes of the Supreme Being. In this profound contemplation many holy men have passed their lives.

Of proper modes of devotion.

Such is a brief statement of Vedic theology, as exhibited in the connected doctrines of the Nature of God, Universal Animation, Transmutation of the World, Emanation of the Soul, Manifestation of Visible Things, Transmigration, Absorption, the uses of Penitential Services, and Contemplation for the attainment of Absolute Happiness in Absolute Rest. The Vedas also recognize a series of creatures superior to man, the gods of the elements and stars; they likewise personify the attributes of the Deity.

The three Vedic divinities, Agni, Indra, and Surya, are not to be looked upon as existing independently, for all spirits are comprehended in the Universal Soul. The later Hindu trinity, Brahma, Vishnu, and Siva, is not recognized by them. They do not authorize the worship of deified men, nor of images, nor of any visible forms. They admit the adoration of subordinate spirits, as those of the planets, or of the demigods who inhabit the air, the waters, the woods; these demigods are liable to death. They inculcate universal charity—charity even to an enemy: "The tree doth not withdraw its shade from the woodcutter." Prayers are to be made thrice a day, morning, noon, evening; fasting is ordained, and ablution before meals; the sacrificial offerings consist of flowers, fruits, money. Considered as a whole their religious tendency is selfish: it puts in prominence the baser motives, and seeks the gratification of the animal appetites, as food, pleasure, good fortune. They suggest no proselyting spirit, but rather adopt the principle that all religions must be equally acceptable to God, since, if it were otherwise, he would have instituted a single one, and, considering his omnipotence, none other could have possibly prevailed. They contain no authorization of the division of castes, which probably had arisen in the necessities of antecedent conquests, but which have imposed a perpetual obstacle to any social progress, keeping each class of society in an immovable state, and concentrating knowledge and power in a hierarchy. Neither in them, nor, it is affirmed, in the whole Indian literature, is there a single passage indicating a love of liberty. The Asiatics cannot understand what value there is in it. They have balanced Freedom against Security; they have deliberately preferred the latter, and left the former for Europe to sigh for. Liberty is alone appreciated in a life of action; but the life of Asia is essentially passive, its desire is for tranquillity. Some have affirmed that this imbecility is due to the fact that that continent has no true temperate zone, and that thus, for ages, the weak nations have been in contact with the strong, and therefore the hopeless aspirations for personal freedom have become extinct. But nations that are cut off from the sea, or that

Minor Vedic doctrines.

have accepted the dogma that to travel upon it is unholy, can never comprehend liberty. From the general tenor of the Vedas, it would appear that the condition of women was not so much restrained as it became in later times, and that monogamy was the ordinary state. From the great extent of these works, their various dates and authorship, it is not easy to deduce from them consistent principles, and their parts being without any connexion, complete copies are very scarce. They have undergone mutilation and restoration, so that great discordances have arisen.

The Institutes of Menu.

In the Institutes of Menu, a code of civil and religious law, written about the ninth century before Christ, though, like the Vedas, betraying a gradual origin, the doctrine of the Divine unity becomes more distinctly mixed up with Pantheistic ideas. They present a description of creation, of the nature of God, and contain prescribed rules for the duty of man in every station of life from the moment of birth to death. Their imperious regulations in all these minute details are a sufficient proof of the great development and paramount power to which the priesthood had now attained, but their morality is discreditable. They indicate a high civilization and demoralization, deal with crimes and a policy such as are incident to an advanced social condition. Their arbitrary and all-reaching spirit reminds one of the papal system; their recommendations to sovereigns, their authorization of immoralities, recall the state of Italian society as reflected in the works of Machiavelli. They hold learning in the most signal esteem, but concede to the prejudices of the illiterate in a worship of the gods with burnt-offerings of clarified butter and libations of the juices of plants. As respects the constitution of man, they make a distinction between the soul and the vital principle, asserting that it is the latter only which expiates sin by transmigration. They divide society into four castes—the priests, the military, the industrial, the servile. They make a Brahmin the chief of all created things, and order that his life shall be divided into four parts, one to be spent in abstinence, one in marriage, one as an anchorite, and one in profound meditation; he may then "quit the body as a bird leaves the branch of a tree." They vest the government of society in an absolute monarch, having seven councillors, who direct the internal administration by a chain of officials, the revenue being derived from a share of agricultural products, taxes on commerce, imposts on shopkeepers, and a service of one day in the month from labourers.

In their essential principles the Institutes therefore follow the Vedas, though, as must be the case in every system intended for men in the various stages of intellectual progress from the least advanced to the highest, they show a leaning toward popular delusions. Both are pantheistic, for both regard the universe as the manifestation of the Creator; both accept the doctrine of Emanation, teaching that the universe lasts only for a definite period of time, and then, the Divine energy being withdrawn, absorption of everything, even of the created gods, takes place, and thus, in great cycles of prodigious duration, many such successive emanations and absorptions of universe occur.

Both the Vedas and Institutes are pantheistic.

The changes that have taken place among the orthodox in India since the period of the Institutes are in consequence of the diminution or disappearance of the highly philosophical classes, and the comparative predominance of the vulgar. They are stated by Mr. Elphinstone as a gradual oblivion of monotheism, the neglect of the worship of some gods and the introduction of others, the worship of deified mortals. The doctrine of human deification is carried to such an extent that Indra and other mythological gods are said to tremble lest they should be supplanted by men. This introduction of polytheism and use of images has probably been connected with the fact that there have been no temples to the Invisible God, and the uneducated mind feels the necessity of some recognizable form. In this manner the Trinitarian conception of Brahma, Vishnu, and Siva, with fourteen other chief gods, has been introduced. Vishnu and Siva are never mentioned in the Institutes, but they now engross the public devotions; besides these there are angels, genii, penates, and lares, like the Roman. Brahma has only one

Disappearance of the philosophical classes, and consequent prominence of anthropocentric ideas.

temple in all India, and has never been much worshipped. Chrishna is the great favourite of the women. The doctrine of incarnation has also become prevalent; the incarnations of Vishnu are innumerable. The opinion has also been spread that faith in a particular god is better than contemplation, ceremonial, or good works. A new ritual, instead of the Vedas, has come into use, these scriptures being the eighteen Puranas, composed between the eighth and sixteenth centuries. They contain theogonies, accounts of the creation, philosophical speculations, fragmentary history, and may be brought to support any sectarian view, having never been intended as one general body, but they are received as incontrovertible authority. In former times great efficacy was attached to sacrifice and religious austerities, but the objects once accomplished in that way are now compassed by mere faith. In the Baghavat Gita, the text-book of the modern school, the sole essential for salvation is dependence on some particular teacher, which makes up for everything else. The efficacy which is thus ascribed to faith, and the facility with which sin may be expiated by penance, have led to great mental debility and superstition. Force has been added to the doctrine of a material paradise of trees, flowers, banquets, hymns; and to a hell, a dismal place of flames, thirst, torment, and horrid spectres.

The philosophical schools.

If such has been the gradual degradation of religion, through the suppression or disappearance of the most highly cultivated minds, the tendency of philosophy is not less strikingly marked. It is said that even in ancient times not fewer than six distinct philosophical schools may be recognized: 1, the prior Mimansa; 2, the later Mimansa, or Vedanta, founded by Vyasa about 1400 B.C. having a Vedanta literature of prodigious extent; 3, the Logical school, bearing a close resemblance to that of Aristotle, even in its details; 4, the Atomic school of Canade; 5, the Atheistical school of Capila; 6, the Theistical school of Patanjali.

The rise of Buddhism.

This great theological system, enforced by a tyrannical hierarchy, did not maintain itself without a conflict. Buddhism arose as its antagonist. By an inevitable necessity, Vedaism must pass onward to Buddhism. The prophetic foresight of the great founder of this system was justified by its prodigious, its unparalleled and enduring success—a success that rested on the assertion of the dogma of the absolute equality of all men, and this in a country that for ages had been oppressed by castes. If the Buddhist admits the existence of God, it is not as a Creator; for matter is equally eternal; and since it possesses a property of inherent organization, even if the universe should perish, this quality would quickly restore it, and carry it on to new regenerations and new decays without any external agency. It also is endued with intelligence and consciousness. The Buddhists agree with the Brahmins in the doctrine of Quietism, in the care of animal life, in transmigration. They deny the Vedas and Puranas, have no castes, and, agreeably to their cardinal principle, draw their priests from all classes like the European monks. They live in monasteries, dress in yellow, go barefoot, their heads and beards being shaved; they have constant services in their chapels, chanting, incense, and candles; erect monuments and temples over the relics of holy men. They place an especial merit in celibacy; renounce all the pleasures of sense; eat in one hall; receive alms. To do these things is incident to a certain phase of human progress.

Buddhism arose about the tenth century before Christ, its founder being Arddha Chiddi, a native of Capila, near Nepaul. Of his epoch there are, however, many statements. The Avars, Siamese, and Cingalese fix it B.C. 600; the Cashmerians, B.C. 1332; the Chinese, Mongols, and Japanese, B.C. 1000. The Sanscrit words occurring in Buddhism attest its Hindu origin, Buddha itself being the Sanscrit for intelligence. After the system had spread widely in India, it was carried by missionaries into Ceylon, Tartary, Thibet, China, Japan, Burmah, and is now professed by a greater portion of the human race than any other religion. Until quite recently, the history of Arddha Chiddi and the system he taught have, notwithstanding their singular interest, been very imperfectly known in Europe. He was born in affluence and of a royal family. In his twenty-ninth year he retired from the world, the pleasures of which he had tasted,

Life of Arddha Chiddi.

and of which he had become weary. The spectacle of a gangrened corpse first arrested his thoughts. Leaving his numerous wives, he became a religious mendicant. It is said that he walked about in a shroud, taken from the body of a female slave. Profoundly impressed with the vanity of all human affairs, he devoted himself to philosophical meditation, by severe self-denial emancipating himself from all wordly hopes and cares. When a man has brought himself to this pass he is able to accomplish great things. For the name by which his parents had called him he substituted that of Gotama, or "he who kills the senses," and subsequently Chakia Mouni, or the Penitent of Chakia. Under the shade of a tree Gotama was born; under the shade of a tree he overcame the love of the world and the fear of death; under the shade of a tree he preached his first sermon in the shroud; under the shade of a tree he died. In four months after he commenced his ministry he had five disciples; at the close of the year they had increased to twelve hundred. In the twenty-nine centuries that have passed since that time, they have given rise to sects counting millions of souls, outnumbering the followers of all other religious teachers. The system still seems to retain much of its pristine vigour; yet religions are perishable. There is no country, except India, which has the same religion now that it had at the birth of Christ.

Gotama died at the advanced age of eighty years; his corpse was burnt eight days subsequently. But several years before this event his system must be considered as thoroughly established. It shows how little depends upon the nature of a doctrine, and how much upon effective organization, that Buddhism, the principles of which are far above the reach of popular thought, should have been propagated with so much rapidity, for it made its converts by preaching, and not, like Mohammedanism, by the sword. Shortly after Gotama's death, a council of five hundred ecclesiastics assembled for the purpose of settling the religion. A century later a second council met to regulate the monastic institution; and in B.C. 241, a third council, for the expulsion of fire-worshippers. Under the auspices of King Asoka, whose

The organization of Buddhism.

character presents singular points of resemblance to that of the Roman emperor who summoned the Council of Nicea, for he, too, was the murderer of his own family, and has been handed down to posterity, because of the success of the policy of his party, as a great, a virtuous, and a pious sovereign—under his auspices missionaries were sent out in all directions, and monasteries richly endowed were everywhere established. The singular efficacy of monastic institutions was rediscovered in Europe many centuries subsequently.

In proclaiming the equality of all men in this life, the Buddhists, as we have seen, came into direct collision with the orthodox creed of India, long carried out into practice in the institution of castes—a collision that was embittered by the abhorrence the Buddhists displayed for any distinction between the clergy and laity. To be a Brahmin a man must be born one, but a Buddhist priest might voluntarily come from any rank—from the very dregs of society. In the former system marriage was absolutely essential to the ecclesiastical caste; in the latter it was not, for the priestly ranks could be recruited without it. And hence there followed a most important advantage, that celibacy and chastity might be extolled as the greatest of all the virtues. The experience of Europe, as well as of Asia, has shown how powerful is the control obtained by the hierarchy in that way. In India there was, therefore, no other course for the orthodox than to meet the danger with bloody persecutions, and in the end, the Buddhists, expelled from their native seats, were scattered throughout Eastern Asia. Persecution is the mother of proselytes.

Contest between the Brahmans and Buddhists.

The fundamental principle of Buddhism is that there is a supreme power, but no Supreme Being. From this it might be inferred that they who adopt such a creed cannot be pantheists, but must be atheists. It is a rejection of the idea of Being, an acknowledgment of that of Force. If it admits the existence of God, it declines him as a Creator. It asserts an impelling power in the universe, a self-existent and plastic principle, but not a self-existent, an eternal a

Buddhism is founded on the conception of Power or Force.

personal God. It rejects inquiry into first causes as being unphilosophical, and considers that phenomena alone can be dealt with by our finite minds. Not without an air of intellectual majesty, it tolerates the Asiatic time-consecrated idea of a trinity, pointing out one not of a corporeal, but of an impersonal kind. Its trinity is the Past, the Present, the Future. For the sake of aiding our thoughts, it images the Past with his hands folded, since he has attained to rest, but the others with their right hands extended in token of activity. Since he has no God, the Buddhist cannot expect absorption; the pantheistic Brahmin looks forward to the return of his soul to the Supreme Being as a drop of rain returns to the sea. The Buddhist has no religion, but only a ceremonial. How can there be a religion where there is no God?

It does not recognize a personal God,

In all this it is plain that the impersonal and immaterial predominates, and that Gotama is contemplating the existence of pure Force without any association of Substance. He necessarily denies the immediate interposition of any such agency as Providence, maintaining that the system of nature, once arising, must proceed irresistibly according to the laws which brought it into being, and that from this point of view the universe is merely a gigantic engine. To the Brahman priesthood such ideas were particularly obnoxious; they were hostile to any philosophical system founded on the principle that the world is governed by law, for they suspected that its tendency would be to leave them without any mediatory functions, and therefore without any claims on the faithful. Equally does Gotama deny the existence of chance, saying that that which we call chance is nothing but the effect of an unknown, unavoidable cause. As to the external world, we cannot tell how far it is a phantasm, how far a reality, for our senses possess no trustworthy criterion of truth. They convey to the mind representations of what we consider to be external things, by which it is furnished with materials for its various operations; but, unless it acts in conjunction with the senses, the operation is lost,

nor a providential government,

but refers all events to resistless law.

Doubts the actual existence of the visible world.

as in that absence which takes place in deep contemplation. It is owing to our inability to determine what share these internal and external conditions take in producing a result that the absolute or actual state of nature is incomprehensible by us. Nevertheless, conceding to our mental infirmity the idea of a real existence of visible nature, we may consider it as offering a succession of impermanent forms, and as exhibiting an orderly series of transmutations, innumerable universes in periods of inconceivable time emerging one after another, and creations and extinctions of systems of worlds taking place according to a primordial law.

Such are his doctrines of a Supreme Force, and of the origin and progress of the visible world. With like

Of the nature of man.

ability Gotama deals with his inquiry into the nature of man. With Oriental imagery he bids us consider what becomes of a grain of salt thrown into the sea; but, lest we should be deceived herein, he tells us that there is no such thing as individuality or personality—that the Ego is altogether a nonentity. In these profound considerations he brings to bear his conception of force, in the light thereof asserting that all sentient beings are homogeneous. If we fail to follow him in these exalted thoughts, bound down to material ideas by the infirmities of the human constitution, and inquire of him how the spirit of man, which obviously displays so much energy, can be conceived of as being without form, without a past, without a future, he demands of us what has become of the flame of a lamp when it is blown out, or to tell him in what obscure condition it lay before it was kindled. Was it a nonentity? Has it been annihilated? By the aid of such imagery he tries to depict the nature of existence, and to convey a vivid idea of the metamorphoses it undergoes. Outward things are to him phantasms; the impressions they make on the mind are phantasms too. In this sense he receives the doctrine of transmigration, conceiving of it very much as we conceive of the accumulation of heat successively in different things. In one sense it may be the same heat which occupies such objects one after another, but in another, since heat is force and not matter, there can be no such individuality. Viewed, however, in the less profound way, he is not unwilling to adopt the doctrine of the transmigration of the soul through various forms, admitting that there may accumulate upon it the effect of all those influences, whether of merit or demerit, of good or of evil, to which it has been exposed. The vital flame is handed down from one generation to another, it is communicated from one animated form to another. He thinks it may carry with it in these movements the modifications which may have been impressed on it, and require opportunity for shaking them off and regaining its original state. At this point the doctrine of Gotama is assuming the aspect of a moral system, and is beginning to suggest means of deliverance from the accumulated evil and consequent demerit to which the spirit has been exposed. He will not, however, recognize any vicarious action. Each one must work out for himself his own salvation, remembering that death is not necessarily a deliverance from worldly ills, it may be only a passage to new miseries. But yet, as the light of the taper must come at last to an end, so there is at length, though it may be after many transmigrations, an end of life. That end he calls Nirwana, a word that has been for nearly three thousand years of solemn import to countless millions of men;—Nirwana, the end of successive existences, that state which has no relation to matter, or space, or time, to which the departing flame of the extinguished taper has gone. It is the supreme end, Nonentity. The attaining of this is the object to which we ought to aspire, and for that purpose we should seek to destroy within ourselves all cleaving to existence, weaning ourselves from every earthly object, from every earthly pursuit. We should resort to monastic life, to penance, to self-denial, self-mortification, and so gradually learn to sink into perfect quietude or apathy, in imitation of that state to which we must come at last, and to which, by such preparation, we may all the more rapidly approach. The pantheistic Brahman expects absorption in God; the Buddhist, having no God, expects extinction.

Of transmigration and penance,

and the passage to nonentity.

India has thus given to the world two distinct philosophical systems: Vedaism, which takes as its resting-point the existence of matter, and Buddhism, of which the resting-point is force. The philosophical ability displayed in the latter is very great; indeed it may be doubted whether Europe has produced its metaphysical equivalent. And yet, if I have correctly presented its principles, it will probably appear that its primary conception is not altogether consistently carried out in the development of the details. Great as was the intellectual ability of its author—so great as to extort our profoundest, though it may be reluctant admiration—there are nevertheless moments in which it appears that his movement is becoming wavering and unsteady—that he is failing to handle his ponderous weapon with self-balanced power. This is particularly the case in that point at which he is passing from the consideration of pure force to the unavoidable consideration of visible nature, the actual existence of which he seems to be obliged to deny. But then I am not sure that I have caught with precision his exact train of thought, or have represented his intention with critical correctness. Considering the extraordinary power he elsewhere displays, it is more probable that I have failed to follow his meaning, than that he has been, on the points in question, incompetent to deal with his task.

Philosophical estimate of Buddhism.

The works of Gotama, under the title of "Verbal Instructions," are published by the Chinese government in four languages—Thibetan, Mongol, Mantchou, Chinese—from the imperial press at Pekin, in eight hundred large volumes. They are presented to the Lama monasteries—a magnificent gift.

In speaking of Vedaism, I have mentioned the manner in which its more elevated conceptions were gradually displaced by those of a base grade coming into prominence; and here it may be useful in like manner to speak of the corresponding debasement of Buddhism. Its practical working was the introduction of an immense monastic system, offering many points of resemblance to the subsequent one of Europe. Since its object was altogether of a personal kind, the attainment of individual happiness, it was not possible that it should do otherwise than engender

Displacement of its higher ideas by base ones.

extreme selfishness. It impressed on each man to secure his own salvation, no matter what became of all others. Of what concern to him were parents, wife, children, friends, country, so long as he attained Nirwana!

Its anthropocentric phase remains, its philosophical declining.

Long before Buddhism had been expelled from India by the victorious Brahmins, it had been overlaid with popular ornaments. It had its fables, legends, miracles. Its humble devotees implicitly believed that Mahamia, the mother of Gotama, an immaculate virgin, conceived him through a divine influence, and that thus he was of the nature of God and man conjoined; that he stood upon his feet and spoke at the moment of his birth; that at five months of age he sat unsupported in the air; that at the moment of his conversion he was attacked by a legion of demons, and that in his penance-fasting he reduced himself to the allowance of one pepper-pod a day; that he had been incarnate many times before, and that on his ascension through the air to heaven he left his footprint on a mountain in Ceylon; that there is a paradise of gems, and flowers, and feasts, and music for the good, and a hell of sulphur, and flames, and torment for the wicked; that it is lawful to resort to the worship of images, but that those are in error who deify men, or pay respect to relics; that there are spirits, and goblins, and other superhuman forms; that there is a queen of heaven; that the reading of the Scriptures is in itself an actual merit, whether its precepts are followed or not; that prayer may be offered by saying a formula by rote, or even by turning the handle of a mill from which invocations written on paper issue forth; that the revealer of Buddhism is to be regarded as the religious head of the world.

Its legends and miracles.

The reader cannot fail to remark the resemblance of these ideas to some of those of the Roman Church. When a knowledge of the Oriental forms of religion was first brought into Europe, and their real origin was not understood, it was supposed that this coincidence had arisen through the labours of Nestorian, or other ancient missionaries from the West, and hopes were entertained that the conversion of Eastern Asia would be promoted thereby. But this expectation was disappointed, and that which many good men regarded as a preparation for Christianity proved to be a stumbling-block in its way. It is not improbable that the pseudo-Christianity of the Chinese revolters, of which so much has recently been said, is of the same nature, and will end with the same result.

Decorated with these extraneous but popular recommendations, Buddhism has been embraced by two-fifths of the human race. It has a prodigious literature, great temples, many monuments. Its monasteries are scattered from the north of Tartary almost to the equinoctial line. In these an education is imparted not unlike that of the European monasteries of the Middle Ages. It has been estimated that in Tartary one-third of the population are Lamas. There are single convents containing more than two thousand individuals; the wealth of the country voluntarily pours into them. Elementary education is more widely diffused than in Europe: it is rare to meet with a person who cannot read. Among the priests there are many who are devout, and, as might be expected, many who are impostors. It is a melancholy fact that, in China, Buddhism has led the entire population not only into indifferentism, but into absolute godlessness. They have come to regard religion as merely a fashion, to be followed according to one's own taste; that as professed by the state it is a civil institution necessary for the holding of office, and demanded by society, but not to be regarded as of the smallest philosophical importance; that a man is entitled to indulge his views on these matters just as he is entitled to indulge his taste in the colour and fashion of his garments; that he has no more right, however, to live without some religious profession than he has a right to go naked. The Chinese cannot comprehend how there should be animosities arising on matters of such doubtful nature and trivial concern. The formula under which they live is: "Religions are many; reason is one; we are brothers." They smile at the credulity of the good-natured Tartars, who believe in the wonders of miracle-workers, for they have miracle-workers who can perform the most supernatural cures, who can lick red-hot

The great diffusion of Buddhism.

Its practical godlessness.

iron, who can cut open their bowels, and, by passing their hand over the wound, make themselves whole again—who can raise the dead. In China, these miracles, with all their authentications, have descended to the conjurer, and are performed for the amusement of children. The common expressions of that country betray the materialism and indifferentism of the people, and their consequent immorality. "The prisons," they say, "are locked night and day, but they are always full; the temples are always open, and yet there is nobody in them." Of the dead they say, with an exquisite refinement of euphemism, "He has saluted the world." The Lazarist Huc, on whose authority many of these statements are made, testifies that they die, indeed, with incomparable tranquillity, just as animals die; and adds, with a bitter, and yet profoundly true sarcasm, they are what many in Europe are wanting to be.

From the theology of India I turn, in the next place, to the civilization of Egypt.

The ancient system of isolation which for many thousand years had been the policy of Egypt was overthrown by Psammetichus about B.C. 670. Up to that time the inhabitants of that country had been shut out from all Mediterranean or European contact by a rigorous exclusion exceeding that until recently practised in China and Japan. As from the inmates of the happy valley, in Rasselas, no tidings escaped to the outer world, so, to the European, the valley of the Nile was a region of mysteries and marvels. At intervals of centuries, individuals, like Cecrops and Danaus, had fled to other countries, and had attached the gratitude of posterity to their memories for the religion, laws, or other institutions of civilization they had conferred. The traditions connected with them served only to magnify those uncertain legends met with all over Asia Minor, Greece, Italy, Sicily, of the prodigies and miracles that adventurous pirates reported they had actually seen in their stealthy visits to the enchanted valley—great pyramids covering acres of land, their tops rising to the heavens, yet each pyramid nothing more than the tombstone of a king; colossi

Egypt a mysterious country to Europe.

Its reported wonders.

sitting on granite thrones, the images of Pharaohs who lived in the morning of the world, still silently looking upon the land which thousands of years before they had ruled; of these, some obedient to the sun, saluted his approach when touched by his morning rays; obelisks of prodigious height, carved by superhuman skill from a single block of stone, and raised by superhuman power erect on their everlasting pedestals, their faces covered with mysterious hieroglyphs, a language unknown to the vulgar, telling by whom and for what they had been constructed; temples, the massive leaning and lowering walls of which were supported by countless ranges of statues; avenues of sphinxes, through the shadows of which, grim and silent, the portals of fanes might be approached; catacombs containing the mortal remains of countless generations, each corpse awaiting, in mysterious embalmment, a future life; labyrinths of many hundred chambers and vaults, into which whoso entered without a clue never again escaped, but in the sameness and solitude of those endless windings found his sepulchre. It is impossible for us to appreciate the sentiment of religious awe with which the Mediterranean people looked upon the enchanted, the hoary, the civilized monarchy on the banks of the Nile. As Bunsen says, "Egypt was to the Greeks a sphinx with an intellectual human countenance."

Its history: the old empire; the Hycksos; the new empire.

Her solitude, however, had not been altogether unbroken. After a duration of 1076 years, and the reign of thirty-eight kings, illustrated by the production of the most stupendous works ever accomplished by the hand of man, some of which, as the Pyramids, remain to our times, the old empire, which had arisen from the union of the upper and lower countries, had been overthrown by the Hycksos, or shepherd kings, a race of Asiatic invaders. These, in their turn, had held dominion for more than five centuries, when an insurrection put an end to their power, and gave birth to the new empire, some of the monarchs of which, for their great achievements, are still remembered. In the middle period of this new empire those events in early Hebrew history took place—the visit of Abram and the elevation of Joseph—which are related with such simplicity in the Holy Scriptures. With varied prosperity, the new empire continued until the time of Psammetichus, who, in a civil war, having attained supreme power by the aid of Greek mercenaries, overthrew the time-honoured policy of all the old dynasties, and occasioned the first grand impulse in the intellectual life of Europe by opening the ports of Egypt, and making that country accessible to the blue-eyed and red-haired barbarians of the North.

Opening of the Egyptian ports.

It is scarcely possible to exaggerate the influence of this event upon the progress of Europe. An immense extension of Greek commerce by the demand for the products of the Euxine as well as of the Mediterranean was the smallest part of the advantage. As to Egypt herself, it entailed a complete change in her policy, domestic and foreign. In the former respect, the employment of the mercenaries was the cause of the entire emigration of the warrior caste, and in the latter it brought things to such a condition, that, if Egypt would continue to exist, she must become a maritime state. Her geographical position for the purposes of commerce was excellent; with the Red Sea on the east and the Mediterranean on the north, she was the natural entrepôt between Asia and Europe, as was shown by the prosperity of Alexandria in later ages. But there was a serious difficulty in the way of her becoming a naval power; no timber suitable for ship-building grew in the country—indeed, scarcely enough was to be found to satisfy the demands for the construction of houses and coffins for the dead. The early Egyptians, like the Hindus, had a religious dread of the sea, but their exclusiveness was, perhaps, not a little dependent on their want of material for ship-building. Egypt was therefore compelled to enter on a career of foreign conquest, and at all hazards possess herself of the timber-growing districts of Syria. It was this urgent necessity which led to her collisions with the Mesopotamian kings, and drew in its train of consequence the sieges, sacks, and captivities of Jerusalem, the metropolis of a little state lying directly between

This compels Egypt to become a maritime state,

and brings on collisions with the Babylonians.

the contending powers, and alternately disturbed by each. Of the necessity of this course of policy in the opinion of the Egyptian kings, we can have no better proof than the fact that Psammetichus himself continued the siege of Azotus for twenty-nine years; that his son Necho re-opened the canal between the Nile at Bubastes and the Red Sea at Suez—it was wide enough for two ships to pass—and on being resisted therein by the priests, who feared that it might weaken the country strategically, attempted the circumnavigation of Africa, and actually accomplished it. In those times such expeditions were not undertaken as mere matters of curiosity. Though this monarch also despatched investigators to ascertain the sources of the Nile, and determine the causes of its rise, it was doubtless in the hope of making such knowledge of use in a material or economical point of view, and therefore it may be supposed that the circumnavigation of Africa was undertaken upon the anticipated or experienced failure of the advantages expected to arise from the reopening of the canal; for the great fleets which Necho and his father had built could not be advantageously handled unless they could be transferred as circumstances required, either by the circumnavigation or by the canal, from one sea to the other. The time occupied in passing round the continent, which appears to have been three years, rendered the former method of little practical use. But the failure experienced, so far from detracting from the estimation in which we must hold those kings who could thus display such a breadth of conception and vigour of execution, must even enhance it. They resumed the policy of the conqueror Rameses II., who had many centuries before possessed the timber-growing countries, and whose engineers originally cut the canal from the Nile to the Red Sea, though the work cost 120,000 lives and countless treasuries of money. The canal of Rameses, which, in the course of so many centuries, has become filled up with sand, was thus cleaned out, as it was again in the reign of the Ptolemies, and again under the khalifs, and galleys passed from sea to sea. The Persians, under Darius Hystaspes, also either repaired

Opening of the Suez Canal.

Circumnavigation of Africa.

History of the Great Canal.

it, or, as some say, attempted a new work of the kind; but their engineering must have been very defective, for they were obliged to abandon their enterprise after carrying it as far as the bitter lakes, finding that salt water would be introduced into the Delta. The Suez mouth of the canal of Rameses was protected by a system of hydraulic works, to meet difficulties arising from the variable levels of the water. It was reserved for the French engineer Lesseps in the nineteenth century to cut the direct canal from the Mediterranean to the Red Sea, an exploit which the Pharaohs and Ptolemies had considered to be impossible.

The Egyptian policy continued by Pharaoh Hophra, who succeeded in the capture of Sidon, brought on hostilities with the Babylonian kings, who were now thoroughly awakened to what was going on in Egypt—a collision which occasioned the expulsion of the Egyptians from Syria, and the seizure of the lower country by Nebuchadnezzar, who also took vengeance on King Zedekiah for the assistance Jerusalem had rendered to the Africans in their projects: that city was razed to the ground, the eyes of the king put out, and the people carried captive to Babylon, B.C. 568. It is a striking exemplification of the manner in which national policy will endure through changes of dynasties, that after the overthrow of Babylon by the Medes, and the transference of power to the Persians, the policy of controlling the Mediterranean was never for an instant lost sight of. Attempts were continually made, by operating alternately on the southern and northern shores, to push westward. The subsequent history of Rome shows what would have been the consequences of an uncontrolled possession of the Mediterranean by a great maritime power. On the occasion of a revolt of Egypt, the Persian King Cambyses so utterly crushed and desolated it, that from that day to this, though twenty-four centuries have intervened, it has never been able to recover its independence. The Persian advance on the south shore toward Carthage failed because of the indisposition of the Phœnicians to assist in any operations against that city. We must particularly remark that the

Attempts of the Asiatics on the south Mediterranean shore.

Egypt overthrown by Cambyses.

ravaging of Egypt by Cambyses was contemporaneous with the cultivation of philosophy in the southern Italian towns—somewhat more than five hundred years before Christ.

Among the incidents occurring during the struggles between the Egyptian and Babylonian kings there is one deserving to be brought into conspicuous prominence, from the importance of its consequences in European history. It was the taking of Tyre by Nebuchadnezzar. So long as that city dominated in the Mediterranean, it was altogether impossible for Greek maritime power to be developed. The strength of Tyre is demonstrated by her resistance to the whole Babylonian power for thirteen years, "until every head was bald and every shoulder peeled." The place was, in the end, utterly destroyed. It was made as bare as the top of a rock on which the fisherman spreads his nets. The blow thus struck at the heart of Tyrian commerce could not but be felt at the utmost extremities. "The isles of the sea were troubled at her departure." It was during this time that Greece fairly emerged as a Mediterranean naval power. Nor did the inhabitants of New Tyre ever recover the ancient position. Their misfortunes had given them a rival. A re-establishment in an island on the coast was not a restoration of their supremacy. Carrying out what Greece instinctively felt to be her national policy, one of the first acts of Alexander's Asiatic campaign, two hundred and fifty years subsequently, was the siege of the new city, and, after almost superhuman exertions, its capture, by building a mole from the mainland. He literally levelled the place to the ground; a countless multitude was massacred, two thousand persons were crucified, and Tyrian influence disappeared for ever.

The Fall of Tyre.

In early Greek history there are, therefore, two leading foreign events: 1st, the opening of the Egyptian ports, B.C. 670; 2nd, the downfall of Old Tyre, 573. The effect of the first was chiefly intellectual; that of the second was to permit the commencement of commercial prosperity and give life to Athens.

Foreign epochs in Greek history.

At the dawn of European civilization, Egypt was, therefore, in process of decadence, gradually becoming less and less able to resist its own interior causes of destruction, or the attempts of its Asiatic rivals, who eventually brought it to ruin. At the first historical appearance of the country of the Nile it is hoary and venerable with age. The beautiful Scripture pictures of the journey of Abram and Sarai, in the famine, the going down of Joseph, the exodus of the Israelites, all point to a long-settled system, a tranquil and prosperous state. Do we ask any proof of the condition of art to which the Egyptians had attained at the time of their earliest monuments? The masonry of the Great Pyramid, built thirty-four hundred years before Christ, has never yet been surpassed. So accurately was that wonder of the world planned and constructed, that at this day the variation of the compass may actually be determined by the position of its sides; yet, when Jacob went into Egypt, that pyramid had been built as many centuries as have intervened from the birth of Christ to the present day. If we turn from the monuments to their inscriptions, there are renewed evidences of antiquity. The hieroglyphic writing had passed through all its stages of formation; its principles had become ascertained and settled long before we gain the first glimpse of it; the decimal and duodecimal systems of arithmetic were in use; the arts necessary in hydraulic engineering, massive architecture, and the ascertainment of the boundaries of land, had reached no insignificant degree of perfection. Indeed, there would be but very little exaggeration in affirming that we are practically as near the early Egyptian ages as was Herodotus himself. Well might the Egyptian priests say to the earliest Greek philosophers, "You Greeks are mere children, talkative and vain; you know nothing at all of the past."

Antiquity of civilization and art in Egypt.

Traces of the prehistoric, premonumental life of Egypt are still preserved in the relics of its language, and the well-known principles of its religion. Of the former, many of the words are referable to Indo-Germanic roots, an indication that the country at an early period must have been conquered from its indigenous African possessors by intrusive expeditions from Asia; and this is supported by the remarkable principles of

Prehistoric life of Egypt.

5*

Egyptian religion. The races of Central Asia had at a very early time attained to the psychical stage of monotheism. Africa is only now emerging from the basest fetichism; the negro priest is still a sorcerer and rain-maker. The Egyptian religion, as is well known, provided for the vulgar a suitable worship of complex idolatry, but for those emancipated from superstition it offered true and even noble conceptions. The coexistence of these apparent incompatibilities in the same faith seems incapable of any other explanation than that of an amalgamation of two distinct systems, just as occurred again many ages subsequently under Ptolemy Soter.

Influence of Egypt on the knowledge and art of Europe.

As a critical attention is being bestowed by modern scholars upon Egyptian remains, we learn more truly what is the place in history of that venerable country. It is their boast that the day is not distant when there will be no more difficulty in translating a page of hieroglyphics than in translating one of Latin or Greek. Even now, what a light has been thrown on all branches of ancient literature, science, art, mythology, domestic life, by researches which it may be said commenced only yesterday! From Egypt, it now appears, were derived the prototypes of the Greek architectural orders, and even their ornaments and conventional designs; thence came the models of the Greek and Etruscan vases; thence came many of the ante-Homeric legends—the accusation of the dead, the trial before the judges of hell; the reward and punishment of every man, from the Pharaoh who had descended from his throne to the slave who had escaped from his chain; the dog Cerberus, the Stygian stream, the Lake of Oblivion, the piece of money, Charon and his boat, the fields of Aahlu or Elysium, and the islands of the blessed; thence came the first ritual for the dead, litanies to the sun, and painted or illuminated missals; thence came the dogma of a queen of heaven. What other country can offer such noble and enduring edifices to the gods; temples with avenues of sphinxes; massive pylons adorned with obelisks in front, which even imperial Rome and modern Paris have not thought it beneath them to appropriate; porticoes and halls of columns, on which were carved the portraits of kings and effigies of the gods? On the walls of the tombs still remain Pthah, the creator, and Neph, the divine spirit, sitting at the potter's wheel, turning clay to form men; and Athor, who receives the setting sun into her arms; and Osiris, the judge of the dead. The granite statues have outlived the gods!

Moreover, the hieroglyphics furnish intrinsic evidence that among this people arose the earliest attempts at the perpetuation and imparting of ideas by writing. Though doubtless it was in the beginning a mere picture-writing, like that of the Mexicans, it had already, at the first moment we meet with it, undergone a twofold development—ideographic and phonetic; the one expressing ideas, the other sounds. Under the Macedonian kings the hieroglyphics had become restricted to religious uses, showing conclusively that the old priesthood had never recovered the terrible blows struck against it by Cambyses and Ochus. From that time forth they were less and less known. It is said that one of the Roman emperors was obliged to offer a reward for the translation of an obelisk. To the early Christian the hieroglyphic inscription was an abomination, as full of the relics of idolatry, and indicating an inspiration of the devil. He defaced the monuments wherever he could make them yield; and in many cases has preserved them for us by plastering them over to hide them from his sight.

The hieroglyphics.

In those enigmatical characters an extensive literature once existed, of which the celebrated books of Hermes were perhaps a corruption or a relic; a literature embracing compositions on music, astronomy, cosmogony, geography, medicine, anatomy, chemistry, magic, and many other subjects that have amused the curiosity of man. Yet of those characters the most singular misconceptions have been entertained almost to our own times. Thus, in 1802, Palin thought that the papyri were the Psalms of David done into Chinese, Lenoir that they were Hebrew documents; it was even asserted that the inscriptions in the temple of Denderah were the 100th Psalm, a pleasant ecclesiastical conceit, reminding one who has seen in Egyptian museums old articles of brass and glass, of the stories delivered down from hand to hand, that brass was first made at the burning of Corinth, and glass first discovered by shipwrecked mariners, who propped their kettle, while it boiled, on pieces of nitre.

Antiquity of the Egyptian monarchy.

Thousands of years have passed since the foundation of the first Egyptian dynasty. The Pyramids have seen the old empire, the Hycksos monarchs, the New Empire, the Persian, the Macedonian, the Roman, the Mohammedan. They have stood while the heavens themselves have changed. They were already "five hundred years old when the Southern Cross disappeared from the horizon of the countries of the Baltic." The pole-star itself is a newcomer to them. Humboldt, referring to these incidents, remarks that "the past seems to be visibly nearer to us when we thus connect its measurement with great and memorable events." No country has had such a varied history as this birthplace of European civilization. Through the darkness of fifty centuries we may not be able to discern the motives of men, but through periods very much longer we can demonstrate the conditions of Nature. If nations, in one sense, depend on the former, in a higher sense they depend on the latter. It was not without reason that the Egyptians took the lead in Mediterranean civilization. The geographical structure of their country surpasses even its hoary monuments in teaching us the conditions under which that people were placed. Nature is a surer guide than the traces of man, whose works are necessarily transitory. The aspect of Egypt has changed again and again; its structure, since man has inhabited it, never. The fields have disappeared, but the land remains.

Causes of the rise of civilization.

Why was it that civilization thus rose on the banks of the Nile, and not upon those of the Danube or Mississippi? Civilization depends on climate and agriculture. In Egypt the harvests may ordinarily be foretold and controlled. Of few other parts of the world can the same be said. In most countries the cultivation of the soil is uncertain. From seed-time to harvest, the meteorological variations are so numerous and great, that no skill can predict the amount of yearly produce. Without any premonition, the crops may be cut off by long-continued droughts, or destroyed by too much rain. Nor is it sufficient that a requisite amount of water should fall; to produce the proper effect, it must fall at particular periods. The labour of the farmer is at the mercy of the winds and clouds.

With difficulty, therefore, could a civilized state originate under such circumstances. So long as life is a scene of uncertainty, the hope of yesterday blighted by the realities of to-day, man is the maker of expedients, but not of laws. In his solicitude as to his approaching lot, he has neither time nor desire to raise his eyes to the heavens to watch and record their phenomena; no leisure to look upon himself, and consider what and where he is. In the imperious demand for a present support, he dares not venture on speculative attempts at ameliorating his state; he is doomed to be a helpless, isolated, spell-bound savage, or, if not isolated, the companion of other savages as careworn as himself. Under such circumstances, however, if once the preliminary conditions and momentum of civilization be imparted to him, the very things which have hitherto tended to depress him produce an opposite effect. Instead of remaining in sameness and apathy, the vicissitudes to which he is now exposed urge him onward; and thus it is that, though the civilization of Europe depended for its commencement on the sameness and stability of an African climate, the conquests of Nature which mark its more advanced stage have been made in the trying life of the temperate zone.

Agriculture in a rainless country.

There is a country in which man is not the sport of the seasons, in which he need have no anxieties for his future well-being—a country in which the sunshines and heats vary very little from year to year. In the Thebaid heavy rain is said to be a prodigy. But, at the time when the Dog-star rises with the sun, the river begins to swell; a tranquil inundation by degrees covering the land, at once watering and enriching it. If the Nilometer which measures the height of the flood indicates eight cubits, the crops will be scanty; but if it reaches fourteen cubits, there will be a plentiful harvest. In the spring of the year it may be known how the fields will be in the autumn. Agriculture is certain in Egypt, and there man first became civilized. The date-tree, moreover, furnishes to Africa a food almost without expense. The climate renders it necessary to use, for the most part, vegetable diet, and but little clothing is required.

The American counterpart of Egypt in this physical condition is Peru, the coast of which is also a rainless district. Peru is the Egypt of civilization of the Western continent. There is also a rainless strand on the Pacific coast of Mexico. It is an incident full of meaning in the history of human progress, that, in regions far apart, civilization thus commenced in rainless countries.

Rainless countries of the West.

In Upper Egypt, the cradle of civilization, the influence of atmospheric water is altogether obliterated, for, in an agricultural point of view, the country is rainless. Variable meteorological conditions are there eliminated.

Where the Nile breaks through the mountain gate at Essouan, it is observed that its waters begin to rise about the end of the month of May, and in eight or nine weeks the inundation is at its height. This flood in the river is due to the great rains which have fallen in the mountainous countries among which the Nile takes its rise, and which have been precipitated from the trade-winds that blow, except where disturbed by the monsoons, over the vast expanse of the tropical Indian Ocean. Thus dried, the east wind pursues its solemn course over the solitudes of Central Africa, a cloudless and a rainless wind, its track marked by desolation and deserts. At first the river becomes red, and then green, because the flood of its great Abyssinian branch, the Blue Nile, arrives first; but, soon after, that of the White Nile makes its appearance, and from the overflowing banks not only water, but a rich and fertilizing mud, is discharged. It is owing to the solid material thus brought down that the river in countless ages has raised its own bed, and has embanked itself with shelving deposits that descend on either side toward the desert. For this reason it is that the inundation is seen on the edge of the desert first, and, as the flood rises, the whole country up to the river itself is laid under water. By the

Inundations of the Nile.

Gradual rise of the whole country.

middle of September the supply begins to fail and the waters abate; by the end of October the stream has returned to its usual limits. The fields are left covered with a fertile deposit, the maximum quantity of which is about six inches thick in a hundred years. It is thought that the bed of the river rises four feet in a thousand years, and the fertilized land in its width continually encroaches on the desert. Since the reign of Amenophis III. it has increased by one-third. He lived B.C. 1430. There have accumulated round the pedestal of his Colossus seven feet of mud.

In the recent examinations made by the orders of the Viceroy of Egypt, close by the fallen statue of Rameses II., at Memphis, who reigned, according to Lepsius, from B.C. 1394 to B.C. 1328, a shaft was sunk to more than 24 feet. The water which then infiltrated compelled a resort to boring, which was continued until 41 feet 4½ inches were reached. The whole consisted of Nile deposits, alternate layers of loam and sand of the same composition throughout. From the greatest depth a fragment of pottery was obtained. Ninety-five of these borings were made in various places, but on no occasion was solid rock reached. The organic remains were all recent; not a trace of an extinct fossil occurred, but an abundance of the residues of burnt bricks and pottery. In their examination from Essouan to Cairo, the French estimated the mud deposit to be five inches for each century. From an examination of the results at Heliopolis, Mr. Horner makes it 3·18 inches. The Colossus of Rameses II. is surrounded by a sediment nine feet four inches deep, fairly estimated. Its date of erection was about 3215 years ago, which gives 3½ inches per century. But beneath it similar layers continue to the depth of 30 feet, which, at the same rate, would give 13,500 years, to A.D. 1854, at which time the examination was made. Every precaution seems to have been taken to obtain accurate results.

Geological age of Egypt.

The extent of surface affected by the inundations of the Nile is, in a geographical point of view, altogether insignificant; yet, such as it was, it constituted Egypt. Commencing at the Cataract of Essouan,

Its geography and topography.

at the sacred island of Philæ, on which to this day here and there the solitary palm-tree looks down, it reached to the Mediterranean Sea, from 24° 3′ N. to 31° 37′ N. The river runs in a valley, bounded on one side by the eastern and on the other by the Libyan chain of mountains, and of which the average breadth is about seven miles, the arable land, however, not averaging more than five and a half. At the widest place it is ten and three-quarters, at the narrowest two. The entire surface of irrigated and fertile land in the Delta is 4500 square miles; the arable land of Egypt, 2255 square miles; and in the Fyoom, 340 square miles, an insignificant surface, yet it supported seven millions of people.

Here agriculture was so precise that it might almost be pronounced a mathematical art. The disturbances arising from atmospheric conditions were eliminated, and the variations, as connected with the supply of river-water, ascertained in advance. The priests proclaimed how the flood stood on the Nilometer, and the husbandman made corresponding preparations for a scanty or an abundant harvest.

In such a state of things, it was an obvious step to improve upon the natural conditions by artificial means; dykes, and canals, and flood-gates, with other hydraulic apparatus, would, even in the beginning of society, unavoidably be suggested, that in one locality the water might be detained longer; in another, shut off when there was danger of excess; in another, more abundantly introduced.

Control of agriculture by the government.

There followed, as a consequence of this condition of things, the establishment of a strong government, having a direct control over the agriculture of the state by undertaking and supporting these artificial improvements, and sustaining itself by a tax cheerfully paid, and regulated in amount by the quantity of water supplied from the river to each estate. Such, indeed, was the fundamental political system of the country. The first king of the old empire undertook to turn the river into a new channel he made for it, a task which might seem to demand very able engineering, and actually accomplished it. It is more than five thousand years since Menes lived. There must have preceded his times many centuries, during which knowledge and skill had been increasing, before such a work could even have been contemplated.

Topographical changes occasioned by the Nile.

I shall not indulge in any imaginary description of the manner in which, under such favourable circumstances, the powers of the human mind were developed and civilization arose. In inaccessible security, the inhabitants of this valley were protected on the west by a burning sandy desert, on the east by the Red Sea. Nor shall I say anything more of those remote geological times when the newly-made river first flowed over a rocky and barren desert on its way to the Mediterranean Sea; nor how, in the course of ages, it had by degrees laid down a fertile stratum, embanking itself in the rich soil it had borne from the tropical mountains. Yet it is none the less true that such was the slow construction of Egypt as a habitable country; such were the gradual steps by which it was fitted to become the seat of man. The pulse of its life-giving artery makes but one beat in a year; what, then, are a few hundreds of centuries in such a process?

The inundations lead to the study of astronomy.

The Egyptians had, at an early period, observed that the rising of the Nile coincided with the heliacal rising of Sirius, the Dog-star, and hence they very plausibly referred it to celestial agencies. Men are ever prone to mistake coincidences for causes; and thus it came to pass that the appearance of that star on the horizon at the rising of the sun was not only viewed as the signal, but as the cause of the inundations. Its coming to the desired position might, therefore, be well expected, and it was soon observed that this took place with regularity at periods of about 360 days. This was the first determination of the length of the year. It is worthy of remark, as showing how astronomy and religious rites were in the beginning connected, that the priests of the mysterious temple of Philæ placed before the tomb of Osiris every morning 360 vases of milk, each one commemorating one day, thus showing that the origin of that rite was in those remote ages when it was thought that the year was

360 days long. It was doubtless such circumstances that led the Egyptians to the cultivation of historical habits. In this they differed from the Hindus, who kept no records.

The phi'osophy of star-worship.

The Dog-star Sirius is the most splendid star in the heavens; to the Egyptian the inundation was the most important event upon earth. Mistaking a coincidence for a cause, he was led to the belief that when that brilliant star emerged in the morning from the rays of the sun, and began to assert its own inherent power, the sympathetic river, moved thereby, commenced to rise. A false inference like this soon dilated into a general doctrine; for if one star could in this way manifest a direct control over the course of terrestrial affairs, why should not another—indeed, why should not all? Moreover, it could not have escaped notice that the daily tides of the Red Sea are connected with the movements and position of the sun and moon, following those luminaries in the time of their occurrence, and being determined by their respective position as to amount at spring and at neap. But the necessary result of such a view is no other than the admission of the astrological influence of the heavenly bodies; first, as respects inanimate nature, and then as respects the fortune and fate of men. It is not until the vast distance of the starry bodies is suspected that man begins to feel the necessity of a mediator between him and them, and star-worship passes to its second phase.

To what part of the world could the Egyptian travel without seeing in the skies the same constellations? Far from the banks of the Nile, in the western deserts, in Syria, in Arabia, the stars are the same. They are omnipresent; for we may lose sight of the things of the earth, but not of those of the heavens. The air of fate-like precision with which their appointed movements are accomplished, their solemn silence, their incomprehensible distances, might satisfy an observer that they are far removed from the influences of all human power, though, perhaps, they may be invoked by human prayer.

Thus star-worship found for itself a plausible justification. The Egyptian system, at its highest development, combined the adoration of the heavenly bodies—the sun, the moon, Venus, &c., with the deified attributes of God. The great and venerable divinities, as Osiris, Pthah, Amun, were impersonations of such attributes, just as we speak of the Creator, the Almighty. It was held that not only has God never appeared upon earth in the human form, but that such is altogether an impossibility, since he is the animating principle of the entire universe, visible nature being only a manifestation of him.

Principles of Egyptian theology.

These impersonated attributes were arranged in various trinities, in each of which the third member is a procession from the other two, the doctrine and even expressions in this respect being full of interest to one who studies the gradual development of comparative theology in Europe. Thus from Amun by Maut proceeds Khonso, from Osiris by Isis proceeds Horus, from Neph by Saté proceeds Anouké. While, therefore, it was considered unlawful to represent God except by his attributes, these trinities and their persons offered abundant means of idolatrous worship for the vulgar. It was admitted that there had been terrestrial manifestations of these divine attributes for the salvation of men. Thus Osiris was incarnate in the flesh: he fell a sacrifice to the evil principle, and, after his death and resurrection, became the appointed judge of the dead. In his capacity of President of the West, or of the region of the setting stars, he dwells in the under world, which is traversed by the sun at night.

God. Trinities and their persons.

The Egyptian priests affirmed that nothing is ever annihilated; to die is therefore only to assume a new form. Herodotus says that they were the first to discover that the soul is immortal, their conception of it being that it is an emanation from or a particle of the universal soul, which in a less degree animates all animals and plants, and even inorganic things. Their dogma that there had been divine incarnations obliged them to assert that there had been a fall of man, this seeming to be necessary to obtain a logical argument in justification of prodigies so great. For the relief of the guilty soul, they prescribed in this

Incarnations; fall of man; redemption.

life fasts and penances, and in the future a transmigration through animals for purification. At death, the merits of the soul were ascertained by a formal trial before Osiris in the shadowy region of Amenti—the under world—in presence of the four genii of that realm, and of forty-two assessors. To this judgment the shade was conducted by Horus, who carried him past Cerberus, a hippopotamus, the gaunt guardian of the gate. He stood by in silence while Anubis weighed his heart in the scales of justice. If his good works preponderated, he was dismissed to the fields of Aahlu—the Elysian Fields; if his evil, he was condemned to transmigration.

The future judgment.

But that this doctrine of a judgment in another world might not decline into an idle legend, it was enforced by a preparatory trial in this—a trial of fearful and living import. From the sovereign to the meanest subject, every man underwent a sepulchral inquisition. As soon as any one died, his body was sent to the embalmers, who kept it forty days, and for thirty-two in addition the family mourned, the mummy, in its coffin, was placed erect in an inner chamber of the house. Notice was then sent to the forty-two assessors of the district; and on an appointed day, the corpse was carried to the sacred lake, of which every nome, and, indeed, every large town, had one toward the west. Arrived on its shore, the trial commenced; any person might bring charges against the deceased, or speak in his behalf; but woe to the false accuser. The assessors then passed sentence according to the evidence before them: if they found an evil life, sepulture was denied, and, in the midst of social disgrace, the friends bore back the mummy to their home, to be redeemed by their own good works in future years; or, if too poor to give it a place of refuge, it was buried on the margin of the lake, the culprit ghost waiting and wandering for a hundred years. On these Stygian shores the bones of some are still dug up in our day; they have remained unsepulchred for more than thirty times their predestined century. Even to wicked kings a burial had thus been denied. But, if the verdict of the assessors was favourable, a coin was paid to the boatman Charon for ferriage; a cake was provided for the

The trial of the dead.

Origin of the Greek Hades.

hippopotamus Cerberus; they rowed across the lake in the baris, or death-boat, the priest announcing to Osiris and the unearthly assessors the good deeds of the deceased. Arriving on the opposite shore, the procession walked in solemn silence, and the mummy was then deposited in its final resting-place—the catacombs.

Ceremonies, creeds, oracles, prophecy.

From this it may be gathered that the Egyptian religion did not remain a mere speculative subject, but was enforced on the people by the most solemn ceremonies. Moreover, in the great temples, grand processional services were celebrated, the precursors of some that still endure. There were sacrifices of meat-offerings, libations, incense. The national double creed, adapted in one branch to the vulgar, in the other to the learned, necessarily implied mysteries; some of these were avowedly transported to Greece. The machinery of oracles was resorted to. The Greek oracles were of Egyptian origin. So profound was the respect paid to their commands that even the sovereigns were obliged to obey them. It was thus that a warning from the oracle of Amun caused Necho to stop the construction of his canal. For the determination of future events, omens were studied, entrails inspected, and nativities were cast.

CHAPTER IV.

GREEK AGE OF INQUIRY.

RISE AND DECLINE OF PHYSICAL SPECULATION.

IONIAN PHILOSOPHY, *commencing from Egyptian Ideas, identifies in Water, or Air, or Fire, the First Principle.—Emerging from the Stage of Sorcery, it founds Psychology, Biology, Cosmogony, Astronomy, and ends in doubting whether there is any Criterion of Truth.*

ITALIAN PHILOSOPHY *depends on Numbers and Harmonies. — It reproduces the Egyptian and Hindu Doctrine of Transmigration.*

ELEATIC PHILOSOPHY *presents a great Advance, indicating a rapid Approach to Oriental Ideas.—It assumes a Pantheistic Aspect.*

RISE OF PHILOSOPHY IN EUROPEAN GREECE.—*Relations and Influence of the Mediterranean Commercial and Colonial System.—Athens attains to commercial Supremacy.—Her vast Progress in Intelligence and Art. —Her Demoralization.—She becomes the Intellectual Centre of the Mediterranean.*

Commencement of the Athenian higher Analysis.—It is conducted by THE SOPHISTS, *who reject Philosophy, Religion, and even Morality, and end in Atheism.*

Political Dangers of the higher Analysis.—Illustration from the Middle Ages.

IN Chapter II. I have described the origin and decline of Greek Mythology; in this, I am to relate the first European attempt at philosophizing. The Ionian systems spring directly out of the contemporary religious opinions, and appear as a phase in Greek comparative theology.

Origin of Greek philosophy.

Contrasted with the psychical condition of India, we cannot but be struck with the feebleness of these first European efforts. They correspond to that period in which the mind has shaken off its ideas of sorcery, but has not advanced beyond geocentral and anthropocentral conceptions. As is uniformly observed, as soon as man has collected what he considers to be trustworthy data, he forthwith applies them to a cosmogony, and develops pseudo-scientific systems. It is not until a later period that he awakens to the suspicion that we have no absolute knowledge of truth.

Its imperfections.

The reader, who might, perhaps, be repelled by the apparent worthlessness of the succession of Greek opinions now to be described, will find them assume an interest, if considered in the aggregate, or viewed as a series of steps or stages of European approach to conclusions long before arrived at in Egypt and India. Far in advance of anything that Greece can offer, the intellectual history of India furnishes systems at once consistent and imposing—systems not remaining useless speculations, but becoming inwoven in social life.

Greek philosophy is considered as having originated with Thales, who, though of Phœnician descent, was born at Miletus, a Greek colony in Asia Minor, about B.C. 640. At that time, as related in the last chapter, the Egyptian ports had been opened to foreigners by Psammetichus. In the civil war which that monarch had been waging with his colleagues, he owed his success to Ionian and other Greek mercenaries whom he had employed; but, though proving victor in the contest, his political position was such as to compel him to depart from the maxims followed in his country for so many thousand years, and to permit foreigners to have access to it. Hitherto the Europeans had been only known to the Egyptians as pirates and cannibals.

Commences in Asia Minor.

From the doctrine of Thales, it may be inferred that, though he had visited Egypt, he had never been in communication with its sources of learning, but had merely mingled among the vulgar, from whom he had gathered the popular notion that the first principle is water. The state of things in Egypt suggests that this primitive dogma of European philosophy was a popular notion in that country. With but little care on the part of men, the fertilizing Nile-water yielded those abundant crops which made Egypt the granary of the Old World. It might therefore be said, both philosophically and facetiously, that the first principle

Doctrine of Thales is derived from Egypt.

of all things is water. The harvests depended on it, and, through them, animals and man. The government of the country was supported by it, for the financial system was founded on a tax paid by the proprietors of the land for the use of the public sluices and aqueducts. There was not a peasant to whom it was not apparent that water is the first principle of all things, even of taxation; and, since it was not only necessary to survey lands to ascertain the surface that had been irrigated, but to redetermine their boundaries after the subsidence of the flood, even the scribes and surveyors might concede that geometry itself was indebted for its origin to water.

Importance of water in Egypt.

If, therefore, in any part of the Old World, this doctrine had both a vulgar and a philosophical significance, that country was Egypt. We may picture to ourselves the inquisitive but ill-instructed Thales carried in some pirate-ship or trading-bark to the mysterious Nile, respecting which Ionia was full of legends and myths. He saw the aqueducts, canals, flood-gates, the great Lake Mœris, dug by the hand of man as many ages before his day as have elapsed from his day to ours; he saw on all sides the adoration paid to the river, for it had actually become deified; he learned from the vulgar, with whom alone he came in contact, their universal belief that all things arise from water—from the vulgar alone, for, had he ever been taught by the priests, we should have found traces in his system of the doctrines of emanation, transmigration, and absorption, which were imported into Greece in later times. We may interpret the story of Thales on the principles which would apply in the case of some intelligent Indian who should find his way to the outposts of a civilized country. Imperfectly acquainted with the language, and coming in contact with the lower class alone, he might learn their vulgar philosophy, and carry back the fancied treasure to his home.

Thales asserts that water is the first principle.

As to the profound meaning which some have been disposed to extract from the dogma of Thales, we shall, perhaps, be warranted in rejecting it altogether. It has been affirmed that he attempted to concentrate all supernatural powers in one; to reduce all possible agents to unity; in short, out of polytheism to bring forth monotheism; to determine the invariable in the variable; and to ascertain the beginning of things: that he observed how infinite is the sea; how necessary moisture is to growth; nay, even how essential it was to the well-being of himself; "that without moisture his own body would not have been what it was, but a dry husk falling to pieces." Nor can we adopt the opinion that the intention of Thales was to establish a coincidence between philosophy and the popular theology as delivered by Hesiod, who affirms that Oceanus is one of the parent-gods of Nature. The imputation of irreligion made against him shows at what an early period the antagonism of polytheism and scientific inquiry was recognized. But it is possible to believe that all things are formed out of one primordial substance, without denying the existence of a creative power. Or, to use the Indian illustration, the clay may not be the potter.

Other doctrines of Thales.

Thales is said to have predicted the solar eclipse which terminated a battle between the Medes and Lydians, but it has been suggestively remarked that it is not stated that he predicted the day on which it should occur. He had an idea that warmth originates from or is nourished by humidity, and that even the sun and stars derived their aliment out of the sea at the time of their rising and setting. Indeed, he regarded them as living beings; obtaining an argument from the phenomena of amber and the magnet, supposed by him to possess a living soul, because they have a moving force. Moreover, he taught that the whole world is an insouled thing, and that it is full of dæmons. Thales had, therefore, not completely passed out of the stage of sorcery.

His system obtained importance not only from its own plausibility, but because it was introduced under favourable auspices and at a favourable time. It came into Asia Minor as a portion of the wisdom of Egypt, and therefore with a prestige sufficient to assure for it an attentive reception. But this would have been of little avail had not the mental culture of Ionia been advanced to a degree suitable for offering to it conditions of development.

Under such circumstances the Egyptian dogma formed the starting-point for a special method of philosophizing.

They constitute the starting-point of Ionian philosophy.

The manner in which that development took place illustrates the vigour of the Grecian mind. In Egypt a doctrine might exist for thousands of years, protected by its mere antiquity from controversy or even examination, and hence sink with the lapse of time into an ineffectual and lifeless state; but the same doctrine brought into a young community full of activity would quickly be made productive and yield new results. As seeds taken from the coffins of mummies, wherein they have been shut up for thousands of years, when placed under circumstances favourable for development in a rich soil, and supplied with moisture, have forthwith, even in our own times, germinated, borne flowers, and matured new seeds, so the rude philosophy of Thales passed through a like development. Its tendency is shown in the attempt it at once made to describe the universe, even before the parts thereof had been determined.

Anaximenes asserts that air is the first principle.

But it is not alone the water or ocean that seems to be infinite, and capable of furnishing a supply for the origin of all other things. The air, also, appears to reach as far as the stars. On it, as Anaximenes of Miletus remarks, "the very earth itself floats like a broad leaf." Accordingly, this Ionian, stimulated doubtless by the hope of sharing in or succeeding to the celebrity that Thales had enjoyed for a century, proposed to substitute for water, as the primitive source of things, atmospheric air. And, in truth, there seem to be reasons for bestowing upon it such a preeminence. To those who have not looked closely into the matter, it would appear that water itself is generated from it, as when clouds are formed, and from them rain-drops, and springs, and fountains, and rivers, and even the sea. He also attributes infinity to it, a dogma scarcely requiring any exercise of the imagination, but being rather the expression of an ostensible fact; for who, when he looks upward, can discern the boundary of the atmosphere.

It is also the soul.

Anaximenes also held that even the human soul itself is nothing but air, since life consists in inhaling and exhaling it, and ceases as soon as that process stops. He taught also that warmth and cold arise from mere rarefaction and condensation, and gave as a proof the fact that when we breathe with the lips drawn together the air is cold, but it becomes warm when we breathe through the widely-opened mouth. Hence he concluded that, with a sufficient rarefaction, air might turn into fire, and that this probably was the origin of the sun and stars, blazing comets, and other meteors; but if by chance it should undergo condensation, it would turn into wind and clouds, or, if that operation should be still more increased, into water, snow, hail, and, at last, even into earth itself. And since it is seen from the results of breathing that the air is a life-giving principle to man, nay, even is actually his soul, it would appear to be a just inference that the infinite air is God and that the gods and goddesses have sprung from it.

The air is God.

Such was the philosophy of Anaximenes. It was the beginning of that stimulation of activity by rival schools which played so distinguished a part in the Greek intellectual movement. Its superiority over the doctrine of Thales evidently consists in this, that it not only assigns a primitive substance, but even undertakes to show by observation and experiment how others arise from it, and transformations occur. As to the discovery of the obliquity of the ecliptic by the aid of a gnomon attributed to Anaximenes, it was merely a boast of his vainglorious countrymen, and altogether beyond the scientific grasp of one who had no more exact idea of the nature of the earth than that it was "like a broad leaf floating in the air."

The doctrines of Anaximenes received a very important development in the hands of Diogenes of Apollonia, who asserted that all things originate from one essence, which, undergoing continual changes, becoming different at different times, turns back again to the same state. He regarded the entire world as a living being, spontaneously evolving and transforming itself, and agreed with Anaximenes that the soul of man is nothing but air, as is also the soul of the world. From this it follows that the air must be eternal, imperishable, and endowed with consciousness. "It knows much; for without reason it would be impossible for all to

Diogenes asserts that air is the soul of the world.

be arranged so duly and proportionately as that all should maintain its fitting measure, winter and summer, night and day, the rain, the wind, and fair weather; and whatever object we consider will be found to have been ordered in the best and most beautiful manner possible." "But that which has knowledge is that which men call air; it is it that regulates and governs all, and hence it is the use of air to pervade all, and to dispose all, and to be in all, for there is nothing that has not part in it."

Difficulty of rising above fetichism.

The early cultivator of philosophy emerges with difficulty from fetichism. The harmony observed among the parts of the world is easily explained on the hypothesis of a spiritual principle residing in things, and arranging them by its intelligent volition. It is not at once that he rises to the conception that all this beauty and harmony are due to the operation of law. We are so prone to judge of the process of external things from the modes of our own personal experience, our acts being determined by the exercise of our wills, that it is with difficulty we disentangle ourselves from such notions in the explanation of natural phenomena. Fetichism may be observed in the infancy of many of the natural sciences. Thus the electrical power of amber was imputed to a soul residing in that substance, a similar explanation being also given of the control of the magnet over iron. The movements of the planetary bodies, Mercury, Venus, Mars, were attributed to an intelligent principle residing in each, guiding and controlling the motions, and ordering all things for the best. It was an epoch in the history of the human mind when astronomy set an example to all other sciences of shaking off its fetichism, and showing that the intricate movements of the heavenly bodies are all capable not only of being explained, but even foretold, if once was admitted the existence of a simple, yet universal, invariable, and eternal law.

Astronomy and chemistry have passed beyond the fetich stage.

Not without difficulty do men perceive that there is nothing inconsistent between invariable law and endlessly varying phenomena, and that it is a more noble view of the government of this world to impute its order to a penetrating primitive wisdom, which could foresee consequences throughout a future eternity, and provide for them in the original plan at the outset, than to invoke the perpetual intervention of an ever-acting spiritual agency for the purpose of warding off misfortunes that might happen, and setting things to rights. Chemistry furnishes us with a striking example--an example very opportune in the case we are considering—of the doctrine of Diogenes of Apollonia, that the air is actually a spiritual being; for, on the discovery of several of the gases by the earlier experimenters, they were not only regarded as of a spiritual nature, but actually received the name under which they pass to this day, gheist or gas, from a belief that they were ghosts. If a labourer descended into a well and was suffocated, as if struck dead by some invisible hand; if a lamp lowered down burnt for a few moments with a lurid flame, and was then extinguished; if, in a coal mine, when the unwary workman exposed a light, on a sudden the place was filled with flashing flames and thundering explosions, tearing down the rocks and destroying every living thing in the way, often, too, without leaving on the dead any marks of violence; what better explanation could be given of such catastrophes than to impute them to some supernatural agent? Nor was there any want, in those times, of well-authenticated stories of unearthly faces and forms seen in such solitudes.

Origin of psychology.

The modification made by Diogenes in the theory of Anaximenes, by converting it from a physical into a psychological system, is important, as marking the beginning of the special philsosophy of Greece. The investigation of the intellectual development of the universe led the Greeks to the study of the intellect itself. In his special doctrine, Diogenes imputed the changeability of the air to its mobility; a property in which he thought it excelled all other substances, because it is among the rarest or thinnest of the elements. It is, however, said by some, who are disposed to transcendentalize his doctrine, that he did not mean the common atmospheric air, but something more attenuated and warm; and since, in its purest state, it constitutes the most perfect intellect, inferior degrees of reason must be owing to an increase of its density and moisture. Upon such a principle, the whole earth is animated by the breath of life; the souls of brutes, which differ from one another so much in intelligence, are only air in its various conditions of moisture and warmth. He explained the production of the world through condensation of the earth from air by cold, the warmth rising upward and forming the sun; in the stars he thought he recognized the respiratory organs of the world. From the preponderance of moist air in the constitution of brutes, he inferred that they are like the insane, incapable of thought, for thickness of the air impedes respiration, and therefore quick apprehension. From the fact that plants have no cavities wherein to receive the air, and are altogether unintelligent, he was led to the principle that the thinking power of man arises from the flowing of that substance throughout the body in the blood. He also explained the superior intelligence of men from their breathing a purer air than the beasts, which carry their nostrils near the ground. In these crude and puerile speculations we have the beginning of mental philosophy.

Modern discoveries as to the relations of the air.

I cannot dismiss the system of the Apollonian without setting in contrast with it the discoveries of modern science respecting the relations of the air. Toward the world of life it stands in a position of wonderful interest. Decomposed into its constituents by the skill of chemistry, it is no longer looked upon as a homogeneous body; its ingredients have not only been separated, but the functions they discharge have been ascertained. From one of these, carbonic acid, all the various forms of plants arise; that substance being decomposed by the rays of the sun, and furnishing to vegetables carbon, their chief solid ingredient. All those beautifully diversified organic productions, from the mosses of the icy regions to the palms characteristic of the landscapes of the tropics—all those we cast away as worthless weeds, and those for the obtaining of which we expend the sweat of our brow—all, without any exception, are obtained from the atmosphere by the influence of the sun. And since without plants the life of animals could not be maintained, they constitute the means by which the aërial material, vivified,

Inter-dependence of animals and plants.

as it may be said, by the rays of the sun, is conveyed even into the composition of man himself. As food, they serve to repair the waste of the body necessarily occasioned in the acts of moving and thinking. For a time, therefore, these ingredients, once a part of the structure of plants, enter as essential constituents in the structure of animals. Yet it is only in a momentary way, for the essential condition of animal activity is that there shall be unceasing interstitial death; not a finger can be lifted without the waste of muscular material; not a thought arise without the destruction of cerebral substance. From the animal system the products of decay are forthwith removed, often by mechanisms of the most exquisite construction; but their uses are not ended, for sooner or later they find their way back again into the air, and again serve for the origination of plants. It is needless to trace these changes in all their details; the same order or cycle of progress holds good for the water, the ammonia; they pass from the inorganic to the living state, and back to the inorganic again; now the same particle is found in the air next aiding in the composition of a plant, then in the body of an animal, and back in the air once more. In this perpetual revolution material particles run, the dominating influence determining and controlling their movement being in that great centre of our system, the sun. From him, in the summer days, plants receive, and, as it were, store up that warmth which, at a subsequent time, is to reappear in the glow of health of man, or to be rekindled in the blush of shame, or to consume in the burning fever. Nor is there any limit of time. The heat we derive from the combustion of stubble came from the sun as it were only yesterday; but that with which we moderate the rigour of winter when we burn anthracite or bituminous coal was also derived from the same source in the ultra-tropical climate of the secondary times, perhaps a thousand centuries ago.

Agency of the sun.

In such perpetually recurring cycles are the movements of material things accomplished, and all takes place under the dominion of invariable law. The air is the source whence all organisms have come; it is the receptacle to which they all return. Its parts are awakened into life, not by the influence of any terrestrial agency or principle concealed in itself, as Diogenes supposed, but by a star which is ninety millions of miles distant, the source, direct or indirect, of every terrestrial movement, and the dispenser of light and life.

Heraclitus asserts that fire is the first principle.

To Thales and Diogenes, whose primordial elements were water and air respectively, we must add Heraclitus of Ephesus, who maintained that the first principle is fire. He illustrated the tendency which Greek philosophy had already assumed of opposition to Polytheism and the idolatrous practices of the age. It is said that in his work, ethical, political, physical, and theological subjects were so confused, and so great was the difficulty of understanding his meaning, that he obtained the surname of "the Obscure." In this respect he has had among modern metaphysicians many successors. He founds his system, however, upon the simple axiom that "all is convertible into fire, and fire into all." Perhaps by the term fire he understood what is at present meant by heat, for he expressly says that he does not mean flame, but something merely dry and warm. He considered that this principle is in a state of perpetual activity, forming and absorbing every individual thing. He says, "All is, and is not; for though it does in truth come into being, yet it forthwith ceases to be." "No one has ever been twice on the same stream, for different waters are constantly flowing down. It dissipates its waters and gathers them again; it approaches and recedes, overflows and fails." And to teach us that we ourselves are changing and have changed, he says, "On the same stream we embark and embark not, we are and we are not." By such illustrations he implies that life is only an unceasing motion, and we cannot fail to remark that the Greek turn of thought is fast following that of the Hindu.

The fictitious permanence of successive forms.

But Heraclitus totally fails to free himself from local conceptions. He speaks of the motion of the primordial principle in the upward and downward directions, in the higher and lower regions. He says that the chief accumulation thereof is above, and the chief deficiency below; and hence he regards the soul of a man as a portion of fire migrated from heaven. He carries his ideas of the transitory nature of all phenomena to their last consequences, and illustrates the noble doctrine that all which appears to us to be permanent is only a regulated and self-renewing concurrence of similar and opposite motions by such extravagances as that the sun is daily destroyed and renewed.

Physical and physiological doctrines of Heraclitus.

In the midst of many wild physical statements many true axioms are delivered. "All is ordered by reason and intelligence, though all is subject to Fate." Already he perceived what the metaphysicians of our own times are illustrating, that "man's mind can produce no certain knowledge from its own interior resources alone." He regarded the organs of sense as being the channels through which the outer life of the world, and therewith truth, enters into the mind, and that in sleep, when the organs of sense are closed, we are shut out from all communion with the surrounding universal spirit. In his view every thing is animated and insouled, but to different degrees, organic objects being most completely or perfectly so. His astronomy may be anticipated from what has been said respecting the sun, which he moreover regarded as being scarcely more than a foot in diameter, and, like all other celestial objects, a mere meteor. His moral system was altogether based upon the physical, the fundamental dogma being the excellence of fire. Thus he accounted for the imbecility of the drunkard by his having a moist soul, and drew the inference that a warm or dry soul is the wisest and best; with justifiable patriotism asserting that the noblest souls must belong to a climate that is dry, intending thereby to indicate that Greece is man's fittest and truest country. There can be no doubt that in Heraclitus there is a strong tendency to the doctrine of a soul of the world. If the divinity is undistinguishable from heat, whither can we go to escape its influences? And in the restless activity and incessant changes it produces in every thing within our reach, do we not recognize the tokens of the illimitable and unshackled?

I have lingered on the chief features of the early Greek philosophy as exhibited in the physical school of Ionia.

They serve to impress upon us its intrinsic imperfection. It is a mixture of the physical, metaphysical, and mystical which, upon the whole, has no other value than this, that it shows how feeble were the beginnings of our knowledge—that we commenced with the importation of a few vulgar errors from Egypt. In presence of the utilitarian philosophy of that country and the theology of India, how vain and even childish are these germs of science in Greece! Yet this very imperfection is not without its use, since it warns us of the inferior position in which we stand as respects the time of our civilization when compared with those ancient states, and teaches us to reject the assertion which so many European scholars have wearied themselves in establishing, that Greece led the way to all human knowledge of any value. Above all, it impresses upon us more appropriate, because more humble views of our present attainments and position, and gives us to understand that other races of men not only preceded us in intellectual culture, but have equalled, and perhaps surpassed every thing that we have yet done in mental philosophy.

The puerility of Ionian philosophy.

Of the other founders of Ionic sects it may be observed that, though they gave to their doctrines different forms, the method of reasoning was essentially the same in them all. Of this a better illustration could not be given than in the philosophy of Anaximander of Miletus, who was contemporary with Thales. He started with the postulate that things arose by separation from a universal mixture of all: his primordial principle was therefore chaos, though he veiled it in the metaphysically obscure designation "The Infinite." The want of precision in this respect gave rise to much difference of opinion as to his tenets. To his chaos he imputed an internal energy, by which its parts spontaneously separated from each other; to those parts he imputed absolute unchangeability. He taught that the earth is of a cylindrical form, its base being one-third of its altitude; it is retained in the centre of the world by the air in an equality of distance from all the boundaries of the universe; that the fixed stars and planets revolved round it, each being fastened to a crystalline ring; and beyond them, in

Anaximander's doctrine of the Infinite.

like manner, the moon, and, still farther off, the sun. He conceived of an opposition between the central and circumferential regions, the former being naturally cold, and the latter hot; indeed, in his opinion, the settling of the cold parts to the centre, and the ascending of the hot, gave origin, respectively, to the formation of the earth and shining celestial bodies, the latter first existing as a complete shell or sphere, which, undergoing destruction, broke up into stars. Already we perceive the tendency of Greek philosophy to shape itself into systems of cosmogony, founded upon the disturbance of the chaotic matter by heat and cold. Nay, more, Anaximander explained the origin of living creatures on like principles, for the sun's heat, acting upon the primal miry earth, produced filmy bladders or bubbles, and these, becoming surrounded with a prickly rind, at length burst open, and, as from an egg, animals came forth. At first they were ill-formed and imperfect, but subsequently elaborated and developed. As to man, so far from being produced in his perfect shape, he was ejected as a fish, and under that form continued in the muddy water until he was capable of supporting himself on dry land. Besides "the Infinite" being thus the cause of generation, it was also the cause of destruction: "things must all return whence they came, according to destiny, for they must all, in order of time, undergo due penalties and expiations of wrong-doing." This expression obviously contains a moral consideration, and is an exemplification of the commencing feeble interconnection between physical and moral philosophy.

Origin of cosmogony.

Origin of biology.

As to the more solid discoveries attributed to this philosopher, we may dispose of them in the same manner that we have dealt with the like facts in the biographies of his predecessors—they are idle inventions of his vainglorious countrymen. That he was the first to make maps is scarcely consistent with the well-known fact that the Egyptians had cultivated geometry for that express purpose thirty centuries before he was born. As to his inventing sun-dials, the shadow had gone back on that of Ahaz a long time before. In reality, the sun-dial was a very ancient Oriental invention. And as to his being the first to make an exact calculation of the size and distance of the heavenly bodies, it need only be remarked that those who have so greatly extolled his labours must have overlooked how incompatible such discoveries are with a system which assumes that the earth is cylindrical in shape, and kept in the midst of the heavens by the atmosphere; that the sun is farther off than the fixed stars; and that each of the heavenly bodies is made to revolve by means of a crystalline wheel.

The philosopher whose views we have next to consider is Anaxagoras of Clazomene, the friend and master of Pericles, Euripides, and Socrates. Like several of his predecessors, he had visited Egypt. Among his disciples were numbered some of the most eminent men of those times.

Anaxagoras teaches the unchangeability of the universe.

The fundamental principle of his philosophy was the recognition of the unchangeability of the universe as a whole, the variety of forms that we see being produced by new arrangements of its constituent parts. Such a doctrine includes, of course, the idea of the eternity of matter. Anaxagoras says, "Wrongly do the Greeks suppose that aught begins or ceases to be, for nothing comes into being or is destroyed, but all is an aggregation or secretion of pre-existent things, so that all becoming might more correctly be called becoming-mixed, and all corruption becoming-separate." In such a statement we cannot fail to remark that the Greek is fast passing into the track of the Egyptian and the Hindu. In some respects his views recall those of the chaos of Anaximander, as when he says, "Together were all things infinite in number and smallness; nothing was distinguishable. Before they were sorted, while all was together, there was no quality noticeable." To the first moving force which arranged the parts of things out of the chaos, he gave the designation of "the Intellect," rejecting Fate as an empty name, and imputing all things to Reason. He made no distinction between the Soul and Intellect. His tenets evidently include a dualism indicated by the moving force and the moved mass, an opposition between the corporeal and mental. This indicated that for philosophy there are two separate

The primal intellect.

routes, the physical and intellectual. While Reason is thus the prime mover in his philosophy, he likewise employed many subordinate agents in the government of things—for instance, air, water, and fire, being evidently unable to explain the state of nature in a satisfactory way by the operation of the Intellect alone. We recognize in the details of his system ideas derived from former ones, such as the settling of the cold and dense below, and the rising of the warm and light above. In the beginning the action of Intellect was only partial; that which was primarily moved was only imperfectly sorted, and contained in itself the capability of many separations. From this point his system became a cosmogony, showing how the elements and fogs, stones, stars, and the sea, were produced. These explanations, as might be anticipated, have no exactness. Among his primary elements are many incongruous things, such as cold, colour, fire, gold, lead, corn, marrow, blood, &c. This doctrine implied that in compound things there was not a formation, but an arrangement. It required, therefore, many elements instead of a single one. Flesh is made of fleshy particles, bones of bony, gold of golden, lead of leaden, wood of wooden, &c. These analogous constituents are homœomeriæ. Of an infinite number of kinds, they composed the infinite all, which is a mixture of them. From such conditions Anaxagoras proves that all the parts of an animal body pre-exist in the food, and are merely collected therefrom. As to the phenomena of life, he explains it on his doctrine of dualism between mind and matter; he teaches that sleep is produced by the reaction of the latter on the former. Even plants he regards as only rooted animals, motionless, but having sensations and desires; he imputes the superiority of man to the mere fact of his having hands. He explains our mental perceptions upon the hypothesis that we have naturally within us the contraries of all the qualities of external things; and that, when we consider an object, we become aware of the preponderance of those qualities in our mind which are deficient in it. Hence all sensation is attended with pain. His doctrine of the production of animals was founded on the action of the sunlight on the miry earth

Cosmogony of Anaxagoras.

The earth he places in the centre of the world, whither it was carried by a whirlwind, the pole being originally in the zenith; but, when animals issued from the mud, its position was changed by the Intellect, so that there might be suitable climates. In some particulars his crude guesses present amusing anticipations of subsequent discoveries. Thus he maintained that the moon has mountains, and valleys like the earth; that there have been grand epochs in the history of our globe, in which it has been successively modified by fire and water; that the hills of Lampsacus would one day be under the sea, if time did not too soon fail.

Doubts whether we have any criterion of truth.

As to the nature of human knowledge, Anaxagoras, asserted that by the Intellect alone do we become acquainted with the truth, the senses being altogether untrustworthy. He illustrated this by putting a drop of coloured liquid into a quantity of clear water, the eye being unable to recognize any change. Upon such principles also he asserted that snow is not white, but black, since it is composed of water, of which the colour is black; and hence he drew such conclusions as that "things are to each man according as they seem to him." It was doubtless the recognition of the unreliability of the senses that extorted from him the well-known complaint: "Nothing can be known; nothing can be learned; nothing can be certain; sense is limited; intellect is weak; life is short."

Anaxagoras is persecuted.

The biography of Anaxagoras is not without interest. Born in affluence, he devoted all his means to philosophy, and in his old age encountered poverty and want. He was accused by the superstitious Athenian populace of Atheism and impiety to the gods, since he asserted that the sun and moon consist of earth and stone, and that the so-called divine miracles of the times were nothing more than common natural effects. For these reasons, and also because of the Magianism of his doctrine—for he taught the antagonism of mind and matter, a dogma of the detested Persians—he was thrown into prison, condemned to death, and barely escaped through the influence of Pericles. He fled to Lampsacus, where he ended his days in exile. His vainglorious countrymen, however, conferred honour upon his memory in their customary exaggerated way, boasting that he was the first to explain the phases of the moon, the nature of solar and lunar eclipses, that he had the power of foretelling future events, and had even predicted the fall of a meteoric stone.

From the biography of Anaxagoras, as well as of several of his contemporaries and successors, we may learn that a popular opposition was springing up against philosophy, not limited to a mere social protest, but carried out into political injustice. The antagonism between learning and Polytheism was becoming every day more distinct. Of the philosophers, some were obliged to flee into exile, some suffered death. The natural result of such a state of things was to force them to practise concealment and mystification, as is strikingly shown in the history of the Pythagoreans.

Pythagoras, biography of.

Of Pythagoras, the founder of this sect, but little is known with certainty; even the date of his birth is contested. Probably he was born at Samos about B.C. 540. If we were not expressly told so, we should recognize from his doctrines that he had been in Egypt and India. Some eminent scholars, who desire on all occasions to magnify the learning of ancient Europe, depreciate as far as they can the universal testimony of antiquity that such was the origin of the knowledge of Pythagoras, asserting that the constitution of the Egyptian priesthood rendered it impossible for a foreigner to become initiated. They forget that the ancient system of that country had been totally destroyed in the great revolution which took place more than a century before those times. If it were not explicitly stated by the ancients that Pythagoras lived for twenty-two years in Egypt, there is sufficient internal evidence in his story to prove that he had been there a long time. As a connoisseur can detect the hand of a master by the style of a picture, so one who has devoted attention to the old systems of thought sees, at a glance, the Egyptian in the philosophy of Pythagoras.

He passed into Italy during the reign of Tarquin the Proud, and settled at Crotona, a Greek colonial city on the Bay of Tarentum. At first he established a school, but, favoured by local dissensions, he gradually organized from the youths who availed themselves of his instructions a secret political society. Already it had passed into a maxim among the learned Greeks that it is not advantageous to communicate knowledge too freely to the people—a bitter experience in persecutions seemed to demonstrate that the maxim was founded on truth. The step from a secret philosophical society to a political conspiracy is but short. Pythagoras appears to have taken it. The disciples who were admitted to his scientific secrets after a period of probation and process of examination constituted a ready instrument of intrigue against the state, the issue of which, after a time, appeared in the supplanting of the ancient senate and the exaltation of Pythagoras and his club to the administration of government. The actions of men in all times are determined by similar principles; and as it would be now with such a conspiracy, so it was then; for, though the Pythagorean influence spread from Crotona to other Italian towns, an overwhelming reaction soon set in, the innovators were driven into exile, their institutions destroyed, and their founder fell a victim to his enemies.

The organization attempted by the Pythagoreans is an exception to the general policy of the Greeks. The philosophical schools had been merely points of reunion for those entertaining similar opinions; but in the state they can hardly be regarded as having had any political existence.

It is difficult, when the political or religious feelings of men have been engaged, to ascertain the truth of events in which they have been concerned; deception, and falsehood, seem to be licensed. In the midst of the troubles befalling Italy as the consequence of these Pythagorean machinations, it is impossible to ascertain facts with certainty. One party exalts Pythagoras to a superhuman state; it pictures him majestic and impassive, clothed in robes of white, with a golden coronet around his brows, listening to the music of the spheres, or seeking relaxation in the more humble hymns of Homer, Hesiod, and Thales; lost in the contemplation of Nature, or rapt in ecstasy in his meditations on God; manifesting his descent from Apollo or Hermes by the working of miracles, predicting future events, conversing with genii in the solitude of a dark cavern, and even surpassing the wonder of speaking simultaneously in different tongues, since it was established, by the most indisputable testimony, that he had accomplished the prodigy of being present with and addressing the people in several different places at the same time. It seems not to have occurred to his disciples that such preposterous assertions cannot be sustained by any evidence whatsoever; and that the stronger and clearer such evidence is, instead of supporting the fact for which it is brought forward, it the more serves to shake our confidence in the truth of man, or impresses on us the conclusion that he is easily lead to the adoption of falsehood, and is readily deceived by imposture.

His miracles.

By his opponents he was denounced as a quack, or, at the best, a visionary mystic, who had deluded the young with the mummeries of a freemasonry; had turned the weak-minded into shallow enthusiasts and grim ascetics; and as having conspired against a state which had given him an honourable refuge, and brought disorder and bloodshed upon it. Between such contradictory statements, it is difficult to determine how much we should impute to the philosopher and how much to the trickster. In this uncertainty, the Pythagoreans reap the fruit of one of their favourite maxims, "Not unto all should all be made known." Perhaps at the bottom of these political movements lay the hope of establishing a central point of union for the numerous Greek colonies of Italy, which, though they were rich and highly civilized, were, by reason of their isolation and antagonism, essentially weak. Could they have been united in a powerful federation by the aid of some political or religious bond, they might have exerted a singular influence on the rising fortunes of Rome, and thereby on humanity.

His character.

The fundamental dogma of the Pythagoreans was that "number is the essence or first principle of things." This led them at once to the study of the mysteries of figures and of arithmetical relations, and plunged them into the wildest fantasies when it took the absurd form that numbers are actually things.

Pythagoras asserts that number is the first principle.

The approval of the doctrines of Pythagoras so generally expressed was doubtless very much due to the fact that they supplied an intellectual void. Those who had been in the foremost ranks of philosophy had come to the conclusion that, as regard external things, and even ourselves, we have no criterion of truth; but in the properties of numbers and their relations, such a criterion does exist.

It would scarcely repay the reader to pursue this system in its details; a very superficial representation of it is all that is necessary for our purpose. It recognizes two species of numbers, the odd and even; and since one, or unity, must be at once both odd and even, it must be the very essence of number, and the ground of all other numbers: hence the meaning of the Pythagorean expression, "All comes from one;" which also took form in the mystical allusion, "God embraces all and actuates all, and is but one." To the number ten extraordinary importance was imputed, since it contains in itself, or arises from the addition of, 1, 2, 3, 4—that is, of even and odd numbers together; hence it received the name of the grand tetractys, because it so contains the first four numbers. Some, however, assert that that designation was imposed on the number thirty-six. To the triad the Pythagoreans likewise attached much significance, since it has a beginning, a middle, and an end. To unity, or one, they gave the designation of the even-odd, asserting that it contained the property both of the even and odd, as is plain from the fact that if one be added to an even number it becomes odd, but if to an odd number it becomes even. They arranged the primary elements of nature in a table of ten contraries, of which the odd and even are one, and light and darkness another. They said that "the nature and energy of number may be traced not only in divine and dæmonish things, but in human works and words everywhere, and in all works of art and in music." They even linked their arithmetical views to morality, through the observation that numbers never lie; that they are hostile to falsehood; and that, therefore, truth belongs to their family: their fanciful speculations led them to infer that in the limitless or infinite, falsehood and envy must

Pythagorean philosophy.

reign. From similar reasoning, they concluded that the number one contained not only the perfect, but also the imperfect; hence it follows that the most good, most beautiful, and most true are not at the beginning, but that they are in the process of time evolved. They held that whatever we know must have had a beginning, a middle, and an end, of which the beginning and end are the boundaries or limits; but the middle is unlimited, and, as a consequence, may be subdivided *ad infinitum.* They therefore resolved corporeal existence into points, as is set forth in their maxim that "all is composed of points or spacial units, which, taken together, constitute a number." Such being their ideas of the limiting which constitutes the extreme, they understood by the unlimited the intermediate space or interval. By the aid of these intervals they obtained a conception of space; for, since the units, or monads, as they were also called, are merely geometrical points, no number of them could produce a line, but by the union of monads and intervals conjointly a line can arise, and also a surface, and also a solid. As to the interval thus existing between monads, some considered it as being mere aërial breath, but the orthodox regarded it as a vacuum; hence we perceive the meaning of their absurd affirmation that all things are produced by a vacuum. As it is not to be overlooked that the monads are merely mathematical points, and have no dimensions or size, substances actually contain no matter, and are nothing more than forms.

The Pythagoreans applied these principles to account for the origin of the world, saying that, since its very existence is an illusion, it could not have any origin in time, but only seemingly so to human thought. As to time itself, they regarded it as "existing only by the distinction of a series of different moments, which, however, are again restored to unity by the limiting moments." The diversity of relations we find in the world they supposed to be occasioned by the bond of harmony. "Since the principles of things are neither similar nor congenerous, it is impossible for them to be brought into order except by the intervention of harmony, whatever may have been the manner in which it took place. Like

Pythagorean cosmogony.

and homogeneous things, indeed, would not have required harmony; but, as to the dissimilar and unsymmetrical, such must necessarily be held together by harmony if they are to be contained in a world of order." In this manner they confused together the ideas of number and harmony, regarding the world not only as a combination of contraries, but as an orderly and harmonical combination thereof. To particular numbers they therefore imputed great significance, asserting that "there are seven chords or harmonies, seven pleiads, seven vowels, and that certain parts of the bodies of animals change in the course of seven years." They carried to an extreme the numerical doctrine, assigning certain numbers as the representatives of a bird, a horse, a man. This doctrine may be illustrated by facts familiar to chemists, who, in like manner, attach significant numbers to the names of things. Taking hydrogen as unity, 6 belongs to carbon, 8 to oxygen, 16 to sulphur. Carrying these principles out, there is no substance, elementary or compound, inorganic or organic, to which an expressive number does not belong. Nay, even an archetypal form, as of man or any other such composite structure, may thus possess a typical number, the sum of the numbers of its constituent parts. It signifies nothing what interpretation we give to these numbers, whether we regarded them as atomic weights, or, declining the idea of atoms, consider them as the representatives of force. As in the ancient philosophical doctrine, so in modern science, the number is invariably connected with the name of a thing, of whatever description the thing may be.

Modern Pythagorisms in chemistry.

The grand standard of harmonical relation among the Pythagoreans was the musical octave. Physical qualities, such as colour and tone, were supposed to appertain to the surface of bodies. Of the elements they enumerated five—earth, air, fire, water, and ether, connecting therewith the fact that man has five organs of sense. Of the planets they numbered five, which, together with the sun, moon, and earth, are placed apart at distances determined by a musical law, and in their movements through space give rise to a sound, the harmony of the spheres, unnoticed by us because we habitually hear it. They place the sun in the centre of the system, round which, with the other planets, the earth revolves. At this point the geocentric doctrine is being abandoned and the heliocentric takes its place. As the circle is the most perfect of forms, the movements of the planets are circular. They maintained that the moon is inhabited, and like the earth, but the people there are taller than men, in the proportion as the moon's periodic rotation is greater than that of the earth. They explained the Milky Way as having been occasioned by the fall of a star, or as having been formerly the path of the sun. They asserted that the world is eternal, but the earth is transitory and liable to change, the universe being in the shape of a sphere. They held that the soul of man is merely an efflux of the universal soul, and that it comes into the body from without. From dreams and the events of sickness they inferred the existence of good and evil dæmons. They supposed that souls can exist without the body, leading a kind of dream-life, and identified the motes in the sunbeam with them. Their heroes and dæmons were souls not yet become embodied, or who had ceased to be so. The doctrine of transmigration which they had adopted was in harmony with such views, and, if it does not imply the absolute immortality of the soul, at least asserts its existence after the death of the body, for the disembodied spirit becomes incarnate again as soon as it finds a tenement which fits it. To their life after death the Pythagoreans added a doctrine of retributive rewards and punishments, and, in this respect, what has been said of animals forming a penitential mechanism in the theology of India and Egypt, holds good for the Pythagoreans too.

Pythagorean physics and psychology.

Of their system of politics nothing can now with certainty be affirmed beyond the fact that its prime element was an aristocracy; of their rule of private life, but little beyond its including a recommendation of moderation in all things, the cultivation of friendship, the observance of faith, and the practice of self-denial, promoted by ascetic exercises. It was a maxim with them that a right education is not only of importance to the individual, but also to the interests of the state. Pythagoras himself, as is well known, paid much attention to the determination of extension and gravity, the ratios of musical tones, astronomy, and medicine. He directed his disciples, in their orgies or secret worship, to practise gymnastics, dancing, music. In correspondence with his principle of imparting to men only such knowledge as they were fitted to receive, he communicated to those who were less perfectly prepared exoteric doctrines, reserving the esoteric for the privileged few who had passed five years in silence, had endured humiliation, and been purged by self-denial and sacrifice.

The Eleatic philosophy.

We have now reached the consideration of the Eleatic philosophy. It differs from the preceding in its neglect of material things, and its devotion to the supra-sensible. It derives its name from Elea, a Greek colonial city of Italy, its chief authors being Xenophanes, Parmenides, and Zeno.

Xenophanes represents a great philosophical advance.

Xenophanes was a native of Ionia, from which having been exiled, he appears to have settled at last in Elea, after leading for many years the life of a wandering rhapsodist. He gave his doctrines a poetical form for the purpose of more easily diffusing them. To the multitude he became conspicuous from his opposition to Homer, Hesiod, and other popular poets, whom he denounced for promoting the base polytheism of the times, and degrading the idea of the divine by the immoralities they attributed to the gods. He proclaimed God as an all-powerful Being, existing from eternity, and without any likeness to man. A strict monotheist, he denounced the plurality of gods as an inconceivable error, asserting that of the all-powerful and all-perfect there could not, in the nature of things, be more than one; for, if there were only so many as two, those attributes could not apply to one of them, much less, then, if there were many. This one principle or power was to him the same as the universe, the substance of which, having existed from all eternity, must necessarily be identical with God; for, since it is impossible that there should be two Omnipresents, so also it is impossible that there should be two Eternals. It therefore may be said that there is a tincture of Orientalism in his ideas, since it would scarcely be possible to offer a more succinct and luminous exposition of the pantheism of India.

The reader who has been wearied with the frivolities of the Ionian philosophy, and lost in the mysticisms of Pythagoras, cannot fail to recognize that here we have something of a very different kind. To an Oriental dignity of conception is added an extraordinary clearness and precision of reasoning.

He approaches the Indian ideas.

To Xenophanes all revelation is a pure fiction; the discovery of the invisible is to be made by the intellect of man alone. The vulgar belief which imputes to the Deity the sentiments, passions, and crimes of man, is blasphemous and accursed. He exposes the impiety of those who would figure the Great Supreme under the form of a man, telling them that if the ox or the lion could rise to a conception of the Deity, they might as well embody him under their own shape; that the negro represents him with a flat nose and black face; the Thracian with blue eyes and a ruddy complexion. "There is but one God; he has no resemblance to the bodily form of man, nor are his thoughts like ours." He taught that God is without parts, and throughout alike; for, if he had parts, some would be ruled by others, and others would rule, which is impossible, for the very notion of God implies his perfect and thorough sovereignty. Throughout he must be Reason, and Intelligence, and Omnipotence, "ruling the universe without trouble by Reason and Insight." He conceived that the Supreme understands by a sensual perception, and not only thinks, but sees and hears throughout. In a symbolical manner he represented God as a sphere, like the heavens, which encompass man and all earthly things.

Theology of Xenophanes.

In his natural philosophy it is said that he adopted the four elements, Earth, Air, Fire, Water; though by some it is asserted that, from observing fossil fish on the tops of mountains, he was led to the belief that the earth itself arose from water; and generally, that the phenomena of nature originate in combinations of the primary elements. From such views he inferred that all things are necessarily transitory, and that men, and even the earth itself, must pass away. As to the latter, he regarded it as a flat surface, the inferior region of which extends indefinitely downward, and so gives a

His physical views.

solid foundation. His physical views he, however, held with a doubt almost bordering on scepticism: "No mortal man ever did, or ever shall know God and the universe thoroughly; for, since error is so spread over all things it is impossible for us to be certain even when we utter the true and the perfect." It seemed to him hopeless that man could ever ascertain the truth, since he has no other aid than truthless appearances.

I cannot dismiss this imperfect account of Xenophanes, who was, undoubtedly, one of the greatest of the Greek philosophers, without an allusion to his denunciation of Homer, and other poets of his country, because they had aided in degrading the idea of the Divinity; and also to his faith in human nature, his rejection of the principle of concealing truth from the multitude, and his self-devotion in diffusing it among all at a risk of liberty and life. He wandered from country to country, withstanding polytheism to its face, and imparting wisdom in rhapsodies and hymns, the form, above all others, calculated most quickly in those times to spread knowledge abroad. To those who are disposed to depreciate his philosophical conclusions, it may be remarked that in some of their most striking features they have been reproduced in modern times, and I would offer to them a quotation from the General Scholium at the end of the third book of the Principia of Newton: "The Supreme God exists necessarily, and by the same necessity he exists *always* and *everywhere*. Whence, also, he is all similar, all eye, all ear, all brain, all arm, all power to perceive, to understand, and to act, but in a manner not at all human, not at all corporeal; in a manner utterly unknown to us. As a blind man has no idea of colours, so have we no idea of the manner by which the all-wise God perceives and understands all things. He is utterly void of all body and bodily figure, and can therefore neither be seen, nor heard, nor touched, nor ought to be worshipped under the representation of any corporeal thing. We have ideas of his attributes, but what the real substance of anything is we know not."

Some of his thoughts reappear in Newton.

To the Eleatic system thus originating with Xenophanes is to be attributed the dialectic phase henceforward so prominently exhibited by Greek philosophy. It abandoned, for the most part, the pursuits which had occupied the Ionians—the investigation of visible nature, the phenomena of material things, and the laws presiding over them; conceiving such to be merely deceptive, and attaching itself to what seemed to be the only true knowledge—an investigation of Being and of God. By the Eleats, since all change appeared to be an impossibility, the phenomena of succession presented by the world were regarded as a pure illusion, and they asserted that Time, and Motion, and Space are phantasms of the imagination, or vain deceptions of the senses. They therefore separated reason from opinion, attributing to the former conceptions of absolute truth, and to the latter imperfections arising from the fictions of sense. It was on this principle that Parmenides divided his work on "Nature" into two books, the first on Reason, the second on Opinion. Starting from the nature of Being, the uncreated and unchangeable, he denied altogether the idea of succession in time, and also the relations of space, and pronounced change and motion, of whatever kind they may be, mere illusions of opinion. His pantheism appears in the declaration that the All is thought and intelligence; and this, indeed, constitutes the essential feature of his doctrine, for, by thus placing thought and being in parallelism with each other, and interconnecting them by the conception that it is for the sake of being that thought exists, he showed that they must necessarily be conceived of as one.

Parmenides on reason and opinion.

Philosophy becoming Pantheism.

Such profound doctrines occupied the first book of the poem of Parmenides; in the second he treated of opinion, which, as we have said, is altogether dependent on the senses, and therefore untrustworthy, not, however, that it must necessarily be absolutely false. It is scarcely possible for us to reconstruct from the remains of his works the details of his theory, or to show his approach to the Ionian doctrines by the assumption of the existence in nature of two opposite species—ethereal fire and heavy night; of an equal proportion of which all things consist, fire being the true, and night the phenomenal. From such an unsubstantial and delusive basis it would not repay us, even if we had the means of accomplishing it, to give an exposition of his physical system. In many respects it degenerated into a wild vagary; as, for example, when he placed an overruling dæmon in the centre of the phenomenal world. Nor need we be detained by his extravagant reproduction of the old doctrine of the generation of animals from miry clay, nor follow his explanation of the nature of man, who, since he is composed of light and darkness, participates in both, and can never ascertain absolute truth. By other routes, and upon far less fanciful principles, modern philosophy has at last come to the same melancholy conclusion.

Doctrines of Parmenides carried out by Zeno;

The doctrines of Parmenides were carried out by Zeno the Eleatic, who is said to have been his adopted son. He brought into use the method of refuting error by the *reductio ad absurdum*. His compositions were in prose, and not in poetry, as were those of his predecessors. As it had been the object of Parmenides to establish the existence of "the One," it was the object of Zeno to establish the non-existence of "the Many." Agreeably to such principles, he started from the position that only one thing really exists, and that all others are mere modifications or appearances of it. He denied motion, but admitted the appearance of it; regarding it as a name given to a series of conditions, each of which is necessarily rest. This dogma against the possibility of motion he maintained by four arguments; the second of them is the celebrated Achilles puzzle. It is thus stated: "Suppose Achilles to run ten times as fast as a tortoise, yet, if the tortoise has the start, Achilles can never overtake him; for, if they are separated at first by an interval of a thousand feet, when Achilles has run these thousand feet the tortoise will have run a hundred, and when Achilles has run these hundred the tortoise will have got on ten, and so on for ever; therefore Achilles may run for ever without overtaking the tortoise." Such were his arguments against the existence of motion; his proof of the existence of One, the indivisible and infinite, may thus be stated: "To suppose that the one is divisible is to suppose it finite. If divisible, it must be infinitely divisible. But suppose two things to exist, then there must necessarily be an interval between those two—something separating and limiting them. What is that something? It is some *other* thing. But then if not the *same* thing, *it also* must be separated and limited, and so on *ad infinitum*. Thus only one thing can exist as the substratum for all manifold appearances." Zeno furnishes us with an illustration of the fallibility of the indications of sense in his argument against Protagoras. It may be here introduced as a specimen of his method: "He asked if a grain of corn, or the ten thousandth part of a grain, would, when it fell to the ground, make a noise. Being answered in the negative, he further asked whether, then, would a measure of corn. This being necessarily affirmed, he then demanded whether the measure was not in some determinate ratio to the single grain; as this could not be denied, he was able to conclude, either, then, the bushel of corn makes no noise on falling, or else the very smallest portion of a grain does the same."

And by Melissus of Samos.

To the names already given as belonging to the Eleatic school may be added that of Melissus of Samos, who also founded his argument on the nature of Being, deducing its unity, unchangeability, and indivisibility. He denied, like the rest of his school, all change and motion, regarding them as mere illusions of the senses. From the indivisibility of being he inferred its incorporeality, and therefore denied all bodily existence.

Biography of Empedocles.

The list of Eleatic philosophers is doubtfully closed by the name of Empedocles of Agrigentum, who in legend almost rivals Pythagoras. In the East he learned medicine and magic, the art of working miracles, of producing rain and wind. He decked himself in priestly garments, a golden girdle, and a crown, proclaiming himself to be a god. It is said by some that he never died, but ascended to the skies in the midst of a supernatural glory. By some it is related that he leaped into the crater of Etna, that, the manner of his death being unknown, he might still continue to pass for a god—an expectation disappointed by an eruption which cast out one of his brazen sandals.

Agreeably to the school to which he belonged, he relied on Reason and distrusted the Senses. From his fragments it has been inferred that he was sceptical of the guidance of the former as well as of the latter, founding his distrust on the imperfection the soul has contracted, and for which it has been condemned to existence in this world, and even to transmigration from body to body. Adopting the Eleatic doctrine that like can be only known by like, fire by fire, love by love, the recognition of the divine by man is sufficient proof that the Divine exists. His primary elements were four—Earth, Air, Fire, and Water; to these he added two principles, Love and Hate. The four elements he regarded as four gods, or divine eternal forces, since out of them all things are made. Love he regards as the creative power, the destroyer or modifier being Hate. It is obvious, therefore, that in him the strictly philosophical system of Xenophanes had degenerated into a mixed and mystical view, in which the physical, the metaphysical, and the moral were confounded together; and that, as the necessary consequence of such a state, the principles of knowledge were becoming unsettled, a suspicion arising that all philosophical systems were untrustworthy, and a general scepticism was already setting in.

He mingles mysticism with philosophy.

To this result also, in no small degree, the labours of Democritus of Abdera tended. He had had the advantages derived from wealth in the procurement of knowledge, for it is said that his father was rich enough to be able to entertain the Persian King Xerxes, who was so gratified thereby that he left several Magi and Chaldeans to complete the education of the youth. On his father's death, Democritus, dividing with his brothers the estate, took as his portion the share consisting of money, leaving to them the lands, that he might be better able to devote himself to travelling. He passed into Egypt, Ethiopia, Persia, and India, gathering knowledge from all those sources.

According to Democritus, "Nothing is true, or, if so, is not certain to us." Nevertheless, as, in his system sensation constitutes thought, and, at the same time, is but a change in the sentient being, "sensations are of necessity true;" from which somewhat obscure passage we may infer that, in the view of Democritus, though sensation is true subjectively, it is

Democritus asserts the untrustworthiness of knowledge.

not true objectively. The sweet, the bitter, the hot, the cold, are simply creations of the mind; but in the outer object to which we append them, atoms and space alone exist, and our opinion of the properties of such objects is founded upon images emitted by them falling upon the senses. Confounding in this manner sensation with thought, and making them identical, he, moreover, included Reflexion as necessary for true knowledge, Sensation by itself being untrustworthy. Thus, though Sensation may indicate to us that sweet, bitter, hot, cold, occur in bodies, Reflexion teaches us that this is altogether an illusion, and that, in reality, atoms and space alone exist.

Devoting his attention, then, to the problem of perception—how the mind becomes aware of the existence of external things—he resorted to the hypothesis that they constantly throw off images of themselves, which are assimilated by the air through which they have to pass, and enter the soul by pores in its sensitive organs. Hence such images, being merely of the superficial form, are necessarily imperfect and untrue, and so, therefore, must be the knowledge yielded by them. Democritus rejected the one element of the Eleatics, affirming that there must be many; but he did not receive the four of Empedocles, nor his principles of Love and Hate, nor the homœomeriæ of Anaxagoras. He also denied that the primary elements had any sensible qualities whatever. He conceived of all things as being composed of invisible, intangible, and indivisible particles or atoms, which, by reason of variation in their configuration, combination, or position, give rise to the varieties of forms: to the atom he imputed self-existence and eternal duration. His doctrine, therefore, explains how it is that the many can arise from the one, and in this particular he reconciled the apparent contradictions of the Ionians and Eleatics. The theory of chemistry, as it now exists, essentially includes his views. The general formative principle of Nature he regarded as being Destiny or Fate; but there are indications that by this he meant nothing more than irreversible law.

He introduces the atomic theory.

Destiny, Fate and resistless law.

A system thus based upon severe mathematical considerations, and taking as its starting-point a vacuum and atoms—the former actionless and passionless; which considers the production of new things as only new aggregations, and the decay of the old as separations; which recognizes in compound bodies specific arrangements of atoms to one another; which can rise to the conception that even a single atom may constitute a world—such a system may commend itself to our attention for its results, but surely not to our approval, when we find it carrying us to the conclusions that even mathematical cognition is a mere semblance; that the soul is only a finely-constituted form fitted into the grosser bodily frame; that even for reason itself there is an absolute impossibility of all certainty; that scepticism is to be indulged in to that degree that we may doubt whether, when a cone has been cut asunder, its two surfaces are alike; that the final result of human inquiry is the absolute demonstration that man is incapable of knowledge; that, even if the truth be in his possession, he can never be certain of it; that the world is an illusive phantasm, and that there is no God.

Is led to atheism.

I need scarcely refer to the legendary stories related of Democritus, as that he put out his eyes with a burning-glass that he might no longer be deluded with their false indications, and more tranquilly exercise his reason—a fiction bearing upon its face the contemptuous accusation of his antagonists, but, by the stolidity of subsequent ages, received as an actual fact instead of a sarcasm. As to his habit of so constantly deriding the knowledge and follies of men that he universally acquired the epithet of the laughing philosopher, we may receive the opinion of the great physician Hippocrates, who. being requested by the people of Abdera to cure him of his madness, after long discoursing with him, expressed himself penetrated with admiration, and even with the most profound veneration for him, and rebuked those who had sent him with the remark that they themselves were the more distempered of the two.

Legends of Democritus.

Thus far European Greece had done but little in the cause of philosophy. The chief schools were in Asia Minor, or among the Greek colonies of Italy. But the time had now arrived when the mother country was to enter upon a distinguished career, though, it must be confessed, from a most unfavourable beginning. This was by no means the only occasion on which the intellectual activity of the Greek colonies made itself felt in the destinies of Europe. The mercantile character in a community has ever been found conducive to mental activity and physical adventure; it holds in light esteem prescriptive opinion, and puts things at the actual value they at the time possess. If the Greek colonies thus discharged the important function of introducing and disseminating speculative philosophy, we shall find them again, five hundred years later, occupied with a similar task on the advent of that period in which philosophical speculation was about to be supplanted by religious faith. For there can be no doubt that, humanly speaking, the cause of the rapid propagation of Christianity, in its first ages, lay in the extraordinary facilities existing among the commercial communities scattered all around the shores of the Mediterranean Sea, from the ports of the Levant to those of France and Spain. An incessant intercourse was kept up among them during the five centuries before Christ; it became, under Roman influence, more and more active, and of increasing political importance. Such a state of things is in the highest degree conducive to the propagation of thought, and, indeed, to its origination, through the constant excitement it furnishes to intellectual activity. Commercial communities, in this respect, present a striking contrast to agricultural. By their aid speculative philosophy was rapidly disseminated everywhere, as was subsequently Christianity. But the agriculturists stedfastly adhered with marvellous stolidity to their ancestral traditions and polytheistic absurdities, until the very designation—paganism—under which their system passes was given as a nickname derived from themselves.

Rise of philosophy in European Greece.

Commercial communities favourable to new ideas.

The intellectual condition of the Greek colonies of Italy and Sicily has not attracted the attention of critics in the manner it deserves. For, though its political result may appear to those whose attention is fixed by mere material aggrandizement to have been totally eclipsed by the subsequent power of the Roman republic, to one who looks at things in a mere general way it may be a probable inquiry whether the philosophy cultivated in those towns has not, in the course of ages, produced as solid and lasting results as the military achievements of the Eternal City. The relations of the Italian peninsula to the career of European civilization are to be classified under three epochs, the first corresponding to the philosophy generated in the southern Greek towns: this would have attained the elevation long before reached in the advanced systems of India had it not been prevented by the rapid development of Roman power; the second presents the military influence of republican and imperial Rome; to the third belongs the agency of ecclesiastical Rome—for the production of the last we shall find hereafter that the preceding two conspire. The Italian effect upon the whole has therefore been philosophical, material, and mixed. We are greatly in want of a history of the first, for which doubtless many facts still remain to a painstaking and enlightened inquirer.

Philosophical influence of the Greek colonies.

It was on account of her small territory and her numerous population that Greece was obliged to colonize. To these motives must be added internal dissensions, and particularly the consequences of unequal marriages. So numerous did these colonies and their offshoots become, that a great Greek influence pervaded all the Mediterranean shores and many of the most important islands, attention more particularly being paid to the latter, from their supposed strategical value; thus, in the opinion of Alexander the Great, the command of the Mediterranean lay in the possession of Cyprus. The Greek colonists were filibusters; they seized by force the women wherever they settled, but their children were taught to speak the paternal language, as has been the case in more recent times with the descendants of the Spaniards in America. The wealth of some of these Greek colonial towns is said to have been incredible. Crotona was more than twelve miles in circumference; and Sybaris, another of the Italiot cities, was so luxurious

Origin of the Greek colonial system.

and dissipated as even to give rise to a proverb. The prosperity of these places was due to two causes: they were not only the centres of great agricultural districts, but carried on also an active commerce in all directions, the dense population of the mother country offering them a steady and profitable market; they also maintained an active traffic with all the Mediterranean cities; thus, if they furnished Athens with corn, they also furnished Carthage with oil. In the Greek cities connected with this colonial system, especially in Athens, the business of ship-building and navigation was so extensively prosecuted as to give a special character to public life. In other parts of Greece, as in Sparta, it was altogether different. In that state the laws of Lycurgus had abolished private property; all things were held in common; savage life was reduced to a system, and therefore there was no object in commerce. But in Athens, commerce was regarded as being so far from dishonourable that some of the most illustrious men, whose names have descended to us as philosophers, were occupied with mercantile pursuits. Aristotle kept a druggist's shop in Athens, and Plato sold oil in Egypt.

It was the intention of Athens, had she succeeded in the conquest of Sicily, to make an attempt upon Carthage, foreseeing therein the dominion of the Mediterranean, as was actually realized subsequently by Rome. The destruction of that city constituted the point of ascendency in the history of the Great Republic. Carthage stood upon a peninsula forty-five miles round, with a neck only three miles across. Her territory has been estimated as having a sea-line of not less than 1400 miles, and containing 300 towns; she had also possessions in Spain, in Sicily, and other Mediterranean islands, acquired, not by conquest, but by colonization. In the silver mines of Spain she employed not less than forty thousand men. In these respects she was guided by the maxims of her Phœnician ancestry, for the Tyrians had colonized for depôts, and had forty stations of that kind in the Mediterranean. Indeed, Carthage herself originated in that way, owing her development to the position she held at the junction of the east and west basins. The Carthaginian merchants did not carry for hire, but dealt in their commodities. This implied an extensive system of depôts and bonding. They had anticipated many of the devices of modern commerce. They effected insurances, made loans on bottomry, and it has been supposed that their leathern money may have been of the nature of our bank notes.

Carthaginian supremacy in the Mediterranean.

In the preceding chapter we have spoken of the attempts of the Asiatics on Egypt and the south shore of the Mediterranean; we have now to turn to their operations on the north shore, the consequences of which are of the utmost interest in the history of philosophy. It appears that the cities of Asia Minor, after their contest with the Lydian kings, had fallen an easy prey to the Persian power. It remained, therefore, only for that power to pass to the European continent. A pretext is easily found where the policy is so clear. So far as the internal condition of Greece was concerned, nothing could be more tempting to an invader. There seemed to be no bond of union between the different towns, and, indeed, the more prominent ones might be regarded as in a state of chronic revolution. In Athens, since B.C. 622, the laws of Draco had been supplanted by those of Solon; and again and again the government had been seized by violence or gained through intrigue by one adventurer after another. Under these circumstances the Persian king passed an army into Europe. The military events of both this and the succeeding invasion under Xerxes have been more than sufficiently illustrated by the brilliant imagination of the lively Greeks. It was needless, however, to devise such fictions as the million of men who crossed into Europe, or the two hundred thousand who lay dead upon the field after the battle of Platæa. If there were not such stubborn facts as the capture and burning of Athens, the circumstance that these wars lasted for fifty years would be sufficient to inform us that all the advantages were not on one side. Wars do not last so long without bringing upon both parties disasters as well as conferring glories; and had these been as exterminating and over-

Attempts of the Persians at dominion in the Mediterranean.

Contest between them and the Greeks.

The fifty years' war, and eventual supremacy of Athens.

whelming as classical authors have supposed, our surprise may well be excited that the Persian annals have preserved so little memory of them. Greece did not perceive that, if posterity must take her accounts as true, it must give the palm of glory to Persia, who could, with unfaltering perseverance, persist in attacks illustrated by such unparalleled catastrophes. She did not perceive that the annals of a nation may be more splendid from their exhibiting a courage which could bear up for half a century against continual disasters, and extract victory at last from defeat.

In pursuance of their policy, the Persians extended their dominion to Cyrene and Barca on the south, as well as to Thrace and Macedonia on the north. The Persian wars gave rise to that wonderful development in Greek art which has so worthily excited the admiration of subsequent ages. The assertion is quite true that after those wars the Greeks could form in sculpture living men. On the part of the Persians, these military undertakings were not of the base kind so common in antiquity; they were the carrying out of a policy conceived with great ability, their object being to obtain countries for tribute and not for devastation. The great critic Niebuhr, by whose opinions I am guided in the views I express of these events, admits that the Greek accounts, when examined, present little that was possible. The Persian empire does not seem to have suffered at all; and Plato, whose opinion must be considered as of very great authority, says that, on the whole, the Persian wars reflect extremely little honour on the Greeks. It was asserted that only thirty-one towns, and most of them small ones, were faithful to Greece. Treason to her seems for years in succession to have infected all her ablest men. It was not Pausanias alone who wanted to be king under the supremacy of Persia. Such a satrap would have borne about the same relation to the great king as the modern pacha does to the grand seignior. However, we must do justice to those able men. A king was what Greece in reality required; had she secured one at this time strong enough to hold her conflicting interests in check, she would have become the mistress of the world. Her leading men saw this.

The elevating effect of the Persian wars was chiefly felt in Athens. It was there that the grand development of pure art, literature, and science took place. As to Sparta, she remained barbarous as she had ever been; the Spartans continuing robbers and impostors, in their national life exhibiting not a single feature that can be commended. Mechanical art reached its perfection at Corinth; real art at Athens, finding a multitude not only of true, but also of new expressions. Before Pericles the only style of architecture was the Doric; his became at once the age of perfect beauty. It also became the age of freedom in thinking and departure from the national faith. In this respect the history of Pericles and of Aspasia is very significant. His, also, was the great age of oratory, but of oratory leading to delusion, the democratical forms of Athens being altogether deceptive, power ever remaining in the hands of a few leading men, who did everything. The true popular sentiment, as was almost always the case under those ancient republican institutions, could find for itself no means of expression. The great men were only too prone to regard their fellow-citizens as a rabble, mere things to be played off against one another, and to consider that the objects of life are dominion and lust, that love, self-sacrifice, and devotion are fictions; that oaths are only good for deception.

The consequence is her vast intellectual progress.

Her progress in art.

Though the standard of statesmanship, at the period of the Persian wars, was very low, there can be no doubt that among the Greek leaders were those who clearly understood the causes of the Asiatic attack; and hence, with an instinct of self-preservation, defensive alliances were continually maintained with Egypt. When their valour and endurance had given to the Greeks a glorious issue to the war, the articles contained in the final treaty manifest clearly the motives and understandings of both parties. No Persian vessel was to appear between the Cyanean Rocks and Chelidonian Islands; no Persian army to approach within three days' journey of the Mediterranean Sea, B.C. 449.

The treaty with Persia.

To Athens herself the war had given political supremacy. We need only look at her condition fifty years after the battle of Platæa. She was mistress of more than a thousand miles of the coast of Asia Minor; she held as dependencies more than forty islands; she controlled the straits between Europe and Asia; her fleets ranged the Mediterranean and the Black Seas; she had monopolized the trade of all the adjoining countries; her magazines were full of the most valuable objects of commerce. From the ashes of the Persian fire she had risen up so supremely beautiful that her temples, her statues, her works of art, in their exquisite perfection, have since had no parallel in the world. Her intellectual supremacy equalled her political. To her, as to a focal point, the rays of light from every direction converged. The philosophers of Italy and Asia Minor directed their steps to her as to the acknowledged centre of mental activity. As to Egypt, an utter ruin had befallen her since she was desolated by the Persian arms. Yet we must not therefore infer that though, as conquerors, the Persians had trodden out the most aged civilization on the globe, as sovereigns they were haters of knowledge, or merciless as kings. We must not forget that the Greeks of Asia Minor were satisfied with their rule, or, at all events, preferred rather to remain their subjects than to contract any permanent political connexions with the conquering Greeks of Europe.

She becomes the centre of policy and philosophy.

In this condition of political glory, Athens became not only the birth-place of new and beautiful productions of art, founded on a more just appreciation of the true than had yet been attained to in any previous age of the world (which, it may be added, have never been surpassed, if, indeed, they have been equalled since), she also became the receptacle for every philosophical opinion, new and old. Ionian, Italian, Egyptian, Persian, all were brought to her, and contrasted and compared together. Indeed, the philosophical celebrity of Greece is altogether due to Athens. The rest of the country participated but little in the cultivation of learning. It is a popular error that Greece, in the aggregate, was a learned country.

We have already seen how the researches of individual inquirers, passing from point to point, had conducted them, in many instances, to a suspicion of the futility of human knowledge; and looking at the results reached by the successive philosophical schools, we cannot fail to remark that there was a general tendency to scepticism. We have seen how, from the material and tangible beginnings of the Ionians, the Eleatics land us not only in a blank atheism, but in a disbelief of the existence of the world. And though it may be said that these were only the isolated results of special schools, it is not to be forgotten that they were of schools the most advanced. The time had now arrived when the name of a master was no more to usurp the place of reason, as had been hitherto the case; when these last results of the different methods of philosophizing were to be brought together, a criticism of a higher order established, and conclusions of a higher order deduced.

State of philosophy at this juncture.

Thus it will ever be with all human investigation. The primitive philosophical elements from which we start are examined, first by one and then by another, each drawing his own special conclusions and deductions, and each firmly believing in the truth of his inferences. Each analyst has seen the whole subject from a particular point of view, without concerning himself with the discordances, contradictions, and incompatibilities obvious enough when his conclusions come to be compared with those of other analysts as skilful as himself. In process of time, it needs must be that a new school of examiners will arise, who, taking the results at which their predecessors have arrived from an examination of the primary elements, will institute a secondary comparison; a comparison of results with results; a comparison of a higher order, and more likely to lead to absolute truth.

Commencement of the higher analysis.

Perhaps I cannot better convey what I here mean by this secondary and higher analysis of philosophical questions than by introducing, as an illustration, what took place subsequently in Rome, through her policy of universal religious toleration. The priests and followers of every god and of every faith were permitted to pursue without molestation their special forms of worship. Of these, it may be supposed that nearly all were perfectly sincere in their adherence to

Illustration from subsequent Roman history.

their special divinity, and, if the occasion had arisen, could have furnished unanswerable arguments in behalf of his supremacy and of the truth of his doctrines. Yet it is very clear that, by thus bringing these several primary systems into contact, a comparison of a secondary and of a higher order, and therefore far more likely to approach to absolute truth, must needs be established among them. It is very well known that the popular result of this secondary examination was the philosophical rejection of polytheism.

The Sophists.

So, in Athens the result of the secondary examination of philosophical systems and deductions was scepticism as regards them all, and the rise of a new order of men—the Sophists—who not only rejected the validity of all former philosophical methods, but carried their infidelity to a degree plainly not warranted by the facts of the case, in this, that they not only denied that human reason had thus far succeeded in ascertaining anything, but even affirmed that it is incapable, from its very nature, as dependent on human organization, or the condition under which it acts, of determining the truth at all; nay, that even if the truth is actually in its possession, since it has no criterion by which to recognize it, it cannot so much as be certain that it is in such possession of it. From these principles it follows that, since we have no standard of the true, neither can we have any standard of the good, and that our ideas of what is good and what is evil are altogether produced by education or by convention. Or, to use the phrase adopted by the Sophists, "it is might that makes right." Right and wrong are hence seen to be mere fictions created by society, having no eternal or absolute existence in nature. The will of a monarch, or of a majority in a community, declares what the law shall be; the law defines what is right and what is wrong; and these, therefore, instead of having an actual existence, are mere illusions, owing their birth to the exercise of force. It is might that has determined and defined what is right.

They reject philosophy, and even morality.

And hence it follows that it is needless for a man to trouble himself with the monitions of conscience, or to be troubled thereby, for conscience, instead of being anything real, is an imaginary fiction, or, at the best, owes its origin to education, and is the creation of our social state. Hence the wise will give himself no concern as to a meritorious act or a crime, seeing that the one is intrinsically neither better nor worse than the other; but he will give himself sedulous concern as respects his outer or external relations —his position in society; conforming his acts to that standard which it in its wisdom or folly, but in the exercise of its might, has declared shall be regarded as right. Or, if his occasions be such as to make it for his interest to depart from the social rule, let him do it in secrecy; or, what is far better, let him cultivate rhetoric, that noble art by which the wrong may be made to appear the right; by which he who has committed a crime may so mystify society as to delude it into the belief that he is worthy of praise; and by which he may prove that his enemy, who has really performed some meritorious deed, has been guilty of a crime. Animated by such considerations, the Sophists passed from place to place, offering to sell for a sum of money a knowledge of the rhetorical art, and disposed of their services in the instruction of the youth of wealthy and noble families.

What shall we say of such a system and of such a state of things? Simply this: that it indicated a complete mental and social demoralization—mental demoralization, for the principles of knowledge were sapped, and man persuaded that his reason was no guide; social demoralization, for he was taught that right and wrong, virtue and vice, conscience, and law, and God, are imaginary fictions; that there is no harm in the commission of sin, though there may be harm, as assuredly there is folly, in being detected therein; that it is excellent for a man to sell his country to the Persian king, provided that the sum of money he receives is large enough, and that the transaction is so darkly conducted that the public, and particularly his enemies, can never find it out. Let him never forget that patriotism is the first delusion of a simpleton, and the last refuge of a knave.

Such were the results of the first attempt to correct the partial philosophies, by submitting them to the measure of a more universal one; such the manner in which, instead of only losing their exclusiveness and imperfections by their contact with one another, they were wrested from their proper object, and made subservient to the purpose of deception. Nor was it science alone that was affected; already might be discerned the foreshadowings of that conviction which many centuries later occasioned the final destruction of polytheism in Rome. Already, in Athens, the voice of philosophers was heard, that among so many gods and so many different worships it was impossible for a man to ascertain what is true. Already, many even of the educated were overwhelmed with the ominous suggestion that, if ever it had been the will of heaven to reveal any form of faith to the world, such a revelation, considering its origin, must necessarily have come with sufficient power to override all opposition; that if there existed only as many as two forms of faith synchronous and successful in the world, that fact would of itself demonstrate that neither of them is true, and that there never had been any revelation from an all-wise and omnipotent God. Nor was it merely among the speculative men that these infidelities were cherished; the leading politicians and statesmen had become deeply infected with them. It was not Anaxagoras alone who was convicted of atheism; the same charge was made against Pericles, the head of the republic—he who had done so much for the glory of Athens—the man who, in practical life, was, beyond all question, the first of his age. With difficulty he succeeded, by the use of what influence remained to him, in saving the life of the guilty philosopher his friend, but in the public estimation he was universally viewed as a participator in his crime. If the foundations of philosophy and those of religion were thus sapped, the foundations of law experienced no better fate. The Sophists, who were wandering all over the world, saw that each nation had its own ideas of merit and demerit, and therefore its own system of law; that even in different towns there were contrary conceptions of right and wrong, and therefore opposing codes. It is evident that in such examinations they applied the same principles which had guided them in their analysis of philosophy and religion, and that the result could be no other than it was, to bring them to

They reject the national religion.

Spread of their opinions among the highest classes.

the conclusion that there is nothing absolute in justice or in law. To what an appalling condition society has arrived, when it reaches the positive conclusion that there is no truth, no religion, no justice, no virtue in the world; that the only object of human exertion is unrestrained physical enjoyment; the only standard of a man's position, wealth; that, since there is no possibility of truth, whose eternal principles might serve for an uncontrovertible and common guide, we should resort to deception and the arts of persuasion, that we may dupe others for our purposes; that there is no sin in undermining the social contract; no crime in blasphemy, or rather there is no blasphemy at all, since there are no gods; that "man is the measure of all things," as Protagoras teaches, and that "he is the criterion of existence;" that "thought is only the relation of the thinking subject to the object thought of, and that the thinking subject, the soul, is nothing more than the sum of the different moments of thinking." It is no wonder that that Sophist who was the author of such doctrines should be condemned to death to satisfy the clamours of a populace who had not advanced sufficiently into the depths of this secondary, this higher philosophy, and that it was only by flight that he could save himself from the punishment awaiting the opening sentiment of his book: "Of the gods I cannot tell whether they are or not, for much hinders us from knowing this—both the obscurity of the subject and the shortness of life." It is no wonder that the social demoralization spread apace, when men like Gorgias, the disciple of Empedocles, were to be found, who laughed at virtue, made an open derision of morality, and proved, by metaphysical demonstration, that nothing at all exists.

They end in blank atheism.

From these statements respecting the crisis at which ancient philosophy had arrived, we might be disposed to believe that the result was unmitigated evil, for it scarcely deserves mention that the quibbles and disputes of the Sophists occasioned an extraordinary improvement of the Greek language, introducing precision into its terms, and a wonderful dialectical skill into its use. For us there may be extracted from these melancholy conclusions at least one instructive lesson—that it is not during the process of decomposition of philosophies, and especially of religions, that social changes occur, for such breakings-up commonly go on in an isolated, and therefore innocuous way; but if by chance the fragments and decomposed portions are brought together, and attempts are made by fusion to incorporate them anew, or to extract from them, by a secondary analysis, what truth they contain, a crisis is at once brought on, and—such is the course of events—in the catastrophe that ensues they are commonly all absolutely destroyed. It was doubtless their foresight of such consequences that inspired the Italian statesmen of the Middle Ages with a resolute purpose of crushing in the bud every encroachment on ecclesiastical authority, and every attempt at individual interpretation of religious doctrines. For it is not to be supposed that men of clear intellect should be insensible to the obvious unreasonableness of many of the dogmas that had been consecrated by authority. But if once permission were accorded to human criticism and human interpretation, what other issue could there be than that doctrine upon doctrine, and sect upon sect should arise; that theological principles should undergo a total decomposition, until two men could scarcely be found whose views coincided; nay, even more than that, that the same man should change his opinion with the changing incidents of the different periods of his life. No matter what might be the plausible guise of the beginning, and the ostensibly cogent arguments for its necessity, once let the decomposition commence, and no human power could arrest it until it had become thorough and complete. Considering the prestige, the authority, and the mass of fact to be dealt with, it might take many centuries for this process to be finished, but that that result would at length be accomplished no enlightened man could doubt. The experience of the ancient European world had shown that in the act of such decompositions there is but little danger, since, for the time being, each sect, and, indeed, each individual, has a guiding rule of life. But as soon as the period of secondary analysis is reached a crisis must inevitably ensue, in all probability involving not only religion, but also the social contract. And though, by the

Political dangers of the higher analysis.

Illustrations from the Middle Ages.

exercise of force on the part of the interests that are disturbed, aided by that popular sentiment which is abhorrent of anarchy, the crisis might, for a time, be put off, it could not be otherwise than that Europe should be left in that deplorable state which must result when the intellect of a people has outgrown its formulas of faith. A fearful condition to contemplate, for such a dislocation must also affect political relations, and necessarily implies revolt against existing law. Nations plunged in the abyss of irreligion must necessarily be nations in anarchy. For a time their tendency to explosion may be kept down by the firm application of the hand of power; but this is simply an antagonism, it is no cure. The social putrefaction proceeds, working its way downward into classes that are lower and lower, until at length it involves the institutions that are relied on for its arrest. Armies, the machinery of compression, once infected, the end is at hand, but no human foresight can predict what the event shall be, especially if the contemporaneous ruling powers have either ignorantly or wilfully neglected to prepare society for the inevitable trial it is about to undergo. It is the most solemn of all the duties of governments, when once they have become aware of such a momentous condition, to prepare the nations for its fearful consequences. For this it may, perhaps, be lawful for them to dissemble in a temporary manner, as it is sometimes proper for a physician to dissemble with his patient; it may be lawful for them even to resort to the use of force, but never should such measures of doubtful correctness be adopted without others directed to a preparation of the mass of society for the trials through which it is about to pass. Such, doubtless, were the profound views of the great Italian statesmen of the Middle Ages; such, doubtless, were the arguments by which they justified to themselves resistance against the beginning of the evil—a course for which Europe has too often and unfairly condemned them.

Danger of intellect outgrowing formulas of faith.

Absolute necessity of preparing communities for these changes.

It remains for us now to review the details presented in the foregoing pages for the purpose of determining the successive phases of development through which the Greek mind passed. It is not with the truth or fallacy of these details that we have to do, but with their order of occurrence. They are points enabling us to describe graphically the curve of Grecian intellectual advance.

Summary of the preceding theories.

The starting point of Greek philosophy is physical and geocentral. The earth is the grand object of the universe, and, as the necessary result. erroneous ideas are entertained as to the relations and dimensions of the sea and air. This philosophy was hardly a century old before it began to cosmogonize, using the principles it considered itself sure of. Long before it was able to get rid of local ideas, such as upward and downward in space, it undertook to explain the origin of the world.

But, as advances were made, it was recognized that creation, in its various parts, displays intention and design, the adaptation of means to secure proposed ends. This suggested a reasoning and voluntary agency, like that of man, in the government of the world; and from a continual reference to human habits and acts, Greek philosophy passed through its stage of anthropoid conceptions.

A little farther progress awakened suspicions that the mind of man can obtain no certain knowledge; and the opinion at last prevailed that we have no trustworthy criterion of truth. In the scepticism thus setting in, the approach to Oriental ideas is each successive instant more and more distinct.

This period of doubt was the immediate forerunner of more correct cosmical opinions. The heliocentric mechanism of the planetary system was introduced, the earth deposed to a subordinate position. The doctrines, both physical and intellectual, founded on geocentric ideas, were necessarily endangered, and, since these had connected themselves with the prevailing religious views, and were represented by important material interests, the public began to practise persecution and the philosophers hypocrisy. Pantheistic notions of the nature of the world became more distinct, and, as their necessary consequence, the doctrines of Emanation, Transmigration, and Absorption were entertained. From this it is but a step to the suspicion that matter, motion, and

Approach to Oriental ideas.

time are phantasms of the imagination—opinions embodied in the atomic theory, which asserts that atoms and space alone exist; and which became more refined when it recognized that atoms are only mathematical points; and still more so when it considered them as mere centres of force. The brink of Buddhism was here approached.

As must necessarily ever be the case where men are coexisting in different psychical stages of advance, some having made a less, some a greater intellectual progress, all these views which we have described successively, were at last contemporaneously entertained. At this point commenced the action of the Sophists, who, by setting the doctrines of one school in opposition to those of another, and representing them all as of equal value, occasioned the destruction of them all, and the philosophy founded on physical speculation came to an end.

Uniformity in the manner of intellectual progress.

Of this phase of Greek intellectual life, if we compare the beginning with the close, we cannot fail to observe how great is the improvement. The thoughts dealt with at the later period are intrinsically of a higher order than those at the outset. From the puerilities and errors with which we have thus been occupied, we learn that there is a definite mode of progress for the mind of man; from the history of later times we shall find that it is ever in the same direction.

CHAPTER V.

THE GREEK AGE OF FAITH.

RISE AND DECLINE OF ETHICAL PHILOSOPHY.

SOCRATES *rejects Physical and Mathematical Speculations, and asserts the Importance of Virtue and Morality, thereby inaugurating an Age of Faith.—His Life and Death.—The schools originating from his Movement teach the Pursuit of Pleasure and Gratification of Self.*

PLATO *founds the Academy.—His three primal Principles.—The Existence of a personal God.—Nature of the World and the Soul.—The ideal Theory, Generals or Types.—Reminiscence.—Transmigration.—Plato's political Institutions.—His Republic.—His Proofs of the Immortality of the Soul.—Criticism on his Doctrines.*

RISE OF THE SCEPTICS, *who conduct the higher Analysis of Ethical Philosophy.—Pyrrho demonstrates the Uncertainty of Knowledge.—Inevitable Passage into tranquil Indifference, Quietude, and Irreligion, as recommended by Epicurus.—Decomposition of the Socratic and Platonic Systems in the later Academies.—Their Errors and Duplicities.—End of the Greek Age of Faith.*

THE Sophists had brought on an intellectual anarchy. It is not in the nature of humanity to be contented with such a state. Thwarted in its expectations from physics, the Greek mind turned its attention to morals. In the progress of life, it is but a step from the age of Inquiry to the age of Faith.

Greek philosophy on the basis of ethics.

Socrates, who led the way in this movement, was born B.C. 469. He exercised an influence in some respects felt to our times. Having experienced the unprofitable results arising from physical speculation, he set in contrast there with the solid advantages to be enjoyed from the cultivation of virtue and morality. His life was a perpetual combat with the Sophists. His manner of instruction was by conversation, in which,

Socrates: his mode of teaching.

according to the uniform testimony of all who heard him, he singularly excelled. He resorted to definitions, and therefrom drew deductions, conveying his argument under the form of a dialogue. Unlike his predecessors, who sought for truth in the investigation of outward things, he turned his attention inward, asserting the supremacy of virtue and its identity with knowledge, and the necessity of an adherence to the strict principles of justice. Considering the depraved condition to which the Sophists had reduced society, he insisted on a change in the manner of education of youth, so as to bring it in accordance with the principle that happiness is only to be found in the pursuit of virtue and goodness. Thus, therefore, he completely substituted the moral for the physical, and in this essentially consists the philosophical revolution he effected. He had no school, properly speaking, nor did he elaborate any special ethical system; for to those who inquired how they should know good from evil and right from wrong, he recommended the decisions of the laws of their country. It does not appear that he ever entered on any inquiry respecting the nature of God, simply viewing his existence as a fact of which there was abundant and incontrovertible proof. Though rejecting the crude religious ideas of his nation, and totally opposed to anthropomorphism, he carefully avoided the giving of public offence by improper allusions to the prevailing superstition; nay, even as a good citizen, he set an example of conforming to its requirements. In his judgment, the fault of the Sophists consisted in this, that they had subverted useless speculation, but had substituted for it no scientific evidence. Nevertheless, if man did not know, he might believe, and demonstration might be profitably supplanted by faith. He therefore insisted on the great doctrines of the immortality of the soul and the government of the world by Providence; but it is not to be denied that there are plain indications, in some of his sentiments, of a conviction that the Supreme Being is the soul of the world. He professed that his own chief wisdom consisted in the knowledge of his own ignorance, and dissuaded his friends from the cultivation of mathematics and physics, since he affirmed

The doctrines of Socrates.

that the former leads to vain conclusions, the latter to atheism. In his system everything turns on the explanation of terms; but his processes of reasoning are often imperfect, his conclusions, therefore, liable to be incorrect. In this way, he maintained that no one would knowingly commit a wrong act, because he that knew a thing to be good would do it; that it is only involuntarily that the bad are bad; that he who knowingly tells a lie is a better man than he who tells a lie in ignorance; and that it is right to injure one's enemies.

Opposes mathemathics and physics.

From such a statement of the philosophy of Socrates, we cannot fail to remark how superficial it must have been; it perpetually mistakes differences of words for distinctions of things; it also possessed little novelty. The enforcement of morality cannot be regarded as anything new, since probably there has never been an age in which good men were not to be found, who observed, as their rule of life, the maxims taught by Socrates; and hence we may reasonably inquire what it was that has spread over the name of this great man such an unfading lustre, and why he stands out in such extraordinary prominence among the benefactors of his race.

Superficiality of his views.

Socrates was happy in two things: happy in those who recorded his life, and happy in the circumstances of his death. It is not given to every great man to have Xenophon and Plato for his biographers: it is not given to every one who has overpassed the limit of life, and, in the natural course of events, has but a little longer to continue, to attain the crown of martyrdom in behalf of virtue and morality. In an evil hour for the glory of Athens, his countrymen put him to death. It was too late when they awoke and saw that they could give no answer to the voice of posterity, demanding why they had perpetrated this crime. With truth Socrates said, at the close of his noble speech to the judges who had condemned him, "It is now time that we depart—I to die, you to live; but which has the better destiny is unknown to all except God." The future has resolved that doubt. For Socrates there was reserved the happier lot.

Causes of the celebrity of Socrates.

No little obscurity still remains as respects the true

nature of this dark transaction. The articles of accusation were three: he rejects the gods of his country; he introduces new ones; he perverts the education of youth. With truth might his friends say it was wonderful that he should be accused of impiety, the whole tenor of whose life was reverence for God—a recognition not only of the divine existence, but of the divine superintendence. "It is only a madman," he would say, "who imputes success in life to human prudence;" and as to the necessity of a right education for the young, "It is only the wise who are fit to govern men." We must conclude that the accusations were only ostensible or fictitious, and that beneath them lay some reality which could reconcile the Athenians to the perpetration of so great a crime.

The ostensible accusations against him.

Shall we find in his private life any explanation of this mystery? Unfortunately, the details of it which have descended to us are few. To the investigations of classical criticism we can scarcely look with any hope, for classical criticism has hitherto been in a state of singular innocence, so far as the actual affairs of life are concerned. It regards Athenians and Romans not as men and women like ourselves, but as the personages presented by fictitious literature, whose lives are exceptions to the common laws of human nature; who live in the midst of scenes of endless surprises and occurrences ever bordering on the marvellous.

If we examine the case according to everyday principles, we cannot fail to remark that the Socrates of our imagination is a very different man from the Socrates of contemporaneous Athenians. To us he appears a transcendent genius, to whom the great names of antiquity render their profound homage; a martyr in behalf of principles, of which, if society be devoid, life itself is scarcely of any worth, and for the defence of which it is the highest glory that a man should be called upon to die. To them Socrates was no more than an idle lounger in the public places and corners of the streets; grotesque, and even repulsive in his person; affecting in the oddities of his walking and in his appearance many of the manners of the mountebank. Neglecting the pursuit of an

The character of Socrates in Athens.

Xantippe his wife.

honest calling, for his trade seems to have been that of a stone-cutter, he wasted his time in discoursing with such youths as his lecherous countenance and satyr-like person could gather around him, leading them astray from the gods of his country, the flimsy veil of his hypocrisy being too transparent to conceal his infidelity. Nevertheless, he was a very brave soldier, as those who served with him testify. It does not appear that he was observant of those cares which by most men are probably considered as paramount, giving himself but little concern for the support of his children and wife. The good woman Xantippe is, to all appearance, one of those characters who are unfairly judged of by the world. Socrates married her because of her singular conversational powers; and though he himself, according to universal testimony, possessed extraordinary merits in that respect, he found to his cost, when too late, so commanding were her excellencies, that he was altogether her inferior. Among the amusing instances related of his domestic difficulties were the consequences of his invitations to persons to dine with him when there was nothing in the house wherewith to entertain them, a proceeding severely trying to the temper of Xantippe, whose cause would unquestionably be defended by the matrons of any nation. It was nothing but the mortification of a high-spirited woman at the acts of a man who was too shiftless to have any concern for his domestic honour. He would not gratify her urgent entreaties by accepting from those upon whom he lavished his time the money that was so greatly needed at home. After his condemnation, she carried her children with her to his prison, and was dismissed by him, as he told his friends, from his apprehension of her deep distress. To the last we see her bearing herself in a manner honourable to a woman and a wife. There is surely something wrong in a man's life when the mother of his children is protesting against his conduct, and her complaints are countenanced by the community. In view of all the incidents of the history of Socrates, we can come to no other conclusion than that the Athenians regarded him as an unworthy, and perhaps troublesome member of society. Tehre can be no doubt that his trial and condemnation were connected with political measures. He himself said that he should have suffered death previously, in the affair of Leon of Salamis, had not the government been broken up. His bias was toward aristocracy, not toward democracy. In common with his party, he had been engaged in undertakings that could not do otherwise than entail mortal animosities; and it is not to be overlooked that his indictment was brought forward by Anytus, who was conspicuous in restoring the old order of things. The mistake made by the Athenians was in applying a punishment altogether beyond the real offence, and in adding thereto the persecution of those who had embraced the tenets of Socrates by driving them into exile. Not only admiration for the memory of their master, but also a recollection of their own wrongs, made these men eloquent eulogists. Had Socrates appeared to the Athenians as he appears to us, it is not consistent with human proceedings that they should have acted in so barbarous and totally indefensible a manner.

He is really the victim of political animosity.

If by the Dæmon to whose suggestions Socrates is said to have listened anything more was meant than conscience, we must infer that he laboured under that mental malady to which those are liable who, either through penury or designedly, submit to extreme abstinence, and, thereby injuring the brain, fall into hallucination. Such cases are by no means of infrequent occurrence. Mohammed was affected in that manner.

The Dæmon of Socrates.

After the death of Socrates there arose several schools professing to be founded upon his principles. The divergences they exhibited when compared with one another prove how little there was of precision in those principles. Among these imitators is numbered Euclid of Megara, who had been in the habit of incurring considerable personal risk for the sake of listening to the great teacher, it being a capital offence for a native of Megara to be found in Athens. Upon their persecution, Plato and other disciples of Socrates fled to Euclid, and were well received by him. His system was a mixture of the Eleatic and Socratic, the ethical preponderating in his doctrine. He maintained the existence of one Being, the Good, having various aspects—Wisdom,

The Megaric school. The wise should be insensible to pain.

God, Reason, and showed an inclination to the tendency afterward fully developed by the Cynical school in his dogma that the wise man should be insensible to pain.

The Cyrenaic school. Pleasure is the object of life.

With the Megaric school is usually classified the Cyrenaic founded by Aristippus. Like Socrates, he held in disdain physical speculations, and directed his attention to the moral. In his opinion, happiness consists in pleasure; and, indeed, he recognized in pleasure and pain the criteria of external things. He denied that we can know anything with certainty, our senses being so liable to deceive us; but, though we may not perceive things truly, it is true that we perceive. With the Cyrenaic school, pleasure was the great end and object of life.

The Cynical school: a contempt for others and gratification of self.

To these may be added the Cynical school, founded by Antisthenes, whose system is personal and ferocious: it is a battle of the mind against the body; it is a pursuit of pleasure of a mental kind, corporeal enjoyment being utterly unworthy of a man. Its nature is very well shown in the character of its founder, who abandoned all the conveniences and comforts of life, voluntarily encountering poverty and exposure to the inclemency of the seasons. His garments were of the meanest kind, his beard neglected, his person filthy, his diet bordering on starvation. To the passers-by this ragged misanthrope indulged in contemptuous language, and offended them by the indecency of his gestures. Abandoned at last by every one except Diogenes of Sinope, he expired in extreme wretchedness. It had been a favourite doctrine with him that friendship and patriotism are altogether worthless; and in his last agony, Diogenes asking him whether he needed a friend, "Will a friend release me from this pain?" he inquired. Diogenes handed him a dagger, saying, "This will." "I want to be free from pain, but not from life." Into such degradation had philosophy, as represented by the Cynical school, fallen, that it may be doubted whether it is right to include a man like Antisthenes among those who derive their title from their love of wisdom—a man who condemned the knowledge of reading and writing, who depreciated the institution of marriage, and professed that

Antisthenes.

he saw no other advantage in philosophy than that it enabled him to keep company with himself.

The wretched doctrines of Cynicism were carried to their utmost application by Diogenes of Sinope. In early life he had been accustomed to luxury and ease; but his father, who was a wealthy banker, having been convicted of debasing the coinage, Diogenes, who in some manner shared in the disgrace, was in a very fit state of mind to embrace doctrines implying a contempt for the goods of the world and for the opinions of men. He may be considered as the prototype of the hermits of a later period in his attempts at the subjugation of the natural appetites by means of starvation. Looking upon the body as a mere clog to the soul, he mortified it in every possible manner, feeding it on raw meat and leaves, and making it dwell in a tub. He professed that the nearer a man approaches to suicide the nearer he approaches to virtue. He wore no other dress than a scanty cloak; a wallet, a stick, and a drinking-cup completed his equipment: the cup he threw away as useless on seeing a boy take water in the hollow of his hand. It was his delight to offend every idea of social decency by performing all the acts of life publicly, asserting that whatever is not improper in itself ought to be done openly. It is said that his death, which occurred in his ninetieth year, was in consequence of devouring a neat's foot raw. From his carrying the Socratic notions to an extreme, he merits the designation applied to him, "the mad Socrates." His contempt for the opinions of others, and his religious disbelief, are illustrated by an incident related of him, that, having in a moment of weakness made a promise to some friends that he would offer a sacrifice to Diana, he repaired the next day to her temple, and, taking a louse from his head, cracked it upon her altar.

Diogenes of Sinope.

His irreverence.

What a melancholy illustration of the tendency of the human mind do these facts offer. What a quick, yet inevitable descent from the morality of Socrates. Selfishness is enthroned; friendship and patriotism are looked upon as the affairs of a fool: happy is the man who stands in no need of a friend; still happier he who has not one. No action is intrinsically bad; even

Decline of morality.

robbery, adultery, sacrilege, are only crimes by public agreement. The sage will take care how he indulges in the weakness of gratitude or benevolence, or any other such sickly sentiment. If he can find pleasure, let him enjoy it; if pain is inflicted on him, let him bear it; but, above all, let him remember that death is just as desirable as life.

If the physical speculations of Greece had ended in sophistry and atheism, ethical investigations, it thus appears, had borne no better fruit. Both systems, when carried to their consequences, had been found to be not only useless to society, but actually prejudicial to its best interests. As far as could be seen, in the times of which we are speaking, the prospects for civilization were dark and discouraging; nor did it appear possible that any successful attempts could be made to extract from philosophy anything completely suitable to the wants of man. Yet, in the midst of these discreditable delusions, one of the friends and disciples of Socrates—indeed, it may be said, his chief disciple, Plato, was laying the foundation of another system, which, though it contained much that was false and more that was vain, contained also some things vigorous enough to descend to our times.

Birth of Plato.

Plato was born about B.C. 426. Antiquity has often delighted to cast a halo of mythical glory around its illustrious names. The immortal works of this great philosopher seemed to entitle him to more than mortal honours. A legend, into the authenticity of which we will abstain from inquiring, asserted that his mother Perictione, a pure virgin, suffered an immaculate conception through the influences of Apollo. The god declared to Ariston, to whom she was about to be married, the parentage of the child. The wisdom of this great writer may justify such a noble descent, and, in some degree, excuse the credulity of his admiring and affectionate disciples, who gave a ready ear to the impossible story.

To the knowledge acquired by Plato during the eight or ten years he had spent with Socrates, he added all that could be obtained from the philosophers of Egypt, Cyrene, Persia, and Tarentum. With every advantage arising from wealth and an illustrious parentage, if even it was only of an earthly kind, for he numbered Solon among his ancestors, he availed himself of the teaching of the chief philosophers of the age, and at length, returning to his native country, founded a school in the grove of Hecademus. Thrice during his career as a teacher he visited Sicily on each occasion returning to the retirement of his academy. He attained the advanced age of eighty-three years. It has been given to few men to exercise so profound an influence on the opinions of posterity, and yet it is said that during his lifetime Plato had no friends. He quarrelled with most of those who had been his fellow-disciples of Socrates; and. as might be anticipated from the venerable age to which he attained, and the uncertain foundation upon which his doctrines reposed, his opinions were very often contradictory, and his philosophy exhibited many variations. To his doctrines we must now attend.

His education and teaching.

It was the belief of Plato that matter is coeternal with God, and that, indeed, there are three primary principles—God, Matter, Ideas; all animate and inanimate things being fashioned by God from matter, which, being capable of receiving any impress, may be designated with propriety the Mother of Forms. He held that intellect existed before such forms were produced, but not antecedently to matter. To matter he imputed a refractory or resisting quality, the origin of the disorders and disturbances occurring in the world; he also regarded it as the cause of evil, accounting thereby for the preponderance of evil, which must exceed the good in proportion as matter exceeds ideas. It is not without reason, therefore, that Plato has been accused of Magianism. These doctrines are of an Oriental cast.

The doctrines of Plato. The three primary principles.

The existence of God, an independent and personal maker of the world, he inferred from proofs of intelligence and design presented by natural objects. "All in the world is for the sake of the rest, and the places of the single parts are so ordered as to subserve to the preservation and excellency of the whole; hence all things are derived from the operation of a Divine intellectual cause." From the marks of unity in that design he deduced the unity of God, the Supreme Intelligence, incorporeal, without beginning, end, or change. His god is the fashioner and father of the

He asserts the existence of a personal God.

universe, in contradistinction to impersonal Nature. In one sense, he taught that the soul is immortal and imperishable; in another, he denied that each individual soul either has had or will continue to have an everlasting duration. From what has been said on a former page, it will be understood that this psychological doctrine is essentially Indian. His views of the ancient condition of and former relations of the soul enabled Plato to introduce the celebrated doctrine of Reminiscence, and to account for what have otherwise been termed innate ideas. They are the recollections of things with which the soul was once familiar.

Nature of the soul.

The reason of God contemplates and comprehends the exemplars or original models of all natural forms, whatever they may be; for visible things are only fleeting shadows, quickly passing away; ideas or exemplars are everlasting. With so much power did he set forth this theory of ideas, and, it must be added, with so much obscurity, that some have asserted his belief in an extramundane space in which exist incorporeal beings, the ideas or original exemplars of all organic and inorganic forms. An illustration may remove some of the obscurity of these views. Thus all men, though they may present different appearances when compared with each other, are obviously fashioned upon the same model, to which they all more or less perfectly conform. All trees of the same kind, though they may differ from one another, are, in like manner, fashioned upon a common model, to which they more or less perfectly conform. To such models, exemplars, or types, Plato gave the designation of Ideas. Our knowledge thereof is clearly not obtained from the senses, but from reflection. Now Plato asserted that these ideas are not only conceptions of the mind, but actually perceptions or entities having a real existence; nay, more, that they are the only real existences. Objects are thus only material embodiments of ideas, and in representation are not exact; for correspondence between an object and its model is only so far as circumstances will permit. Hence we can never determine all the properties or functions of the idea from an examination of its imperfect material representation, any more

Plato's Ideal theory.

Exemplars or types.

than we can discover the character or qualities of a man from pictures of him, no matter how excellent those pictures may be.

The Ideal theory of Plato, therefore, teaches that, beyond this world of delusive appearances, this world of material objects, there is another world, invisible, eternal, and essentially true; that, though we cannot trust our senses for the correctness of the indications they yield, there are other impressions upon which we may fall back to aid us in coming to the truth, the reminiscences or recollections still abiding in the soul of the things it formerly knew, either in the realm of pure ideas, or in the states of former life through which it has passed. For Plato says that there are souls which, in periods of many thousand years, have successively transmigrated through bodies of various kinds. Of these various conditions they retain a recollection, more faintly or vividly, as the case may be. Ideas seeming to be implanted in the human mind, but certainly never communicated to us by the senses, are derived from those former states. If this recollection of ancient events and conditions were absolutely precise and correct, then man would have an innate means for determining the truth. But such reminiscences being, in their nature, imperfect and uncertain, we never can attain to absolute truth. With Plato, the Beautiful is the perfect image of the true. Love is the desire of the soul for Beauty, the attraction of like for like, the longing of the divinity within us for the divinity beyond us; and the Good, which is beauty, truth, justice, is God—God in his abstract state.

Doctrine of Reminiscence.

Recollections during transmigration.

From the Platonic system it therefore followed that science is impossible to man, and possible only to God; that, however, recollecting our origin, we ought not to despair, but elevate our intellectual aim as high as we may; that all knowledge is not attributable to our present senses; for, if that were the case, all men would be equally wise, their senses being equal in acuteness; but a very large portion, and by far the surest portion, is derived from reminiscence of our former states; that each individual soul is an idea; and that, of ideas generally, the lower are held together by the higher, and hence, finally by one which is supreme; that God is the sum of ideas, and is therefore eternal and unchangeable, the sensuous conditions of time and space having no relation to him, and being inapplicable in any conception of his attributes; that he is the measure of all things, and not man, as Protagoras supposed; that the universe is a type of him; that matter itself is an absolute negation, and is the same as space; that the forms presented by our senses are unsubstantial shadows, and no reality; that, so far from there being an infinity of worlds, there is but one, which, as the work of God, is neither subject to age nor decay, and that it consists of a body and a soul; in another respect it may be said to be composed of fire and earth, which can only be made to cohere through the intermedium of air and water, and hence the necessity of the existence of the four elements; that of geometrical forms, the pyramid corresponds to fire, the cube to earth, the octahedron to air, these forms being produced from triangles connected by certain numerical ratios; that the entire sum of vitality is divided by God into seven parts, answering to the divisions of the musical octave, or to the seven planets; that the world is an animal having within it a soul; for man is warm, and so is the world; man is made of various elements, and so is the world; and, as the body of man has a soul, so too must the world have one; that there is a race of created, generated, and visible gods, who must be distinguished from the eternal, their bodies being composed for the most part of fire, their shape spherical; that the earth is the oldest and first of the starry bodies, its place being in the centre of the universe, or in the axis thereof, where it remains, balanced by its own equilibrium; that perhaps it is an ensouled being and a generated god; that the mortal races are three, answering to Earth, Air, and Water; that the male man was the first made of mortals, and that from him the female, and beasts, and birds, and fishes issued forth; that the superiority of man depends upon his being a religious animal; that each mortal consists of two portions, a soul and a body—their separation constitutes death; that of the soul

God is the sum of ideas.

The nature of the world and of the gods.

there are two primitive component parts, a mortal and an immortal, the one being made by the created gods, and the other by the Supreme; that, for the purpose of uniting these parts together, it is necessary that there should be an intermedium, and that this is the dæmonic portion or spirit; that our mental struggles arise from this triple constitution of Appetite, Spirit, and Reason; that Reason alone is immortal, and the others die; that the number of souls in the universe is invariable or constant; that the sentiment of pre-existence proves the soul to have existed before the body; that, since the soul is the cause of motion, it can neither be produced nor decay, else all motion must eventually cease; that, as to the condition of departed souls, they hover as shades around the graves, pining for restoration to their lifeless bodies, or migrating through various human or brute shapes, but that an unembodied life in God is reserved for the virtuous philosopher; that valour is nothing but knowledge, and virtue a knowledge of good; that the soul, on entering the body, is irrational or in a trance, and that the god, the star who formed its created part, influences its career, and hence its fortunes may be predicted by astrological computations; that there are future rewards and punishments, a residence being appointed for the righteous in his kindred star; for those whose lives have been less pure there is a second birth under the form of a woman, and, if evil courses are still persisted in, successive transmigrations through various brutes are in reserve—the frivolous passing into birds, the unphilosophical into beasts, the ignorant into fishes; that the world undergoes periodical revolutions by fire and water, its destructions and reproductions depending upon the coincidences of the stars. Of Plato's views of human physiology I can offer no better statement than the following from Ritter: "All in the human body is formed for the sake of the Reason, after certain determinate ends. Accordingly, first of all, a seat must be provided for the god-like portion of the soul, the head, viz., which is round, and similar to the perfect shape of the whole, furnished with the organs of cognition, slightly

Triple constitution of the soul.

Transmigration and future rewards and punishments.

The physiology of Plato.

covered with flesh, which impedes the senses. To the head is given the direction of the whole frame, hence its position at the top; and, since the animal creation possesses all the six irregular motions, and the head ought not to roll upon the ground, the human form is long, with legs for walking and arms for serving the body, and the anterior part is fashioned differently from the posterior. Now, the reason being seated in the head, the spirit or irascible soul has its seat in the breast, under the head, in order that it may be within call and command of the Reason, but yet separated from the head by the neck, that it might not mix with it. The concupiscible has likewise its particular seat in the lower part of the trunk, the abdomen, separated by the diaphragm from that of the irascible, since it is destined, being separate from both, to be governed and held in order both by the spirit and the Reason. For this end God has given it a watch, the liver, which is dense, smooth, and shining, and, containing in combination both bitter and sweet, is fitted to receive and reflect, as a mirror, the images of thoughts. Whenever the Reason disapproves, it checks inordinate desires by its bitterness, and, on the other hand, when it approves, all is soothed into gentle repose by its sweetness; moreover, in sleep, in sickness, or in inspiration it becomes prophetic, so that even the vilest portion of the body is in a certain degree participant of truth. In other respects the lower portion of the trunk is fashioned with equal adaptation for the ends it has to serve. The spleen is placed on the left side of the liver, in order to secrete and carry off the impurities which the diseases of the body might produce and accumulate. The intestines are coiled many times, in order that the food may not pass too quickly through the body, and so occasion again an immoderate desire for more; for such a constant appetite would render the pursuit of philosophy impossible, and make man disobedient to the commands of the divinity within him."

The reader will gather from the preceding paragraph how much of wisdom and of folly, of knowledge and of ignorance, the doctrines of Plato present. I may be permitted to continue this analysis of his writings a little farther, with the intention of exhibiting the manner in which he carried his views into practice; for Plato asserted that, though the supreme good is unattainable by our reason, we must try to resemble God as far as it is possible for the changeable to copy the eternal; remembering that pleasure is not the end of man, and, though the sensual part of the soul dwells on eating and drinking, riches and pleasure, and the spiritual on worldly honours and distinctions, the reason is devoted to knowledge. Pleasure, therefore, cannot be attributed to the gods, though knowledge may; pleasure, which is not a good in itself, but only a means thereto. Each of the three parts of the soul has its own appropriate virtue, that of reason being wisdom; that of the spirit, courage; that of the appetite, temperance; and for the sake of perfection, justice is added for the mutual regulation of the other three.

His ethical deas.

In carrying his ethical conceptions into practice, Plato insists that the state is everything, and that what is in opposition to it ought to be destroyed. He denies the right of property; strikes at the very existence of the family, pressing his doctrines to such an extreme as to consider women as public property, to be used for the purposes of the state; he teaches that education should be a governmental duty, and that religion must be absolutely subjected to the politician; that children do not belong to their parents, but to the state; that the aim of government should not be the happiness of the individual, but that of the whole; and that men are to be considered not as men, but as elements of the state, a perfect subject differing from a slave only in this, that he has the state for his master. He recommends the exposure of deformed and sickly infants, and requires every citizen to be initiated into every species of falsehood and fraud. Distinguishing between mere social unions and true polities, and insisting that there should be an analogy between the state and the soul as respects triple constitution, he establishes a division of ruler, warriors, and labourers, preferring, therefore, a monarchy reposing on aristocracy, particularly of talent. Though he considers music essential to education, his opinion of the fine arts is so low that he would admit

His proposed political institutions.

into his state painters and musicians only under severe restrictions, or not at all. It was for the sake of having this chimerical republic realized in Sicily that he made a journey to Dionysius; and it may be added that it was well for those whom he hoped to have subjected to the experiment that his wild and visionary scheme was never permitted to be carried into effect. In our times extravagant social plans have been proposed, and some have been attempted; but we have witnessed nothing so absurd as this vaunted republic of Plato. It shows a surprising ignorance of the acts and wants of man in his social condition.

The Republic of Plato.

Some of the more important doctrines of Plato are worthy of further reflection. I shall therefore detain the reader a short time to offer a few remarks upon them.

It was a beautiful conception of this philosophy that ideas are connected together by others of a higher order, and these, in their turn, by others still higher, their generality and power increasing as we ascend, until finally a culminating point is reached—a last, a supreme, an all-ruling idea, which is God. Approaching in this elevated manner to the doctrine of an Almighty Being, we are free from those fallacies we are otherwise liable to fall into when we mingle notions derived from time and space with the attributes of God; we also avoid those obscurities necessarily encountered when we attempt the consideration of the illimitable and eternal.

Grandeur of Plato's conceptions of God

Plato's views of the immortality of the soul offer a striking contrast to those of the popular philosophy and superstition of his time. They recall, in many respects, the doctrines of India. In Greece, those who held the most enlarged views entertained what might be termed a doctrine of semi-immortality. They looked for a continuance of the soul in an endless futurity, but gave themselves no concern about the eternity which is past. But Plato considered the soul as having already eternally existed the present life being only a moment in our career; he looked forward with an undoubting faith to the changes through which we must hereafter pass. As sparks issue forth from a flame, so doubtless to his imagination did the soul of man issue forth from the soul

and of the soul.

of the world. Innate ideas and the sentiment of pre-existence indicate our past life. By the latter is meant that on some occasion perhaps of trivial concern, or perhaps in some momentous event, it suddenly occurs to us that we have been in like circumstances, and surrounded by the things at that instant present on some other occasion before; but the recollection, though forcibly impressing us with surprise, is misty and confused. With Plato shall we say it was in one of our prior states of existence, and the long-forgotten transactions are now suddenly flashing upon us?

The sentiment of pre-existence.

But Plato did not know the double structure and the double action of the brain of man; he did not remember that the mind may lose all recognition of the lapse of time, and, with equal facility, compress into the twinkling of an eye events so numerous that for their occurrence days and even years would seem to be required; or, conversely, that it can take a single, a simple idea, which one would suppose might be disposed of in a moment, and dwell upon it, dilating or swelling it out, until all the hours of a long night are consumed. Of the truth of these singular effects we have not only such testimony as that offered by those who have been restored from death by drowning, who describe the flood of memory rushing upon them in the last moment of their mortal agony, the long train of all the affairs in which they have borne a part seen in an instant, as we see the landscape, with all its various objects, by a flash of lightning at night, and that with appalling distinctness, but also from our own experience in our dreams. It is shown in my Physiology how the phenomena of the sentiment of pre-existence may, upon these principles, be explained, each hemisphere of the brain thinking for itself, and the mind deluded as respects the lapse of time, mistaking these simultaneous actions for successive ones, and referring one of the two impressions to an indistinct and misty past. To Plato such facts as these afforded copious proofs of the prior existence of the soul, and strong foundations for a faith in its future life.

But this arises from the anatomical construction of the brain.

Thus Plato's doctrine of the immortality of the soul

implies a double immortality; the past eternity, as well as that to come, falls within its scope. In the national superstition of his time, the spiritual principle seemed to arise without author or generator, finding its chance residence in the tabernacle of the body, growing with its growth and strengthening with its strength, acquiring for each period of life a correspondence of form and of feature with its companion the body, successively assuming the appearance of the infant, the youth, the adult, the white-bearded patriarch. The shade who wandered in the Stygian fields, or stood before the tribunal of Minos to receive his doom, was thought to correspond in aspect with the aspect of the body at death. It was thus that Ulysses recognized the forms of Patroclus and Achilles, and other heroes of the ten years' siege; it was thus that the peasant recognized the ghost of his enemy or friend. As a matter of superstition, these notions had their use, but in a philosophical sense it is impossible to conceive anything more defective.

The double immortality, past and future.

Man differs from a lifeless body or a brute in this, that it is not with the present moment alone that he has to deal. For the brute the past, when gone, is clean gone for ever; and the future, before it approaches, is as if it were never to be. Man, by his recollection, makes the past a part of the present, and his foreknowledge adds the future thereto, thereby uniting the three in one.

Relations of the past and future to man.

Some of the illustrations commonly given of Plato's Ideal theory may also be instructively used for showing the manner in which his facts are dealt with by the methods of modern science. Thus Plato would say that there is contained in every acorn the ideal type of an oak, in accordance with which as soon as suitable circumstances occur, the acorn will develop itself into an oak, and into no other tree. In the act of development of such a seed into its final growth there are, therefore, two things demanding attention, the intrinsic character of the seed and the external forces acting upon it. The Platonic doctrine draws such a distinction emphatically; its essential purpose is to assert

Criticism on the Ideal theory.

the absolute existence and independence of that innate type and its imperishability. Though it requires the agency of external circumstances for its complete realization, its being is altogether irrespective of them. There are, therefore, in such a case, two elements concerned—an internal and an external. A like duality is perceived in many other physiological instances, as in the relationship of mind and matter, thought and sensation. It is the aim of the Platonic philosophy to magnify the internal at the expense of the external in the case of man, thereby asserting the absolute supremacy of intellect; this being the particular in which man is distinguished from the brutes and lower organisms, in whom the external relatively predominates. The development of any such organism, be it plant or animal, is therefore nothing but a manifestation of the Divine idea of Platonism. Many instances of natural history offer striking illustrations, as when that which might have been a branch is developed into a flower, the parts thereof showing a disposition to arrange themselves by fives or by threes. The persistency with which this occurs in organisms of the same species, is, in the Platonic interpretation, a proof that, though individuals may perish, the idea is immortal. How else, in this manner, could the like extricate itself from the unlike: the one deliver itself from, and make itself manifest among the many?

Such is an instance of Plato's views; but the very illustration, thus serving to bring them so explicitly before us, may teach us another, and, perhaps, a more correct doctrine. For, considering the duality presented by such cases, the internal and external, the immortal hidden type and the power acting upon it without, the character and the circumstances, may we not pertinently inquire by what authority does Plato diminish the influence of the latter and enhance the value of the former? Why are facts to be burdened with such hypothetical creations, when it is obvious that a much simpler explanation is sufficient? Let us admit, as our best physiological views direct, that the starting-point of every organism, low or high, vegetable or animal, or whatever else, is a simple cell, the manner of development of which depends altogether on the circumstances and influences to which it is exposed; that, so long as those circumstances are the same the resulting form will be the same, and that as soon as those circumstances differ the resulting form differs too. The offspring is like its parent, not because it includes an immortal typical form, but because it is exposed in development to the same conditions as was its parent. Elsewhere I have endeavoured to show that we must acknowledge this absolute dominion of physical agents over organic forms as the fundamental principle in all the sciences of organization; indeed, the main object of my work on Physiology was to enforce this very doctrine. But such a doctrine is altogether inconsistent with the Ideal theory of Platonism. It is no latent imperishable type existing from eternity that is dominating in such developments, but they take place as the issue of a resistless law, variety being possible under variation of environment. Hence we may perhaps excuse ourselves from that suprasensual world in which reside typical forms, universals, ideas of created things, declining this complex machinery of Platonism, and substituting for it a simple notion of law. Nor shall we find, if from this starting-point we direct our thoughts upward, as Plato did from subordinate ideas to the first idea, anything incompatible with the noble conclusion to which he eventually came, anything incompatible with the majesty of God, whose existence and attributes may be asserted with more precision and distinctness from considerations of the operation of immutable law than they can be from the starting-point of fantastic, imaginary, ideal forms.

Rise of the Sceptics.

We have seen how the pre-Socratic philosophy ended in the Sophists; we have now to see how the post-Socratic ended in the Sceptics. Again was repeated the same result exhibited in former times, that the doctrines of the different schools, even those supposed to be matters of absolute demonstration, were not only essentially different, but in contradiction to one another. Again, therefore, the opinion was resumed that the intellect of man possesses no criterion of truth, being neither able to distinguish among the contradictions of the impressions of the senses, nor to judge of the correctness of philosophical deductions, nor even to determine the intrinsic morality of acts. And, if there be no criterion of truth, there can be no certain ground of science, and there remains nothing for us but doubt. Such was the conclusion to which Pyrrho, the founder of the Sceptics, came. He lived about B.C. 300. His philosophical doctrine of the necessity of suspending or refusing our assent from want of a criterion of judgment led by a natural transition to the moral doctrine that virtue and happiness consist in perfect quiescence or freedom from all mental perturbation. This doctrine, it is said, he had learned in India from the Brahmans, whither he had been in the expedition of Alexander. On his return to Europe he taught these views in his school at Elis; but Greek philosophy, in its own order of advancement, was verging on the discovery of these conclusions.

The Sceptical school was thus founded on the assertion that man can never ascertain the true among phenomena, and therefore can never know whether things are in accordance or discordance with their appearances, for the same object appears differently to us in different positions and at different times. Doubtless it also appears differently to various individuals. Among such appearances, how shall we select the true one, and, if we make a selection, how shall we be absolutely certain that we are right? Moreover, the properties we impute to things, such as colour, smell, taste, hardness, and the like, are dependent upon our senses; but we very well know that our senses are perpetually yielding to us contradictory indications, and it is in vain that we expect Reason to enable us to distinguish with correctness, or furnish us a criterion of the truth. The Sceptical school thus made use of the weapon which the Sophists had so destructively employed, directing it, however, chiefly against ethics. But let us ascend a step higher. If we rely upon Reason, how do we know that Reason itself is trustworthy? Do we not want some criterion for it? And, even if such a criterion existed, must we not have for it, in its turn, some higher criterion? The Sceptic thus justified his assertion that to man there is no criterion of truth.

Secondary analysis of ethical philosophy.

In accordance with these principles, the Sceptics denied

that we can ever attain to a knowledge of existence from a knowledge of phenomena. They carried their doubt to such an extreme as to assert that we can never know the truth of anything that we have asserted, no, not even the truth of this very assertion itself. "We assert nothing," said they; "no, not even that we assert nothing." They declared that the system of induction is at best only a system of probability, for an induction can only be certain when every one and all of the individual things have been examined and demonstrated to agree with the universal. If one single exception among myriads of examples be discovered, the induction is destroyed. But how shall we be sure, in any one case, that we have examined all the individuals? therefore we must ever doubt. As to the method of definitions, it is clear that it is altogether useless; for, if we are ignorant of a thing, we cannot define it, and if we know a thing, a definition adds nothing to our knowledge. In thus destroying definitions and inductions they destroyed all philosophical method.

The doctrines of Pyrrho.

No certainty in knowledge.

But if there be this impossibility of attaining knowledge, what is the use of man giving himself any trouble about the matter? Is it not best to accept life as it comes, and enjoy pleasure while he may? And this is what Epicurus, B.C. 342, had already advised men to do. Like Socrates, he disparages science, and looks upon pleasure as the main object of life and the criterion of virtue. Asserting that truth cannot be determined by Reason alone, he gives up philosophy in despair, or regards it as an inferior or ineffectual means of contributing to happiness. In his view the proper division of philosophy is into Ethics, Canonic, and Physics, the two latter being of very little importance compared with the first. The wise man or sage must seek in an Oriental quietism for the chief happiness of life, indulging himself in a temperate manner as respects his present appetite, and adding thereto the recollection of similar sensual pleasures that are past, and the expectation of new ones reserved for the future. He must look on philosophy as the art of enjoying life. He should give himself no concern as to death or the power of the gods, who are only a

The doctrines of Epicurus.

delusion; none as respects a future state, remembering that the soul, which is nothing more than a congeries of atoms, is resolved into those constituents at death. There can be no doubt that such doctrines were very well suited to the times in which they were introduced; for so great was the social and political disturbance, so great the uncertainty of the tenure of property, that it might well be suggested what better could a man do than enjoy his own while it was yet in his possession? nor was the inducement to such a course lessened by extravagant dissipations when courtesans and cooks, jesters and buffoons, splendid attire and magnificent appointments had become essential to life. Demetrius Poliorcetes, who understood the condition of things thoroughly, says, "There was not, in my time, in Athens, one great or noble mind." In such a social state, it is not at all surprising that Epicurus had many followers, and that there were many who agreed with him in thinking that happiness is best found in a tranquil indifference, and in believing that there is nothing in reality good or bad; that it is best to decide upon nothing, but to leave affairs to chance; that there is, after all, little or no difference between life and death: that a wise man will regard philosophy as an activity of ideas and arguments which may tend to happiness; that its physical branch is of no other use than to correct superstitious fancies as to death, and remove the fear of meteors, prodigies, and other phenomena by explaining their nature; that the views of Democritus and Aristotle may be made to some extent available for the procurement of pleasure; and that we may learn from the brutes, who pursue pleasure and avoid pain, what ought to be our course. Upon the whole, it will be found that there is a connexion between pleasure and virtue, especially if we enlarge our views and seek for pleasure, not in the gratification of the present moment, but in the aggregate offered by existence. The pleasures of the soul all originate in the pleasures of the flesh; not only those of the time being, but also those recollected in the past and anticipated in the future. The sage will therefore provide for all these, and, remembering that pain is in its nature transient, but pleasure is enduring, he will not

Tranquil indifference is best for man.

hesitate to encounter the former if he can be certain that it will procure him the latter; he will dismiss from his mind all idle fears of the gods and of destiny, for these are fictions beneficial only to women and the vulgar; yet, since they are the objects of the national superstition, it is needless to procure one's self disfavour by openly deriding them. It will therefore be better for the sage to treat them with apparent solemnity, or at least with outward respect, though he may laugh at the imposition in his heart. As to the fear of death, he will be especially careful to rid himself from it, remembering that death is only a deliverer from the miseries of life.

Imperfections of the Canonic of Epicurus,

Under the title of Canonic Epicurus delivers his philosophical views; they are, however, of a very superficial kind. He insists that our sensuous impressions are the criterion of truth, and that even the sensations of a lunatic and a dreamer are true. But, besides the impressions of the moment, memory is also to be looked upon as a criterion—memory, which is the basis of experience.

and contradictions of his Physics.

In his Physics he adopts the Atomic theory of Democritus, though in many respects it ill accords with his Ethics or Canonic; but so low is his esteem of its value that he cares nothing for that. Though atoms and a void are in their nature imperceptible to the senses, he acknowledges their existence, asserting the occurrence of an infinite number of atoms of different kinds in the infinite void, which, because of their weight, precipitate themselves perpendicularly downward with an equable motion; but some of them, through an unaccountable internal force, have deviated from their perpendicular path, and, sticking together after their collision, have given rise to the world. Not much better than these vague puerilities are his notions about the size of the sun, the nature of eclipses, and other astronomical phenomena; but he justifies his contradictions and superficiality by asserting that it is altogether useless for a man to know such things, and that the sage ought to give himself no trouble about them. As to the soul, he says that it must be of a material or corporeal nature, for this simple reason, that there is nothing incorporeal but a vacuum; he inclines to the belief that it is a rarefied body, easily movable, and somewhat of the nature of a vapour; he divides it into four activities, corresponding to the four elements entering into its constitution; and that, so far from being immortal, it is decomposed into its integral atoms, dying when the body dies. With the atomic doctrines of Democritus, Epicurus adopts the notions of that philosopher respecting sensation, to the effect that eidola or images are sloughed off from all external objects, and find access to the brain through the eye. In his theology he admits, under the circumstances we have mentioned, anthropomorphic gods, pretending to account for their origin in the chance concourse of atoms, and suggesting that they display their quietism and blessedness by giving themselves no concern about man or his affairs. By such derisive promptings does Epicurus mock at the religion of his country—its rituals, sacrifices, prayers, and observances. He offers no better evidence of the existence of God than that there is a general belief current among men in support of such a notion; but, when brought to the point, he does not hesitate to utter his disbelief in the national theology, and to declare that, in his judgment, it is blind chance that rules the world.

His irreligion.

Such are the opinions to which the name of Epicurus has been attached; but there were Epicureans ages before that philosopher was born, and Epicureans there will be in all time to come. They abound in our own days, ever characterized by the same features—an intense egoism in their social relations, superficiality in their philosophical views, if the term philosophical can be justly applied to intellects so narrow; they manifest an accordance often loud and particular with the religion of their country, while in their hearts and in their lives they are utter infidels. These are they who constitute the most specious part of modern society, and are often the self-proclaimed guardians of its interests. They are to be found in every grade of life; in the senate, in the army, in the professions, and especially in commercial pursuits, which, unhappily, tend too frequently to the development of selfishness. It is to them that society is

Epicureans of modern times.

indebted for more than half its corruptions, all its hypocrisy, and more than half its sins. It is they who infuse into it falsehood as respects the past, imposture as respects the present, fraud as respects the future; who teach it by example that the course of a man's life ought to be determined upon principles of selfishness; that gratitude and affection are well enough if displayed for effect, but that they should never be felt; that men are to be looked upon not as men, but as things to be used; that knowledge and integrity, patriotism and virtue, are the delusions of simpletons; and that wealth is the only object which is really worthy of the homage of man.

It now only remains in this chapter to speak of the later Platonism. The Old Academy, of which Plato was the founder, limited its labours to the illustration and defence of his doctrines. The Middle Academy, originating with Arcesilaus, born B.C. 316, maintained a warfare with the Stoics, developed the doctrine of the uncertainty of sensual impressions and the nothingness of human knowledge. The New Academy was founded by Carneades, born B.C. 213, and participated with the preceding in many of its fundamental positions. On the one side Carneades leans to scepticism, on the other he accepts probability as his guide. This school so rapidly degenerated that at last it occupied itself with rhetoric alone. The gradual increase of scepticism and indifference throughout this period is obvious enough; thus Arcesilaus said that he knew nothing, not even his own ignorance, and denied both intellectual and sensuous knowledge. Carneades, obtaining his views from the old philosophy, found therein arguments suitable for his purpose against necessity, God, soothsaying; he did not admit that there is any such thing as justice in the abstract, declaring that it is a purely conventional thing; indeed, it was his rhetorical display, alternately in praise of justice and against it, on the occasion of his visit to Rome, that led Cato to have him expelled from the city. Though Plato had been the representative of an age of faith, a secondary analysis of all his works, implying an exposition of their contradictions, ended in

The Middle Academy of Arcesilaus.

The New Academy of Carneades.

The duplicity of the later Academicians.

scepticism. If we may undertake to determine the precise aim of a philosophy whose representatives stood in such an attitude of rhetorical duplicity, it may be said to be the demonstration that there is no criterion of truth in this world. Persuaded thus of the impossibility of philosophy, Carneades was led to recommend his theory of the probable. "That which has been most perfectly analyzed and examined, and found to be devoid of improbability, is the most probable idea." The degeneration of philosophy now became truly complete, the labours of so many great men being degraded to rhetorical and artistic purposes. It was seen by all that Plato had troyed all trust in the indications of the senses, and substituted for it the Ideal theory. Aristotle had destroyed that, and there was nothing left to the world but scepticism. A fourth Academy was founded by Philo of Larissa, a fifth by Antiochus of Ascalon. It was reserved for this teacher to attach the Porch to the Academy, and to merge the doctrines of Plato in those of the Stoics. Such a heterogeneous mixture demonstrates the pass to which speculative philosophy had come, and shows us clearly that her disciples had abandoned her in despair.

The fourth and fifth Academies.

So ends the Greek age of Faith. How strikingly does its history recall the corresponding period of individual life—the trusting spirit and the disappointment of youth. We enter on it full of confidence in things and men, never suspecting that the one may disappoint, the other deceive. Our early experiences, if considered at all, afford only matter of surprise that we could ever have been seriously occupied in such folly, or actuated by motives now seeming so inadequate. It never occurs to us that, in our present state, though the pursuits may have changed, they are none the less vain, the objects none the less delusive.

End of the Greek age of Faith.

The second age of Greek philosophy ended in sophism, the third in scepticism. Speculative philosophy strikes at last upon a limit which it can not overpass. This is its state even in our own times. It reverberates against the wall that confines it without the least chance of making its way through.

CHAPTER VI.

THE GREEK AGE OF REASON.

RISE OF SCIENCE.

THE MACEDONIAN CAMPAIGN.—*Disastrous in its political Effects to Greece, but ushering in the Age of Reason.*

ARISTOTLE *founds the Inductive Philosophy.—His Method the Inverse of that of Plato.—Its great power.—In his own hands it fails for want of Knowledge, but is carried out by the Alexandrians.*

ZENO.—*His Philosophical Aim is the Cultivation of Virtue and Knowledge.—He is in the Ethical Branch the Counterpart of Aristotle in the Physical.*

FOUNDATION OF THE MUSEUM OF ALEXANDRIA.—*The great Libraries, Observatories, Botanical Gardens, Menageries, Dissecting Houses.—Its Effect on the rapid Development of exact Knowledge.—Influence of Euclid, Archimedes, Eratosthenes, Apollonius, Ptolemy, Hipparchus, on Geometry, Natural Philosophy, Astronomy, Chronology, Geography. Decline of the Greek Age of Reason.*

The Greek invasion of Persia.

THE conquest of Persia by Alexander the Great is a most important event in European history. That adventurer, carrying out the intentions of his father Philip, commenced his attack with apparently very insignificant means, having, it is said, at the most, only thirty-four thousand infantry, four thousand cavalry, and seventy talents in money. The result of his expedition was the ruin of the Persian empire, and also the ruin of Greece. It was not without reason that his memory was cursed in his native country. Her life-blood was drained away by his successes. In view of the splendid fortunes to be made in Asia, Greece ceased to be the place for an enterprising man. To such an extent did military emigration go, that Greek recruits were settled all over the Persian empire; their number was sufficient to injure irreparably the country from which they had parted, but not sufficient to Hellenize the dense and antique populations among whom they had settled.

Its ruinous effect on Greece.

Not only was it thus by the drain of men that the Macedonian expedition was so dreadfully disastrous to Greece, the political consequences following those successful campaigns added to the baneful result. Alexander could not have more effectually ruined Athens had he treated her as he did Thebes, which he levelled with the ground, massacring six thousand of her citizens, and selling thirty thousand for slaves. The founding of Alexandria was the commercial end of Athens, the finishing stroke to her old colonial system. It might have been well for her had he stopped short in his projects with the downfall of Tyre, destroyed, not from any vindictive reasons, as is sometimes said, but because he discovered that that city was an essential part of the Persian system. It was never his intention that Athens should derive advantage from the annihilation of her Phœnician competitor; his object was effectually carried out by the building and prosperity of Alexandria.

Injury to Athens from the founding of Alexandria.

Though the military celebrity of this great soldier may be diminished by the history of the last hundred years, which shows a uniform result of victory when European armies are brought in contact with Asiatic, even under the most extraordinary disadvantages, there cannot be denied to him a profound sagacity and statesmanship excelled by no other conqueror. Before he became intoxicated with success, and, unfortunately, too frequently intoxicated with wine, there was much that was noble in his character. He had been under the instruction of Aristotle for several years, and, on setting out on his expedition, took with him so many learned men as almost to justify the remark applied to it, that it was as much a scientific as a military undertaking. Among those who thus accompanied him was Callisthenes, a relative and pupil of Aristotle, destined for an evil end. Perhaps the assertion

Scientific tendency of the Macedonian campaigns.

that Alexander furnished to his master 250,000*l.* and the services of several thousand men, for the purpose of obtaining and examining the specimens required in the composition of his work on the "History of Animals" may be an exaggeration, but there can be no doubt that in these transactions was the real beginning of that policy which soon led to the institution of the Museum at Alexandria. The importance of this event, though hitherto little understood, admits of no exaggeration, so far as the intellectual progress of Europe is concerned. It gave to the works of Aristotle their wonderful duration; it imparted to them not only a Grecian celebrity, but led to their translation into Syriac by the Nestorians in the fifth century, and from Syriac by the Arabs into their tongue four hundred years later. They exercised a living influence over Christians and Mohammedans indifferently, from Spain to Mesopotamia.

Origin of the influence of Aristotle through Alexander.

If the letter quoted by Plutarch as having been written by Alexander to Aristotle be authentic, it not only shows how thoroughly the pupil had been indoctrinated into the wisdom of the master, but warns us how liable we are to be led astray in the exposition we are presently to give of the Aristotelian philosophy. There was then, as unfortunately there has been too often since, a private as well as a public doctrine. Alexander upbraids the philosopher for his indiscretion in revealing things that it was understood should be concealed. Aristotle defends himself by asserting that the desired concealment had not been broken. By many other incidents of a trifling kind the attachment of the conqueror to philosophy is indicated; thus Harpalus and Nearchus, the companions of his youth, were the agents employed in some of his scientific undertakings, the latter being engaged in sea explorations, doubtless having in the main a political object, yet full of interest to science. Had Alexander lived, Nearchus was to have repeated the circumnavigation of Africa. Harpalus, while governor of Babylon, was occupied in the attempt to exchange the vegetation of Europe and Asia; he intertransplanted the productions of Persia and Greece, succeeding, as is related,

Scientific training and undertakings of Alexander.

in his object of making all European plants that he tried, except the ivy, grow in Mesopotamia. The journey to the Caspian Sea, the expedition into the African deserts, indicate Alexander's personal taste for natural knowledge; nor is it without significance that, while on his death-bed, and, indeed, within a few days of his decease, he found consolation and amusement in having Nearchus by his side relating the story of his voyages. Nothing shows more strikingly how correct was his military perception than the intention he avowed of equipping a thousand ships for the conquest of Carthage, and thus securing his supremacy in the Mediterranean. Notwithstanding all this, there were many points of his character, and many events of his life, worthy of the condemnation with which they have been visited; the drunken burning of Persepolis, the prisoners he slaughtered in honour of Hephæstion, the hanging of Callisthenes, were the results of intemperance and unbridled passion. Even so steady a mind as his was incapable of withstanding the influence of such enormous treasures as those he seized at Susa; the plunder of the Persian empire; the inconceivable luxury of Asiatic life; the uncontrolled power to which he attained. But he was not so imbecile as to believe himself the descendant of Jupiter Ammon; that was only an artifice he permitted for the sake of influencing those around him. We must not forget that he lived in an age when men looked for immaculate conceptions and celestial descents. These Asiatic ideas had made their way into Europe. The Athenians themselves were soon to be reconciled to the appointment of divine honours to such as Antigonus and Demetrius, adoring them as gods—saviour gods—and instituting sacrifices and priests for their worship.

His unbridled passions and iniquities.

Great as were the political results of the Macedonian expedition, they were equalled by the intellectual. The times were marked by the ushering in of a new philosophy. Greece had gone through her age of Credulity, her age of Inquiry, her age of Faith; she had entered on her age of Reason, and, had freedom of action been permitted to her, she would have given a decisive tone to the forthcoming civilization of Europe.

The Greek age of Reason ushered in.

As will be seen in the following pages, that great destiny did not await her. From her eccentric position at Alexandria she could not civilize Europe. In her old age, the power of Europe, concentrated in the Roman empire, overthrew her. There are very few histories of the past of more interest to modern times, and none, unfortunately, more misunderstood, than this Greek age of Reason manifested at Alexandria. It illustrates, in the most signal manner, that affairs control men more than men control affairs. The scientific associations of the Macedonian conqueror directly arose from the contemporaneous state of Greek philosophy in the act of reaching the close of its age of faith, and these influences ripened under the Macedonian captain who became King of Egypt. As it was, the learning of Alexandria, though diverted from its most appropriate and desirable direction by the operation of the Byzantine system, in the course of a few centuries acting forcibly upon it, was not without an influence on the future thought of Europe. Even at this day Europe will not bear to be fully told how great that influence has been.

Its inability to accomplish the civilization of Europe.

The age of Reason, to which Aristotle is about to introduce us, stands in striking contrast to the preceding ages. It cannot escape the reader that what was done by the men of science in Alexandria resembles what is doing in our own times; their day was the foreshadowing of ours. And yet a long and dreary period of almost twenty centuries parts us from them. Politically, Aristotle, through his friendship with Alexander and the perpetuation of the Macedonian influence in Ptolemy, was the connecting link between the Greek age of Faith and that of Reason, as he was also philosophically by the nature of his doctrines. He offers us an easy passage from the speculative methods of Plato to the scientific methods of Archimedes and Euclid. The copiousness of his doctrines, and the obscurity of many of them, might, perhaps, discourage a superficial student, unless he steadily bears in mind the singular authority they maintained for so many ages, and the brilliant results in all the exact parts of human knowledge to which they so quickly led. The history of Aristotle and his philosophy is therefore

The writings of Aristotle are its prelude.

our necessary introduction to the grand, the immortal achievements of the Alexandrian school.

Biography of Aristotle.

Aristotle was born at Stagira, in Thrace, B.C. 384. His father was an eminent author of those times on subjects of Natural History; by profession he was a physician. Dying while his son was yet quite young, he bequeathed to him not only very ample means, but also his own tastes. Aristotle soon found his way to Athens, and entered the school of Plato, with whom it is said he remained for nearly twenty years. During this period he spent most of his patrimony, and in the end was obliged to support himself by the trade of a druggist. At length differences arose between them, for, as we shall soon find, the great pupil was by no means a blind follower of the great master. In a fortunate moment, Philip, the King of Macedon, appointed him preceptor to his son Alexander, an incident of importance in the intellectual history of Europe. It was to the friendship arising through this relation that Aristotle owed the assistance he received from the conqueror during his Asiatic expedition for the composition of "the Natural History," and also gained that prestige which gave his name such singular authority for more than fifteen centuries. He eventually founded a school in the Lyceum at Athens, and, as it was his habit to deliver his lectures while walking, his disciples received the name of Peripatetics, or walking philosophers. These lectures were of two kinds, esoteric and exoteric, the former being delivered to the more advanced pupils only. He wrote a very large number of works, of which about one-fourth remain.

He founds the inductive philosophy.

The philosophical method of Aristotle is the inverse of that of Plato, whose starting-point was universals, the very existence of which was a matter of faith, and from these he descended to particulars or details. Aristotle, on the contrary, rose from particulars to universals, advancing to them by inductions; and his system, thus an inductive philosophy, was in reality the true beginning of science.

Plato therefore trusts to the Imagination, Aristotle to Reason. The contrast between them is best seen by the attitude in which they stand as respects the Ideal theory.

Plato regards universals, types, or exemplars as having an actual existence; Aristotle declares that they are mere abstractions of reasoning. For the fanciful reminiscences derived from former experience in another life by Plato, Aristotle substitutes the reminiscences of our actual experience in this. These ideas of experience are furnished by the memory, which enables us not only to recall individual facts and events witnessed by ourselves, but also to collate them with one another, thereby discovering their resemblances and their differences. Our induction becomes the more certain as our facts are more numerous, our experience larger. "Art commences when, from a great number of experiences, one general conception is formed which will embrace all similar cases." "If we properly observe celestial phenomena, we may demonstrate the laws which regulate them." With Plato, philosophy arises from faith in the past; with Aristotle, reason alone can constitute it from existing facts. Plato is analytic, Aristotle synthetic. The philosophy of Plato arises from the decomposition of a primitive idea into particulars, that of Aristotle from the union of particulars into a general conception. The former is essentially an idealist, the latter a materialist.

His method compared with that of Plato.

From this it will be seen that the method of Plato was capable of producing more splendid, though they were necessarily more unsubstantial results; that of Aristotle was more tardy in its operation, but much more solid. It implied endless labour in the collection of facts, the tedious resort to experiment and observation, the application of demonstration. In its very nature it was such that it was impossible for its author to carry by its aid the structure of science to completion. The moment that Aristotle applies his own principles we find him compelled to depart from them through want of a sufficient experience and sufficient precision in his facts. The philosophy of Plato is a gorgeous castle in the air, that of Aristotle is a solid structure, laboriously, and, with many failures, founded on the solid rock.

The results of Platonism and Aristotelism.

Under Logic, Aristotle treats of the methods of arriving at general propositions, and of reasoning from them. His logic is at once the art of thinking and the instrument

9*

of thought. The completeness of our knowledge depends on the extent and completeness of our experience. His manner of reasoning is by the syllogism, an argument consisting of three propositions, such that the concluding one follows of necessity from the two premises, and of which, indeed, the whole theory of demonstration is only an example. Regarding logic as the instrument of thought, he introduces into it, as a fundamental feature, the ten categories. These predicaments are the genera to which everything may be reduced, and denote the most general of the attributes which may be assigned to a thing.

Aristotle's logic

His metaphysics overrides all the branches of the physical sciences. It undertakes an examination of the postulates on which each one of them is founded, determining their truth or fallacy. Considering that all science must find a support for its fundamental conditions in an extensive induction from facts, he puts at the foundation of his system the consideration of the individual; in relation to the world of sense, he regards four causes as necessary for the production of a fact—the material cause, the substantial cause, the efficient cause, the final cause.

and metaphysics.

But as soon as we come to the Physics of Aristotle we see at once his weakness. The knowledge of his age does not furnish him facts enough whereon to build, and the consequence is that he is forced into speculation. It will be sufficient for our purpose to allude to a few of his statements, either in this or in his metaphysical branch, to show how great is his uncertainty and confusion. Thus he asserts that matter contains a triple form—simple substance, higher substance, which is eternal, and absolute substance, or God himself; that the universe is immutable and eternal, and, though in relation with the vicissitudes of the world, it is unaffected thereby; that the primitive force which gives rise to all the motions and changes we see is Nature; it also gives rise to Rest; that the world is a living being, having a soul; that, since every thing is for some particular end, the soul of man is the end of his body; that Motion is the condition of all nature; that the world has a definite boundary

Temporary failure of his system.

The Peripatetic philosophy.

Substance, Motion, Space, Time.

and a limited magnitude; that Space is the immovable vessel in which whatever is may be moved; that Space, as a whole, is without motion, though its parts may move: that it is not to be conceived of as without contents; that it is impossible for a vacuum to exist, and hence there is not beyond and surrounding the world a void which contains the world; that there could be no such thing as Time unless there is a soul, for time being the number of motion, number is impossible except there be one who numbers; that, perpetual motion in a finite right line being impossible, but in a curvilinear path possible, the world, which is limited and ever in motion, must be of a spherical form; that the earth is its central part, the heavens the circumferential: hence the heaven is nearest to the prime cause of motion; that the orderly, continuous, and unceasing movement of the celestial bodies implies an unmoved mover, for the unchangeable alone can give birth to uniform motion; that unmoved existence is God; that the stars are passionless beings, having attained the end of existence, and worthy above other things of human adoration; that the fixed stars are in the outermost heaven, and the sun, moon, and planets beneath: the former receive their motion from the prime moving cause, but the planets are disturbed by the stars; that there are five elements—earth, air, fire, water, and ether; that the earth is in the centre of the world, since earthy matter settles uniformly round a central point; that fire seeks the circumferential region, and intermediately water floats upon the earth, and air upon water; that the elements are transmutable into one another, and hence many intervening substances arise; that each sphere is in interconnection with the others; the earth is agitated and disturbed by the sea, the sea by the winds, which are movements of the air, the air by the sun, moon, and planets. Each inferior sphere is controlled by its outlying or superior one, and hence it follows that the earth, which is thus disturbed by the conspiring or conflicting action of all above it, is liable to the most irregularities; that, since animals are nourished by the earth, it needs must enter into their composition, but that water is required to hold the earthy matters together; that every element must be

The world.

looked upon as living, since it is pervaded by the soul of the world; that there is an unbroken chain from the simple element through the plant and animal up to man, the different groups merging by insensible shades into one another: thus zoophytes partake partly of the vegetable and partly of the animal, and serve as an intermedium between them; that plants are inferior to animals in this, that they do not possess a single principle of life or soul, but many subordinate ones, as is shown by the circumstance that, when they are cut to pieces, each piece is capable of perfect or independent growth or life. Their inferiority is likewise betrayed by their belonging especially to the earth to which they are rooted, each root being a true mouth; and this again displays their lowly position, for the place of the mouth is ever an indication of the grade of a creature: thus in man, who is at the head of the scale, it is in the upper part of the body; that in proportion to the heat of an animal is its grade higher: thus those that are aquatic are cold, and therefore of very little intelligence, and the same may be said of plants; but of man, whose warmth is very great, the soul is much more excellent; that the possession of locomotion by an organism always implies the possession of sensation; that the senses of taste and touch indicate the qualities of things in contact with the organs of the animal, but that those of smell, hearing, and sight extend the sphere of its existence, and indicate to it what is at a distance: that the place of reception of the various sensations is the soul, from which issue forth the motions; that the blood, as the general element of nutrition, is essential to the support of the body, though insensible itself: it is also essential to the activity of the soul; that the brain is not the recipient of sensations: that function belongs to the heart; all the animal activities are united in the last; it contains the principle of life, being the principle of motion: it is the first part to be formed and the last to die; that the brain is a mere appendix to the heart, since it is formed after the heart, is the coldest of the organs, and is devoid of blood; that the soul is the reunion of all the functions of the body: it is an energy or active essence; being neither body nor magnitude, it cannot have extension, for

Organic beings.

Physiological conclusions.

thought has no parts, nor can it be said to move in space; it is as a sailor, who is motionless in a ship which is moving; that, in the origin of the organism, the male furnishes the soul and the female the body; that the body being liable to decay, and of a transitory nature, it is necessary for its well-being that its disintegration and nutrition should balance one another; that sensation may be compared to the impression of a seal on wax, the wax receiving form only, but no substance or matter; that imagination arises from impressions thus made, which endure for a length of time, and that this is the origin of memory; that man alone possesses recollection, but animals share with him memory—memory being unintentional or spontaneous, but recollection implying voluntary exertion or a search; that recollection is necessary for acting with design. It is doubtful whether Aristotle believed in the immortality of the soul, no decisive passage to that effect occurring in such of his works as are extant.

Causes of Aristotle's success and failure.

Aristotle, with a correct and scientific method, tried to build up a vast system when he was not in possession of the necessary data. Though a very learned man, he had not sufficient knowledge; indeed, there was not sufficient knowledge at that time in the world. For many of the assertions I have quoted in the preceding paragraph there was no kind of proof; many of them also, such as the settling of the heavy and the rise of the light, imply very poor cosmic ideas. It is not until he deals with those branches, such as comparative anatomy and natural history, of which he had a personal and practical knowledge, that he begins to write well. Of his physiological conclusions, some are singularly felicitous; his views of the connected chain of organic forms, from the lowest to the highest, are very grand. His metaphysical and physical speculations—for in reality they are nothing but speculations—are of no kind of value. His successful achievements, and also his failures, conspicuously prove the excellence of his system. He expounded the true principles of science, but failed to apply them merely for want of materials. His ambition could not brook restraint. He would rather attempt to construct the universe without the necessary means than not construct it at all.

Aristotle failed when he abandoned his own principles, and the magnitude of his failure proves how just his principles were; he succeeded when he adhered to them. If anything were wanting to vindicate their correctness and illustrate them, it is supplied by the glorious achievements of the Alexandrian school, which acted in physical science as Aristotle had acted in natural history, laying a basis solidly in observation and experiment, and accomplishing a like durable and brilliant result.

From Aristotle it is necessary to turn to Zeno, for the Peripatetics and Stoics stand in parallel lines. The social conditions existing in Greece at the time of Epicurus may in some degree palliate his sentiments, but virtue and honour will make themselves felt at last. Stoicism soon appeared as the antagonist of Epicureanism, and Epicurus found in Zeno of Citium a rival. The passage from Epicurus to Zeno is the passage from sensual gratification to self-control.

Biography of Zeno.

The biography of Zeno may be dismissed in a few words. Born about B.C. 300, he spent the early part of his life in the vocation of his father, who was a merchant, but, by a fortunate shipwreck, happily losing his goods during a voyage he was making to Athens, he turned to philosophy for consolation. Though he had heretofore been somewhat acquainted with the doctrines of Socrates, he became a disciple of the Cynics, subsequently studying in the Megaric school, and then making himself acquainted with Platonism. After twenty years of preparation, he opened a school in the stoa or porch in Athens, from which his doctrine and disciples have received their name. He presided over his school for fifty-eight years, numbering many eminent men among his disciples. When nearly a hundred years old he chanced to fall and break his finger, and, receiving this as an admonition that his time was accomplished, he forthwith strangled himself. The Athenians erected to his memory a statue of brass. His doctrines long survived him, and, in times when there was no other consolation for man, offered a support in their hour of trial, and an unwavering guide in the vicissitudes of life, not only to many illustrious Greeks, but also to some of the great philosophers, statesmen, generals, and emperors of Rome.

It was the intention of Zeno to substitute for the visionary speculations of Platonism a system directed to the daily practices of life, and hence dealing chiefly with morals. To make men virtuous was his aim. But this is essentially connected with knowledge, for Zeno was persuaded that if we only know what is good we shall be certain to practise it. He therefore rejected Plato's fancies of Ideas and Reminiscences, leaning to the common-sense doctrines of Aristotle, to whom he approached in many details. With him Sense furnishes the data of knowledge, and Reason combines them: the soul being modified by external things, and modifying them in return, he believed that the mind is at first, as it were, a blank tablet, on which sensation writes marks, and that the distinctness of sensuous impressions is the criterion of their truth. The changes thus produced in the soul constitute ideas; but, with a prophetic inspiration, he complained that man will never know the true essence of things.

Intention of Stoicism.

In his Physics Zeno adopted the doctrine of Strato, that the world is a living being. He believed that nothing incorporeal can produce an effect, and hence that the soul is corporeal. Matter and its properties he considered to be absolutely inseparable, a property being actually a body. In the world there are two things, matter and God, who is the Reason of the world. Essentially, however, God and matter are the same thing, which assumes the aspect of matter from the passive point of view, and God from the active: he is, moreover, the prime moving force, Destiny, Necessity, a life-giving Soul, evolving things as the vital force evolves a plant out of a seed; the visible world is thus to be regarded as the material manifestation of God. The transitory objects which it on all sides presents will be reabsorbed after a season of time, and reunited in him. The Stoics pretended to indicate, even in a more definite manner, the process by which the world has arisen, and also its future destiny; for, regarding the Supreme as a vital heat, they supposed that a portion of that fire, declining in energy, became transmuted into matter, and hence the origin of the world; but that that fire, hereafter resuming its activity, would cause a universal conflagration, the end of things. During

The Physics of Zeno.

the present state everything is in a condition of uncertain mutation, decays being followed by reproductions, and reproductions by decays; and, as a cataract shows from year to year an invariable form, though the water composing it is perpetually changing, so the objects around us are nothing more than a flux of matter offering a permanent form. Thus the visible world is only a moment in the life of God, and after it has vanished away like a scroll that is burned, a new period shall be ushered in, and a new heaven and a new earth, exactly like the ancient ones, shall arise. Since nothing can exist without its contrary, no injustice unless there was justice, no cowardice unless there was courage, no lie unless there was truth, no shadow unless there was light, so the existence of good necessitates that of evil. The Stoics believed that the development of the world is under the dominion of paramount law, supreme law, Destiny, to which God himself is subject, and that hence he can only develop the world in a predestined way, as the vital warmth evolves a seed into the predestined form of a plant.

Exoteric philosophy of the Stoics.

The Stoics held it indecorous to offend needlessly the religious ideas of the times, and, indeed, they admitted that there might be created gods like those of Plato; but they disapproved of the adoration of images and the use of temples, making amends for their offences in these particulars by offering a semi-philosophical interpretation of the legends, and demonstrating that the existence, and even phenomenal display of the gods was in accordance with their principles. Perhaps to this exoteric philosophy we must ascribe the manner in which they expressed themselves as to final causes—expressions sometimes of amusing quaintness—thus, that the peacock was formed for the sake of his tail, and that a soul was given to the hog instead of salt, to prevent his body from rotting; that the final cause of plants is to be food for brutes, of brutes to be food for men, though they discreetly checked their irony in its ascending career, and abstained from saying that men are food for the gods, and the gods for all.

The Stoics concluded that the soul is mere warm breath, and that it and the body mutually interpervade one another.

They thought that it might subsist after death until the general conflagration, particularly if its energy were great, as in the strong spirits of the virtuous and wise. Its unity of action implies that it has a principle of identity, the I, of which the physiological seat is the heart. Every appetite, lust, or desire is an imperfect knowledge. Our nature and properties are forced upon us by Fate, but it is our duty to despise all our propensities and passions, and to live so that we may be free, intelligent, and virtuous.

Their opinions of the nature of the soul.

This sentiment leads us to the great maxim of Stoical Ethics, "Live according to Reason;" or, since the world is composed of matter and God, who is the Reason of the world, "Live in harmony with Nature." As Reason is supreme in Nature, it ought to be so in man. Our existence should be intellectual, and all bodily pains and pleasures should be despised. A harmony between the human will and universal Reason constitutes virtue. The free-will of the sage should guide his actions in the same irresistible manner in which universal Reason controls nature. Hence the necessity of a cultivation of physics, without which we cannot distinguish good from evil. The sage is directed to remember that Nature, in her operations, aims at the universal, and never spares individuals, but uses them as means for accomplishing her ends. It is for him, therefore, to submit to his destiny, endeavouring continually to establish the supremacy of Reason, and cultivating, as the things necessary to virtue, knowledge, temperance, fortitude, justice. He is at liberty to put patriotism at the value it is worth when he remembers that he is a citizen of the world; he must train himself to receive in tranquillity the shocks of Destiny, and to be above all passion and all pain. He must never relent and never forgive. He must remember that there are only two classes of men, the wise and the fools, as "sticks can only either be straight or crooked, and very few sticks in this world are absolutely straight."

Their ethical rules of wisdom.

From the account I have given of Aristotle's philosophy, it may be seen that he occupied a middle ground between the speculation of the old philosophy and the strict science of the Alexandrian school. He is the true connecting link, in the history of European intellectual progress, between philosophy and science. Under his teaching, and the material tendencies of the Macedonian campaigns, there arose a class of men in Egypt who gave to the practical a development it had never before attained; for that country, upon the breaking up of Alexander's dominion, B.C. 323, falling into the possession of Ptolemy, that general found himself at once the depositary of spiritual and temporal power. Of the former, it is to be remembered that, though the conquest by Cambyses had given it a severe shock, it still not only survived, but displayed no inconsiderable tokens of strength. Indeed, it is well known that the surrender of Egypt to Alexander was greatly accelerated by hatred to the Persians, the Egyptians welcoming the Macedonians as their deliverers. In this movement we perceive at once the authority of the old priesthood. It is hard to tear up by the roots an ancient religion, the ramifications of which have solidly insinuated themselves among a populace. That of Egypt had already been the growth of more than three thousand years. The question for the intrusive Greek sovereigns to solve was how to co-ordinate this hoary system with the philosophical scepticism that had issued as the result of Greek thought. With singular sagacity, they saw that this might be accomplished by availing themselves of Orientalism, the common point of contact of the two systems; and that, by its formal introduction and development, it would be possible not only to enable the philosophical king, to whom all the pagan gods were alike equally fictitious and equally useful, to manifest respect even to the ultra-heathenish practices of the Egyptian populace, but, what was of far more moment, to establish an apparent concord between the old sacerdotal Egyptian party—strong in its unparalleled antiquity; strong in its reminiscences; strong in its recent persecutions; strong in its Pharaonic relics, regarded by all men with a superstitious or reverent awe—and the free-thinking and versatile Greeks. The occasion was like some others in history, some even in our own times; a small but energetic

Rise of Greek science.

Political position of the Ptolemies.

They co-ordinate Egyptian idolatry and Greek scepticism.

body of invaders was holding in subjection an ancient and populous country.

To give practical force to this project, a grand state institution was founded at Alexandria. It became celebrated as the Museum. To it, as to a centre, philosophers from all parts of the world converged. It is said that at one time not less than fourteen thousand students were assembled there. Alexandria, in confirmation of the prophetic foresight of the great soldier who founded it, quickly became an immense metropolis, abounding in mercantile and manufacturing activity. As is ever the case with such cities, its higher classes were prodigal and dissipated, its lower only to be held in restraint by armed force. Its public amusements were such as might be expected—theatrical shows, music, horse-racing. In the solitude of such a crowd, or in the noise of such dissipation, anyone could find a retreat—atheists who had been banished from Athens, devotees from the Ganges, monotheistic Jews, blasphemers from Asia Minor. Indeed, it has been said that in this heterogeneous community blasphemy was hardly looked upon as a crime; at the worst, it was no more than an unfortunate, and, it might be, an innocent mistake. But, since uneducated men need some solid support on which their thoughts may rest, mere abstract doctrines not meeting their wants, it became necessary to provide a corporeal representation for this eclectic philosophical Pantheism, and hence the Ptolemies were obliged to restore, or, as some say, to import the worship of the god Serapis. Those who affirm that he was imported say that he was brought from Sinope; modern Egyptian scholars, however, give a different account. As setting forth the Pantheistic doctrine of which he was the emblem, his image, subsequently to attain world-wide fame, was made of all kinds of metals and stones. "All is God." But still the people, with that instinct which other nations and ages have displayed, hankered after a female divinity, and this led to the partial restoration of the worship of Isis. It is interesting to remark how the humble classes never shake off the reminiscences of early life, leaning rather to the maternal than to the paternal attachment. Perhaps

The Museum of Alexandria.

Establishment of the worship of Serapis.

it is for that reason that they expect a more favourable attention to their supplications from a female divinity than a god. Accordingly, the devotees of Isis soon outnumbered those of Serapis, though a magnificent temple had been built for him at Rhacotis, in the quarter adjoining the Museum, and his worship was celebrated with more than imperial splendour. In subsequent ages the worship of Serapis diffused itself throughout the Roman empire, though the authorities—consuls, senate, emperors—knowing well the idea it foreshadowed, and the doctrine it was meant to imply, used their utmost power to put it down.

The Alexandrian Museum soon assumed the character of a University. In it those great libraries were collected, the pride and boast of antiquity. Demetrius Phalareus was instructed to collect all the writings in the world. So powerfully were the exertions of himself and his successors enforced by the government that two immense libraries were procured. They contained 700,000 volumes. In this literary and scientific retreat, supported in ease and even in luxury—luxury, for allusions to the sumptuous dinners have descended to our times—the philosophers spent their time in mental culture by study, or mutual improvement by debates. The king himself conferred appointments to these positions; in later times, the Roman emperors succeeded to the patronage, the government thereby binding in golden chains intellect that might otherwise have proved troublesome. At first, in honour of the ancient religion, the presidency of the establishment was committed to an Egyptian priest; but in the course of time that policy was abandoned. It must not, however, be imagined that the duties of the inmates were limited to reading and rhetorical display; a far more practical character was imparted to them. A botanical garden, in connection with the Museum, offered an opportunity to those who were interested in the study of the nature of plants; a zoological menagerie afforded like facilities to those interested in animals. Even these costly establishments were made to minister to the luxury of the times: in the zoological garden pheasants were raised for the royal table. Besides these elegant and fashionable appointments,

The Alexandrian libraries.

Botanical gardens; menageries; dissecting-houses; observatories.

another, of a more forbidding and perhaps repulsive kind, was added; an establishment which, in the light of our times, is sufficient to confer immortal glory on those illustrious and high-minded kings, and to put to shame the ignorance and superstition of many modern nations: it was an anatomical school, suitably provided with means for the dissection of the human body, this anatomical school being the basis of a medical college for the education of physicians. For the astronomers Ptolemy Euergetes placed in the Square Porch an equinoctial and a solstitial armil, the graduated limbs of these instruments being divided into degrees and sixths. There were in the observatory stone quadrants, the precursors of our mural quadrants. On the floor a meridian line was drawn for the adjustment of the instruments. There were also astrolabes and dioptras. Thus, side by side, almost in the king's palace, were noble provisions for the cultivation of exact science and for the pursuit of light literature. Under the same roof were gathered together geometers, astronomers, chemists, mechanicians, engineers. There were also poets, who ministered to the literary wants of the dissipated city—authors who could write verse, not only in correct metre, but in all kinds of fantastic forms—trees, hearts, and eggs. Here met together the literary dandy and the grim theologian. At their repasts occasionally the king himself would preside, enlivening the moment with the condescensions of royal relaxation. Thus, of Philadelphus it is stated that he caused to be presented to the Stoic Sphærus a dish of fruit made of wax, so beautifully coloured as to be undistinguishable from the natural, and on the mortified philosopher detecting too late the fraud that had been practised upon him, inquired what he now thought of the maxim of his sect that "the sage is never deceived by appearances." Of the same sovereign it is related that he received the translators of the Septuagint Bible with the highest honours, entertaining them at his table. Under the atmosphere of the place their usual religious ceremonial was laid aside, save that the king courteously requested one of the aged priests to offer an extempore prayer. It is naively related that the Alexandrians present, ever quick to discern rhetorical merit,

Life in the Museum.

testified their estimation of the performance with loud applause. But not alone did literature and the exact sciences thus find protection. As if no subjects with which the human mind has occupied itself can be unworthy of investigation, in the Museum were cultivated the more doubtful arts, magic and astrology. Philadelphus, who, toward the close of his life, was haunted with an intolerable dread of death, devoted himself with intense assiduity to the discovery of the elixir of life and to alchemy. Such a comprehensive organization for the development of human knowledge never existed in the world before, and, considering the circumstances, never has since. To be connected with it was the passport to the highest Alexandrian society and to court favour.

To the Museum, and, it has been asserted, particularly to Ptolemy Philadelphus, the Christian world is thus under obligation for the ancient version of the Hebrew Scriptures —the Septuagint. Many idle stories have been related respecting the circumstances under which that version was made, as that the seventy-two translators by whom it was executed were confined each in a separate cell, and, when their work was finished, the seventy-two copies were found identically the same, word for word. From this it was supposed that the inspiration of this translation was established. If any proof of that kind were needed, it would be much better found in the fact that whenever occasion arises in the New Testament of quoting from the Old, it is usually done in the words of the Septuagint. The story of the cells underwent successive improvements among the early fathers, but is now rejected as a fiction; and, indeed, it seems probable that the translation was not made under the splendid circumstances commonly related, but merely by the Alexandrian Jews for their own convenience. As the Septuagint grew into credit among the Christians, it lost favour among the Jews, who made repeated attempts in after years to supplant it by new versions, such as those of Aquila, of Theodotion, of Symmachus, and others. From the first the Syrian Jews had looked on it with disapproval; they even held the time of its translation as a day of mourning, and with malicious grief pointed out its errors, as, for instance,

The Septuagint translators.

they affirmed that it made Methusaleh live until after the Deluge. Ptolemy treated all those who were concerned in providing books for the library with consideration, remunerating his translators and transcribers in a princely manner.

But the modern world is not indebted to these Egyptian kings only in the particular here referred to. The Museum made an impression upon the intellectual career of Europe so powerful and enduring that we still enjoy its results. That impression was twofold, theological and physical. The dialectical spirit and literary culture diffused among the Alexandrians prepared that people, beyond all others, for the reception of Christianity. For thirty centuries the Egyptians had been familiar with the conception of a triune God. There was hardly a city of any note without its particular triad. Here it was Amum, Maut, and Khonso; there Osiris, Isis, and Horus. The apostolic missionaries, when they reached Alexandria, found a people ready to appreciate the profoundest mysteries. But with these advantages came great evils. The Trinitarian disputes, which subsequently deluged the world with blood, had their starting-point and focus in Alexandria. In that city Arius and Athanasius dwelt. There originated that desperate conflict which compelled Constantine the Great to summon the Council of Nicea, to settle, by a formulary or creed, the essentials of our faith.

Lasting influence of the Museum, theological and scientific.

But it was not alone as regards theology that Alexandria exerted a power on subsequent ages: her influence was as strongly marked in the impression it gave to science. Astronomical observatories, chemical laboratories, libraries, dissecting-houses, were not in vain. There went forth from them a spirit powerful enough to tincture all future times. Nothing like the Alexandrian Museum was ever called into existence in Greece or Rome, even in their palmiest days. It is the unique and noble memorial of the dynasty of the Ptolemies, who have thereby laid the whole human race under obligations, and vindicated their title to be regarded as a most illustrious line of kings. The Museum was, in truth, an attempt at the organization of human knowledge, both for its development and its diffusion. It was conceived and executed in a practical manner worthy of Alexander. And though, in the night through which Europe has been passing—a night full of dreams and delusions—men have not entertained a right estimate of the spirit in which that great institution was founded, and the work it accomplished, its glories being eclipsed by darker and more unworthy things, the time is approaching when its action on the course of human events will be better understood, and its influences on European civilization more clearly discerned.

The Museum was the issue of the Macedonian campaigns.

Thus, then, about the beginning of the third century before Christ, in consequence of the Macedonian campaign, which had brought the Greeks into contact with the ancient civilization of Asia, a great degree of intellectual activity was manifested in Egypt. On the site of the village of Rhacotis, once held as an Egyptian post to prevent the ingress of strangers, the Macedonians erected that city which was to be the entrepôt of the commerce of the East and West, and to transmit an illustrious name to the latest generations. Her long career of commercial prosperity, her commanding position as respects the material interests of the world, justified the statesmanship of her founder, and the intellectual glory which has gathered round her has given an enduring lustre to his name.

There can be no doubt that the philosophical activity here alluded to was the direct issue of the political and military event to which we have referred it. The tastes and genius of Alexander were manifested by his relations to Aristotle, whose studies in natural history he promoted by the collection of a menagerie; and in astronomy, by transmitting to him, through Callisthenes, the records of Babylonian observations extending over 1903 years. His biography, as we have seen, shows a personal interest in the cultivation of such studies. In this particular other great soldiers have resembled him; and perhaps it may be inferred that the practical habit of thought and accommodation of theory to the actual purposes of life preeminently required by their profession, leads them spontaneously to decline speculative uncertainties, and to be satisfied only with things that are real and exact.

Under the inspiration of the system of Alexander, and guided by the suggestions of certain great men who had caught the spirit of the times, the Egyptian kings thus created, under their own immediate auspices, the Museum. State policy, operating in the manner I have previously described, furnished them with an additional theological reason for founding this establishment. In the Macedonian campaign a vast amount of engineering and mathematical talent had been necessarily stimulated into existence, for great armies cannot be handled, great marches cannot be made, nor great battles fought without that result. When the period of energetic action was over, and to the military operations succeeded comparative repose and temporary moments of peace, the talent thus called forth found occupation in the way most congenial to it by cultivating mathematical and physical studies. In Alexandria, itself a monument of engineering and architectural skill, soon were to be found men whose names were destined for futurity—Apollonius, Eratosthenes, Manetho. Of these, one may be selected for the remark that, while speculative philosophers were occupying themselves with discussions respecting the criterion of truth, and, upon the whole, coming to the conclusion that no such thing existed, and that, if the truth was actually in the possession of man, he had no means of knowing it, Euclid of Alexandria was writing an immortal work, destined to challenge contradiction from the whole human race, and to make good its title as the representative of absolute and undeniable truth—truth not to be gainsaid in any nation or at any time. We still use the geometry of Euclid in our schools.

The great men it produced.

It is said that Euclid opened a geometrical school in Alexandria about B.C. 300. He occupied himself not only with mathematical, but also with physical investigation. Besides many works of the former class supposed to have been written by him, as on Fallacies, Conic Sections, Divisions, Porisms, Data, there are imputed to him treatises on Harmonics, Optics, and Catoptrics, the two latter subjects being discussed, agreeably to the views of those times, on the hypothesis of rays issuing from the eye to the object, instead of passing, as we consider them to do,

The writings of Euclid.

from the object to the eye. It is, however, on the excellencies of his Elements of Geometry that the durable reputation of Euclid depends; and though the hypercriticism of modern mathematicians has perhaps successfully maintained such objections against them as that they might have been more precise in their axioms, that they sometimes assume what might be proved, that they are occasionally redundant, and their arrangement sometimes imperfect, yet they still maintain their ground as a model of extreme accuracy, of perspicuity, and as a standard of exact demonstration. They were employed universally by the Greeks, and, in subsequent ages, were translated and preserved by the Arabs.

The writings and works of Archimedes.

Great as is the fame of Euclid, it is eclipsed by that of Archimedes the Syracusan, born B.C. 287, whose connection with Egyptian science is not alone testified by tradition, but also by such facts as his acknowledged friendship with Conon of Alexandria, and his invention of the screw still bearing his name, intended for raising the waters of the Nile. Among his mathematical works, the most interesting, perhaps, in his own estimation, as we may judge from the incident that he directed the diagram thereof to be engraved on his tombstone, was his demonstration that the solid content of a sphere is two-thirds that of its circumscribing cylinder. It was by this mark that Cicero, when Quæstor of Sicily, discovered the tomb of Archimedes grown over with weeds. This theorem was, however, only one of a large number of a like kind, which he treated of in his two books on the sphere and cylinder in an equally masterly manner, and with equal success. His position as a geometer is perhaps better understood from the assertion made respecting him by a modern mathematician, that he came as near to the discovery of the Differential Calculus as can be done without the aid of algebraic transformations. Among the special problems he treated of may be mentioned the quadrature of the circle, his determination of the ratio of the circumference to the diameter being between 3·1428 and 3·1408, the true value, as is now known, being 3·1416 nearly. He also wrote on Conoids and Spheroids, and upon that spiral still passing under his name, the genesis of which had been suggested to him by Conon. In his work entitled "Psammites" he alludes to the astronomical system subsequently established by Copernicus, whose name has been given to it. He also mentions the attempts which had been made to measure the size of the earth; the chief object of the work being, however, to prove not only that the sands upon the sea-shore can be numbered, but even those required to fill the entire space within the sphere of the fixed stars; the result being, according to our system of arithmetic, a less number than is expressed by unity followed by 63 ciphers. Such a book is the sport of a geometrical giant wantonly amusing himself with his strength. Among his mathematical investigations must not be omitted the quadrature of the parabola. His fame depends, however, not so much on his mathematical triumphs as upon his brilliant discoveries in physics and his mechanical inventions. How he laid the foundation of Hydrostatics is familiar to everyone, through the story of Hiero's crown. A certain artisan having adulterated the gold given him by King Hiero to form a crown, Archimedes discovered while he was accidentally stepping into a bath, that the falsification might be detected, and thereby invented the method for the determination of specific gravity. From these investigations he was naturally led to the consideration of the equilibrium of floating bodies; but his grand achievement in the mechanical direction was his discovery of the true theory of the lever: his surprising merit in these respects is demonstrated by the fact that no advance was made in theoretical mechanics during the eighteen centuries intervening between him and Leonardo da Vinci. Of minor matters not fewer than forty mechanical inventions have been attributed to him. Among these are the endless screw, the screw pump, a hydraulic organ, and burning mirrors. His genius is well indicated by the saying popularly attributed to him, "Give me whereon to stand, and I will move the earth," and by the anecdotes told of his exertions against Marcellus during the siege of Syracuse; his invention of catapults and other engines for throwing projectiles, as darts and heavy stones; claws which, reaching over the walls, lifted up into the air ships and their crews, and then suddenly dropped them into the sea; burning mirrors, by which, at a great distance, the Roman fleet was set on fire. It is related that Marcellus, honouring his intellect, gave the strictest orders that no harm should be done to him at the taking of the town, and that he was killed, unfortunately, by an ignorant soldier—unfortunately, for Europe was not able to produce his equal for nearly two thousand years.

The writings and works of Eratosthenes.

Eratosthenes was contemporary with Archimedes. He was born at Cyrene, B.C. 276. The care of the library appears to have been committed to him by Euergetes; but his attention was more specially directed to mathematical, astronomical, geographical, and historical pursuits. The work entitled "Catasterisms," doubtfully imputed to him, is a catalogue of 475 of the principal stars; but it was probably intended for nothing more than a manual. He also is said to have written a poem upon terrestrial zones. Among his important geographical labours may be mentioned his determination of the interval between the tropics. He found it to be eleven eighty-thirds of the circumference. He also attempted the measurement of the size of the earth by ascertaining the distance between Alexandria and Syene, the difference of latitude between which he had found to be one-fiftieth of the earth's circumference. It was his object to free geography from the legends with which the superstition of ages had adorned and oppressed it. In effecting this he well deserves the tribute paid to him by Humboldt, the modern who of all others could best appreciate his labours. He considered the articulation and expansion of continents; the position of mountain chains; the action of clouds; the geological submersion of lands; the elevation of ancient sea-beds; the opening of the Dardanelles and of the Straits of Gibraltar; the relations of the Euxine Sea; the problem of the equal level of the circumfluous ocean; and the necessary existence of a mountain chain running through Asia in the diaphragm of Dicæarchus. What an advance is all this beyond the meditations of Thales! Herein we see the practical tendencies of the Macedonian wars. In his astronomical observations he had the advantage of using the armils and other instruments in the Observatory. He ascertained that the direction of terrestrial gravity is not constant, but that the verticals converge. He composed a complete systematic description of the earth in three books—physical, mathematical, historical—accompanied by a map of all the parts then known. Of his skill as a geometer, his solution of the problem of two mean proportionals, still extant, offers ample evidence; and it is only of late years that the fragments remaining of his Chronicles of the Theban Kings have been properly appreciated. He hoped to free history as well as geography from the myths that deform it, a task which the prejudices and interests of man will never permit to be accomplished. Some amusing anecdotes of his opinions in these respects have descended to us. He ventured to doubt the historical truth of the Homeric legends. "I will believe in it when I have been shown the currier who made the wind-bags which Ulysses on his homeward voyage received from Æolus." It is said that, having attained the age of eighty years, he became weary of life, and put an end to himself by voluntary starvation.

Chronology of Eratosthenes.

I shall here pause to make a few remarks suggested by the chronological and astronomical works of Eratosthenes. Our current chronology was the offspring of erroneous theological considerations, the nature of which required not only a short historical term for the various nations of antiquity, but even for the existence of man upon the globe. This necessity appears to have been chiefly experienced in the attempt to exalt certain facts in the history of the Hebrews from their subordinate position in human affairs, and, indeed, to give the whole of that history an exaggerated value. This was done in a double way: by elevating Hebrew history from its true grade, and depreciating or falsifying that of other nations. Among those who have been guilty of this literary offence, the name of the celebrated Eusebius, the Bishop of Cæsarea in the time of Constantine, should be designated, since in his chronography and synchronal tables he purposely "perverted chronology for the sake of making synchronisms" (Bunsen). It is true, as Niebuhr asserts, "He is a very dishonest writer." To a great extent, the superseding of the Egyptian annals was brought about by his influence. It was forgotten, however, that of all things chronology is the least suited to be an object of inspiration; and that, though men may be wholly indifferent to truth for its own sake, and consider it not improper to wrest it unscrupulously to what they may suppose to be a just purpose, yet that it will vindicate itself at last. It is impossible to succeed completely in perverting the history of a nation which has left numerous enduring records. Egypt offers us testimonials reaching over five thousand years. As Bunsen remarks, from the known portion of the curve of history we may determine the whole. The Egyptians, old as they are, belong to the middle ages of mankind, for there is a period antecedent to monumental history, or indeed, to history of any kind, during which language and mythology are formed, for these must exist prior to all political institutions, all art, all science. Even at the first moment that we gain a glimpse of the state of Egypt she had attained a high intellectual condition, as is proved by the fact that her system of hieroglyphics was perfected before the fourth dynasty. It continued unchanged until the time of Psammetichus. A stationary condition of language and writing for thousands of years necessarily implies a long and very remote period of active improvement and advance. It was doubtless such a general consideration, rather than a positive knowledge of the fact, which led the Greeks to assert that the introduction of geometry into Egypt must be attributed to kings before the times of Menes. Not alone do her artificial monuments attest for that country an extreme antiquity; she is herself her own witness; for, though the Nile raises its bed only four feet in a thousand years, all the alluvial portion of Egypt has been deposited from the waters of that river. A natural register thus re-enforces the written records, and both together compose a body of evidence not to be gainsaid. Thus the depth of muddy silt accumulated round the pedestals of monuments is an irreproachable index of their age. In the eminent position he occupied, Eusebius might succeed in perverting the received book-chronology; but he had no power to make the endless trade-wind that sweeps over the tropical Pacific blow a day more or a day less; none to change the weight of water precipitated from it by the African mountains; none to arrest the annual mass of mud brought down by the river. It is by collating such different orders of evidence together—the natural and the monumental, the latter gaining strength every year from the cultivation of hieroglyphic studies—that we begin to discern the true Egyptian chronology, and to put confidence in the fragments that remain of Eratosthenes and Manetho.

At the time of which we are speaking—the time of Eratosthenes—general ideas had been attained to respecting the doctrine of the sphere, its poles, axis, the equator, arctic and antarctic circles, equinoctial points, solstices, colures, horizon, etc. No one competent to form an opinion any longer entertained a doubt respecting the globular form of the earth, the arguments adduced in support of that fact being such as are still popularly resorted to—the different positions of the horizon at different places, the changes in elevation of the pole, the phenomena of eclipses, and the gradual disappearance of ships as they sail from us. As to eclipses, once looked upon with superstitious awe, their true causes had not only been assigned, but their periodicities so well ascertained that predictions of their occurrence could be made. The Babylonians had thus long known that after a cycle of 223 lunations the eclipses of the moon return. The mechanism of the phases of that satellite was clearly understood. Indeed, Aristarchus of Samos attempted to ascertain the distance of the sun from the earth on the principle of observing the moon when she is dichotomized, a method quite significant of the knowledge of the time, though in practice untrustworthy; Aristarchus thus finding that the sun's distance is eighteen times that of the moon, whereas it is in reality 400. In like manner, in a general way, pretty clear notions were entertained of the climatic distribution of heat upon the earth, exaggerated, however, in this respect, that the torrid zone was believed to be too hot for human life, and the frigid too cold. Observations, as good as could be made by simple instruments,

Astronomy of Eratosthenes.

Attempts of Aristarchus to find the distance of the sun.

had not only demonstrated in a general manner the progressions, retrogradations and stations of the planets, but attempts had been made to account for, or rather to represent them, by the aid of epicycles.

It was thus in Alexandria, under the Ptolemies, that modern astronomy arose. Ptolemy Soter, the founder of this line of kings, was not only a patron of science, but likewise an author. He composed a history of the campaigns of Alexander. Under him the collection of the library was commenced, probably soon after the defeat of Antigonus at the battle of Ipsus, B.C. 301. The museum is due to his son Ptolemy Philadelphus, who not only patronized learning in his own dominions, but likewise endeavoured to extend the boundaries of human knowledge in other quarters. Thus he sent an expedition under his admiral Timosthenes as far as Madagascar. Of the succeeding Ptolemies, Euergetes and Philopator were both very able men, though the later was a bad one; he murdered his father, and perpetrated many horrors in Alexandria. Epiphanes, succeeding his father when only five years old, was placed by his guardians under the protection of Rome, thus furnishing to the ambitious republic a pretence for interfering in the affairs of Egypt. The same policy was continued during the reign of his son Philometor, who, upon the whole, was an able and good king. Even Physcon, who succeeded in B.C. 146, and who is described as sensual, corpulent, and cruel—cruel, for he cut off the head, hands, and feet of his son, and sent them to Cleopatra his wife—could not resist the inspirations to which the policy of his ancestors, continued for nearly two centuries, had given birth, but was an effective promoter of literature and the arts, and himself the author of an historical work. A like inclination was displayed by his successors, Lathyrus and Auletes, the name of the latter indicating his proficiency in music. The surnames under which all these Ptolemies pass were nicknames, or titles of derision imposed upon them by their giddy and satirical Alexandrian subjects. The political state of Alexandria was significantly said to be a tyranny tempered by ridicule. The dynasty ended in the person of the celebrated Cleopatra, who, after the

Biography of the Ptolemies.

battle of Actium, caused herself, as is related in the legends, to be bitten by an asp. She took poison that she might not fall captive to Octavianus, and be led in his triumph through the streets of Rome.

If we possessed a complete and unbiassed history of these Greek kings, it would doubtless uphold their title to be regarded as the most illustrious of all ancient sovereigns. Even after their political power had passed into the hands of the Romans—a nation who had no regard to truth and to right—and philosophy, in its old age, had become extinguished or eclipsed by the faith of the later Cæsars, enforced by an unscrupulous use of their power, so strong was the vitality of the intellectual germ they had fostered, that, though compelled to lie dormant for centuries, it shot up vigorously on the first occasion that favouring circumstances allowed.

This Egyptian dynasty extended its protection and patronage to literature as well as to science. Thus Philadelphus did not consider it beneath him to count among his personal friends the poet Callimachus, who had written a treatise on birds, and honourably maintained himself by keeping a school in Alexandria. The court of that sovereign was, moreover, adorned by a constellation of seven poets, to which the gay Alexandrians gave the nickname of the Pleiades. They are said to have been Lycophron, Theocritus, Callimachus, Aratus, Apollonius Rhodius, Nicander, and Homer the son of Macro. Among them may be distinguished Lycophron, whose work, entitled Cassandra, still remains; and Theocritus, whose exquisite bucolics prove how sweet a poet he was.

They patronize literature as well as science.

To return to the scientific movement. The school of Euclid was worthily represented in the time of Euergetes by Apollonius Pergæus, forty years later than Archimedes. He excelled both in the mathematical and physical department. His chief work was a treatise on Conic Sections. It is said that he was the first to introduce the words ellipse and hyperbola. So late as the eleventh century his complete works were extant in Arabic. Modern geometers describe him as handling his subjects with less power than his great predecessor

The writings of Apollonius.

Archimedes, but nevertheless displaying extreme precision and beauty in his methods. His fifth book, on Maxima and Minima, is to be regarded as one of the highest efforts of Greek geometry. As an example of his physical inquiries may be mentioned his invention of a clock.

Fifty years after Apollonius, B.C. 160–125, we meet with the great astronomer Hipparchus. He does not appear to have made observations himself in Alexandria, but he uses those of Aristyllus and Timochares of that place. Indeed, his great discovery of the precession of the equinoxes was essentially founded on the discussion of the Alexandrian observations on Spica Virginis made by Timochares. In pure mathematics he gave methods for solving all triangles plane and spherical: he also constructed a table of chords. In astronomy, besides his capital discovery of the precession of the equinoxes just mentioned, he also determined the first inequality of the moon, the equation of the centre, and all but anticipated Ptolemy in the discovery of the evection. To him also must be attributed the establishment of the theory of epicycles and eccentrics, a geometrical conception for the purpose of resolving the apparent motions of the heavenly bodies, on the principle of circular movement. In the case of the sun and moon, Hipparchus succeeded in the application of that theory, and indicated that it might be adapted to the planets. Though never intended as a representation of the actual motions of the heavenly bodies, it maintained its ground until the era of Kepler and Newton, when the heliocentric doctrine, and that of elliptic motions, were incontestably established. Even Newton himself, in the 37th proposition of the third book of the "Principia," availed himself of its aid. Hipparchus also undertook to make a register of the stars by the method of alineations—that is, by indicating those which were in the same apparent straight line. The number of stars catalogued by him was 1,080. If he thus depicted the aspect of the sky for his times, he also endeavoured to do the same for the surface of the earth by marking the position of towns and other places by lines of latitude and longitude.

The writings of Hipparchus.

The theory of epicycles and eccentrics.

Subsequently to Hipparchus, we find the astronomers Geminus and Cleomedes; their fame, however, is totally eclipsed by that of Ptolemy, A.D. 138, the author of the great work "Syntaxis," or the mathematical construction of the heavens—a work fully deserving the epithet which has been bestowed upon it, "a noble exposition of the mathematical theory of epicycles and eccentrics." It was translated by the Arabians after the Mohammedan conquest of Egypt; and, under the title of Almagest, was received by them as the highest authority on the mechanism and phenomena of the universe. It maintained its ground in Europe in the same eminent position for nearly fifteen hundred years, justifying the encomium of Synesius on the institution which gave it birth, "the divine school of Alexandria." The Almagest commences with the doctrine that the earth is globular and fixed in space; it describes the construction of a table of chords and instruments for observing the solstices, and deduces the obliquity of the ecliptic. It finds terrestrial latitudes by the gnomon; describes climates; shows how ordinary may be converted into sidereal time; gives reasons for preferring the tropical to the sidereal year; furnishes the solar theory on the principle of the sun's orbit being a simple eccentric; explains the equation of time; advances to the discussion of the motions of the moon; treats of the first inequality, of her eclipses, and the motion of the node. It then gives Ptolemy's own great discovery—that which has made his name immortal—the discovery of the moon's evection or second inequality, reducing it to the epicyclic theory. It attempts the determination of the distances of the sun and moon from the earth, with, however, only partial success, since it makes the sun's distance but one-twentieth of the real amount. It considers the precession of the equinoxes, the discovery of Hipparchus, the full period for which is twenty-five thousand years. It gives a catalogue of 1,022 stars; treats of the nature of the Milky Way; and discusses, in the most masterly manner, the motions of the planets. This point constitutes Ptolemy's second claim to scientific fame. His determination of the planetary orbits was accomplished by comparing his own observations with those of former astronomers, especially with those of Timochares on Venus.

The writings of Ptolemy.

His great work: the mechanical construction of the heavens.

To Ptolemy we are also indebted for a work on Geography used in European schools as late as the fifteenth century. The known world to him was from the Canary Islands eastward to China, and from the equator northward to Caledonia. His maps, however, are very erroneous; for, in the attempt to make them correspond to the spherical figure of the earth, the longitudes are too much to the east; the Mediterranean Sea is twenty degrees too long. Ptolemy's determinations are, therefore, inferior in accuracy to those of his illustrious predecessor Eratosthenes, who made the distance from the sacred promontory in Spain to the eastern mouth of the Ganges to be seventy thousand stadia. Ptolemy also wrote on Optics, the Planisphere, and Astrology. It is not often given to an author to endure for so many ages; perhaps, indeed, few deserve it. The mechanism of the heavens, from his point of view, has however, been greatly misunderstood. Neither he nor Hipparchus ever intended that theory as anything more than a geometrical fiction. It is not to be regarded as a representation of the actual celestial motions. And, as might be expected, for such is the destiny of all unreal abstractions, the theory kept advancing in complexity as facts accumulated, and was on the point of becoming altogether unmanageable, when it was supplanted by the theory of universal gravitation, which has ever exhibited the inalienable attribute of a true theory—affording an explanation of every new fact as soon as it was discovered, without requiring to be burdened with new provisions, and prophetically foretelling phenemona which had not as yet been observed.

His geography.

From the time of the Ptolemies the scientific spirit of the Alexandrian school declined; for though such mathematicians as Theodosius, whose work on Spherical Geometry was greatly valued by the Arab geometers; and Pappus, whose mathematical collections, in eight books, still for the most part remain; and Theon, doubly celebrated for his geometrical attainments, and as being the father of the unfortunate Hypatia, A.D. 415, lived in the next three centuries, they were not men like their great predecessors. That mental strength which gives birth to original discovery had passed away.

The later Alexandrian geometers.

The commentator had succeeded to the philosopher. No new development illustrated the physical sciences; they were destined long to remain stationary. Mechanics could boast of no trophy like the proposition of Archimedes on the equilibrium of the lever; no new and exact ideas like those of the same great man on statical and hydrostatical pressure; no novel and clear views like those developed in his treatise on floating bodies; no mechanical invention like the first of all steam-engines—that of Hero. Natural Philosophy had come to a stop. Its great, and hitherto successfully cultivated department, Astronomy, exhibited no farther advance. Men were content with what had been done, and continued to amuse themselves with reconciling the celestial phenomena to a combination of equable circular motions. To what are we to attribute this pause? Something had occurred to enervate the spirit of science. A gloom had settled on the Museum.

Decline of the Greek age of Reason.

There is no difficulty in giving an explanation of this unfortunate condition. Greek intellectual life had passed the period of its maturity, and was entering on old age. Moreover, the talent which might have been devoted to the service of science was in part allured to another pursuit, and in part repressed. Alexandria had sapped Athens, and in her turn Alexandria was sapped by Rome. From metropolitan pre-eminence she had sunk to be a mere provincial town. The great prizes of life were not so likely to be met with in such a declining city as in Italy or, subsequently, in Constantinople. Whatever affected these chief centres of Roman activity, necessarily influenced her; but, such is the fate of the conquered, she must await their decisions. In the very institutions by which she had once been glorified, success could only be attained by a conformity to the manner of thinking fashionable in the imperial metropolis, and the best that could be done was to seek distinction in the path so marked out. Yet even with all this restraint Alexandria asserted her intellectual power, leaving an indelible impress on the new theology of her conquerors. During three centuries the intellectual atmosphere of the Roman empire had been changing. Men were unable to resist the steadily increasing

Causes of that decline.

pressure. Tranquillity could only be secured by passiveness. Things had come to such a state that the thinking of men was to be done for them by others, or, if they thought at all, it must be in accordance with a prescribed formula or rule. Greek intellect was passing into decrepitude, and the moral condition of the European world was in antagonism to scientific progress.

CHAPTER VII.

THE GREEK AGE OF INTELLECTUAL DECREPITUDE.

THE DEATH OF GREEK PHILOSOPHY.

Decline of Greek Philosophy: it becomes Retrospective, and in Philo the Jew and Apollonius of Tyana leans on Inspiration, Mysticism, Miracles.
NEO-PLATONISM *founded by Ammonius Saccas, followed by Plotinus, Porphyry, Iamblicus, Proclus.—The Alexandrian Trinity.—Ecstasy. —Alliance with Magic, Necromancy.*
The Emperor Justinian closes the philosophical Schools.
Summary of Greek Philosophy.—Its four Problems: 1. Origin of the World; 2. Nature of the Soul; 3. Existence of God; 4. Criterion of Truth.—Solution of these Problems in the Age of Inquiry—in that of Faith—in that of Reason—in that of Decrepitude.
Determination of the Law of Variation of Greek Opinion.—The Development of National Intellect is the same as that of Individual.
Determination of the final Conclusions of Greek Philosophy as to God, the World, the Soul, the Criterion of Truth.—Illustrations and Criticisms on each of these Points.

Decline of Greek philosophy.

IN this chapter it is a melancholy picture that I have to present—the old age and death of Greek philosophy. The strong man of Aristotelism and Stoicism is sinking into the superannuated dotard; he is settling

"Into the lean and slipper'd pantaloon,
With spectacles on nose and pouch on side;
His youthful hose, well saved, a world too wide
For his shrunk shank; and his big manly voice,
Turning again toward childish treble, pipes
And whistles in his sound. Last scene of all,
That ends this strange, eventful history,
Is second childishness and mere oblivion—
Sans teeth, sans eyes, sans taste, sans everything."

He is full of admiration for the past and of contemptuous disgust at the present; his thoughts are wandering to the things that occupied him in his youth, and even in his infancy. Like those who are ready to die, he delivers himself up to religious preparation, without any farther concern whether the things on which he is depending are intrinsically true or false.

In this, the closing scene, no more do we find the vivid faith of Plato, the mature intellect of Aristotle, the manly self-control of Zeno. Greek philosophy is ending in garrulity and mysticism. It is leaning for help on the conjurer, juggler, and high-priest of Nature.

There are also new-comers obtruding themselves on the stage. The Roman soldier is about to take the place of the Greek thinker, and assert his claim to the effects of the intestate—to keep what suits him, and to destroy what he pleases. The Romans, advancing towards their age of Faith, are about to force their ideas on the European world.

Under the shadow of the Pyramids Greek philosophy was born; after many wanderings for a thousand years round the shores of the Mediterranean, it came back to its native place, and under the shadow of the Pyramids it died.

From the period of the New Academy the decline of Greek philosophy was uninterrupted. Inventive genius no longer existed; its place was occupied by the commentator. Instead of troubling themselves with inquiries

It becomes retrospective.

after absolute truth, philosophers sought support in the opinions of the ancient times, and the real or imputed views of Pythagoras, Plato, or Aristotle were received as a criterion. In this, the old age of philosophy, men began to act as though there had never been such things as original investigation and discovery among the human race, and that whatever truth there was in the world was not the product of thought, but the remains of an ancient and now all but forgotten revelation from heaven—forgotten through the guilt and fall of man. There is something very melancholy in this total cessation of inquiry. The mental impetus, which one would have expected to continue for a season by reason of the momentum that had been gathered in so many ages, seems to have been all at once abruptly lost. So complete a pause is surprising: the arrow still flies on after it has parted from the bow; the potter's wheel runs round though all the vessels are finished. In producing this sudden stoppage, the policy of the early Cæsars greatly assisted. The principle of liberty of thought, which the very existence of the divers philosophical schools necessarily implied, was too liable to make itself manifest in aspirations for political liberty. While through the emperors the schools of Greece, of Alexandria, and Rome were depressed from that supremacy to which they might have aspired, and those of the provinces, as Marseilles and Rhodes, were relatively exalted, the former, in a silent and private way, were commencing those rivalries, the forerunners of the great theological struggles between them in after ages for political power. Christianity in its dawn was attended by a general belief that in the East there had been preserved a purer recollection of the ancient revelation, and that hence from that quarter the light would presently shine forth. Under the favouring influence of such an expectation, Orientalism, to which, as we have seen, Grecian thought had spontaneously arrived, was greatly re-enforced.

Has arrived at Oriental ideas.

In this final period of Greek philosophy, the first to whom we must turn is Philo the Jew, who lived in the time of the Emperor Caligula. In harmony with the ideas of his nation, he derives all philosophy and useful knowledge from the Mosaic record, not hesitating to wrest Scripture to his use by various allegorical interpretations, asserting that man has fallen from his primitive wisdom and purity; that physical inquiry is of very little avail, but that an innocent life and a burning faith are what we must trust to. He persuaded himself that a certain inspiration fell upon him while he was in the act of writing, somewhat like that of the penmen of the Holy Scriptures. His readers may, however, be disposed to believe that herein he was self-deceived, judging both from the character of his composition and the nature of his doctrine. As

Philo the Jew thinks he is inspired.

respects the former, he writes feebly, is vacillating in his views, and, when watched in his treatment of a difficult point, is seen to be wavering and unsteady. As respects the latter, among other extraordinary things he teaches that the world is the chief angel or first son of God; he combines all the powers of God into one force, the Logos or holy Word, the highest powers being creative wisdom and governing mercy. From this are emitted all the mundane forces; and, since God cannot do evil, the existence of evil in the world must be imputed to these emanating forces. It is very clear, therefore, that though Philo declined Oriental pantheism, he laid his foundation on the Oriental theory of Emanation.

His mystical philosophy.

As aiding very greatly in the popular introduction of Orientalism, Apollonius of Tyana must be mentioned. Under the auspices of the Empress Julia Domna, in a biographical composition, Philostratus had the audacity to institute a parallel between this man and our Saviour. He was a miracle-worker, given to soothsaying and prophesying, led the life of an ascetic, his raiment and food being of the poorest. He attempted a reformation of religious rites and morals; denied the efficacy of sacrifice, substituting for it a simple worship and a pure prayer, scarce even needing words. He condemned the poets for propagating immoral fables of the gods, since they had thereby brought impurity into religion. He maintained the doctrine of transmigration.

Apollonius of Tyana.

Is a miracle-worker and prophet.

Plutarch, whose time reaches to the Emperor Hadrian, has exercised an influence, through certain peculiarities of his style, which has extended even to us. As a philosopher he is to be classed among the Platonists, yet with a predominance of the prevailing Orientalism. His mental peculiarities seem to have unfitted him for an acceptance of the national faith, and his works commend themselves rather by the pleasant manner in which he deals with the topic on which he treats than by a deep philosophy. In some respects an analogy may be discerned between his views and those of Philo, the Isis of the one corresponding to the Word of the other. This disposition to Orientalism occurs still

Plutarch leans to patronizing Orientalism.

more strongly in succeeding writers; for example, Lucius Apuleius the Numidian, and Numenius: the latter embracing the opinion that had now become almost universal—that all Greek philosophy was originally brought from the East. In his doctrine a trinity is assumed, the first person of which is reason; the second the principle of becoming, which is a dual existence, and so gives rise to a third person, these three persons constituting, however, only one God. Having indicated the occurrence of this idea, it is not necessary for us to inquire more particularly into its details. As philosophical conceptions, none of the trinities of the Greeks will bear comparison with those of ancient Egypt, Amun, Maut, and Khonso, Osiris, Isis, and Horus; nor with those of India, Brahma, Vishnu, and Siva, the Creator, Preserver, and Destroyer, or, the Past, the Present, and the Future of the Buddhists.

Numenius inclines to a trinitarian philosophy.

The doctrines of Numenius led directly to those of Neo-Platonism, of which, however, the origin is commonly imputed to Ammonius Saccas of Alexandria, toward the close of the second century after Christ. The views of this philosopher do not appear to have been committed to writing. They are known to us through his disciples Longinus and Plotinus chiefly. Neo-Platonism, assuming the aspect of a philosophical religion, is distinguished for the conflict it maintained with the rising power of Christianity. Alexandria was the scene of this contest. The school which there arose lasted for about 300 years. Its history is not only interesting to us from its antagonism to that new power which soon was to conquer the Western world, but also because it was the expiring effort of Grecian philosophy.

Ammonius Saccas founds Neo-Platonism.

Plotinus, an Egyptian, was born about A.D. 204. He studied at Alexandria, and is said to have spent eleven years under Ammonius Saccas. He accompanied the expedition of the Emperor Gordian to Persia and India, and, escaping from its disasters, opened a philosophical school in Rome. In that city he was held in the highest esteem by the Emperor Gallienus; the Empress Salonina intended to

Plotinus, a Mystic. Reunion with God.

build a city, in which Plotinus might inaugurate the celebrated Republic of Plato. The plan was not, however, carried out. With the best intention for promoting the happiness of man, Plotinus is to be charged with no little obscurity and mysticism. Eunapius says truly that the heavenly elevation of his mind and his perplexed style make him very tiresome and unpleasant. His repulsiveness is, perhaps, in a measure due to his want of skill in the art of composition, for he did not learn to write till he was fifty years old. He professed a contempt for the advantages of life and for its pursuits. He disparaged patriotism. An ascetic in his habits, eating no flesh and but little bread, he held his body in utter contempt, saying that it was only a phantom and a clog to his soul. He refused to remember his birthday. As has frequently been the case with those who have submitted to prolonged fasting and meditation, he believed that he had been privileged to see God with his bodily eye, and on six different occasions had been reunited to him. In such a mental condition, it may well be supposed that his writings are mysterious, inconsequent and diffuse. An air of Platonism mingled with many Oriental ideas and ancient Egyptian recollections, pervades his works.

Like many of his predecessors, Plotinus recognized a difference between the mental necessities of the educated and the vulgar, justifying mythology on the ground that it was very useful to those who were not yet emancipated from the sensible. Aristotle, in his Metaphysics, referring to mythology and the gods in human form, had remarked, "Much has been mythically added for the persuasion of the multitude, and also on account of the laws and for other useful ends." But Plotinus also held that the gods are not to be moved by prayer, and that both they and the dæmons occasionally manifest themselves visibly; that incantations may be lawfully practised, and are not repugnant to philosophy. In the body he discerns a penitential mechanism for the soul. He believes that the external world is a mere phantom—a dream—and the indications of the senses altogether deceptive. The union with the divinity of which he speaks he describes as an intoxication of the soul which, forgetting all external things, becomes lost in the contemplation of "the One." The doctrinal philosophy of Plotinus presents a trinity in accordance with the Platonic idea. (1.) The One, or Prime essence. (2.) The Reason. (3.) The Soul. Of the first he declares that it is impossibe to speak fully, and in what he says on this point there are many apparent contradictions, as when he denies oneness to the one. His ideas of the trinity are essentially based on the theory of emanation. He describes how the second principle issues by emanation out of the first, and the third out of the second. The mechanism of this process may be illustrated by recalling how from the body of the sun issues forth light, and from light emerges heat. In the procession of the third from the second principle it is really Thought arising from Reason; but Thought is the Soul. The mundane soul he considers as united to nothing; but on these details he falls into much mysticism, and it is often difficult to see clearly his precise meaning, as when he says that Reason is surrounded by Eternity, but the Soul is surrounded by Time. He carries Idealism to its last extreme, and, as has been said, looks upon the visible world as a semblance only, deducing from his doctrine moral reflections to be a comfort in the trials of life. Thus he says that "sensuous life is a mere stage-play; all the misery in it is only imaginary, all grief a mere cheat of the players." "The soul is not in the game; it looks on, while nothing more than the external phantom weeps and laments." "Passive affections and misery light only on the outward shadow of man." The great end of existence is to draw the soul from external things and fasten it in contemplation on God. Such considerations teach us a contempt for virtue as well as for vice: "Once united with God, man leaves the virtues, as on entering the sanctuary he leaves the images of the gods in the ante-temple behind." Hence we should struggle to free ourselves from everything low and mean: to cultivate truth, and devote life to intimate communion with God, divesting ourselves of all personality, and passing into the condition of ecstasy, in which the soul is loosened from its material prison, separated from individual consciousness,

The trinity of Plotinus.

Ecstasy; communion with the invisible.

and absorbed in the infinite intelligence from which it emanated. "In ecstasy it contemplates real existence; it identifies itself with that which it contemplates." Our reminiscence passes into intuition. In all these views of Plotinus the tincture of Orientalism predominates; the principles and practices are altogether Indian. The Supreme Being of the system is the "unus qui est omnia;" the intention of the theory of emanation is to find a philosophical connexion between him and the soul of man; the process for passing into ecstacy by sitting long in an invariable posture, by looking stedfastly at the tip of the nose, or by observing for a long time an unusual or definite manner of breathing, had been familiar to the Eastern devotees, as they are now to the impostors of our own times; the result is not celestial, but physiological. The pious Hindus were, however, assured that, as water will not wet the lotus, so, though sin may touch, it can never defile the soul after a full intuition of God.

Porphyry—his writings destroyed;

The opinions of Plotinus were strengthened and diffused by his celebrated pupil Porphyry, who was born at Tyre A.D. 233. After the death of Plotinus he established a school in Rome, attaining great celebrity in astronomy, music, geography, and other sciences. His treatise against Christianity was answered by Eusebius, St. Jerome, and others; the Emperor Theodosius the Great, however, silenced it more effectually by causing all the copies to be burned. Porphyry asserts his own unworthiness when compared with his master, saying that he had been united to God but once in eighty six years, whereas Plotinus had been so united six times in sixty years. In him is to be seen all the mysticism, and, it may be added, all the piety of Plotinus. He speaks of dæmons shapeless, and therefore invisible; requiring food, and not immortal; some of which rule the air, and may be propitated or restrained by magic: he admits also the use of necromancy. It is scarcely possible to determine how much this inclination of the Neo-Platonists to the unlawful art is to be regarded as a concession to the popular sentiment of the times, for elsewhere Porphyry does not hesitate to condemn soothsaying and divination, and to dwell upon the folly of

resorts to magic and necromancy.

invoking the gods in making bargains, marriages, and such-like trifles. He strenously enjoins a holy life in view of the fact that man has fallen both from his ancient purity and knowledge. He recommends a worship in silence and pure thought, the public worship being of very secondary importance. He also insists on an abstinence from animal food.

The cultivation of magic and the necromantic art was fully carried out in Iamblicus, a Cœlo-Syrian, who died in the reign of Constantine the Great. It is scarcely necessary to relate the miracles and prodigies he performed, though they received full credence in those superstitious times; how, by the intensity of his prayers, he raised himself unsupported nine feet above the ground; how he could make rays of a blinding effulgence play round his head; how, before the bodily eyes of his pupils, he evoked two visible dæmonish imps. Nor is it necessary to mention the opinions of Ædesius, Chrysanthus, or Maximus.

Iamblicus a wonder-worker.

For a moment, however, we may turn to Proclus, who was born in Constantinople A.D. 412. When Vitalian laid siege to Constantinople, Proclus is said to have burned his ships with a polished brass mirror. It is scarcely possible for us to determine how much truth there is in this, since similar authority affirms that he could produce rain and earthquakes. His theurgic propensities are therefore quite distinct. Yet, notwithstanding these superhuman powers, together with special favours displayed to him by Apollo, Athene, and other divinities, he found it expedient to cultivate his rites in secret, in terror of persecution by the Christians, whose attention he had drawn upon himself by writing a work in opposition to them. Eventually they succeeded in expelling him from Athens, thereby teaching him a new intrepretation of the moral maxim he had adopted, "Live concealed." It was the aim of Proclus to construct a complete theology, which should include the theory of emanation, and be duly embellished with mysticism. The Orphic poems and Chaldæan oracles were the basis upon which he commenced; his character may be understood from the dignity he assumed as "high priest of

Proclus unites emanation with mysticism.

the universe" He recommended to his disciples the study of Aristotle for the sake of cultivating the reason, but enjoined that of Plato, whose works he found to be full of sublime allegories suited to his purpose. He asserted that to know one's own mind is to know the whole universe, and that that knowledge is imparted to us by revelations and illuminations of the gods.

He speculates on the manner in which absorption is to take place; whether the last form can pass at once into the primitive, or whether it is needful for it to resume, in a returning succession, the intervening states of its career. From such elevated ideas, considering the mystical manner in which they were treated, there was no other prospect for philosophy than to end as Neo-Platonism did under Damasius. The final days were approaching. The Emperor Justinian prohibited the teaching of philosophy, and closed its schools in Athens A.D. 529. Its last representatives, Damasius, Simplicius, and Isidorus, went as exiles to Persia, expecting to find a retreat under the protection of the great king, who boasted that he was a philosopher and a Platonist. Disappointed, they were fain to return to their native land; and it must be recorded to the honour of Chosroes that, in his treaty of peace with the Romans, he stipulated safety and toleration for these exiles, vainly hoping that they might cultivate their philosophy and practise their rites without molestation.

Justinian puts an end to philosophy.

So ends Greek philosophy. She is abandoned, and preparation made for crowning Faith in her stead. The inquiries of the Ionians, the reasoning of the Eleatics, the labours of Plato, of Aristotle, have sunk into mysticism and the art of the conjurer. As with the individual man, so with philosophy in its old age: when all else had failed it threw itself upon devotion, seeking consolation in the exercises of piety—a frame of mind in which it was ready to die. The whole period from the New Academy shows that the grand attempt, every year becoming more and more urgent, was to find a system which should be in harmony with that feeling of religious devotion into which the Roman empire had fallen—a feeling continually gathering force. An air of piety, though of a most delusive kind, had settled upon the whole pagan world.

From the long history of Greek philosophy presented in the foregoing pages, we turn, 1st, to an investigation of the manner of progress of the Greek mind; and, 2nd, to the results to which it attained.

Summary of Greek philosophy.

The period occupied by the events we have been considering extends over almost twelve centuries. It commences with Thales, B.C. 636, and ends A.D. 529.

1st. Greek philosophy commenced on the foundation of physical suggestions. Its first object was the determination of the origin and manner of production of the world. The basis upon which it rested was in its nature unsubstantial, for it included intrinsic errors due to imperfect and erroneous observations. It diminished the world and magnified man, accepting the apparent aspect of Nature as real, and regarding the earth as a flat surface, on which the sky was sustained like a dome. It limited the boundaries of the terrestrial plane to an insignificant extent, and asserted that it was the special and exclusive property of man. The stars and other heavenly bodies it looked upon as mere meteors or manifestations of fire. With superficial simplicity, it received the notions of absolute directions in space, up and down, above and below. In a like spirit is adopted, from the most general observation, the doctrine of four elements, those forms of substance naturally presented to us in a predominating quantity—earth, water, air, fire. From these slender beginnings it made its first attempt at a cosmogony, or theory of the mode of creation, by giving to one of these elements a predominance or superiority over the other three, and making them issue from it. With one teacher the primordial element was water; with another, air; with another, fire. Whether a genesis had thus taken place, or whether all four elements were coordinate and equal, the production of the world was of easy explanation; for, by calling in the aid of ordinary observation, which assures us that mud will sink to the bottom of water, that water will fall through air, that it is the apparent nature of fire to ascend, and, combining these illusory facts with the erroneous notion of up and down in space, the arrangement of the visible world became clear—

Age of Inquiry—Its solutions.

First problem. Origin of the world.

the earth down below, the water floating upon it, the air above, and, still higher, the region of fire. Thus it appears that the first inquiry made by European philosophy was, Whence and in what manner came the world?

The principles involved in the solution of this problem evidently led to a very important inference, at this early period betraying what was before long to become a serious point of dispute. It is natural for man to see in things around him visible tokens of divinity, continual providential dispensations. But in this, its very first act, Greek philosophy had evidently excluded God from his own world. This settling of the heavy, this ascending of the light, was altogether a purely physical affair; the limitless sea, the blue air, and the unnumbered shining stars, were set in their appropriate places, not at the pleasure or by the hand of God, but by innate properties of their own. Popular superstition was in some degree appeased by the localization of deities in the likeness of men in a starry Olympus above the sky, a region furnishing unsubstantial glories and a tranquil abode. And yet it is not possible to exclude altogether the spiritual from this world. The soul, ever active and ever thinking, asserts its kindred with the divine. What is that soul? Such was the second question propounded by Greek philosophy.

Its irreligious solution thereof.

A like course of superficial observation was resorted to in the solution of this inquiry. To breathe is to live; then the breath is the life. If we cease to breathe we die. Man only becomes a living soul when the breath of life enters his nostrils; he is a senseless and impassive form when the last breath is expired. In this life-giving principle, the air, must therefore exist all those noble qualities possessed by the soul. It must be the source from which all intellect arises, the store to which all intellect again returns. The philosophical school whose fundamental principle was that the air is the primordial element thus brought back the Deity into the world, though under a material form. Yet still it was in antagonism to the national polytheism, unless from that one god, the air, the many gods of Olympus arose.

Second problem. What is the soul?

Its material solution thereof.

But who is that one God? This is the third question put forth by Greek philosophy. Its answer betrays that in this, its beginning, it is tending to Pantheism,

Third problem. What is God?

In all these investigations the starting-point had been material conceptions, depending on the impressions or information of the senses. Whatever the conclusion arrived at, its correctness turned on the correctness of that information. When we put a little wine into a measure of water, the eye may no longer see it, but the wine is there. When a rain-drop falls on the leaves of a distant forest, we cannot hear it, but the murmur of many drops composing a shower is audible enough. But what is that murmur except the sum of the sounds of all the individual drops?

And so it is plain our senses are prone to deceive us. Hence arises the fourth great question of Greek philosophy: Have we any criterion of truth?

Fourth problem. Has man a criterion of truth?

The moment a suspicion that we have not crosses the mind of man, he realizes what may be truly termed intellectual despair. Is this world an illusion, a phantasm of the imagination? If things material and tangible, and therefore the most solid props of knowledge, are thus abruptly destroyed, in what direction shall we turn? Within a single century Greek philosophy had come to this pass, and it was not without reason that intelligent men looked on Pythagoras almost as a divinity upon earth when he pointed out to them a path of escape; when he bid them reflect on what it was that had thus taught them the fallibility of sense. For what is it but reason that has been thus warning us, and, in the midst of delusions, has guided us to the truth—reason, which has objects of her own, a world of her own? Though the visible and audible may deceive, we may nevertheless find absolute truth in things altogether separate from material nature, particularly in the relations of numbers and properties of geometrical forms. There is no illusion in this, that two added to two make four; or in this, that any two sides of a triangle taken together are greater than the third. If, then, we are living in a region

Importance of the views of Pythagoras.

of deceptions, we may rest assured that it is surrounded by a world of truth.

Influence of the Eleatic school and the Sophists.

From the material basis speculative philosophy gradually disengaged itself through the labours of the Eleatic school, the controversy as to the primary element receding into insignificance, and being replaced by investigations as to Time, Motion, Space, Thought, Being, God. The general result of these inquiries brought into prominence the suspicion of the untrustworthiness of the senses, the tendency of the whole period being manifested in the hypothesis at last attained, that atoms and space alone exist; and, since the former are mere centres of force, matter is necessarily a phantasm. When, therefore, the Athenians themselves commenced the cultivation of philosophy, it was with full participation in the doubt and uncertainty thus overspreading the whole subject. As Sophists, their action closed this speculative period, for, by a comparison of all the partial sciences thus far known, they arrived at the conclusion that there is no conscience, no good or evil, no philosophy, no religion, no law, no criterion of truth.

Age of faith—its solutions.

But man cannot live without some guiding rule. If his speculations in Nature will yield him nothing on which he may rely, he will seek some other aid. If there be no criterion of truth for him in philosophy, he will lean on implicit, unquestioning faith. If he cannot prove by physical arguments the existence of God, he will, with Socrates, accept that great fact as self evident and needing no demonstration. He will, in like manner, take his stand upon the undeniable advantages of virtue and good morals, defending the doctrine that pleasure should be the object of life—pleasure of that pure kind which flows from a cultivation of ennobling pursuits, or instinctive, as exhibited in the life of brutes. But when he has thus cast aside demonstration as needless for his purposes, and put his reliance in this manner on faith, he has lost the restraining, the guiding principle that can set bounds to his conduct. If he considers, with Socrates, who opens the third age of Greek development—its age of faith—the existence of God as not needing any proof, he may, in like manner, add thereto the existence of matter and ideas. To faith there will be no difficulty in such doctrines as those of Reminiscence, the double immortality of the soul, the actual existence of universals; and, if such faith, unrestrained and unrestricted, be directed to the regulation of personal life, there is nothing to prevent a falling into excess and base egoism. For ethics, in such an application, ends either in the attempt at the procurement of extreme personal sanctity or the obtaining of individual pleasure—the foundation of patriotism is sapped, the sentiment of friendship is destroyed. So it was with the period of Grecian faith inaugurated by Socrates, developed by Plato, and closed by the Sceptics. Antisthenes and Diogenes of Sinope, in their outrages on society and their self-mortifications, show to what end a period of faith, unrestrained by reason, will come; and Epicurus demonstrated its tendency when guided by self.

Its continuation by Plato, and its end by the Sceptics.

Thus closes the third period of Greek philosophical development.

In introducing us to a fourth, Aristotle insists that, though we must rely on reason, Reason itself must submit to be guided by Experience; and Zeno, taking up the same thought, teaches us that we must appeal to the decisions of common sense. He disposes of all doubt respecting the criterion of truth by proclaiming that the distinctness of our sensuous impressions is a sufficient guide. In all this, the essential condition involved is altogether different from that of the speculative ages, and also of the age of faith. Yet, though under the ostensible guidance of reason, the human mind ever seeks to burst through such self-imposed restraints, attempting to ascertain things for which it possesses no suitable data. Even in the age of Aristotle, the age of Reason in Greece, philosophy resumed such questions as those of the creation of the world, the emanation of matter from God, the existence and nature of evil, the immortality, or, alas! it might perhaps be more truly said, judging from its conclusions, the death of the soul, and this even after the Sceptics had, with increased force, denied that we have any criterion of truth, and showed to their own satisfaction that man, at the best, can do nothing but doubt; and, in

Age of Reason —its solutions.

view of his condition here upon earth, since it has not been permitted him to know what is right and what is wrong, what is true and what is false, his wisest course is to give himself no concern about the matter, but tranquilly sink into a state of complete indifference and quietism.

How uniformly do we see that through such variations of opinion individual man approaches his end. For Greek philosophy, what other prospect was there but decrepitude, with its contempt for the present, its attachment to the past, its distrust of man, its reliance on the mysterious—the unknown? And this imbecility how plainly we witness before the scene finally is closed.

If now we look back upon this career of the Grecian mind, we find that after the legendary pre-historic period—the age of credulity—there came in succession an age of speculative inquiry, an age of faith, an age of reason, an age of decrepitude—the first, the age of credulity, was closed by geographical discovery; the second by the criticism of the Sophists; the third by the doubts of the Sceptics; the fourth, eminently distinguished by the greatness of its results, gradually declined into the fifth, an age of decrepitude, to which the hand of the Roman put an end. In the mental progress of this people we therefore discern the foreshadowing of a course like that of individual life, its epochs answering to Infancy, Childhood Youth, Manhood, Old Age; and which, on a still grander scale, as we shall hereafter find, has been repeated by all Europe in its intellectual development.

Duration of these ages.

In a space of 1150 years, ending about A.D. 529, the Greek mind had completed its philosophical career. The ages into which we have divided that course pass by insensible gradations into each other. They overlap and intermingle, like a gradation of colours, but the characteristics of each are perfectly distinct.

Boundaries of these ages.

2nd. Having thus determined the general law of the variation of opinions, that it is the same in this nation as in an individual, I shall next endeavour to disentangle the final results attained, considering Greek philosophy as a whole. To return to the illustration, to us more than an empty metaphor, though in individual life there is a successive

Determination of the law of variation of opinions.

passage through infancy, childhood, youth, and manhood to old age, a passage in which the characteristics of each period in their turn disappear, yet, nevertheless, there are certain results in another sense permanent, giving to the whole progress its proper individuality. A critical eye may discern in the successive stages of Greek philosophical development decisive and enduring results. These it is for which we have been searching in this long and tedious discussion.

Philosophical conclusions finally arrived at by the Greeks.

There are four grand topics in Greek philosophy: 1st, the existence and attributes of God; 2nd, the origin and destiny of the world; 3rd, the nature of the human soul; 4th, the possibility of a criterion of truth. I shall now present what appear to me to be the results at which the Greek mind arrived on each of these points.

(1.) Of the existence and attributes of God. On this point the decision of the Greek mind was the absolute rejection of all anthropomorphic conceptions, even at the risk of encountering the pressure of the national superstition. Of the all-powerful, all-perfect, and eternal there can be but one, for such attributes are absolutely opposed to anything like a participation, whether of a spiritual or material nature; and hence the conclusion that the universe itself is God, and that all animate and inanimate things belong to his essence. In him they live, and move, and have their being. It is conceivable that God may exist without the world, but it is inconceivable that the world should exist without God. We must not, however, permit ourselves to be deluded by the varied aspect of things; for, though the universe is thus God, we know it not as it really is, but only as it appears. God has no relations to space and time. They are only the fictions of our finite imagination.

As to God—His unity.

But this ultimate effort of the Greek mind is Pantheism. It is the same result which the more aged branch of the Indo-European family had long before reached. "There is no God independent of Nature; no other has been revealed by tradition, perceived by the sense, or demonstrated by argument."

But their solution is Pantheism.

Yet never will man be satisfied with such a conclusion. It offers him none of that aspect of personality which his yearnings demand. This infinite, and eternal, and universal is no intellect at all. It is passionless, without motive, without design. It does not answer to those lineaments of which he catches a glimpse when he considers the attributes of his own soul. He shudderingly turns from Pantheism, this final result of human philosophy, and, voluntarily retracing his steps, subordinates his reason to his instinctive feelings; declines the impersonal as having nothing in unison with him, and asserts a personal God, the Maker of the universe and the Father of men.

As to the world—a manifestation of God.

(2.) Of the origin and destiny of the world. In an examination of the results at which the Greek mind arrived on this topic, our labour is rendered much lighter by the assistance we receive from the decision of the preceding inquiry. The origin of all things is in God, of whom the world is only a visible manifestation. It is evolved by and from him, perhaps, as the Stoics delighted to say, as the plant is evolved by and from the vital germ in the seed. It is an emanation of him. On this point we may therefore accept as correct the general impression entertained by philosophers, Greek, Alexandrian, and Roman after the Christian era, that, at the bottom, the Greek and Oriental philosophies were alike, not only as respects the questions they proposed for solution, but also in the decisions they arrived at. As we have said, this impression led to the belief that there must have been in the remote past a revelation common to both, though subsequently obscured and vitiated by the infirmities and wickedness of man. This doctrine of emanation, reposing on the assertion that the world existed eternally in God, that it came forth into visibility from him, and will be hereafter absorbed into him, is one of the most striking features of Veda theology. It is developed with singular ability by the Indian philosophers as well as by the Greeks, and is illustrated by their poets.

This solution identical with the Oriental.

The following extract from the Institutes of Menu will convey the Oriental conclusion: "This universe existed only in the first divine idea, yet unexpanded, as if involved in darkness; imperceptible, undefinable, undiscoverable by reason, and undiscovered by revelation, as if it were wholly immersed in sleep. Then the sole self-existing power, himself undiscerned, but making this world discernible, with five elements and other principles of nature, appeared with undiminished glory, expanding his idea, or dispelling the gloom. He whom the mind alone can perceive, whose essence eludes the external organs, who has no visible parts, who exists from eternity—even He, the soul of all beings, whom no being can comprehend, shone forth in person. He, having willed to produce various beings from his own divine substance, first with a thought created the waters. The waters are so called (nárá) because they were the production of *Nara*, or the spirit of God; and, since they were his first *ayaná*, or place of motion, he thence is named Narayana, or moving on the waters. From that which is the first cause, not the object of sense existing everywhere in substance, not existing to our perception, without beginning or end, was produced the divine male. He framed the heaven above, the earth beneath, and in the midst placed the subtle ether, the light regions, and the permanent receptacle of waters. He framed all creatures. He gave being to time and the divisions of time—to the stars also and the planets. For the sake of distinguishing actions, he made a total difference between right and wrong. He whose powers are incomprehensible, having created this universe, was again absorbed in the spirit, changing the time of energy for the time of repose."

Illustrations of the origin, duration, and absorption of the world.

From such extracts from the sacred writings of the Hindus we might turn to their poets, and find the same conceptions of the emanation, manifestation, and absorption of the world illustrated. "The Infinite being is like the clear crystal, which receives into itself all the colours and emits them again, yet its transparency or purity is not thereby injured or impaired." "He is like the diamond, which absorbs the light surrounding it, and glows in the dark from the emanation thereof." In similes of a less noble nature they sought to convey their idea to the illiterate "Thou hast seen the spider spin his web, thou hast seen its excellent geometrical form, and how well adapted it is to its use; thou hast seen the play of tinted colours making it shine like a rainbow in the rays of the morning sun. From his bosom the little artificer drew forth the wonderful thread, and into his bosom, when it pleases him, he can withdraw it again. So Brahm made, and so will he absorb the world." In common the Greek and Indian asserted that being exists for the sake of thought, and hence they must be one; that the universe is a thought in the mind of God, and is unaffected by the vicissitudes of the worlds of which it is composed. In India this doctrine of emanation had reached such apparent precision that some asserted it was possible to demonstrate that the entire Brahm was not transmuted into mundane phenomena, but only a fourth part; that there occur successive emanations and absorptions, a periodicity in this respect being observed; that, in these considerations, we ought to guard ourselves from any deception arising from the visible appearance of material things, for there is reason to believe that matter is nothing more than forces filling space. Democritus raised us to the noble thought that, small as it is, a single atom may constitute a world.

The doctrine of Emanation has thus a double interpretation. It sets forth the universe either as a part of the substance of God, or as an unsubstantial something proceeding from him: the former a conception more tangible and readily grasped by the mind; the latter of unapproachable sublimity, when we recall the countless beautiful and majestic forms which Nature on all sides presents. This visible world is only the shadow of God.

In the further consideration of this doctrine of the issue forthcoming, or emanation of the universe from God, and its return into or absorption by him, an illustration may not be without value. Out of the air, which may be pure and tranquil, the watery vapour often comes forth in a visible form, a misty fleece, perhaps no larger than the hand of a man at first, but a great cloud in the end. The external appearance the forthcoming form presents is determined by the incidents of the times; it may have a pure whiteness or a threatening blackness; its edges may be fringed with gold. In the bosom of such a cloud the lightning may be pent up, from it the thunder may be heard; but, even if it should not offer these manifestations of power, if its disappearance should be as tranquil as its formation, it has not existed in vain. No cloud ever yet formed on the sky without leaving an imperishable impression on the earth, for while it yet existed there was not a plant whose growth was not delayed, whose substance was not lessened. And of such a cloud the production of which we have watched, how often has it happened to us to witness its melting away into the untroubled air. From the untroubled air it came, and to the pure untroubled air it has again returned.

Now such a cloud is made up of countless hosts of microscopic drops, each maintaining itself separate from the others, and each, small though it may be, having an individuality of its own. The grand aggregate may vary its colour and shape; it may be the scene of unceasing and rapid interior movements of many kinds, yet it presents its aspect unchanged, or changes tranquilly and silently, still glowing in the light that falls on it, still casting its shadow on the ground. It is an emblem of the universe according to the ancient doctrine, showing us how the visible may issue from the invisible, and return again thereto; that a drop too small for the unassisted eye to see may be the representative of a world. The spontaneous emergence and disappearance of a cloud is the emblem of a transitory universe issuing forth and disappearing, again to be succeeded by other universes, other like creations in the long lapse of time.

As to the soul—a part of the divinity.

(3.) Of the nature of the soul. From the material quality assigned to the soul by the early Ionian schools, as that it was air, fire, or the like, there was a gradual passage to the opinion of its immateriality. To this, precision was given by the assertion that it had not only an affinity with, but even is a part of God. Whatever were the views entertained of the nature and attributes of the Supreme Being, they directly influenced the conclusions arrived at respecting the nature of the soul.

Greek philosophy, in its highest state of development, regarded the soul as something more than the sum of the moments of thinking. It held it to be a portion of the

Deity himself. This doctrine is the necessary corollary of Pantheism. It contemplated a past eternity, a future immortality. It entered on such inquiries as whether the number of souls in the universe is constant. As upon the foregoing point, so upon this: there was a complete analogy beween the decision arrived at in Grecian and that in Indian philosophy. Thus the latter says, "I am myself an irradiated manifestation of the supreme BRAHM." "Never was there a time in which I was not, nor thou, nor these princes of the people, and never shall I not be; henceforth we all are." Viewing the soul as merely a spectator and stranger in this world, they regarded it as occupying itself rather in contemplation than in action, asserting that in its origin it is an immediate emanation from the Divinity—not a modification nor a transformation of the Supreme, but a portion of him; "its relation is not that of a servant to his master, but of a part to the whole." It is like a spark separated from a flame; it migrates from body to body, sometimes found in the higher, then in the lower, and again in the higher tribes of life, occupying first one, then another body, as circumstances demand. And, as a drop of water pursues a devious career in the cloud, in the rain, in the river, a part of a plant, or a part of an animal, but sooner or later inevitably finds its way back to the sea from which it came, so the soul, however various its fortunes may have been, sinks back at last into the divinity from which it emanated.

Its immortality and final absorption.

Both Greeks and Hindus turned their attention to the delusive phenomena of the world. Among the latter many figuratively supposed that what we call visible nature is a mere illusion befalling the soul, because of its temporary separation from God. In the Buddhist philosophy the world is thus held to be a creature of the imagination. But among some in those ancient, as among others in more modern times, it was looked upon as having a more substantial condition, and the soul as a passive mirror in which things reflected themselves, or perhaps it might, to some extent, be the partial creator of its own forms. However that may be, its final destiny is a perfect repose after its absorption in the Supreme.

On this third topic of ancient philosophy an illustration may not be without use. As a bubble floats upon the sea, and, by reason of its form, reflects whatever objects may be present, whether the clouds in the sky, or the stationary and moving things on the shore, nay, even to a certain extent depicts the sea itself on which it floats, and from which it arose, offering these various forms not only in shapes resembling the truth in the proper order of light and shade, the proper perspective, the proper colours, but, in addition thereto, tincturing them all with a play of hues arising from itself, so it is with the soul. From a boundless and unfathomable sea the bubble arose. It does not in any respect differ in nature from its source. From water it came, and mere water it ever is. It gathers its qualities, so far as external things are concerned, only from its form, and from the environment in which it is placed. As the circumstances to which it is exposed vary, it floats here and there, merging into other bubbles it meets, and emerging from the collected foam again. In such migrations it is now larger, now smaller; at one moment passing into new shapes, at another lost in a coalescence with those around it. But whatever these its migrations, these its vicissitudes, there awaits it an inevitable destiny, an absorption, a reincorporation with the ocean. In that final moment, what is it that is lost? what is it that has come to an end? Not the essential substance, for water it was before it was developed, water it was during its existence, and water it still remains, ready to be re-expanded.

Illustration of the nature of the soul.

Nor does the resemblance fail when we consider the general functions discharged while the bubble maintained its form. In it were depicted in their true shapes and relative magnitudes surrounding things. It hence had a relation to Space. And, if it was in motion, it reflected in succession the diverse objects as they passed by. Through such successive representations it maintained a relation to Time. Moreover, it imparted to the images it thus produced a coloration of its own, and in all this was an emblem of the Soul. For Space and Time are the outward conditions with which it is concerned, and it adds thereto abstract ideas, the product of its own nature.

But when the bubble bursts there is an end of all these relations. No longer is there any reflection of external forms, no longer any motion, no longer any innate qualities to add. In one respect the bubble is annihilated, in another it still exists. It has returned to that infinite expanse in comparison with which it is altogether insignificant and imperceptible. Transitory, and yet eternal: transitory, since all its relations of a special and individual kind have come to an end; eternal in a double sense—the sense of Platonism—since it was connected with a past of which there was no beginning, and continues in a future to which there is no end.

Its continued existence—its Nirwana.

(4.) Of the possibility of a criterion of truth. An absolute criterion of truth must at once accredit itself, as well as other things. At a very early period in philosophy the senses were detected as being altogether untrustworthy. On numberless occasions, instead of accrediting, they discredit themselves. A stick, having a spark of fire at one end, gives rise to the appearance of a circle of light when it is turned round quickly. The rainbow seems to be an actually existing arch until the delusion is detected by our going to the place over which it seems to rest. Nor is it alone as respects things for which there is an exterior basis or foundation, such as the spark of fire in one of these cases, and the drops of water in the other. Each of our organs of sense can palm off delusions of the most purely fictitious kind. The eye may present apparitions as distinct as the realities among which they place themselves; the ear may annoy us with the continual repetition of a murmuring sound, or parts of a musical strain, or articulate voices, though we well know that it is all a delusion; and in like manner, in their proper way, in times of health, and especially in those of sickness, will the other senses of taste, and touch, and smell practise upon us their deceptions.

As to the criterion of truth—sense-delusions.

This being the case, how shall we know that any information derived from such unfaithful sources is true? Pythagoras rendered a great service in telling us to remember that we have within ourselves a means of detecting fallacy and demonstrating truth. What is it that assures us of the unreality of the fiery circle, the rainbow, the spectre, the voices, the crawling of insects upon the skin? Is it not reason? To reason may we not then trust?

With such facts before us, what a crowd of inquiries at once presses upon our attention—inquiries which even in modern times have occupied the thoughts of the greatest metaphysicians. Shall we begin our studies by examining sensations or by examining ideas? Shall we say with Descartes that all clear ideas are true? Shall we inquire with Spinoza whether we have any ideas independent of experience? With Hobbes, shall we say that all our thoughts are begotten by and are the representatives of objects exterior to us; that our conceptions arise in material motions pressing on our organs, producing motion in them, and so affecting the mind; that our sensations do not correspond with outward qualities; that sound and noise belong to the bell and the air, and not to the mind, and, like colour, are only agitations occasioned by the object in the brain; that imagination is a conception gradually dying away after the act of sense, and is nothing more than a decaying sensation; that memory is the vestige of former impressions, enduring for a time; that forgetfulness is the obliteration of such vestiges; that the succession of thought is not indifferent, at random, or voluntary, but that thought follows thought in a determinate and predestined sequence; that whatever we imagine is finite, and hence we cannot conceive of the infinite, nor think of anything not subject to sense? Shall we say with Locke that there are two sources of our ideas, sensation and reflection; that the mind cannot know things directly, but only through ideas? Shall we suggest with Leibnitz that reflection is nothing more than attention to what is passing in the mind, and that between the mind and the body there is a sympathetic synchronism? With Berkeley shall we assert that there is no other reason for inferring the existence of matter itself than the necessity of having some synthesis for its attributes; that the objects of knowledge are ideas and nothing else; and that the mind is active in sensation? Shall we listen to the demonstration of Hume, that, if matter be an unreal

Uncertainties in philosophizing.

fiction, the mind is not less so, since it is no more than a succession of impressions and ideas; that our belief in causation is only the consequence of habit; and that we have better proof that night is the cause of day, than of thousands of other cases in which we persuade ourselves that we know the right relation of cause and effect; that from habit alone we believe the future will resemble the past? Shall we infer with Condillac that memory is only transformed sensation, and comparison double attention; that every idea for which we cannot find an exterior object is destitute of significance; that our innate ideas come by development, and that reasoning and running are learned together. With Kant shall we conclude that there is but one source of knowledge, the union of the object and the subject—but two elements thereof, space and time; and that they are forms of sensibility, space being a form of internal sensibility, and time both of internal and external, but neither of them having any objective reality; and that the world is not known to us as it is, but only as it appears?

I admit the truth of the remark of Posidonius that a man might as well be content to die as to cease philosophizing; for, if there are contradictions in philosophy, there are quite as many in life. In the light of this remark, I shall therefore not hesitate to offer a few sugges-

Remarks on the criterion.

tions respecting the criterion of human knowledge, undiscouraged by the fact that so many of the ablest men have turned their attention to it. In this there might seem to be presumption, were it not that the advance of the sciences, and especially of human physiology has brought us to a more elevated point of view, and enabled us to see the state of things much more distinctly than was possible for our predecessors.

Defective information of the old philosophy.

I think that the inability of ancient philosophers to furnish a true solution of this problem was altogether owing to the imperfect, and, indeed, erroneous idea they had of the position of man. They gave too much weight to his personal individuality. In the mature period of his life they regarded him as isolated, independent, and complete in himself. They forgot that this is only a momentary phase in his existence, which, commencing from small beginnings, exhibits a continuous expansion or progress. From a single cell, scarcely more than a step above the inorganic state, not differing, as we may infer both from the appearance it offers and the forms through which it runs in the earlier stages of life, from the cell out of which any other animal or plant, even the humblest, is derived, a passage is made through form after form in a manner absolutely depending upon surrounding physical conditions. The history is very long, and the forms are very numerous, between the first appearance of the primitive trace and the hoary aspect of seventy years. It is not correct to take one moment in this long procession and make it a representative of the whole. It is not correct to say, even if the body of the mature man undergoes unceasing changes to an extent implying the reception, incorporation, and dismissal of nearly a ton and a half of material in the course of a year, that in this flux of matter there is not only a permanence of form, but, what is of infinitely more importance, an unchangeableness in his intellectual powers. It is not correct to say this; indeed, it is wholly untrue. The intellectual principle passes forward in a career as clearly marked as that in which the body runs. Even if we overlook the time antecedent to birth, how complete is the imbecility of his early days! The light shines upon his eyes, he sees not; sounds fall upon his ear, he hears not. From these low beginnings we might describe the successive re-enforcements through infancy, childhood, and youth to maturity. And what is the result to which all this carries us? Is it not that, in the philosophical contemplation of man, we are constrained to reject the idea of personality, of individuality, and to adopt that of a cycle of progress; to abandon all contemplation of his mere substantial form, and consider his abstract relation? All organic forms, if compared together and examined from one common point of view, are found to be constructed upon an identical scheme. It is as in some mathematical expression containing constants and variables; the actual result changes accordingly as we assign successively different values to the variables, yet in those

Necessity of a more general conception as to man.

The whole cycle must be included.

different results, no matter how numerous they may be, the original formula always exists. From such a universal conception of the condition and career of man, we rise at once to the apprehension of his relations to others like himself—that is to say, his relations as a member of society. We perceive, in this light, that society must run a course the counterpart of that we have traced for the individual, and that the appearance of isolation presented by the individual is altogether illusory. Each individual man drew his life from another, and to another man he gives rise, losing, in point of fact, his aspect of individuality when these his race connexions are considered. One epoch in life is not all life. The mature individual cannot be disentangled from the multitudinous forms through which he has passed; and, considering the nature of his primitive conception and the issue of his reproduction, man cannot be separated from his race.

And also his race connexions.

By the aid of these views of the nature and relationship of man, we can come to a decision respecting his possession of a criterion of truth. In the earliest moments of his existence he can neither feel nor think, and the universe is to him as though it did not exist. Considering the progress of his sensational powers—his sight, hearing, touch, etc.—these, as his cycle advances to its maximum, become, by nature or by education, more and more perfect; but never, at the best, as the ancient philosophers well knew, are they trustworthy. And so of his intellectual powers. They, too, begin in feebleness and gradually expand. The mind alone is no more to be relied on than the organs of sense alone. If any doubt existed on this point, the study of the phenomena of dreaming is sufficient to remove it, for dreaming manifests to us how wavering and unsteady is the mind in its operations when it is detached from the solid support of the organs of sense. How true is the remark of Philo the Jew, that the mind is like the eye; for, though it may see all other objects, it cannot see itself, and therefore cannot judge of itself. And thus we may conclude that neither are the senses to be trusted alone, nor is the mind to be trusted alone. In the conjoint action of the two, by reason of the mutual checks established, a far higher degree of certainty is attained to, yet even in this, the utmost vouchsafed to the individual, there is not, as both Greeks and Indians ascertained, an absolute sureness. It was the knowledge of this which extorted from them so many melancholy complaints, which threw them into an intellectual despair, and made them, by applying the sad determination to which they had come to the course of their daily life, sink down into indifference and infidelity.

But yet there is something more in reserve for man. Let him cast off the clog of individuality, and remember that he has race connexions—connexions which, in this matter of a criterion of truth, indefinitely increase his chances of certainty, If he looks with contempt on the opinions of his childhood, with little consideration on those of his youth, with distrust on those of his manhood, what will he say about the opinions of his race? Do not such considerations teach us that, through all these successive conditions, the criterion of truth is ever advancing in precision and power, and that its maximum is found in the unanimous opinion of the whole human race?

Though no absolute criterion exists, a practical one does.

Upon these principles I believe that, though we have not philosophically speaking, any absolute criterion of truth, we rise by degrees to higher and higher certainties along an ascending scale which becomes more and more exact. I think that metaphysical writers who have treated of this point have been led into error from an imperfect conception of the true position of man; they have limited their thoughts to a single epoch of his course, and have not taken an enlarged and philosophical view. In thus declining the Oriental doctrine that the individual is the centre from which the universe should be regarded, and transferring our stand-point to a more comprehensive and solid foundation, we imitate, in metaphysics, the course of astronomy when it substituted the heliocentric for the geocentric point of view, and the change promises to be equally fertile in sure results. If it were worth while, we might proceed to enforce this doctrine by an appeal to the experience of ordinary life. How often, when we distrust our own judgment, do we seek support in the advice of a friend. How strong is our persuasion that we are in the right when public opinion is with us. For this even the Church has not disdained to call together Councils, aiming thereby at a surer means of arriving at the truth. The Council is more trustworthy than an individual, whoever he may be. The probabilities increase with the number of consenting intellects, and hence I come to the conclusion that in the unanimous consent of the entire human race lies the human criterion of truth—a criterion, in its turn, capable of increased precision with the diffusion of enlightenment and knowledge. For this reason, I do not look upon the prospects of humanity in so cheerless a light as they did of old. On the contrary, ever thing seems full of hope. Good auguries may be drawn for philosophy from the great mechanical and material inventions which multiply the means of intercommunication, and, it may be said, annihilate terrestrial distances. In the intellectual collisions that must ensue, in the melting down of opinions, in the examinations and analyses of nations, truth will come forth. Whatever cannot stand that ordeal must submit to its fate. Lies and imposture, no matter how powerfully sustained, must prepare to depart. In that supreme tribunal man may place implicit confidence. Even though, philosophically, it is far from absolute, it is the highest criterion vouchsafed to him, and from its decision he has no appeal.

The maximum of certainty in the human race.

In delivering thus emphatically my own views on this profound topic perhaps I do wrong. It is becoming to speak with humility on that which has been glorified by the great writers of Greece, of India, of Alexandria, and, in later times, of Europe.

In conclusion, I would remark that the view here presented of the results of Greek philosophy is that which offers itself to me after a long and careful study of the subject. It is, however, the affirmative, not the negative result; for we must not forget that if, on the one hand, the pantheistic doctrines of the Nature of God, Universal Animation, the theory of Emanation, Transmutation, Absorption, Transmigration, etc., were adopted, on

Complete analogy between Greek and Indian process of thought.

the other there was by no means an insignificant tendency to atheism and utter infidelity. Even of this negative state a corresponding condition occurred in the Buddhism of India, of which I have previously spoken; and, indeed, so complete is the parallel between the course of mental evolution in Asia and Europe, that it is difficult to designate a matter of minor detail in the philosophy of the one which cannot be pointed out in that of the other. It was not without reason, therefore, that the Alexandrian philosophers, who were profoundly initiated in the detail of both systems, came to the conclusion that such surprising coincidences could only be accounted for upon the admission that there had been an ancient revelation, the vestiges of which had descended to their time. In this, however, they judged erroneously; the true explanation consisting in the fact that the process of development of the intellect of man, and the final results to which he arrives in examining similar problems, are in all countries the same.

Variation of practical application explained.

It does not fall within my plan to trace the application of these philosophical principles to practice in daily life, yet the subject is of such boundless interest that perhaps the reader will excuse a single paragraph. It may seem to superficial observation that, whatever might be the doctrinal resemblances of these philosophies, their application was very different. In a general way, it may be asserted that the same doctrines which in India led to the inculcation of indifference and quietism, led to Stoic activity in Greece and Italy. If the occasion permitted, I could, nevertheless, demonstrate in this apparent divergence an actual coincidence; for the mode of life of man is chiefly determined by geographical conditions, his instinctive disposition to activity increasing with the latitude in which he lives. Under the equinoctial line he has no disposition for exertion, his physiological relations with the climate making quietism most agreeable to him. The philosophical formula which, in the hot plains of India, finds its issue in a life of tranquillity and repose, will be interpreted in the more bracing air of Europe by a life of activity. Thus, in later ages, the monk of Africa, willingly persuading himself that any intervention to improve Nature is a revolt against the providence of God, spent his worthless life in weaving baskets and mats, or in solitary meditation in the caves of the desert of Thebais; but the monk of Europe encountered the labours of agriculture and social activity, and thereby aided, in no insignificant manner, in the civilization of England, France, and Germany. These things, duly considered, lead to the conclusion that human life, in its diversities, is dependent upon and determined by primary conditions in all countries and climates essentially the same.

CHAPTER VIII.

DIGRESSION ON THE HISTORY AND PHILOSOPHICAL INFLUENCES OF ROME.

PREPARATION FOR RESUMING THE EXAMINATION OF THE INTELLECTUAL PROGRESS OF EUROPE.

Religious Ideas of the primitive Europeans.—The Form of their Variations is determined by the Influence of Rome.—Necessity of Roman History in these Investigations.

Rise and Development of Roman Power, its successive Phases, territorial Acquisitions.—Becomes Supreme in the Mediterranean.—Consequent Demoralization of Italy.—Irresistible Concentration of Power.—Development of Imperialism.—Eventual Extinction of the true Roman Race.

Effect on the intellectual, religious, and social Condition of the Mediterranean Countries.—Produces homogeneous Thought.—Imperialism prepares the Way for Monotheism.—Momentous Transition of the Roman World in its religious Ideas.

Opinions of the Roman Philosophers.—Coalescence of the new and old Ideas.—Seizure of Power by the Illiterate, and consequent Debasement of Christianity in Rome.

Transition from Greece to Europe.

FROM the exposition of the intellectual progress of Greece given in the preceding pages, we now turn, agreeably to the plan laid down, to an examination of that of all Europe. The movement in that single nation is typical of the movement of the entire continent.

European age of Inquiry.

The first European intellectual age—that of Credulity—has already, in part, been considered in Chapter II., more especially so far as Greece is concerned. I propose now, after some necessary remarks in conclusion of that topic, to enter on the description of the second European age—that of Inquiry.

For these remarks, what has already been said of Greece

prepares the way. Mediterranean Europe was philosophically and socially in advance of the central and northern countries. The wave of civilization passed from the south to the north; in truth, it has hardly yet reached its extreme limit. The adventurous emigrants who in remote times had come from Asia left to the successive generations of their descendants a legacy of hardship. In the struggle for life, all memory of an Oriental parentage was lost; knowledge died away; religious ideas became debased; and the diverse populations sank into the same intellectual condition that they would have presented had they been proper autochthons of the soil.

The religion of the barbarian Europeans was in many respects like that of the American Indians. They recognized a Great Spirit—ommiscient, omnipotent, omnipresent.

Religion of the old Europeans.

In the earliest times they made no representation of him under the human form, nor had they temples; but they propitiated him by sacrifices, offering animals, as the horse, and even men, upon rude altars. Though it was believed that this Great Spirit might sometimes be heard in the sounds of the forests at night, yet, for the most part, he was too far removed from human supplication, and hence arose, from the mere sorcerous ideas of a terrified fancy, as has been the case in so many other countries, star worship—the second stage of comparative theology. The gloom and shade of dense forests, a solitude that offers an air of sanctity, and seems a fitting resort for mysterious spirits, suggested the establishment of sacred groves and holy trees. Throughout Europe there was a confused idea that the soul exists after the death of the body; as to its particular state there was a diversity of belief. As among other people, also, the offices of religion were not only directed to the present benefit of individuals, but also to the discovery of future events by various processes of divination and augury practised among the priests.

Their priesthood,

Although the priests had thus charge of the religious rites, they do not seem to have been organized in such a manner as to be able to act with unanimity or to pursue a steady system of policy. A class of female religious officials—prophetesses—joined in the ceremonials

These holy women, who were held in very great esteem, prepared the way for the reception of Mariolatry. Instead of temples—rock-altars, cromlechs, and other rustic structures were used among the Celtic nations by the Druids, who were at the same time priests, magicians, and medicine-men. Their religious doctrines, which recall in many particulars those of the Rig-Veda, were perpetuated from generation to generation by the aid of songs.

The essential features of this system were its purely local form and its want of a well-organized hierarchy. Even the Celts offer no exception, though they had a subordination from the Arch-Druid downward. This was the reason of the weakness of the old faith and eventually the cause of its fall. When the German nations migrated to the south in their warlike expeditions, they left behind them their consecrated groves and sacred oaks, hallowed by immemorial ages. These objects the devotee could not carry with him, and no equivalent substitute could be obtained for them. In the civilized countries to which they came they met with a very different state of things; a priesthood thoroughly organized and modelled according to the ancient Roman political system; its objects of reverence tied to no particular locality; its institutions capable of universal action; its sacred writings easy of transportation anywhere; its emblems moveable to all countries—the cross on the standards of its armies, the crucifix on the bosom of its saints. In the midst of the noble architecture of Italy and the splendid remains of those Romans who had once given laws to the world, in the midst of a worship distinguished by the magnificence of its ceremonial and the solemnity of its mysteries, they found a people whose faith taught them to regard the present life as offering only a transitory occupation, and not for a moment to be weighed against the eternal existence hereafter—an existence very different from that of the base transmigration of Druidism or the Drunken Paradise of Woden, where the brave solace themselves with mead from cups made of the skulls of their enemies killed in their days upon earth.

and objects of adoration.

Influence of Roman Christianity upon them

The European age of inquiry is therefore essentially connected with Roman affairs. It is distinguished by the religious direction it took. In place of the dogmas of rival philosophical schools, we have now to deal with the tenets of conflicting sects. The whole history of those unhappy times displays the organizing and practical spirit characteristic of Rome. Greek democracy, tending to the decomposition of things, led to the Sophists and Sceptics. Roman imperialism, ever constructive, sought to bring unity out of discords, and draw the line between orthodoxy and heresy by the authority of councils like that of Nicea. Following the ideas of St. Augustine in his work, "The City of God," I adopt, as the most convenient termination of this age, the sack of Rome by Alaric. This makes it overlap the age of Faith, which had, as its unmistakable beginning, the foundation of Constantinople.

Importance of Roman history in this investigation.

Greek intellectual life displays all its phases completely, but not so was it with that of the Romans, who came to an untimely end. They were men of violence, who disappeared in consequence of their own conquests and crimes. The consumption of them by war bore, however, an insignificant proportion to that fatal diminution, that mortal adulteration occasioned by their merging in the vast mass of humanity with which they came in contact.

I approach the consideration of Roman affairs, which is thus the next portion of my task, with no little diffidence. It is hard to rise to a point of view sufficiently elevated and clear, where the extent of dominion is so great geographically, and the reasons of policy are obscured by the dimness and clouds of so many centuries. Living in a social state the origin of which is in the events now to be examined, our mental vision can hardly free itself from the illusions of historical perspective, or bring things into their just proportions and position. Of a thousand acts, all of surpassing interest and importance, how shall we identify the master ones? how shall we discern with correctness the true relation of the parts of this wonderful phenomenon of empire, the vanishing events of which glide like dissolving views into each other? Warned by the example of those who have permitted the shadows of their own imagination to fall upon the scene, and have mistaken them for a part of it, I

Great difficulty of treating it.

shall endeavour to apply the test of common sense to the facts of which it will be necessary to treat; and, believing that man has ever been the same in his modes of thought and motives of action, I shall judge of past occurrences in the same way as of those of our own times.

Triple form of Roman power.

In its entire form the Roman power consists of two theocracies, with a military domination intercalated. The first of these theocracies corresponds to the fabulous period of the kings; the military domination to the time of the republic and earlier Cæsars; the second theocracy to that of the Christian emperors and the Popes.

The first theocracy and legendary times.

The first theocracy is so enveloped in legends and fictions that it is impossible to give a satisfactory account of it. The biographies of the kings offer such undeniable evidence of being mere romances, that, since the time of Niebuhr, they have been received by historians in that light. But during the reigns of the pagan emperors it was not safe in Rome to insinuate publicly any disbelief in such honoured legends as those of the wolf that suckled the foundlings; the ascent of Romulus into heaven; the nymph Egeria; the duel of the Horatii and Curiatii; the leaping of Curtius into the gulf on his horse; the cutting of a flint with a razor by Tarquin; the Sibyl and her books. The modern historian has, therefore, only very little reliable material. He may admit that the Romans and Sabines coalesced; that they conquered the Albans and Latins; that thousands of the latter were transplanted to Mount Aventine and made plebeians; these movements being the origin of the castes which long afflicted Rome, the vanquished people constituting a subordinate class; that at first the chief occupation was agriculture, the nature of which is not only to accustom men to the gradations of rank, such as the proprietor of the land, the overseer, the labourer, but also to the cultivation of religious sentiment, and even the cherishing of superstition; that, besides the more honourable occupations in which the rising state was engaged, she had, from the beginning, indulged in aggressive war, and was therefore perpetually liable to reprisal—one of her

Early Roman history.

first acts was the founding of the town of Ostia, at the mouth of the Tiber, on account of piracy; that, through some conspiracy in the army, indicated in the legend of Lucretia, since armies have often been known to do such things, the kings were expelled, and a military domination fancifully called a republic, but consisting of a league of some powerful families, arose.

Throughout the regal times, and far into the republican, the chief domestic incidents turn on the strife of the upper caste or patricians with the lower or plebeians, manifesting itself by the latter asserting their right to a share in the lands conquered by their valour; by the extortion of the Valerian law; by the admission of the Latins and Hernicans to conditions of equality; by the transference of the election of tribunes from the centuries to the tribes; by the repeal of the law prohibiting the marriage of plebeians with patricians and by the eventual concession to the former of the offices of consul, dictator, censor, and prætor.

The domestic necessity for foreign war.

In these domestic disputes we see the origin of the Roman necessity for war. The high caste is steadily diminishing in number, the low caste as steadily increasing. In imperious pride, the patrician fills his private jail with debtors and delinquents; he usurps the lands that have been conquered. Insurrection is the inevitable consequence, foreign war the only relief. As the circle of operations extends, both parties see their interest in a cordial coalescence on equal terms, and jointly tyrannize exteriorly.

Gradual spread of Roman influence to the south.

The geographical dominion of Rome was extended at first with infinite difficulty. Up to the time of the capture of the city by the Gauls a doubtful existence was maintained in perpetual struggles with the adjacent towns and chieftains. There is reason to believe that in the very infancy of the republic, in the contest that ensued upon the expulsion of the kings, the city was taken by Porsenna. The direction in which her influence first spread was toward the south of the peninsula. Tarentum, one of the southern states, brought over to its assistance Pyrrhus the Epirot. He did little in the way of assisting his allies—he only saw Rome from the Acropolis of Præneste; but from him the Romans learned the art of fortifying camps, and caught the idea of invading Sicily. Here the rising republic came in contact with the Carthaginians, and in the conflict that ensued discovered the military value of Spain and Gaul, from which the Carthaginians drew an immense supply of mercenaries and munitions of war. The advance to greatness which Rome now made was prodigious. She saw that everything turned on the possession of the sea, and with admirable energy built a navy. In this her expectations were more than realized. The assertion is quite true that she spent more time in acquiring a little earth in Italy than was necessary for subduing the world after she had once obtained possession of the Mediterranean. From the experience of Agathocles she learned that the true method of controlling Carthage was by invading Africa. The principles involved in the contest, and the position of Rome at its close, are shown by the terms of the treaty of the first Punic War—that Carthage should evacuate every island in the Mediterranean, and pay a war-fine of six hundred thousand pounds. In her devotion to the acquisition of wealth Carthage had become very rich; she had reached a high state of cultivation of art; yet her prosperity, or rather the mode by which she had attained it, had greatly weakened her, as also had the political anomaly under which she was living, for it is an anomaly that an Asiatic people should place itself under democratic forms. Her condition in this respect was evidently the consequence of her original subordinate position as a Tyrian trading station, her rich men having long been habituated to look to the mother city for distinction. As in other commercial states, her citizens became soldiers with reluctance, and hence she had often to rely on mercenary troops. From her the Romans received lessons of the utmost importance. She confirmed them in the estimate they had formed of the value of naval power; taught them how to build ships properly and handle them; how to make military roads. The tribes of Northern Italy were hardly included in the circle of Roman dominion when a fleet was built in the Adriatic, and, under the pretence of

Rome builds a navy,

and invades Africa.

Results of the first Punic War.

putting down piracy, the sea power of the Illyrians was extinguished. From time immemorial the Mediterranean had been infested with pirates; man-stealing had been a profitable occupation, great gains being realized by ransoms of captives, or by selling them at Delos or other slave-markets. At this time it was clear that the final mastery of the Mediterranean turned on the possession of Spain, the great silver-producing country. The rivalry for Spain occasioned the second Punic War. It is needless to repeat the well-known story of Hannibal, how he brought Rome to the brink of ruin.

Results of the second Punic War.

The relations she maintained with surrounding communities had been such that she could not trust to them. Her enemy found allies in many of the Greek towns in the south of Italy. It is enough for us to look at the result of that conflict in the treaty that closed it. Carthage had to give up all her ships of war except ten triremes, to bind herself to enter into no war without the consent of the Roman people, and to pay a war-fine of two millions of pounds. Rome now entered, on the great scale, on the policy of disorganizing states for the purpose of weakening them. Under pretext of an invitation from the Athenians to protect them from the King of Macedon, the ambitious republic secured a footing in Greece, the principle developed in the invasion of Africa of making war maintain war being again resorted to. There may have been truth in the Roman accusation that the intrigues of Hannibal with Antiochus, king of Syria, occasioned the conflict between Rome and that monarch. Its issue was a prodigious event in the material aggrandizement of Rome—it was the cession of all his possessions in Europe and those of Asia north of Mount Taurus, with a war-fine of three millions of pounds. Already were seen the effects of the wealth that was pouring into Italy in the embezzlement of the public money by the Scipios. The resistance of Perses, king of Macedon, could not restore independence to Greece; it ended in the annexation of that country, Epirus and Illyricum. The results of this war were to the last degree pernicious to the victors and the

Rome invades Greece, and compels the cession of all the European provinces of Antiochus.

Revolt of Perses.

vanquished; the moral greatness of the former is truly affirmed to have disappeared, and the social ruin of the latter was so complete that for long marriage was replaced by concubinage. The policy and practices of Rome now literally became infernal; she forced a quarrel upon her old antagonist Carthage, and the third Punic War resulted in the utter destruction of that city. Simultaneously her oppressions in Greece provoked revolt, which was ended by the sack and burning of Corinth, Thebes, Chalcis, and the transference of the plundered statues, paintings, and works of art to Italy. There was nothing now in the way of the conquest of Spain except the valour of its inhabitants. After the assassination of Viriatus, procured by the Consul Cæpio, and the horrible siege of Numantia, that country was annexed as a province. Next we see the gigantic republic extending itself over the richest parts of Asia Minor, through the insane bequest of Attalus, king of Pergamus. The wealth of Africa, Spain, Greece, and Asia, was now concentrating in Italy, and the capital was becoming absolutely demoralized. In vain the Gracchi attempted to apply a remedy. The Roman aristocracy was intoxicated, insatiate, irresistible. The middle class was gone; there was nothing but profligate nobles and a diabolical populace. In the midst of inconceivable corruption, the Jugurthine War served only to postpone for a moment an explosion which was inevitable. The Servile rebellion in Sicily broke out; it was closed by the extermination of a million of those unhappy wretches: vast numbers of them were exposed, for the popular amusement, to the wild beasts in the arena. It was followed closely by the revolt of the Italian allies, known as the Social War—this ending, after the destruction of half a million of men, with a better result, in the extortion of the freedom of the city by several of the revolting states. Doubtless it was the intrigues connected with these transactions that brought the Cimbri and Teutons into Italy, and furnished an opening for the rivalries of Marius and Sylla, who, in turn, filled Rome with slaughter. The same spirit broke

Dreadful social effects on Rome.

Plunder of Greece and annexation of Spain.

Seizure of Asia Minor.

The Servile and Social wars.

out under the gladiator Spartacus: it was only checked for a time by resorting to the most awful atrocities, such as the crucifixion of prisoners, to appear under another form in the conspiracy of Catiline. And now it was plain that the contest for supreme power lay between a few leading men. It found an issue in the first triumvirate—a union of Pompey, Crassus, and Cæsar, who usurped the whole power of the senate and people, and bound themselves by oath to permit nothing to be done without their unanimous consent. Affairs then passed through their inevitable course. The death of Crassus and the battle of Pharsalia left Cæsar the master of the world. At this moment nothing could have prevented the inevitable result. The dagger of Brutus merely removed a man, but it left the fact. The battle of Actium reaffirmed the destiny of Rome, and the death of the republic was illustrated by the annexation of Egypt. The circle of conquest around the Mediterranean was complete; the function of the republic was discharged: it did not pass away prematurely.

Gradual convergence of power.

Cæsar the master of the world.

From this statement of the geographical career of Rome, we may turn to reflect on the political principles which inspired her. From a remote antiquity wars had been engaged in for the purpose of obtaining a supply of labour, the conqueror compelling those whom he had spared to cultivate his fields and serve him as slaves. Under a system of transitory military domination, it was more expedient to exhaust a people at once by the most unsparing plunder than to be content with a tribute periodically paid, but necessarily uncertain in the vicissitudes of years. These elementary principles of the policy of antiquity were included by the Romans in their system with modifications and improvements.

Ancient necessity for slave-wars.

The republic, during its whole career, illustrates the observation that the system on which it was founded included no conception of the actual relations of man. It dealt with him as a thing, not as a being endowed with inalienable rights. Recognizing power as its only measure of value, it could never accept the principle of the equality of all men in the eye of the law. The subjugation of Sicily, Africa, Greece, was quickly followed by the depopulation of those countries, as Livy, Plutarch, Strabo, and Polybius testify. Can there be a more fearful instance than the conduct of Paulus Æmilius, who, at the conquest of Epirus, murdered or carried into slavery 150,000 persons? At the taking of Thebes whole familes were thus disposed of, and these not of the lower, but of the respectable kind, of whom it has been significantly said that they were transported into Italy to be melted down. In Italy itself the consumption of life was so great that there was no possibility of the slaves by birth meeting the requirement, and the supply of others by war became necessary. To these slaves the laws were atrociously unjust. Tacitus has recorded that on the occasion of the murder of Pedanius, after a solemn debate in the senate, the particulars of which he furnishes, the ancient laws were enforced, and four hundred slaves of the deceased were put to death, when it was obvious to every one that scarcely any of them had known of the crime. The horrible maxim that not only the slaves within a house in which a master was murdered, but even those within a circle supposed to be measured by the reach of his voice, should be put to death, shows us the small value of the life of these unfortunates, and the facility with which they could be replaced. Their vast numbers necessarily made every citizen a soldier; the culture of the land and the manufacturing processes, the pursuits of labour and industry, were assigned to them with contempt. The relation of the slave in such a social system is significantly shown by the fact that the courts estimated the amount of any injury he had received by the damage his master had thereby sustained. To such a degree had this system been developed, that slave labour was actually cheaper than animal labour, and, as a consequence, much of the work that we perform by cattle was then done by men. The class of independent hirelings, which should have constituted the chief strength of the country, disappeared, labour itself becoming so ignoble that the poor citizen could not be an artisan, but must remain a pauper—a sturdy

Depopulation of countries after Roman conquest.

Atrocity of the Roman slave-laws.

Social effects of the Roman slave-system.

beggar, expecting from the state bread and amusements. The personal uncleannesss and shiftless condition of these lower classes were the true causes of the prevalence of leprosy and other loathsome diseases. Attempts at sanitary improvement were repeatedly made, but they so imperfectly answered the purpose that epidemics, occurring from time to time, produced a dreadful mortality. Even under the Cæsars, after all that had been done, there was no essential amendment. The assertion is true that the Old World never recovered from the great plague in the time of M. Antoninus, brought by the army from the Parthian War. In the reign of Titus ten thousand persons died in one day in Rome.

The slave system bred that thorough contempt for trade which animated the Romans. They never grudged even the Carthaginians a market. It threw them into the occupation of the demagogue, making them spend their lives, when not engaged in war, in the intrigues of political factions, the turbulence of public elections, the excitement of lawsuits. They were the first to discover that the privilege of interpreting laws is nearly equal to that of making them; and to this has been rightly attributed their turn for jurisprudence, and the prosperity of advocates among them. The disappearance of the hireling class was the immediate cause of the downfall of the republic and the institution of the empire, for the aristocracy were left without any antagonist, and therefore without any restraint. They broke up into factions, involving the country in civil war by their struggles with each other for power.

The political maxims of the republic, for the most part, rejected the ancient system of devastating a vanquished state by an instant, unsparing, and crushing plunder, which may answer very well where the tenure is expected to be brief, but does not accord with the formula subdue, retain, advance. Yet depopulation was the necessary incident. Italy, Sicily, Asia Minor, Gaul, Germany, were full of people, but they greatly diminished under Roman occupation. Her maxims were capable of being realized with facility through her military organization, particularly that of the legion. In some nations

The war system.

colonies are founded for commercial purposes, in others for getting rid of an excess of population: the Roman colony implies the idea of a garrison and an active military intent. Each legion was, in fact, so constructed as to be a small but complete army. In whatever country it might be encamped, it was in quick communication with the head-quarters at Rome; and this not metaphorically, but materially, as was shown by the building of the necessary military roads. The idea of permanent occupation, which was thus implied, did not admit the expediency of devastating a country, but, on the contrary, led to the encouragement of provincial prosperity, because the greater the riches the greater the capacity for taxation. Such principles were in harmony with the conditions of solidity and security of the Roman power, which proverbially had not risen in a single day—was not the creation of a single fortunate soldier, but represented the settled policy of many centuries. In the act of conquest Rome was inhuman; she tried to strike a blow that there would never be any occasion to repeat; no one was spared who by possibility might inconvenience her; but, the catastrophe once over, as a general thing, the vanquished had no occasion to complain of her rule. Of course, in the shadow of public justice, private wrong and oppression were often concealed. Through injustice and extortion, her officers accumulated enormous fortunes, which have never since been equalled in Europe. Sometimes the like occurred in times of public violence; thus Brutus made Asia Minor pay five years' tribute at once, and shortly after Antony compelled it to do it again. The extent to which recognized and legitimate exactions were carried is shown by the fact that upon the institution of the empire the annual revenues were about forty millions of pounds sterling.

The comparative value of metals in Rome is a significant political indication. Bullion rapidly increased in amount during the Carthaginian wars. At the opening of the first Punic War silver and copper were as 1 to 960; at the second Punic War the ratio had fallen, and was 1 to 160; soon after there was another fall, and it became 1 to 128. The republic debased the coinage by reducing its weight, the empire by alloying it.

Value of gold and silver.

The science, art, and political condition of nations are often illustrated by their coinage. An interesting view of the progress of Europe might be obtained from a philosophical study of its numismatic remains. The simplicity of the earlier ages is indicated by the pure silver, such as that coined at Crotona, B.C. 600—that of the reign of Philip of Macedon by the native unalloyed gold. A gradual decline in Roman prosperity is more than shadowed forth by the gradual deterioration of its money; for, as evil times befell the state, the emperors were compelled to utter a false coinage. Thus, under Vespasian, A.D. 69, the silver money contained about one fourth of its weight of copper; under Antoninus Pius, A.D. 138, more than one third; under Commodus, A.D. 180, nearly one half; under Gordian, A.D. 236, there was added to the silver more than twice its weight of copper. Nay, under Gallienus, a coinage was issued of copper, tin and silver, in which the first two metals exceed the last by more than two hundred times its weight. It shows to what a hopeless condition the state had come.

Connexion between debasement of coinage and political decline.

The Roman demagogues, as is the instinct of their kind, made political capital by attacking industrial capital. They lowered the rate of interest, prohibited interest, and often attempted the abolition of debts.

The concentration of power and increase of immorality proceeded with an equal step. In its earlier ages, the Roman dominion was exercised by a few thousand persons; then it passed into the hands of some score families; then it was sustained for a moment by individuals, and at last was seized by one man, who became the master of 120 millions. As the process went on, the virtues which had adorned the earlier times disappeared, and in the end were replaced by crimes such as the world had never before witnessed and never will again. An evil day is approaching when it becomes recognized in a community that the only standard of social distinction is wealth. That day was soon followed in Rome by its unavoidable consequence, a government founded upon two domestic elements, corruption and terrorism. No language can describe the state

Indescribable depravity in the Roman decline.

of that capital after the civil wars. The accumulation of power and wealth gave rise to a universal depravity. Law ceased to be of any value. A suitor must deposit a bribe before a trial could be had. The social fabric was a festering mass of rottenness. The people had become a populace; the aristocracy was demoniac; the city was a hell. No crime that the annals of human wickedness can show was left unperpetrated—remorseless murders; the betrayal of parents, husbands, wives, friends; poisoning reduced to a system; adultery degenerating into incests, and crimes that cannot be written. Women of the higher class were so lascivious, depraved, and dangerous, that men could not be compelled to contract matrimony with them; marriage was displaced by concubinage; even virgins were guilty of inconceivable immodesties; great officers of state and ladies of the court, of promiscuous bathings and naked exhibitions. In the time of Cæsar it had become necessary for the government to interfere, and actually put a premium on marriage. He gave rewards to women who had many children; prohibited those who were under forty five years of age, and who had no children, from wearing jewels and riding in litters, hoping by such social disabilities to correct the evil. It went on from bad to worse, so that Augustus, in view of the general avoidance of legal marriage and resort to concubinage with slaves, was compelled to impose penalties on the unmarried—to enact that they should not inherit by will except from relations. Not that the Roman women refrained from the gratification of their desires; their depravity impelled them to such wicked practices as cannot be named in a modern book. They actually reckoned the years, not by the consuls, but by the men they had lived with. To be childless, and therefore without the natural restraint of a family, was looked upon as a singular felicity. Plutarch correctly touched the point when he said that the Romans married to be heirs and not to have heirs. Of offences that do not rise to the dignity of atrocity, but which excite our loathing, such as gluttony and the most debauched luxury, the annals of the times furnish disgusting proofs. It was said, "They eat that they may vomit, and vomit that they

Dissoluteness of the women, and avoidance of marriage.

may eat." At the taking of Perusium, three hundred of the most distinguished citizens were solemnly sacrificed at the altar of Divus Julius by Octavian! Are these the deeds of civilized men, or the riotings of cannibals drunk with blood?

The whole system is past cure.

The higher classes on all sides exhibited a total extinction of moral principle; the lower were practical atheists. Who can peruse the annals of the emperors without being shocked at the manner in which men died, meeting their fate with the obtuse tranquillity that characterizes beasts? A centurion with a private mandate appears, and forthwith the victim opens his veins and dies in a warm bath. At the best, all that was done was to strike at the tyrant. Men despairingly acknowledged that the system itself was utterly past cure.

Testimony of Tacitus.

That in these statements I do not exaggerate, hear what Tacitus says: "The holy ceremonies of religion were violated; adultery reigning without control; the adjacent islands filled with exiles; rocks and desert places stained with clandestine murders, and Rome itself a theatre of horrors, where nobility of descent and splendour of fortune marked men out for destruction; where the vigour of mind that aimed at civil dignities, and the modesty that declined them, were offences without distinction; where virtue was a crime that led to certain ruin; where the guilt of informers and the wages of their iniquity were alike detestable; where the sacerdotal order, the consular dignity, the government of provinces, and even the cabinet of the prince, were seized by that execrable race as their lawful prey; where nothing was sacred, nothing safe from the hand of rapacity; where slaves were suborned, or by their own malevolence excited against their masters; where freemen betrayed their patrons, and he who had lived without an enemy died by the treachery of a friend."

Effects in the provinces. Free trade.

But, though these were the consequences of the concentration of power and wealth in the city of Rome, it was otherwise in the expanse of the empire. The effect of Roman domination was the cessation of all the little wars that had heretofore been waged between adjacent peoples. They exchanged independence for peace. Moreover, and this, in the end, was of the utmost importance to them all, unrestricted commerce ensued, direct trade arising between all parts of the empire. The Mediterranean nations were brought closer to each other, and became common inheritors of such knowledge as was then in the world. Arts, sciences, improved agriculture, spread among them; the most distant countries could boast of noble roads, aqueducts, bridges, and great works of engineering. In barbarous places, the legions that were intended as garrisons proved to be foci of civilization. For the provinces, even the wickedness of Rome was not without some good. From one quarter corn had to be brought; from another, clothing; from another, luxuries; and Italy had to pay for it all in coin. She had nothing to export in return. By this there was a tendency to equalization of wealth in all parts of the empire, and a perpetual movement of money. Nor was the advantage altogether material; there were conjoined intellectual results of no little value. Superstition and the amazing credulity of the old times disappeared. In the first Punic War, Africa was looked upon as a land of monsters; it had serpents large enough to stop armies, it had headless men. Sicily had its Cyclops, giants, enchantresses; golden apples grew in Spain; the mouth of Hell was on the shores of the Euxine. The marches of the legions and the voyages of merchants made all these phantasms vanish.

Intellectual advancement.

It was the necessary consequence of her military aggrandizement that the ethnical element which really constituted Rome should expire. A small nucleus of men had undertaken to conquer the Mediterranean world, and had succeeded. In doing this they had diffused themselves over an immense geographical surface, and necessarily became lost in the mass with which they mingled. On the other hand, the deterioration of Italy was insured by the slave system, and the ruin of Rome was accomplished before the barbarians touched it. Whoever inquires the cause of the fall of the Roman empire will find his answer in ascertaining what had become of the Romans.

Disappearance of the Roman ethnical element.

The extinction of prodigies and superstitious legends was occasioned by increased travel, through the merging of many separate nations into one great empire. Intellectual communication attends material communication. The spread of Roman influence around the borders of the Mediterranean produced a tendency to homogeneous thought eminently dangerous to the many forms of faith professed by so many different people.

Roman conquest produces homogeneous thought,

After Tarquin was expelled the sacerdotal class became altogether subordinate to the military, whose whole history shows that they regarded religion as a mere state institution, without any kind of philosophical significance, and chiefly to be valued for the control it furnished over vulgar minds. It presented itself to them in the light of a branch of industry, from which profit might be made by those who practised it. They thought no more of concerning themselves individually about it than in taking an interest in any other branch of lucrative trade. As to any examination of its intellectual basis, they were not sophists, but soldiers, blindly following the prescribed institutions of their country with as little question as its military commands. For these reasons, throughout the time of the republic, and also under the early emperors, there never was much reluctance to the domestication of any kind of worship in Rome. Indeed, the gods of the conquered countries were established there to the gratification of the national vanity. From this commingling of worship in the city, and intercommunication of ideas in the provinces, the most important events arose.

and revolutionizes religious ideas.

For it very soon was apparent that the political unity which had been established over so great a geographical surface was the forerunner of intellectual, and therefore religious unity. Polytheism became practically inconsistent with the Roman empire, and a tendency arose for the introduction of some form of monotheism. Apart from the operations of Reason, it is clear that the recognition by so many nations of one emperor must soon be followed by the acknowledgment of one God. There is a disposition to uniformity among people who are associated by a common political

Imperialism prepares the way for monotheism.

bond. Moreover, the rivalries of a hundred priesthoods imparted to polytheism an intrinsic weakness; but monotheism implies centralization, an organized hierarchy, and therefore concentration of power. The different interests and collisions of multitudinous forms of religion sapped individual faith; a diffusion of practical atheism, manifested by a total indifference to all ceremonies, except so far as they were shows, was the result, the whole community falling into an unbelieving and godless state. The form of superstition through which the national mind had passed was essentially founded upon the recognition of an incessant intervention of many divinities determining human affairs; but such a faith became extinct by degrees among the educated. How was it possible that human reason should deal otherwise with all the contradictions and absurdities of a thousand indigenous and imported deities, each asserting his inconsistent pretensions. A god who in his native grove or temple has been paramount and unquestioned, sinks into insignificance when he is brought into a crowd of compeers. In this respect there is no difference between gods and men. Great cities are great levellers of both. He who has stood forth in undue proportions in the solitude of the country, sinks out of observation in the solitude of a crowd.

Roman philosophy.

The most superficial statement of philosophy among the Romans, if philosophy it can be called, shows us how completely religious sentiment was effaced. The presence of sceptical thought is seen in the explanations of Terentius Varro, B.C. 110, that the anthropomorphic gods are to be received as mere emblems of the forces of matter; and the general tendency of the times may be gathered from the poem of Lucretius: his recommendations that the mind should be emancipated from the fear of the gods; his arguments against the immortality of the soul; his setting forth Nature as the only God to be worshipped. In Cicero we see how feeble and wavering a guide to life in a period of trouble philosophy had become, and how one who wished to stand in the attitude of chief thinker of his times was no more than a servile copyist of Grecian predecessors, giving to his works not an air of masculine

Varro. Lucretius.

and independent thought, but aiming at present effect rather than a solid durability; for Cicero addresses himself more to the public than to philosophers, exhibiting herein his professional tendency as an advocate. Under a thin veil he hides an undisguised scepticism, and, with the instinct of a placeman, leans rather to the investigation of public concerns than to the profound and abstract topics of philosophy. As is the case with superficial men, he sees no difference between the speculative and the exact, confusing them together. He feels that it is inexpedient to communicate truth publicly, especially that of a religious kind. Doubtless herein we shall agree when we find that he believes God to be nothing more than the soul of the world; discovers many serious objections to the doctrine of Providence; insinuates that the gods are only poetical creations; is uncertain whether the soul be immortal, but is clear that popular doctrine of punishment in the world to come is only an idle fable.

Cicero.

It was the attribute of the Romans to impress upon every thing a practical character. In their philosophy we continually see this displayed, along with a striking inferiority in original thought. Quintus Sextius admonishes us to pursue a virtuous life, and, as an aid thereto, enjoins an abstinence from meat. In this opinion many of the Cynical school acquiesced, and some it is said, even joined the Brahmans. In the troublous times of the first Cæsars, men had occasion to derive all the support they could from philosophy; there was no religion to sustain them. Among the Stoics there were some, as Seneca, to whom we can look back with pleasure. Through his writings he exercised a considerable influence on subsequent ages, though, when we attentively read his works, we must attribute this not so much to their intrinsic value as to their happening to coincide with the prevalent tone of religious thought. He enforces the necessity of a cultivation of good morals, and yet he writes against the religion of his country, its observances, and requirements. Of a far higher grade was Epictetus, at once a slave and a philosopher, though scarcely to be classed as a true Stoic. He considers man as a mere spectator of God and his works, and teaches that

Quintus Sextius. Seneca.

Epictetus. Antoninus.

every one who can no longer bear the miseries of life is upon just deliberation, and a conscientious belief that the gods will not disapprove, free to commit suicide. His maxim is that all have a part to play, and he has done well who has done his best—that he must look to conscience as his guide. If Seneca said that time alone is our absolute and only possession, and that nothing else belongs to man, Epictetus taught that his thoughts are all that man has any power over, every thing else being beyond his control. M. Aurelius Antoninus, the emperor, did not hesitate to acknowledge his thankfulness to Epictetus, the slave, in his attempt to guide his life according to the principles of the Stoics. He recommends every man to preserve his dæmon free from sin, and prefers religious devotions to the researches of physics, in this departing to some extent from the original doctrines of the sect; but the evil times on which men had fallen led them to seek support in religious consolations rather than in philosophical inquiries. In Maximus Tyrius, A.D. 146, we discover a corresponding sentiment, enveloped, it is true, in an air of Platonism, and countenancing an impression that image worship and sanctuaries are unnecessary for those who have a lively remembrance of the view they once enjoyed of the divine, though excellent for the vulgar, who have forgotten their past. Alexander of Aphrodisias exhibits the tendency, which was becoming very prevalent, to combine Plato and Aristotle. He treats upon Providence, both absolute and contingent; considers its bearings upon religion, and shows a disposition to cultivate the pious feelings of the age.

Maximus Tyrius.

Alexander of Aphrodisias.

Galen, the physician, asserts that experience is the only source of knowledge; lays great stress on the culture of mathematics and logic, observing that he himself should have been a Pyrrhonist had it not been for geometry. In the teleological doctrine of physiology he considers that the foundations of a true theology must be laid. The physicians of the times exerted no little influence on the promotion of such views; for the most part they embraced the Pantheistic doctrine. As one of them, Sextus Empiricus may be mentioned; his works, still remaining, indicate to us the tendency of this school to materialism.

Ancient Physicians.

Such was the tone of thought among the cultivated Romans; and to this philosophical atheism among them was added an atheism of indifference among the vulgar. But, since man is so constituted that he cannot live for any length of time without a form of worship, it is evident that there was great danger, whenever events should be ripe for the appearance of some monotheistic idea, that it might come in a base aspect. At a much later period than that we are here considering, one of the emperors expressed himself to the effect that it would be necessary to give liberty for the exercise of a sound philosophy among the higher classes, and provide a gorgeous ceremonial for the lower; he saw how difficult it is, by mere statesmanship to co-ordinate two such requirements, in their very nature contradictory. Though polytheism had lost all intellectual strength, the nations who had so recently parted with it could not be expected to have ceased from all disposition to an animalization of religion and corporealization of God. In a certain sense the emperor was only a more remote and more majestic form of the conquered and vanished kings, but, like them, he was a man. There was danger that the theological system, thus changing with the political, would yield only expanded anthropomorphic conceptions.

Philosophical atheism among the educated.

History perpetually demonstrates that nations cannot be permanently modified except by principles or actions conspiring with their existing tendency. Violence perpetrated upon them may pass away, leaving, perhaps in a few generations, no vestige of itself. Even Victory is conquered by Time. Profound changes only ensue when the operating force is in unison with the temper of the age. International peace among so many people once in conflict—peace under the auspices of a great overshadowing power; the unity of sentiment and brotherhood of feeling fast finding its way around the Mediterranean shores; the interests of a vast growing commerce, unfettered through the absorption of so many little kingdoms into one great republic, were silently bringing things to a condition that political force could be given to any religious dogma founded upon sentiments of mutual regard and interest. Nor could it

Principles, to be effective, must coincide with existing tendencies.

be otherwise than that among the great soldiers of those times one would at last arise whose practical intellect would discover the personal advantages that must accrue from putting himself in relation with the universally prevailing idea. How could he better find adherents from the centre to the remotest corner of the empire? And, even if his own personal intellectual state should disable him from accepting in its fulness the special form in which the idea had become embodied, could there be any doubt, if he received it, and was true to it as a politician, though he might decline it as a man, of the immense power it would yield him in return—a power sufficient, if the metropolis should resist, or be otherwise unsuited to his designs, to enable him to found a rival to her in a more congenial place, and leave her to herself, "the skeleton of so much glory and of so much guilt."

Thus, after the event, we can plainly see that the final blow to Polytheism was the suppression of the ancient independent nationalities around the Mediterranean Sea; and that, in like manner, Monotheism was the result of the establishment of an imperial government in Rome. But the great statesmen of those times, who were at the general point of view, must have foreseen that, in whatever form the expected change came, its limits of definition would inevitably be those of the empire itself, and that wherever the language of Rome was understood the religion of Rome would prevail. In the course of ages, an expansion beyond those limits might ensue wherever the state of things was congenial. On the south, beyond the mere verge of Africa, nothing was to be hoped for—it is the country in which man lives in degradation and is happy. On the east there were great unsubdued and untouched monarchies, having their own types of civilization, and experiencing no want in a religious respect. But on the north there were nations who, though they were plunged in hideous barbarism, filthy in an equal degree in body and mind, polygamists, idolaters, drunkards out of their enemies' skulls, were yet capable of an illustrious career. For these there was a glorious participation in store.

The coming Monotheism must be bounded by the limits of Roman influence.

Except the death of a nation, there is no event in human

history more profoundly solemn than the passing away of an ancient religion, though religious ideas are transitory, and creeds succeed one another with a periodicity determined by the law of continuous variation of human thought. The intellectual epoch at which we have now arrived has for its essential characteristic such a change—the abandonment of a time-honoured but obsolete system, the acceptance of a new and living one; and, in the incipient stages, opinion succeeding opinion in a well-marked way, until at length, after a few centuries of fusion and solution, there crystallized on the remnant of Roman power, as on a nucleus, a definite form, which, slowly modifying itself into the Papacy, served the purposes of Europe for more than a thousand years throughout its age of Faith.

The new ideas coalesce with the old.

In this abandonment, the personal conduct of the educated classes very powerfully assisted. They outwardly conformed to the ceremonial of the times, reserving their higher doctrines to themselves, as something beyond vulgar comprehension. Considering themselves as an intellectual aristocracy, they stood aloof, and, with an ill-concealed smile, consented to the transparent folly around them. It had come to an evil state when authors like Polybius and Strabo apologized to their compeers for the traditions and legends they ostensibly accepted, on the ground that it is inconvenient and needless to give popular offence, and that those who are children in understanding must, like those who are children in age, be kept in order by bugbears. It had come to an evil state when the awful ceremonial of former times had degenerated into a pageant, played off by an infidel priesthood and unbelieving aristocracy; when oracles were becoming mute, because they could no longer withstand the sly wit of the initiated; when the miracles of the ancients were regarded as mere lies, and of contemporaries as feats of legerdemain. It had come to an evil pass when even statesmen received it as a maxim that when the people have advanced in intellectual culture to a certain point, the sacerdotal class must either deceive them or oppress them, if it means to keep its power.

Conduct of the Roman educated men at this period.

In Rome, at the time of Augustus, the intellectual

classes—philosophers and statesmen—had completely emerged from the ancient modes of thought. To them, the national legends, so jealously guarded by the populace, had become mere fictions. The miraculous conception of Rhea Sylvia by the god Mars, an event from which their ancestors had deduced with pride the celestial origin of the founder of their city, had dwindled into a myth; as a source of actual reliance and trust, the intercession of Venus, that emblem of female loveliness, with the father of the gods in behalf of her human favourites, was abandoned; the Sibylline books, once believed to contain all that was necessary for the prosperity of the republic, were suspected of an origin more sinister than celestial; nor were insinuations wanting that from time to time they had been tampered with to suit the expediency of passing interests, or even that the true ones were lost and forgeries put in their stead. The Greek mythology was to them, as it is to us, an object of reverence, not because of any inherent truth, but because of the exquisite embodiments it can yield in poetry, in painting, in marble. The existence of those illustrious men who, on account of their useful lives or excellent example, had, by the pious ages of old, been sanctified or even deified, was denied, or, if admitted, they were regarded as the exaggerations of dark and barbarous times. It was thus with Æsculapius, Bacchus, and Hercules. And as to the various forms of worship, the multitude of sects into which the pagan nations were broken up offered themselves as a spectacle of imbecile and inconsistent devotion altogether unworthy of attention, except so far as they might be of use to the interests of the state.

Religious condition of the intellectual classes in Rome.

Such was the position of things among the educated. In one sense they had passed into liberty, in another they were in bondage. Their indisposition to encounter those inflictions with which their illiterate contemporaries might visit them may seem to us surprizing: they acted as if they thought that the public was a wild beast that would bite if awakened too abruptly from its dream; but their pusillanimity, at the most, could only postpone for a little an inevitable day. The ignorant classes, whom they had so much feared, awoke

Their irresolution.

in due season spontaneously, and saw in the clear light how matters stood.

Of the Roman emperors there were some whose intellectual endowments were of the highest kind; yet, though it must have been plain to them, as to all who turned their attention to the matter, in what direction society was drifting, they let things take their course, and no one lifted a finger to guide. It may be said that the genius of Rome manifested itself rather in physical than in intellectual operations; but in her best days it was never the genius of Rome to abandon great events to freedmen, eunuchs, and slaves. By such it was that the ancient gods were politically cast aside, while the government was speciously yielding a simulated obedience to them, and hence it was not at all surprizing that, soon after the introduction of Christianity, its pure doctrines were debased by a commingling with ceremonies of the departing creed. It was not to be expected that the popular mind could spontaneously extricate itself from the vicious circle in which it was involved. Nothing but philosophy was competent to deliver it, and philosophy failed of its duty at the critical moment. The classical scholar need scarcely express his surprize that the Feriæ Augusti were continued in the Church as the Festival St. Petri in vinculis; that even to our own times an image of the holy Virgin was carried to the river in the same manner as in the old times was that of Cybele, and that many pagan rites still continue to be observed in Rome. Had it been in such incidental particulars only that the vestiges of paganism were preserved, the thing would have been of little moment; but, as all who have examined the subject very well know, the evil was far more general, far more profound. When it was announced to the Ephesians that the Council of that place, headed by Cyril, had decreed that the Virgin should be called "the Mother of God," with tears of joy they embraced the knees of their bishop; it was the old instinct peeping out; their ancestors would have done the same for Diana. If Trajan, after ten centuries, could have revisited Rome, he would, without difficulty, have recognized the drama, though the

Surrender of affairs to the illiterate classes,

and consequent debasement of Christianity in Rome.

actors and scenery had all changed; he would have reflected how great a mistake had been committed in the legislation of his reign, and how much better it is, when the intellectual basis of a religion is gone, for a wise government to abstain from all compulsion in behalf of what has become untenable, and to throw itself into the new movement so as to shape the career by assuming the lead. Philosophy is useless when misapplied in support of things which common sense has begun to reject; she shares in the discredit which is attaching to them. The opportunity of rendering herself of service to humanity once lost, ages may elapse before it occurs again. Ignorance and low interests seize the moment, and fasten a burden on man which the struggles of a thousand years may not suffice to cast off. Of all the duties of an enlightened government, this of allying itself with Philosophy in the critical moment in which society is passing through so serious a metamorphosis of its opinions as is involved in the casting off of its ancient investiture of Faith, and its assumption of a new one, is the most important, for it stands connected with things that outlast all temporal concerns.

CHAPTER IX.

THE EUROPEAN AGE OF INQUIRY.

THE PROGRESSIVE VARIATION OF OPINIONS CLOSED BY THE INSTITUTION OF COUNCILS AND THE CONCENTRATION OF POWER IN A PONTIFF.

RISE, EARLY VARIATIONS, CONFLICTS, AND FINAL ESTABLISHMENT OF CHRISTIANITY.

Rise of Christianity.—Distinguished from ecclesiastical Organization.—It is demanded by the deplorable Condition of the Empire.—Its brief Conflict with Paganism.—Character of its first Organization.—Variations of Thought and Rise of Sects: their essential Difference in the East and West.—The three primitive Forms of Christianity: the Judaic Form, its End—the Gnostic Form, its End—the African Form, continues.

Spread of Christianity from Syria.—Its Antagonism to Imperialism, their Conflicts.—Position of Affairs under Diocletian.—The Policy of Constantine.—He avails himself of the Christian Party, and through it attains supreme Power.—His personal Relations to it.

The Trinitarian Controversy.—Story of Arius.—The Council of Nicea.

The Progress of the Bishop of Rome to Supremacy.—The Roman Church; its primitive subordinate Position.—Causes of its increasing Wealth, Influence, and Corruptions.—Stages of its Advancement through the Pelagian, Nestorian, and Eutychian Disputes.—Rivalry of the Bishops of Constantinople, Alexandria, and Rome.

Necessity of a Pontiff in the West and ecclesiastical Councils in the East.—Nature of those Councils and of pontifical Power.

The Period closes at the Capture and Sack of Rome by Alaric.—Defence of that Event by St. Augustine.—Criticism on his Writings.

Character of the Progress of Thought through this Period.—Destiny of the three great Bishops.

Subject of the chapter.

FROM the decay of Polytheism and the decline of philosophy, from the moral and social disorganization of the Roman empire, I have now to turn to the most important of all events, the rise of

Christianity. I have to show how a variation of opinion proceeded and reached its culmination; how it was closed by the establishment of a criterion of truth, under the form of ecclesiastical councils, and a system developed which supplied the intellectual wants of Europe for nearly a thousand years.

The reader, to whom I have thus offered a representation of the state of Roman affairs, must now prepare to look at the consequences thereof. Together we must trace out the progress of Christianity, examine the adaptation of its cardinal principles to the wants of the empire, and the variations it exhibited—a task supremely difficult, for even sincerity and truth will sometimes offend. For my part, it is my intention to speak with veneration on this great topic, and yet with liberty, for freedom of thought and expression is to me the first of all earthly things.

Introduction to the study of Christianity.

But, that I may not be misunderstood, I here, at the outset, emphatically distinguish between Christianity and ecclesiastical organizations. The former is the gift of God; the latter are the product of human exigencies and human invention, and therefore open to criticism, or, if need be, to condemnation.

Distinction between Christianity and ecclesiastical organizations.

From the condition of the Roman empire may be indicated the principles of any new system adapted to its amelioration. In the reign of Augustus, violence paused only because it had finished its work. Faith was dead; morality had disappeared. Around the shores of the Mediterranean the conquered nations looked at one another—partakers of a common misfortune, associates in a common lot. Not one of them had found a god to help her in her day of need. Europe, Asia, and Africa were tranquil, but it was the silence of despair.

Moral state of the world at this period.

Rome never considered man as an individual, but only as a thing. Her way to political greatness was pursued utterly regardless of human suffering. If advantages accrued to the conquered under her dominion, they arose altogether from incident, and never from her purposed intent. She was no self-conscious,

Unpitying tyranny of Rome.

deliberate civilizer. Conquest and rapine, the uniform aim of her actions, never permitted her, even at her utmost intellectual development, to comprehend the equal rights of all men in the eye of the law. Unpitying in her stern policy, few were the occasions when, for high state reasons, she stayed her uplifted hand. She might in the wantonness of her power, stoop to mercy; she never rose to benevolence.

When Syria was paying one third of its annual produce in taxes, is it surprising that the Jewish peasant sighed for a deliverer, and eagerly listened to the traditions of his nation that a temporal Messiah, "a king of the Jews" would soon come? When there was announced the equality of all men before God, "who maketh his sun to shine on the good and the evil, and sendeth his rain on the just and the unjust," is it surprising that men looked for equal rights before the law? Universal equality means universal benevolence; it substitutes for the impersonal and easily-eluded commands of the state the dictates of an ever-present conscience; it accepts the injunction, "Do unto others as you would they should do to you."

Prepares the way for the recognition of the equality of all men.

In the spread of a doctrine two things are concerned—its own intrinsic nature, and the condition of him on whom it is intended to act. The spread of Christianity is not difficult to be understood. Its antagonist, Paganism, presented inherent weakness, infidelity, and a cheerless prospect; a system, if that can be called so, which had no ruling idea, no principles, no organization; caring nothing for proselytes; its rival pontiffs devoted to many gods, but forming no political combination; occupying themselves with directing public worship and foretelling future events, but not interfering in domestic life; giving itself no concern for the lowly and unfortunate; not recognizing, or, at the best, doubtfully admitting a future life; limiting the hopes and destiny of man to this world; teaching that temporal prosperity may be selfishly gained at any cost, and looking to suicide as the relief of the brave from misfortune.

Attitude of Paganism.

On the other side was Christianity, with its enthusiasm and burning faith; its rewards in this life, and everlasting happiness or damnation in the next; the precise doctrines it by degrees gathered of sin, repentance, pardon; the efficacy of the blood of the Son of God; its proselytizing spirit; its vivid dogmas of a resurrection from the dead, the approaching end of the world, the judgment-day. Above all, in a worldly point of view, the incomparable organization it soon attained, and its preaching in season and out of season. To the needy Christian the charities of the faithful were freely given; to the desolate, sympathy. In every congregation there were prayers to God that he would listen to the sighing of the prisoner and captive, and have mercy on those who were ready to die. For the slave and his master there was one law and one hope, one baptism, one Saviour, one Judge. In times of domestic bereavement the Christian slave doubtless often consoled his pagan mistress with the suggestion that our present separations are only for a little while, and revealed to her willing ear that there is another world—a land in which we rejoin our dead. How is it possible to arrest the spread of a faith which can make the broken heart leap with joy?

Attitude of Christianity.

At its first organization Christianity embodied itself in a form of communism, the merging of the property of the disciples into a common stock, from which the necessary provision for the needy was made. Such a system, carried out rigorously, is, however, only suited to small numbers and a brief period. In its very nature it is impracticable on a great scale. Scarcely had it been resorted to before such troubles as that connected with the question of the Hebrew and Greek widows showed that it must be modified. By this relief or maintenance out of the funds of the Church, the spread of the faith among the humbler classes was greatly facilitated. In warm climates, where the necessities of life are small, an apparently insignificant sum will accomplish much in this way. But, as wealth accumulated, besides this inducement for the poor, there were temptations for the ambitious: luxurious appointments and a splendid maintenance, the ecclesiastical dignitaries becoming more than rivals to those of the state.

Its first organization.

From the modification which the primitive organization thus underwent, we may draw the instructive conclusion that the special forms of embodiment which the Christian principle from time to time has assumed, and of which many might be mentioned, were, in reality, of only secondary importance. The sects of the early ages have so totally died away that we hardly recall the meaning of their names, or determine their essential dogmas. From fasting, penance, and the gift of money, things which are of precise measurement, and therefore well suited to intellectual infancy, there may be perceived an advancing orthodoxy up to the highest metaphysical ideas. Yet it must not be supposed that new observances and doctrines, as they emerged, were the disconnected inventions of ambitious men. If rightly considered, they are, in the aggregate, the product of the uniform progression of human opinions.

Gradual sectarian divergences.

Authors who have treated of the sects of earlier times will point out to the curious reader how, in the beginning, the Church was agitated by a lingering attachment to the Hebrew rites, and with difficulty tore itself away from Judaism, which for the first ten years was paramount in it; how then, for several centuries, it became engrossed with disputes respecting the nature of Christ, and creed after creed arose therefrom; to the Ebionites he was a mere man; to the Docetes, a phantasm; to the Jewish Gnostic, Cerinthus, possessed of a twofold nature; how, after the spread of Christianity, in succeeding ages, all over the empire, the intellectual peculiarites of the East and West were visibly impressed upon it—the East filled with speculative doctrines, of which the most important were those brought forward by the Platonists of Alexandria, for the Platonists, of all Philosophical sects, furnished most converts; the West, in accordance with its utilitarian genius, which esteems the practical and disparages the intellectual, singularly aided by propitious opportunity, occupying itself with material aggrandizement and territorial power. The vanishing point of all Christian sectarian ideas of the East was in God, of those of the West in Man. Herein

Early variation of opinions.

Eastern theology tends to Divinity,

consists the essential difference between them. The one was rich in doctrines respecting the nature of the Divinity, the other abounded in regulations for the improvement and consolation of humanity. For long there was a tolerance, and even liberality toward differences of opinion. Until the Council of Nicea, no one was accounted a heretic if only he professed his belief in the Apostles' Creed.

Western to Humanity.

A very astute ecclesiastical historian, referring to the early contaminations of Christianity, makes this remark: "A clear and unpolluted fountain fed by secret channels with the dew of Heaven, when it grows a large river, and takes a long and winding course, receives a tincture from the various soils through which it passes."

Foreign modifications of Christianity.

Thus influenced by circumstances, the primitive modifications of Christianity were three—Judaic Christianity, Gnostic Christianity, African Christianity.

Of these, the first consisted of contaminations from Judaism, from which true Christianity disentangled itself with extreme difficulty, at the cost of dissensions among the Apostles themselves. From the purely Hebrew point of view of the early disciples, who surrendered with reluctance their expectation that the Saviour was the long-looked-for temporal Messiah, the King of the Jews, under which name he suffered, the faith gradually expanded, including successively proselytes of the Gate, the surrounding Gentiles, and at last the whole world, irrespective of nation, climate, or colour. With this truly imperial extension, there came into view the essential doctrines on which it was based. But Judaic Christianity, properly speaking, soon came to an untimely end. It was unable to maintain itself against the powerful apostolic influences in the bosom of the Church, and the violent pressure exerted by the unbelieving Jews, who exhibited toward it an inflexible hatred. Moreover, the rapid advance of the new doctrines through Asia Minor and Greece offered a tempting field for enthusiasm. The first preachers in the Roman empire were Jews; for the first years circumcision and conformity to the law of Moses were insisted on; but the first council

Judaic Christianity.

determined that point, at Jerusalem, probably about A.D. 49, in the negative. The organization of the Church, originally modelled upon that of the Synagogue, was changed. In the beginning the creed and the rites were simple; it was only necessary to profess belief in the Lord Jesus Christ, and baptism marked the admission of the convert into the community of the faithful. James, the brother of our Lord, as might, from his relationship, be expected, occupied the position of headship in the Church. The names of the bishops of the church of Jerusalem, as given by Eusebius, succeed to James, the brother of Christ, in the following order: Simeon, Justus, Zaccheus, Tobias, Benjamin, John, Matthew, Philip, Simeon, Justus, Levi, Ephraim, Joseph, and Judas. The names are indicative of the nationality. It was the boast of this Church that it was not corrupted with any heresy until the last Jewish bishop, a boast which must be received with some limitation, for very early we find traces of two distinct parties in Jerusalem—those who received the account of the miraculous conception and those who did not. The Ebionites, who were desirous of tracing our Saviour's lineage up to David, did so according to the genealogy given in the Gospel of St. Mathew, and therefore they would not accept what was said respecting the miraculous conception, affirming that it was apocryphal, and in obvious contradiction to the genealogy in which our Saviour's line was traced up through Joseph, who, it would thus appear, was not his father. They are to be considered as the national or patriotic party.

Causes of the arrest of Jewish conversion.

Two causes seem to have been concerned in arresting the spread of conversion among the Jews: the first was their disappointment as respects the temporal power of the Messiah; the second, the prominence eventually given to the doctrine of the Trinity. Their jealousy of anything that might touch the national doctrine of the unity of God became almost a fanaticism. Judaic Christianity may be said to have virtually ended with the destruction of Jerusalem by the Romans; its last trace, however, was the dispute respecting Easter, which was terminated by the Council of Nicea. The conversion of the Jews had ceased before the reign of Constantine.

The second form, Gnostic Christianity, had reached its full development within a century after the death of Christ; it maintained an active influence through the first four centuries, and gave birth, during that time, to many different subordinate sects. It consisted essentially in ingrafting Christianity upon Magianism. It made the Saviour an emanated intelligence, derived from the eternal, self-existing mind; this intelligence, and not the Man-Jesus, was the Christ, who thus, being an impassive phantom, afforded to Gnosticism no idea of an expiatory sacrifice, none of an atonement. It was arrested by the reappearance of pure Magianism in the Persian empire under Ardeschir Babhegan; not, however, without communicating to orthodox Christianity an impression far more profound than is commonly supposed, and one of which indelible traces may be perceived in our day.

Gnostic Christianity.

The third form, African or Platonic Christianity, arose in Alexandria. Here was the focus of those fatal disputes respecting the Trinity, a word which does not occur in the Holy Scriptures, and which, it appears, had been first introduced by Theophilus, the Bishop of Antioch, the seventh from the apostles. In the time of Hadrian, Christianity had become diffused all over Egypt, and had found among the Platonizing philosophers of the metropolis many converts. These men modified the Gnostic idea to suit their own doctrines, asserting that the principle from which the universe originated was something emitted from the Supreme Mind, and capable of being drawn into it again, as they supposed was the case with a ray and the sun. This ray, they affirmed, was permanently attached to our Saviour, and hence he might be considered as God. Thus, therefore, there were in his person three parts, a body, a soul, and the logos; hence he was both God and man. But, as a ray is inferior to the sun, it seemed to follow that the Christ must be inferior to the Father.

Platonic Christianity.

In all this it is evident that there is something transcendental, and the Platonizing Christians, following the habit of the Greek philosophers, considered it as a mysterious doctrine; they spoke of it as "meat for strong men," but the popular current doctrine was "milk for babes." Justin Martyr, A.D. 132, who had been a Platonic philosopher, believed that the divine ray, after it was attached to Christ, was never withdrawn from him, and never separated from its source. He offers two illustrations of his idea. As speech (logos), going forth from one man, enters into another, conveying to him meaning, while the same meaning remains in the person who speaks, thus the logos of the Father continues unimpaired in himself, though imparted to the Christ; or, as from one lamp another may be lighted without any loss of splendour, so the divinity of the Father is transferred to the Son. This last illustration subsequently became very popular, and was adopted into the Nicene Creed. "God of God, Light of Light."

The Logos.

It is obvious that the intention of this reasoning was to preserve intact, the doctrine of the unity of God, for the great body of Christians were at this time monarchists, the word being used in its theological acceptation.

Thus the Jewish and Gnostic forms both died out, but the African, Platonic, or Alexandrian, was destined to be perpetuated. The manner in which this occurred, can only be understood by a study of the political history of the times. To such facts as are needful for the purpose, I shall therefore with brevity allude.

Permanence of Alexandrian ideas.

From its birthplace in Judea, Christianity advanced to the conquest of the Roman world. In its primitive form it received an urgency from the belief that the end of all things was close at hand, and that the earth was on the point of being burnt up by fire. From the civil war it waged in Judea, it emerged to enter on a war of invasion and foreign annexation. In succession, Cyprus, Phrygia, Galatia, and all Asia Minor, Greece, and Italy, were penetrated. The persecutions of Nero, incident on the burning of Rome, did not for a moment retard its career; during his reign it rapidly spread, and in every direction Petrine and Pauline, or Judaizing and Hellenizing churches were springing up. The latter gained the superiority, and the former passed away. The constitution of the churches changed, the

Spread of Christianity from Syria.

congregations gradually losing power, which became concentrated in the bishop. By the end of the first century the episcopal form was predominant, and the ecclesiastical organization so imposing as to command the attention of the emperors, who now began to discover the mistake that had hitherto been made in confounding the new religion with Judaism. Their dislike to it, soon manifested in measures of repression, was in consequence of the peculiar attitude it assumed. As a body, the Christians not only kept aloof from all the amusements of the times, avoiding theatres and public rejoicings, but in every respect constituted themselves an empire within the empire. Such a state of things was altogether inconsistent with the established government, and its certain inconveniences and evils were not long in making themselves felt. The triumphant march of Christianity was singularly facilitated by free intercommunication over the Mediterranean, in consequence of that sea being in the hands of one sovereign power. The Jewish and Greek merchants afforded it a medium; their trading towns were its posts. But it is not to be supposed that its spread was without resistance; for at least the first century and a half the small farmers and land labourers entertained a hatred to it, looking upon it as a peculiarity of the trading communities, whom they ever despised. They persuaded themselves that the earthquakes, inundations and pestilences were attributable to it. To these incitements was added a desire to seize the property of the faithful confiscated by the law. Of this the early Christians unceasingly and bitterly complained. But the rack, the fire, wild beasts were unavailingly applied. Out of the very persecutions themselves advantages arose. Injustice and barbarity bound the pious but feeble communities together, and repressed internal dissent.

Modifications of organization become necessary.

Becomes antagonistic to Imperialism.

Persecution consolidates it.

In several instances, however, there can be no doubt that persecution was brought on by the defiant air the churches assumed as they gathered strength. To understand this, we have only to peruse such documents as the address of Tertullian to Scapula. Full of intolerant spirit, it accuses the national

Defiant air of the young churches.

religion of being the cause of all the public calamities, the floods, the fires, the eclipses; it denounces the vengeance of God on the national idolatry. As was the opinion of the Christians at that time, it acknowledges the reality of the pagan gods, whom it stigmatizes as demons, and proclaims its determination to expel them. It warns its opponents that they may be stricken blind, devoured by worms, or visited with other awful calamities. Such a sentiment of scorn and hatred, gathering force enough to make itself politically felt, was certain to provoke persecution. That of Decius, A.D. 250, was chiefly aimed against the clergy, not even the bishops of Jerusalem, Antioch, and Rome escaping. Eight years afterwards occurred that in which Sextus, the Bishop of Rome, and Cyprian of Carthage perished.

Opposition of the emperors.

Under Diocletian it had become apparent that the self-governed Christian corporations everywhere arising were altogether incompatible with the imperial system. If tolerated much longer, they would undoubtedly gain such strength as to become politically quite formidable. There was not a town, hardly a village in the empire—nay, what was indeed far more serious, there was not a legion in which these organizations did not exist. The uncompromising and inexorable spirit animating them brought on necessarily a triple alliance of the statesmen, the philosophers, and the polytheists. These three parties, composing or postponing their mutual disputes, cordially united to put down the common enemy before it should be too late. It so fell out that the conflict first broke out in the army. When the engine of power is affected, it behoves a prince to take heed. The Christian soldiers in some of the legions refused to join in the time-honoured solemnities for propitiating the gods. It was in the winter A.D. 302–3. The emergency became so pressing that a council was held by Diocletian and Galerius to determine what should be done. The difficulty of the position may perhaps be appreciated when it is understood that even the wife and daughter of Diocletian himself were adherents of the new religion. He was a man of such capacity and enlarged political views that, at the second council of the leading statesmen and generals, he would

Position of things under Diocletian.

not have been brought to give his consent to repression if it had not been quite clear that a conflict was unavoidable. His extreme reluctance to act is shown by the express stipulation he made that there should be no sacrifice of life. It is scarcely necessary to relate the events which ensued; how the Church of Nicomedia was razed to the ground; how, in retaliation, the imperial palace was set on fire; how an edict was openly insulted and torn down; how the Christian officers in the army were compelled to resign; and, as Eusebius, an eye-witness, relates, a vast number of martyrs soon suffered in Armenia, Syria, Mauritania, Egypt, and elsewhere. So resistless was the march of events that not even the emperor himself could stop the persecution. The Christians were given over to torture, the fire, wild beasts, beheading; many of them, in the moment of condemnation, simply returning thanks to God that he had thought them worthy to suffer. The whole world was filled with admiration. The greatness of such holy courage could have no other result. An internecine conflict between the disputants seemed to be inevitable. But, in the dark and bloody policy of the times, the question was settled in an unexpected way. To Constantine, who had fled from the treacherous custody of Galerius, it naturally occurred that if he should ally himself to the Christian party, conspicuous advantages must forthwith accrue to him. It would give him in every corner of the empire men and women ready to encounter fire and sword; it would give him partisans, not only animated by the traditions of their fathers, but—for human nature will even in the religious assert itself—demanding retribution for the horrible barbarities and injustice that had been inflicted on themselves; it would give him, and this was the most important of all, unwavering adherents in every legion of the army. He took his course. The events of war crowned him with success. He could not be otherwise than outwardly true to those who had given him power, and who continued to maintain him on the throne. But he never conformed to the ceremonial requirements of the Church till the close of his evil life.

Imperial persecutions.

Their great political consequences.

Successful policy of Constantine.

The attempt to make an alliance with this great and rapidly growing party was nothing new. Maximin tried it, but was distrusted. Licinius, foreseeing the policy that Constantine would certainly pursue, endeavoured to neutralize it by feebly reviving the persecution, A.D. 316, thinking thereby to conciliate the pagans. The aspirants for empire at this moment so divided the strength of the state that, had the Christian party been weaker than it actually was, it so held the balance of power as to be able to give a preponderance to the candidate of its choice. Much more, therefore, was it certain to prevail, considering its numbers, its ramifications, its compactness. Force, argument, and persuasion had alike proved ineffectual against its strength.

Influence of the reign of Constantine.

To the reign of Constantine the Great must be referred the commencement of those dark and dismal times which oppressed Europe for a thousand years. It is the true close of the Roman empire, the beginning of the Greek. The transition from one to the other is emphatically and abruptly marked by a new metropolis, a new religion, a new code, and, above all, a new policy. An ambitious man had attained to imperial power by personating the interests of a rapidly growing party. The unavoidable consequences were a union between the Church and State; a diverting of the dangerous classes from civil to ecclesiastical paths, and the decay and materialization of religion. This, and not the reign of Leo the Isaurian, as some have said, is the true beginning of the Byzantine empire; it is also the beginning of the age of Faith in Europe, though I consider the age of Inquiry as overlapping this epoch, and as terminating with the military fall of Rome.

Ecclesiastical authors have made everything hinge on the conversion of Constantine and the national establishment of Christianity. The medium through which they look distorts the position of objects, and magnifies the subordinate and the collateral into the chief. Events had been gradually shaping themselves in such a way that the political fall of the city of Rome was inevitable. The Romans, as a people, had disappeared, being absorbed among other nations; the centre of power was in the army. One after another, the legions put forth competitors for the purple—soldiers of fortune, whose success could never remove low habits due to a base origin, the coarseness of a life of camps—who found no congeniality in the elegance and refinement of those relics of the ancient families which were expiring in Rome. They despised the military decrepitude of the superannuated city; her recollections they hated. To such men the expediency of founding a new capital was an obvious device; or, if indisposed to undertake so laborious a task, the removal of the imperial residence to some other of the great towns was an effectual substitute. It was thus that the residence of Diocletian at Nicomedia produced such disastrous consequences in a short time to Rome.

After Constantine had murdered his son Crispus, his nephew Licinius, and had suffocated in a steam-bath his wife Fausta, to whom he had been married twenty years, and who was the mother of three of his sons, the public abhorrence of his crimes could no longer be concealed. A pasquinade, comparing his reign to that of Nero, was affixed to the palace gate. The guilty emperor, in the first burst of anger, was on the point of darkening the tragedy, if such a thing had been possible, by a massacre of the Roman populace who had thus insulted him. It is said that his brothers were consulted on this measure of vengeance. The result of their counsel was even more deadly, for it was resolved to degrade Rome to a subordinate rank, and build a metropolis elsewhere.

He resolves on removing the metropolis.

Political conditions thus at once suggested and rendered possible the translation of the seat of government: the temporary motive was the vengeance of a great criminal. Perhaps, also, in the mental occupation incident to such an undertaking, the emperor found a refuge from the accusations of conscience. But it is altogether erroneous to suppose that either at this time, or for many years subsequently, he was a Christian. His actions are not those of a devout convert; he was no proselyte, but a protector; never guiding himself by religious principles, but now giving the most valuable support to his new allies, now exhibiting the impartiality

He is a protector, but not a convert.

of a statesman for both forms of faith. In his character of Pontifex Maximus he restored pagan temples, and directed that the haruspices should be consulted. On the festival of the birthday of the new city he honoured the statue of Fortune. The continued heathen sacrifices and open temples seemed to indicate that he intended to do no more than place the new religion on a level with the old. His recommendation to the Bishop of Alexandria and to Arius of the example of the philosophers, who never debated profound questions before ignorant audiences, and who could differ without hating one another, illustrates the indifferentism of his personal attitude, and yet he clearly recognized his obligations to the party that had given him power.

His tendencies to Paganism.

This conclusion is confirmed by the works of Constantine himself. They must be regarded as far better authority than the writings of religious polemics. A medal was struck, on which was impressed his title of "God," together with the monogram of Christ. Another represented him as raised by a hand from the sky while seated in the chariot of the Sun. But more particularly the great porphyry pillar, a column 120 feet in height, exhibited the true religious condition of the founder of Constantinople. The statue on its summit mingled together the Sun, the Saviour, and the Emperor. Its body was a colossal image of Apollo, whose features were replaced by those of Constantine, and round the head, like rays, were fixed the nails of the cross of Christ recently discovered in Jerusalem.

The position of a patron assumed by Constantine may be remarked in many of the incidents of his policy. The edict of Milan gave liberty both to Pagans and Christians; but his necessity for showing in some degree a preponderance of favour for the latter obliged him to issue a rescript exempting the clergy from civil offices. It was this also which led him to conciliate the bishops by the donation of large sums of money for the restoration of their churches and other purposes, and to exert himself, often by objectionable means, for destroying that which they who were around him considered to be heresy. A better motive, perhaps, led him to restore those Christians who had been degraded; to surrender to the legal heirs the confiscated estates of martyrs, or, if no heirs were to be found, to convey them to the Church; to set at liberty those who had been condemned to the mines; to recall those who had been banished. If, as a tribute to the Christians, who had sustained him politically, he made the imperial treasury responsible for many of their losses; if he caused costly churches to be built not only in the great cities, but even in the Holy Land; if he vindicated the triumphant position of his supporters by forbidding any Jew to have a Christian slave; if he undertook to enforce the decisions of councils by means of the power of the state; if he forbade all schism in the Church, himself determining the degrees of heresy under the inspirations of his ecclesiastical entourage, his vacillations show how little he was guided by principle, how much by policy. After the case of the Donatists had been settled by repeated councils, he spontaneously recalled them from banishment; after he had denounced Arius as "the very image of the Devil," he, through the influence of court females, received him again into favour; after the temple of Æsculapius at Ægæ had been demolished, and the doors and roofs of others removed, the pagans were half conciliated by perceiving that no steady care was taken to enforce the obnoxious decrees, and that, after all, the Christians would have to accept the declarations of the emperor for deeds.

His relations to the Church.

In a double respect the removal of the seat of empire was important to Christianity. It rendered possible the assumption of power by the bishops of Rome, who were thereby secluded from imperial observation and inspection, and whose position, feeble at first, under such singularly auspicious circumstances was at last developed into papal supremacy. In Constantinople, also, there were no pagan recollections and interests to contend with. At first the new city was essentially Roman, and its language Latin; but this was soon changed for Greek, and thus the transference of the seat of government tended in the end to make Latin a sacred tongue.

Consequences of building a new metropolis.

Constantine knew very well where Roman power had for many years lain. His own history, from the time of his father's death and his exaltation by the legions at York, had taught him that, for the perpetuation of his dynasty and system, those formidable bodies must be disposed of.

The policy of Constantine.

It was for this reason, and that no future commander might do what himself and so many of his predecessors had done, that he reduced the strength of the legion from 6000 to 1500 or 1000 men. For this reason, too, he opened to ambition the less dangerous field of ecclesiastical wealth and dignity, justly concluding that, since the clergy came from every class of society, the whole people would look to the prosperity of the Church. By exempting the priesthood from burdensome municipal offices, such as the decurionate, he put a premium on apostacy from paganism. The interest he personally took in the Trinitarian controversy encouraged the spreading of theological disputation from philosophers and men of capacity to the populace. Under the old polytheism heresy was impossible, since every man might select his god and his worship; but under the new monotheism it was inevitable—heresy, a word that provokes and justifies a black catalogue of crimes. Occupied in those exciting pursuits, men took but little heed of the more important political changes that were in progress. The eyes of the rabble were easily turned from the movements of the government by horse-racing, theatres, largesses. Yet already this diversion of ambition into new fields gave tokens of dangers to the state in future times. The Donatists, whom Constantine had attempted to pacify by the Councils of Rome, Arles, and Milan, maintained a more than religious revolt, and exhibited the bitterness that may be infused among competitors for ecclesiastical spoils. These enthusiasts assumed to themselves the title of God's elect, proclaimed that the only true apostolic succession was in their bishops, and that whosoever denied the right of Donatus to be Bishop of Carthage should be eternally damned. They asked, with a truth that lent force to their demand, "What has the emperor to do with the Church, what have Christians to do with kings, what have bishops to do at court?" Already the Catholic party, in preparation of its commencing atrocities, ominously inquired, "Is the vengeance of God to be defrauded of its victims?" Already

Constantine, by bestowing on the Church the right of receiving bequests, had given birth to that power which, reposing on the influence that always attaches to the possession of land, becomes at last overwhelming when it is held by a corporation which may always receive and can never alienate, which is always renewing itself and can never die. It was by no miraculous agency, but simply by its organization, that the Church attained to power an individual who must die, and a family which must become extinct, had no chance against a corporation whose purposes were ever unchanged, and its life perpetual. But it was not the state alone which thus took detriment from her connection with the Church; the latter paid a full price for the temporal advantages she received in admitting civil intervention in her affairs. After a retrospect of a thousand years, the pious Fratricelli loudly proclaimed their conviction that the fatal gift of a Christian emperor had been the doom of true religion.

From the rough soldier who accepted the purple at York, how great the change to the effeminate emperor of the Bosphorus, in silken robes stiffened with threads of gold, a diadem of sapphires and pearls, and false hair stained of various tints; his steps stealthily guarded by mysterious eunuchs flitting through the palace, the streets full of spies, and an ever-watchful police! The same man who approaches us as the Roman imperator retires from us as the Asiatic despot. In the last days of his life, he put aside the imperial purple, and, assuming the customary white garment, prepared for baptism, that the sins of his long and evil life might all be washed away. Since complete purification can thus be only once obtained, he was desirous to procrastinate that ceremony to the last moment. Profoundly politic, even in his relations with heaven, he thenceforth reclined on a white bed, took no further part in worldly affairs, and, having thus insured a right to the continuance of that prosperity in a future life which he had enjoyed in this, expired, A.D. 337.

His conversion and death.

In a theological respect, among the chief events of this emperor's reign are the Trinitarian controversy and the open materialization of Christianity. The former, commencing among the Platonizing ecclesiastics of Alexandria, continued for ages to exert a formidable influence. From time immemorial, as we have already related, the Egyptians had been familiar with various trinities, different ones being worshipped in different cities, the devotees of each exercising a peaceful toleration toward those of others. But now things were greatly changed. It was the settled policy of Constantine to divert ambition from the state to the Church, and to make it not only safer, but more profitable to be a great ecclesiastic than a successful soldier. A violent competition, for the chief offices was the consequence—a competition, the prelude of that still greater one for episcopal supremacy.

The Trinitarian controversy.

We are now again brought to a consideration of the variations of opinion which marked this age. It would be impossible to give a description of them all. I therefore propose to speak only of the prominent ones. They are a sufficient guide in our investigation; and of the Trinitarian controversy first.

Prelude of sectarian dissent.

For some time past dissensions had been springing up in the Church. Even out of persecution itself disunion had arisen. The martyrs who had suffered for their faith, and the confessors who had nobly avowed it, gained a worthy consideration and influence, becoming the intermedium of reconciliation of such of their weaker brethren as had apostatized in times of peril by authoritative recommendations to "the peace of the Church." From this abuses arose. Martyrs were known to have given the use of their names to "a man and his friends;" nay, it was even asserted that tickets of recommendation had been bought for money; and as it was desirable that a uniformity of discipline should obtain in all the churches, so that he who was excommunicated from one should be excommunicated from all, it was necessary that these abuses should be corrected. In the controversies that ensued, Novatus founded his sect on the principle that penitent apostates should, under no circumstances, be ever again received. Besides this dissent on a question of discipline, already there were abundant elements of dispute, such as the time of observance of Easter, the nature of Christ, the millennium upon earth, and rebaptism. Already, in Syria, Noetus, the Unitarian, had foreshadowed what was coming; already there were Patripassians; already Sabellianism existed.

Arius, his doctrines.

But it was in Alexandria that the tempest burst forth. There lived in that city a presbyter of the name of Arius, who, on occasion of a vacancy occurring, desired to be appointed bishop. But one Alex ander supplanted him in the coveted dignity. Both relied on numerous supporters, Arius counting among his not less than seven hundred virgins of the Mareotic nome. In his disappointment he accused his successful antagonist of Sabellianism, and, in retaliation, was anathematized. It was no wonder that, in such an atmosphere, the question quickly assumed a philosophical aspect. The point of difficulty was to define the position of the Son in the Holy Trinity. Arius took the ground that there was a time when, from the very nature of sonship, the Son did not exist, and a time at which he commenced to be, asserting that it is the necessary condition of the filial relation that a father must be older than his son. But this assertion evidently might imply subordination or inequality among the three persons of the Holy Trinity The partisans of Alexander raised up their voices against such a blasphemous lowering of the Redeemer; the Arians answered them that, by exalting the Son in every respect to an equality with the Father, they impugned the great truth of the unity of God. The new bishop himself edified the giddy citizens, and perhaps, in some degree, justified his appointment to his place by displaying his rhetorical powers in public debates on the question. The Alexandrians, little anticipating the serious and enduring results soon to arise, amused themselves, with characteristic levity, by theatrical representations of the contest upon the stage. The passions of the two parties were roused; the Jews and Pagans, of whom the town was full, exasperated things by their mocking derision. The dissension spread: the whole country became convulsed. In the hot climate of Africa, theological controversy soon ripened into political disturbance. In all Egypt there was not a Christian man, and not a woman, who did not proceed to settle the nature of the unity of God. The tumult rose to such a pitch that it became necessary for the emperor to interfere. Doubtless, at first, he congratulated himself on such a course of events. It was better that the provinces should be fanatically engaged in disputes than secretly employed in treason against his person or conspiracies against his policy. A united people is an inconvenience to one in power. Nevertheless, to compose the matter somewhat, he sent Hosius, the Bishop of Cordova, to Alexandria; but, finding that the remedy was altogether inadequate, he was driven at last to the memorable expedient of summoning the Council of Nicea, A.D. 325. It attempted a settlement of the trouble by a condemnation of Arius, and the promulgation of authoritative articles of belief as set forth in the Nicene Creed. As to the main point, the Son was declared to be of the same substance with the Father —a temporizing and convenient, but, as the event proved, a disastrous ambiguity. The Nicene Council, therefore, settled the question by evading it, and the emperor enforced the decision by the banishment of Arius.

Constantine attempts to check the controversy,

and summons the Council of Nicea.

"I am persecuted," Arius plaintively said, "because I have taught that the Son had a beginning and the Father had not." It was the influence of the court theologians that had made the emperor his personal enemy. Constantine, as we have seen, had looked upon the dispute, in the first instance, as altogether frivolous, if he did not, in truth, himself incline to the assertion of Arius, that, in the very nature of the thing, a father must be older than his son. The theatrical exhibitions at Alexandria in mockery of the question were calculated to confirm him in his opinion: his judgment was lost in the theories that were springing up as to the nature of Christ; for on the Ebionitish, Gnostic, and Platonic doctrines, as well as on the new one that "the logos" was made out of nothing, it equally followed that the current opinion must be erroneous, and that there was a time before which the Son did not exist.

The fortunes of Arius.

But, as the contest spread through churches and even

families, Constantine had found himself compelled to intervene. At first he attempted the position of a moderator, but soon took ground against Arius, advised to that course by his entourage at Constantinople. It was at this time that the letter was circulated in which he denounced Arius as the image of the Devil. Arius might now have foreseen what must certainly occur at Nicea. Before that council was called everything was settled. No contemporary for a moment supposed that this was an assembly of simple-hearted men, anxious by a mutual comparison of thought, to ascertain the truth. Its aim was not to compose such a creed as would give unity to the Church, but one so worded that the Arians would be compelled to refuse to sign it, and so ruin themselves. To the creed was attached an anathema precisely defining the point of dispute, and leaving the foreordained victims no chance of escape. The original Nicene Creed differed in some essential particulars from that now current under that title. Among other things, the fatal and final clause has been dropped. Thus it ran: "The Holy Catholic and Apostolic Church anathematizes those who say that there was a time when the Son of God was not; and that before he was begotten he was not, and that he was made out of nothing, or out of another substance or essence, and is created, or changeable, or alterable." The emperor enforced the decision of the council by the civil power; he circulated letters denouncing Arius, and initiated those fearful punishments unhappily destined in future ages to become so frequent, by ordaining that whoever should find one of the books of Arius and not burn it should actually be put to death.

His condemnation as a heretic.

The Nicene Creed.

It might be thought that, after such a decisive course, it would be impossible to change, and yet in less than ten years Constantine is found agreeing with the convict Arius. A presbyter in the confidence of Constantia, the emperor's sister, had wrought upon him. Athanasius, now Bishop of Alexandria, the representative of the other party, is deposed and banished. Arius is invited to Constantinople. The emperor orders Alexander, the bishop of that city, to receive him into

Arius received again into court favour,

communion to-morrow. It is Saturday. Alexander flees to the church, and, falling prostrate, prays to God that he will interpose and save his servant from being forced into this sin, even if it should be by death. That same evening Arius was seized with a sudden and violent illness as he passed along the street, and in a few moments he was found dead in a house, whither he had hastened. In Constantinople, where men were familiar with Asiatic crimes, there was more than a suspicion of poison. But when Alexander's party proclaimed that his prayer had been answered, they forgot what then that prayer must have been, and that the difference is little between praying for the death of a man and compassing it.

and is poisoned.

The Arians affirmed that it was the intention of Constantine to have called a new council, and have the creed rectified according to his more recent ideas; but, before he could accomplish this, he was overtaken by death. So little efficacy was there in the determination of the Council of Nicea, that for many years afterward creed upon creed appeared. What Constantine's new creed would have been may be told from the fact that the Consubstantialists had gone out of power, and from what his son Constantius soon after did at the Council of Ariminium.

Constantine prepares for a new creed.

So far, therefore, from the Council of Nicea ending the controversies afflicting religion, they continued with increasing fury. The sons and successors of Constantine set an example of violence in these disputes; and, until the barbarians burst in upon the empire, the fourth century wore away in theological feuds. Even the populace, scarcely emerged from paganism, set itself up for a judge on questions from their very nature incapable of being solved; and to this the government gave an impetus by making the profits of public service the reward of sectarian violence. The policy of Constantine began to produce its results. Mental activity and ambition found their true field in ecclesiastical affairs. Orthodoxy triumphed, because it was more in unison with the present necessity of the court, while asserting the predominance of Christianity, to offend as little as might

Spread of theological disputes.

be the pagan party. The heresy of Arius, though it might suit the monotheistic views of the educated, did not commend itself to that large mass who had been so recently pagan. Already the elements of dissension were obvious enough; on one side there was an illiterate, intolerant, unscrupulous, credulous, numerous body, on the other a refined, better-informed, yet doubting sect. The Emperor Constantius, guided by his father's latest principles, having sided with the Arian party, soon found that under the new system a bishop would, without hesitation, oppose his sovereign. Athanasius, the Bishop of Alexandria, as the head of the orthodox party, became the personal antagonist of the emperor, who attempted, after vainly using physical compulsion, to resort to the celestial weapons in vogue by laying claim to Divine inspiration. Like his father, he had a celestial vision; but, as his views were Arian, the orthodox rejected without scruple his supernatural authority, and Hilary of Poictiers wrote a book to prove that he was Antichrist. The horrible bloodshed and murders attending these quarrels in the great cities, and the private life of persons both of high and low degree, clearly showed that Christianity, through its union with politics, had fallen into such a state that it could no longer control the passions of men. The biography of the sons of Constantine is an awful relation of family murders. Religion had disappeared, theology had come in its stead. Even theology had gone mad. But in the midst of these disputes worldly interests were steadily kept in view. At the Council of Ariminium, A.D. 359, an attempt was made to have the lands belonging to the churches exempt from all taxation; to his credit, the emperor steadfastly refused. Macedonius, the Bishop of Constantinople, who had passed over the slaughtered bodies of three thousand people to take possession of his episcopal throne, exceeded in heresy even Arius himself, by not only asserting the inferiority of the Son to the Father, but by absolutely denying the divinity of the Holy Ghost.

Athanasius rebels against the emperor.

Steady aggression of the Church and crimes of ecclesiastics.

As the fruits of these broils, two facts appear: 1st, that there is a higher law, which the faithful may obey, in opposition to the law of the land, when

Two results of these events.

it suits their views; the law of God, as expounded by the bishop, who can eternally punish the soul, must take precedence of the law of Cæsar, who can only kill the body and seize the goods; 2d, that there is a supremacy in the Bishop of Rome, to whom Athanasius, the leader of the orthodox, by twice visiting that city, submitted his cause. The significance of these facts becomes conspicuous in later ages. Things were evidently shaping themselves for a trial of strength between the imperial and ecclesiastical powers, heretofore allied. They were about to quarrel over their booty.

We have now to consider this asserted supremacy of the Bishop of Rome, and how it came to be established as a political fact. We must also turn from the Oriental variations of opinion to those of the West. Except by thus enlarging the field to be traversed, we can gain no perfect conception of the general intellectual tendency.

History of Papal supremacy.

For long after its introduction to Western Europe, Christianity was essentially a Greek religion. Its Oriental aspect had become Hellenized. Its churches had, in the first instance, a Greek organization, conducted their worship in that tongue, and composed their writings in it. Though it retained much of this foreign aspect so long as Rome continued to be the residence, or was more particularly under the eye of the emperors, it was gradually being affected by the influences to which it was exposed. On Western Europe, the questions which had so profoundly agitated the East, such as the nature of God, the Trinity, the cause of evil, had made but little impression, the intellectual peculiarity of the people being unsuited to such exercises. The foundation of Constantinople, by taking off the political pressure, permitted native peculiarities to manifest themselves, and Latin Christianity emerged in contradistinction to Greek.

Hellenized Christianity.

Yet still it cannot be said that Europe owes its existing forms of Christianity to a Roman origin. It is indebted to Africa for them. We live under African domination.

Modified by Africanism.

I have now with brevity to relate the progress of this interesting event; how African conceptions were firmly established in Rome, and, by the time that Greek Christianity had lost its expansive power and ceased to be aggressive, African Christianity took its place, extending to the North and West, and obtaining for itself an organization copied from that of the Roman empire; sacerdotal prætors, proconsuls, and a Cæsar; developing its own jurisprudence, establishing its own magistracy, exchanging the Greek tongue it had hitherto used for the Latin, which, soon becoming a sacred language, conferred upon it the most singular advantages.

Subordinate position of the early Roman Church.

The Greek churches were of the nature of confederated republics; the Latin Church instinctively tended to monarchy. Far from assuming an attitude of conspicuous dignity, the primitive bishops of Rome led a life of obscurity. In the earliest times, the bishops of Jerusalem, of whom James, the brother of our Lord, was the first, are spoken of as the heads of the Church, and so regarded even in Rome itself. The controversy respecting Easter, A.D. 109, shows, however, how soon the disposition for Western supremacy was exhibited, Victor, the Bishop of Rome, requiring the Asiatic bishops to conform to the view of his Church respecting the time at which the festival of Easter should be observed, and being resisted therein by Polycrates, the Bishop of Ephesus, on behalf of the Eastern churches, the feud continuing until the determination of the Council of Nicea. It was not in Asia alone that the growth of Roman supremacy was resisted. There is no difficulty in selecting from ecclesiastical history proofs of the same feeling in many other quarters. Thus, when the disciples of Montanus, the Phrygian, who pretended to be the Paraclete, had converted to their doctrines and austerities the Bishop of Rome and Tertullian the Carthaginian, on the former backsliding from that faith, the latter denounced him as a Patripassian heretic. Yet, for the most part, a good understanding obtained not only between Rome and Carthage, but also among the Gallic and Spanish churches, who looked upon Rome as conspicuous and illustrious, though as no more than equal to themselves. At the Council of Carthage St. Cyprian said, "None of us ought to set himself up as a bishop of bishops, or pretend tyrannically to restrain his colleagues, because each bishop has a liberty and power to act as he thinks fit, and can no more be judged by another bishop than he can judge another. But we must all wait for the judgment of Jesus Christ, to whom alone belongs the power to set us over the Church, and to judge of our actions."

Its gradual increase in wealth and influence,

Rome by degrees emerged from this equality, not by the splendid talents of any illustrious man, for among her early bishops none rose above mediocrity, but partly from her political position, partly from the great wealth she soon accumulated, and partly from the policy she happened to follow. Her bishop was not present at the Council of Nicea, A.D. 325, nor at that of Sardica, A.D. 345; perhaps on these occasions, as on others of a like kind subsequently, the immediate motive of his standing aloof was the fear that he might not receive the presidency. Soon, however, was discerned the advantage of the system of appearing by representatives. Such an attitude, moreover, offered the opportunity of frequently holding the balance of power in the fierce conflicts that soon arose, made Rome a retreat for the discomfited ecclesiastic, and her bishop, apparently, an elevated and unbiased arbiter on his case. It was thus that Athanasius, in his contests with the emperor, found a refuge and protector. With this elevated position in the esteem of strangers came also domestic dignity. The prodigal gifts of the rich Roman ladies had already made the bishopric to be sought after by those who esteem the ease and luxuries of life, as well as by the ambitious. Fierce contests arose on the occurrence of vacancies. At the election of Damasus, one hundred and thirty of the slain lay in the basilica of Sisinnius: the competitors had called in the aid of a rabble of gladiators, charioteers, and other ruffians; nor could the riots be ended except by the intervention of the imperial troops.

and early corruptions.

It was none too soon that Jerome introduced the monastic system at Rome—there was need of a change to austerity; none too soon that legacy-hunting on the part of the clergy was prohibited by law—it had become a public scandal; none too soon that Jerome struggled for the patronage of the rich Roman women;

none too soon that this stern fanatic denounced the immorality of the Roman clergy, when even the Bishop Damasus himself was involved in a charge of adultery. It became clear, if the clergy would hold their ground in public estimation against their antagonists the monks, that celibacy must be insisted on. The doctrine of the pre-eminent value of virginity was steadily making progress; but it cost many years of struggle before the monks carried their point, and the celibacy of the clergy became compulsory.

Necessity for an apostolic head.

It had long been seen by those who hoped for Roman supremacy that there was a necessity for the establishment of a definite and ascertained doctrine—a necessity for recognizing some apostolic man, who might be the representative of a criterion of truth. The Eastern system of deciding by councils was in its nature uncertain. The councils themselves had no ascertained organization. Experience had shown that they were too much under the control of the court at Constantinople.

Necessity for Councils or a pontiff.

This tendency to accept the republican decisions of councils in the East, and monarchical ones by a supreme pontiff in the West, in reality, however, depended on a common sentiment entertained by reflecting men everywhere. Something must be done to check the anarchy of opinion.

To show how this tendency was satisfied, it will be sufficient to select, out of the numberless controversies of the times, a few leading ones. A clear light is thrown upon the matter by the history of the Pelagian, Nestorian, and Eutychian heresies. Their chronological period is from about A.D. 400 to A.D. 450.

The Pelagian controversy.

Pelagius was the assumed name of a British monk, who, about the first of those dates, passed through Western Europe and Northern Africa, teaching the doctrines that Adam was by nature mortal, and that, if he had not sinned, he nevertheless would have died; that the consequences of his sin were confined to himself, and did not affect his posterity; that new-born infants are in the same condition as Adam before his fall; that we are at birth as pure as he was; that we sin by our own free will, and in the same manner may reform, and thereby work out our own salvation; that the grace of God is given according to our merits. He was repelled from Africa by the influence of St. Augustine, and denounced in Palestine from the cell of Jerome. He specially insisted on this, that it is not the mere act of baptizing by water that washes away sin, sin can only be removed by good works. Infants are baptized before it is possible that they could have sinned. On the contrary, Augustine resisted these doctrines, resting himself on the words of Scripture that baptism is for the remission of sins. The case of children compelled that father to introduce the doctrine of original sin as derived from Adam, notwithstanding the dreadful consequences if they die unbaptized. In like manner also followed the doctrines of predestination, grace, atonement.

Effect of Pelagianism on papal superiority.

Summoned before a synod at Diospolis, Pelagius was unexpectedly acquitted of heresy—an extraordinary decision, which brought Africa and the East into conflict. Under these circumstances, perhaps without a clear foresight of the issue, the matter was referred to Rome as arbiter or judge.

In his decision, Innocent I., magnifying the dignity of the Roman see and the advantage of such a supreme tribunal, determined in favour of the African bishops. But scarcely had he done this when he died, and his successor, Zosimus, annulled his judgment, and declared the opinions of Pelagius to be orthodox. Carthage now put herself in an attitude of resistance. There was danger of a metaphysical or theological Punic war. Meantime the wily Africans quietly procured from the emperor an edict denouncing Pelagius as a heretic. Through the influence of Count Valerius the faith of Europe was settled; the heresiarchs and their accomplices were condemned to exile and forfeiture of their estates; the contested doctrine that Adam was created without any liability to death was established by law; to deny it was a state crime. Thus it appears that the vacillating papacy was not yet strong enough to exalt itself above its equals, and the orthodoxy of Europe was for ever determined by an obscure court intrigue.

Settlement of the Pelagian question by the Africans.

Scarcely was the Pelagian controversy disposed of when

a new heresy appeared. Nestorius, the Bishop of Antioch, attempted to distinguish between the divine and human nature of Christ; he considered that they had become too much confounded, and that "the God" ought to be kept separate from "the Man." Hence it followed that the Virgin Mary should not be regarded as the "Mother of God," but only the "Mother of Christ—the God-man." Called by the Emperor Theodosius the Younger to the episcopate of Constantinople, A.D. 427, Nestorius was very quickly plunged by the intrigues of a disappointed faction of that city into disputes with the populace.

The Nestorian controversy.

Let us hear the Bishop of Constantinople himself; he is preaching in the great metropolitan church, setting forth, with all the eloquence of which language is capable, the attributes of the illimitable, the everlasting, the Almighty God. "And can this God have a mother? The heathen notion of a god born of a mortal mother is directly confuted by St. Paul, who declares the Lord to be without father and without mother. Could a creature bear the uncreated?" He thus insisted that what was born of Mary was human, and the divine was added afterwards. At once the monks raised a riot in the city, and Cyril, the Bishop of Alexandria, espoused their cause.

The doctrines of Nestorius.

Beneath the outraged orthodoxy of Cyril lay an ill-concealed motive, the desire of the Bishop of Alexandria to humble the Bishop of Constantinople. The uproar commenced with sermons, epistles, addresses. Instigated by the monks of Alexandria, the monks of Constantinople took up arms in behalf of "the Mother of God." Again we remark the eminent position of Rome. Both parties turn to her as an arbiter. Pope Celestine assembles a synod. The Bishop of Constantinople is ordered by the Bishop of Rome to recant, or hold himself under excommunication. Italian supremacy is emerging through Oriental disputes, yet not without a struggle. Relying on his influence at court, Nestorius resists, excommunicates Cyril, and the emperor summons a council to meet at Ephesus.

To that council Nestorius repaired, with sixteen bishops

and some of the city populace. Cyril collected fifty, together with a rabble of sailors, bath-men, and women of the baser sort. The imperial commissioner with his troops with difficulty repressed the tumult of the assembly.

Overthrow of Nestorianism by the Africans.

The rescript was fraudulently read before the arrival of the Syrian bishops. In one day the matter was completed; the Virgin's party triumphed, and Nestorius was deposed. On the arrival of the Syrian ecclesiastics, a meeting of protest was held by them. A riot, with much bloodshed, occurred in the Cathedral of St. John. The emperor was again compelled to interfere; he ordered eight deputies from each party to meet him at Chalcedon. In the meantime court intrigues decided the matter. The emperor's sister was in after times celebrated by the party of Cyril as having been the cause of the discomfiture of Nestorius: "the Holy Virgin of the court of Heaven had found an ally of her own sex in the holy virgin of the emperor's court." But there were also other very efficient auxiliaries. In the treasury of the chief eunuch, which some time after there was occasion to open, was discovered an acknowledgment of many pounds of gold received by him from Cyril, through Paul, his sister's son. Nestorius was abandoned by the court, and eventually exiled to an Egyptian oasis. An edifying legend relates that his blasphemous tongue was devoured by worms, and that from the heats of an Egyptian desert he escaped only into the hotter torments of Hell.

Worship of the Virgin Mary.

So, again, in the affair of Nestorius as in that of Pelagius, Africa triumphed, and the supremacy of Rome, her ally or confederate, was becoming more and more distinct.

A very important result in this gradual evolution of Roman supremacy arose from the affair of Eutyches, the Archimandrite of a convent of monks at Constantinople. He had distinguished himself as a leader in the riots occurring at the time of Nestorius and in other subsequent troubles. Accused before a synod held in Constantinople of denying the two natures of Christ, of saying that if there be two natures there must be two Sons, Eutyches was convicted, and

The Eutychian controversy.

sentence of excommunication passed upon him. This was, however, only the ostensible cause of his condemnation; the true motive was connected with a court intrigue. The chief eunuch, who was his godson, was occupied in a double movement to elevate Eutyches to the see of Constantinople, and to destroy the authority of Pulcheria, the emperor's sister, by Eudocia, the emperor's wife. On his condemnation, Eutyches appealed to the emperor, who summoned, at the instigation of the eunuch, a council to meet at Ephesus. This was the celebrated "Robber Synod," as it was called. It pronounced in favour of the orthodoxy of Eutyches, and ordered his restoration, deposing the Bishop of Constantinople, Flavianus, who was his rival, and at the synod had been his judge and also Eusebius, who had been his accuser. A riot ensued, in which the Bishop of Constantinople was murdered by the Bishop of Alexandria and one Barsumas, who beat him with their fists amid cries of "Kill him! kill him!" The Italian legates made their escape from the uproar with difficulty.

The success of these movements was mainly due to Dioscorus, the Bishop of Alexandria, who thus accomplished the overthrow of his rivals of Antioch and Constantinople. An imperial edict gave force to the determination of the council. At this point the Bishop of Rome intervened, refusing to acknowledge the proceedings. It was well that Alexandria and Constantinople should be perpetually struggling, but it was not well that either should become paramount. Dioscorus thereupon broke off communion with him. Rome and Alexandria were at issue.

In a fortunate moment the emperor died; his sister, the orthodox Pulcheria, the friend of Leo, married Marcian, and made him emperor. A council was summoned at Chalcedon. Leo wished it to be in Italy, where no one could have disputed his presidency. As it was, he fell back on the ancient policy, and appeared by representatives. Dioscorus was overthrown, and sentence pronounced against him, in behalf of the council, by one of the representatives of Leo. It set forth that "Leo, therefore, by their voice, and with the authority of the council, in the name of the Apostle

Another advance of Rome to power through Eutychianism.

Peter, the Rock and foundation of the Church, deposes Dioscorus from his episcopal dignity, and excludes him from all Christian rites and privileges."

The rivalry of Constantinople.

But, perhaps that no permanent advantage might accrue to Rome from the eminent position she was attaining in these transactions, when most of the prelates had left the council, a few, who were chiefly of the diocese of Constantinople, passed, among other canons, one to the effect that the supremacy of the Roman see was not in right of its descent from St. Peter, but because it was the bishopric of an imperial city. It assigned, therefore, to the Bishop of Constantinople equal civil dignity and ecclesiastical authority. Rome ever refused to recognize the validity of this canon.

Rivalries of the three great bishops.

In these contests of Rome, Constantinople, and Alexandria for supremacy—for, after all, they were nothing more than the rivalries of ambitious placemen for power—the Roman bishop uniformly came forth the gainer. And it is to be remarked that he deserved to be so; his course was always dignified, often noble; theirs exhibited a reckless scramble for influence, an unscrupulous resort to bribery, court intrigue, murder.

Nature of ecclesiastical councils.

Thus the want of a criterion of truth, and a determination to arrest a spirit of inquiry that had become troublesome, led to the introduction of councils, by which, in an authoritative manner, theological questions might be settled. But it is to be observed that these councils did not accredit themselves by the coincidence of their decisions on successive occasions, since they often contradicted one another; nor did they sustain those decisions only with a moral influence arising from the understanding of man, enlightened by their investigations and conclusions. Their human character is clearly shown by the necessity under which they laboured of enforcing their arbitrary conclusions by the support of the civil power. The same necessity which, in the monarchical East, led thus to the republican form of a council, led in the democratic West to the development of the autocratic papal power: but in both it was found that the final authority thus appealed to had no innate or divinely derived energy. It was altogether helpless except by the aid of military or civil compulsion against any one disposed to resist it.

No other opinion could be entertained of the character of these assemblages by men of practical ability who had been concerned in their transactions. Gregory of Nazianzen, one of the most pious and able men of his age, and one who, during a part of its sittings, was president of the Council of Constantinople, A.D. 381, refused subsequently to attend any more, saying that he had never known an assembly of bishops terminate well; that, instead of removing evils, they only increased them, and that their strifes and lust of power were not to be described. A thousand years later, Æneas Sylvius, Pope Pius II., speaking of another council, observes that it was not so much directed by the Holy Ghost as by the passions of men.

Progressive variation of human thought manifested by these councils.

Notwithstanding the contradictions and opposition they so frequently exhibit, there may be discerned in the decisions of these bodies the traces of an affiliation indicating the continuous progression of thought. Thus, of the four œcumenical councils that were concerned with the facts spoken of in the preceding pages, that of Nicea determined the Son to be of the same substance with the Father; that of Constantinople, that the Son and Holy Spirit are equal to the Father; that of Ephesus, that the two natures of Christ make but one person; and that of Chalcedon, that these natures remain two, notwithstanding their personal union. But that they failed of their object in constituting a criterion of truth is plainly demonstrated by such simple facts as that, in the fourth century alone, there were thirteen councils adverse to Arius, fifteen in his favour, and seventeen for the semi-Arians—in all, forty-five. From such a confusion, it was necessary that the councils themselves must be subordinate to a higher authority—a higher criterion, able to give to them or refuse to them authenticity. That the source of power, both for the council in the East and the papacy in the West, was altogether political, is proved by almost every transaction in which they were concerned. In the case of the papacy, this was well seen in the contest between Hilary the Bishop of Arles, and Leo, on which occasion an edict was issued by the Emperor Valentinian denouncing the contumacy of Hilary, and setting forth that "though the sentence of so great a pontiff as the Bishop of Rome did not need imperial confirmation, yet that it must now be understood by all bishops that the decrees of the apostolic see should henceforth be law, and that whoever refused to obey the citation of the Roman pontiff should be compelled to do so by the Moderator of the province." Herein we see the intrinsic nature of Papal power distinctly. It is allied with physical force.

Pontifical power sustained by physical force.

In the midst of these theological disputes occurred that great event which I have designated as marking the close of the age of Inquiry. It was the fall of Rome.

The fall of Rome.

In the Eastern empire the Goths had become permanently settled, having laws of their own, a magistracy of their own, paying no taxes, but contributing 40,000 men to the army. The Visigoths were spreading through Greece, Spain, Italy. In their devastations of the former country, they had spared Athens for the sake of her souvenirs. The Eleusinian mysteries had ceased. From that day Greece never saw prosperity again. Alaric entered Italy. Stilicho, the imperial general, forced him to retreat. Rhadogast made his invasion. Stilicho compelled him to surrender at discretion. The Burgundians and Vandals overflowed Gaul; the Suevi, Vandals, and Alans overflowed Spain. Stilicho, a man worthy of the old days of the republic, though a Goth, was murdered by the emperor his master. Alaric appeared before Rome. It was 619 years since she had felt the presence of a foreign enemy, and that was Hannibal. She still contained 1780 senatorial palaces, the annual income of some of the owners of which was 160,000*l*. The city was eighteen miles in circumference, and contained above a million of people—of people, as in old times clamorous for distributions of bread, and wine, and oil. In its conscious despair, the apostate city, it is said, with the

Spread of the barbarians.

Capture and sack of Rome by Alaric.

consent of the pope, offered sacrifice to Jupiter, its repudiated, and, as it now believed, its offended god. 200,000*l.*, together with many costly goods, were paid as a ransom. The barbarian general retired. He was insulted by the emperor from his fastness at Ravenna. Altercations and new marches ensued; and at last, for the third time, Alaric appeared before Rome. At midnight on the 24th of April, A.D. 410, eleven hundred and sixty-three years from the foundation of the city, the Salarian gate was opened to him by the treachery of slaves; there was no god to defend her in her dire extremity, and Rome was sacked by the Goths.

Has the Eternal City really fallen! was the universal exclamation throughout the empire when it became known that Alaric had taken Rome. Though paganism had been ruined in a national sense, the true Roman ethnical element had never given it up, but was dying out with it, a relic of the population of the city still adhering to the ancient faith. Among this were not wanting many of the aristocratic families and philosophers, who imputed the disaster to the public apostasy, and in their shame and suffering loudly proclaimed that the nation was justly punished for its abandonment of the gods of its forefathers, the gods who had given victory and empire. It became necessary for the Church to meet this accusation, which, while it was openly urged by thousands, was doubtless believed to be true by silent, and timid, and panic-stricken millions. With the intention of defending Christianity, St. Augustine, one of the ablest of the fathers, solemnly devoted thirteen years of his life to the composition of his great work entitled "The City of God." It is interesting for us to remark the tone of some of these replies of the Christians to their pagan adversaries.

Accusations of the Pagans against the Christians.

"For the manifest deterioration of Roman manners, and for the impending dissolution of the state, paganism itself is responsible. Our political power is only of yesterday; it is in no manner concerned with the gradual development of luxury and wickedness, which has been going on for the last thousand years. Your ancestors made war a trade; they laid under tribute and

The Christian reply.

enslaved the adjacent nations; but were not profusion, extravagance, dissipation, the necessary consequences of conquest? was not Roman idleness the inevitable result of the filling of Italy with slaves? Every hour rendered wider that bottomless gulf which separates immense riches from abject poverty. Did not the middle class, in which reside the virtue and strength of a nation, disappear, and aristocratic families remain in Rome, whose estates in Syria or Spain, Gaul or Africa, equalled, nay, even exceeded in extent and revenue illustrious kingdoms, provinces for the annexation of which the republic of old had decreed triumphs? Was there not in the streets a profligate rabble living in total idleness, fed and amused at the expense of the state? We are not answerable for the grinding oppression perpetrated on the rural populations until they have been driven to despair, their numbers so diminishing as to warn us that there is danger of their being extinguished. We did not suggest to the Emperor Trajan to abandon Dacia, and neglect that policy which fixed the boundaries of the empire at strong military posts. We did not suggest to Caracalla to admit all sorts of people to Roman citizenship, nor dislocate the population by a wild pursuit of civil offices or the discharge of military duties. We did not crowd Italy with slaves, nor make those miserable men more degraded than the beasts of the field, compelling them to labours which are the business of the brutes. We have taught and practised a very different doctrine. We did not nightly put into irons the population of provinces and cities reduced to bondage. We are not responsible for the inevitable insurrections, poisonings, assassinations, vengeance. We did not bring on that state of things in which a man having a patrimony found it his best interest to abandon it without compensation and flee. We did not demoralize the populace by providing them food, games, races, theatres; we have been persecuted because we would not set our feet in a theatre. We did not ruin the senate and aristocracy by sacrificing everything, even ourselves, for the Julian family. We did not neutralize the legions by setting them to fight against one another. We were not the first to degrade Rome · Diocletian, who persecuted us, gave the example by establishing his residence at Nicomedia. As to the sentiment of patriotism of which you vaunt, was it not destroyed by your own emperors? When they had made Roman citizens of Gauls and Egyptians, Africans and Huns, Spaniards and Syrians, how could they expect that such a motley crew would remain true to the interests of an Italian town, and that town their hated oppressor. Patriotism depends on concentration; it cannot bear diffusion. Something more than such a worldly tie was wanted to bind the diverse nations together; they have found it in Christianity. A common language imparts community of thought and feeling; but what was to be expected when Greek is the language of one half of the ruling classes, and Latin of the other? we say nothing of the thousand unintelligible forms of speech in use throughout the Roman world. The fall of the senate preceded, by a few years, the origin of Christianity; you surely will not say that we were the inciters of the usurpations of the Cæsars? What have we had to do with the army, that engine of violence, which in ninety-two years gave you thirty-two emperors and twenty-seven pretenders to the throne? We did not suggest to the Prætorian Guards to put up the empire to auction.

"Can you really wonder that all this should come to an end? We do not wonder; on the contrary, we thank God for it. It is time that the human race had rest. The sighing of the prisoner, the prayer of the captive, are heard at last. Yet the judgment has been tempered with mercy. Had the pagan Rhadogast taken Rome, not a life would have been spared, no stone left on another. The Christian Alaric, though a Goth, respects his Christian brethren, and for their sakes you are saved. As to the gods, those dæmons in whom you trust, did they always save you from calamity? How long did Hannibal insult them? Was it a goose or a god that saved the Capitol from Brennus? Where were the gods in all the defeats, some of them but recent, of the pagan emperors? It is well that the purple Babylon has fallen, the harlot who was drunk with the blood of nations.

"In the place of this earthly city, this vaunted mistress, of the world, whose fall closes a long career of superstition and sin, there shall arise "the City of God." The purifying fire of the barbarian shall remove her heathenish defilements, and make her fit for the kingdom of Christ. Instead of a thousand years of that night of crime, to which in your despair you look back, there is before her the day of the millennium, predicted by the prophets of old. In her regenerated walls there shall be no taint of sin, but righteousness and peace; no stain of the vanities of the world, no conflicts of ambition, no sordid hunger for gold, no lust after glory, no desire for domination, but holiness to the Lord."

St. Augustine's "City of God."

Of those who in such sentiments defended the cause of the new religion St. Augustine was the chief. In his great work, "the City of God," which may be regarded as the ablest specimen of the early Christian literature, he pursues this theme, if not in the language, at least in the spirit here presented, and through a copious detail of many books. On the later Christianity of the Western churches he has exerted more influence than any other of the fathers. To him is due much of the precision of our views on original sin, total depravity, grace, predestination, election.

Life and writings of St. Augustine.

In his early years St. Augustine had led a frivolous and evil life, plunging into all the dissipations of the gay city of Carthage. Through the devious paths of Manichæism, astrology, and scepticism, he at last arrived at the truth. It was not, however, the Fathers, but Cicero, to whom the good change was due; the writings of that great orator won him over to a love of wisdom, weaning him from the pleasures of the theatre, the follies of divination and superstition. From his Manichæan errors, he was snatched by Ambrose, the Bishop of Milan, who baptized him, together with his illegitimate son Adeodatus. In his writings we may, without difficulty, recognize the vestiges of Magianism, not as regards the duality of God, but as respects the division of mankind—the elect and lost; the kingdoms of grace and perdition, of God and the devil; answering to the Oriental ideas of the rule of light and darkness. From Ambrose, St. Augustine learned those high Trinitarian doctrines which were soon enforced in the West.

In his philosophical disquisitions on Time, Matter, Memory, this far-famed writer is, however, always unsatisfactory, often trivial. His doctrine that Scripture, as the word of God, is capable of a manifold meaning, led him into many delusions, and exercised, in subsequent ages, a most baneful influence on true science. Thus he finds in the Mosaic account of the creation proofs of the Trinity; that the firmament spoken of therein is the type of God's word; and that there is a correspondence between creation itself and the Church. His numerous books have often been translated, especially his Confessions, a work that has delighted and edified fifty generations, but which must, after all, yield the palm, as a literary production, to the writings of Bunyan, who, like Augustine, gave himself up to all the agony of unsparing personal examination and relentless self-condemnation, anatomizing his very soul, and dragging forth every sin into the face of day.

The ecclesiastical influence of St. Augustine has so completely eclipsed his political biography, that but little attention has been given to his conduct in the interesting time in which he lived. Sismondi recalls to his disadvantage that he was the friend of Count Boniface, who invited Genseric and his Vandals into Africa; the bloody consequences of that conspiracy cannot be exaggerated. It was through him that the count's name has been transmitted to posterity without infamy. Boniface was with him when he died, at Hippo, August 28th, A.D. 440.

Propitious effect of Alaric's siege.

When Rome thus fell before Alaric, so far from the provincial Christians bewailing her misfortune, they actually gloried in it. They critically distinguished between the downfall of the purple pagan harlot and the untouched city of God. The vengeance of the Goth had fallen on the temples, but the churches had been spared. Though in subsequent and not very distant calamities of the city these triumphant distinctions could scarcely be maintained, there can be no doubt that that catastrophe singularly developed papal power. The abasement of the ancient aristocracy brought into relief the bishop. It has been truly said that, as Rome rose from her ruins, the bishop was discerned to be her most conspicuous man. Most opportunely, at this period Jerome had completed his Latin translation of the Bible. The Vulgate henceforth became the ecclesiastical authority of the West. The influence of the heathen classics, which that austere anchorite had in early life admired, but had vainly attempted to free himself from by unremitting nocturnal flagellations, appears in this great version. It came at a critical moment for the West. In the politic non-committalism of Rome, it was not expedient that a pope should be an author. The Vulgate was all that the times required. Henceforth the East might occupy herself in the harmless fabrication of creeds and of heresies; the West could develop her practical talent in the much more important organization of ecclesiastical power.

Doubtless not without interest will the reader of these pages remark how closely the process of ecclesiastical events resembles that of civil. In both there is an irresistible tendency to the concentration of power. As in Roman history we have seen a few families, and, indeed, at last, one man grasp the influence which in earlier times was disseminated among the people, so in the Church the congregations are quickly found in subordination to their bishops, and these, in their turn, succumbing to a perpetually diminishing number of their compeers. In the period we are now considering, the minor episcopates, such as those of Jerusalem, Antioch, Carthage, had virtually lost their pristine force, everything having converged into the three great sees of Constantinople, Alexandria, and Rome. The history of the time is a record of the desperate struggles of the three chief bishops for supremacy. In this conflict Rome possessed many advantages; the two others were more immediately under the control of the imperial government, the clashing of interests between them more frequent, their rivalry more bitter. The control of ecclesiastical power was hence perpetually in Rome, though she was, both politically and intellectually, inferior to her competitors. As of old, there was a triumvirate in the world destined to concentrate into a despotism. And, as if to remind men that the principles involved in the movements of the

The fate of the three great bishops.

Church are of the same nature as those involved in the movements of the state, the resemblances here pointed out are sometimes singularly illustrated in trifling details. The Bishop of Alexandria was not the first triumvir who came to an untimely end on the banks of the Nile; the Roman pontiff was not the first who consolidated his power by the aid of Gallic legions.

CHAPTER X.

THE EUROPEAN AGE OF FAITH.

AGE OF FAITH IN THE EAST.

Consolidation of the Byzantine System, or the Union of Church and State.—The consequent Paganization of Religion and Persecution of Philosophy.

Political Necessity for the enforcement of Patristicism, or Science of the Fathers.—Its peculiar Doctrines.

Obliteration of the Vestiges of Greek Knowledge by Patristicism.—The Libraries and Serapion of Alexandria.—Destruction of the latter by Theodosius.—Death of Hypatia.—Extinction of Learning in the East by Cyril, his Associates and Successors.

THE policy of Constantine the Great inevitably tended to the paganization of Christianity. An incorporation of its pure doctrines with decaying pagan ideas was the necessary consequence of the control that had been attained by unscrupulous politicians and placemen. The faith, thus contaminated, gained a more general and ready popular acceptance, but at the cost of a new lease of life to those ideas. So thorough was the adulteration, that it was not until the Reformation, a period of more than a thousand years, that a separation of the true from the false could be accomplished.

The age of Faith.

Considering how many nations were involved in these events, and the length of time over which they extend, a clear treatment of the subject requires its subdivision. I shall therefore speak, 1st, of the Age of Faith in the East; 2nd, of the Age of Faith in the West. The former was closed prematurely by the Mohammedan conquest; the latter, after undergoing slow metamorphosis,

Subdivision of the subject.

passed into the European Age of Reason during the pontificate of Nicholas V.

In this and the following chapter I shall therefore treat of the age of Faith in the East, and of the catastrophe that closed it. I shall then turn to the Age of Faith in the West—a long but an instructive story.

The paganization of religion was in no small degree accomplished by the influence of the females of the court of Constantinople. It soon manifested all the essential features of a true mythology and hero-worship. Helena, the empress-mother, superintended the building of monumental churches over the reputed places of interest in the history of our Saviour—those of his birth, his burial, his ascension. A vast and ever-increasing crowd of converts from paganism, who had become such from worldly considerations, and still hankered after wonders like those in which their forefathers had from time immemorial believed, lent a ready ear to assertions which, to more hesitating or better-instructed minds, would have seemed to carry imposture on their very face. A temple of Venus, formerly erected on the site of the Holy Sepulchre, being torn down, there were discovered, in a cavern beneath, three crosses, and also the inscription written by Pilate. The Saviour's cross, being by miracle distinguished from those of the thieves, was divided, a part being kept at Jerusalem and a part sent to Constantinople, together with the nails used in the crucifixion, which were also fortunately found. These were destined to adorn the head of the emperor's statue on the top of the porphyry pillar. The wood of the cross, moreover, displayed a property of growth, and hence furnished an abundant supply for the demands of pilgrims, and an unfailing source of pecuniary profit to its possessors. In the course of subsequent years there was accumulated in the various churches of Europe, from this particular relic, a sufficiency to have constructed many hundred crosses. The age that could accept such a prodigy, of course found no difficulty in the vision of Constantine and the story of the Labarum.

The paganization of Christianity.

Discovery of the true cross and nails.

Such was the tendency of the times to adulterate

Christianity with the spirit of paganism, partly to conciliate the prejudices of worldly converts, partly in the hope of securing its more rapid spread. There is a solemnity in the truthful accusation which Faustus makes to Augustine: "You have substituted your agapæ for the sacrifices of the pagans; for their idols your martyrs, whom you serve with the very same honours. You appease the shades of the dead with wine and feasts; you celebrate the solemn festivals of the Gentiles, their calends and their solstices; and as to their manners, those you have retained without any alteration. Nothing distinguishes you from the pagans except that you hold your assemblies apart from them."

Political causes of paganization.

As we have seen in the last chapter, the course of political affairs had detached the power of the state from the philosophical and polytheistic parties. Joined to the new movement, it was not long before it gave significant proofs of the sincerity of its friendship by commencing an active persecution of the remnant of philosophy. It is to be borne in mind that the direction of the proselytism, which was thus leading to important results, was from below upward through society. As to philosophy, its action had been in the other direction; its depository in the few enlightened, in the few educated; its course, socially, from above downward. Under these circumstances, it was obvious enough that the prejudices of the ignorant populace would find, in the end, a full expression; that learning would have no consideration shown to it, or would be denounced as mere magic; that philosophy would be looked upon as a vain, and therefore sinful pursuit. When once a political aspirant has bidden with the multitude for power, and still depends on their pleasure for effective support, it is no easy thing to refuse their wishes or hold back from their demands. Even Constantine himself felt the pressure of the influence to which he was allied, and was compelled to surrender his friend Sopater, the philosopher, who was accused of binding the winds in an adverse quarter by the influence of magic, so that the corn-ships could not reach Constantinople; and the emperor was obliged to give orders for

Relative action of faith and philosophy.

The emperors resist their ecclesiastical allies.

his decapitation to satisfy the clamours in the theatre. Not that such requisitions were submitted to without a struggle, or that succeeding sovereigns were willing to make their dignity tacitly subordinate to ecclesiastical domination. It was the aim of Constantine to make theology a branch of politics; it was the hope of every bishop in the empire to make politics a branch of theology. Already, however, it was apparent that the ecclesiastical party would, in the end, get the upper hand, and that the reluctance of some of the emperors to obey its behests was merely the revolt of individual minds, and therefore ephemeral in its nature, and that the popular wishes would be abundantly gratified as soon as emperors arose who not merely, like Constantine, availed themselves of Christianity, but absolutely and sincerely adopted it.

The Emperor Julian.

Julian, by his brief but ineffectual attempt to restore paganism, scarcely restrained for a moment the course of the new doctrines now strengthening themselves continually in public estimation by incorporating ideas borrowed from paganism. Through the reign of Valentinian, who was a Nicenist, and of Valens, who was an Arian, things went on almost as if the episode of Julian had never occurred. The ancient gods, whose existence no one seems ever to have denied, were now thoroughly identified with dæmons; their worship was stigmatized as the practice of magic. Against this crime, regarded by the laws as equal to treason, a violent persecution arose. Persons resorting to Rome for the purposes of study were forbidden to remain there after they were twenty-one years of age. The force of this persecution fell practically upon the old religion, though nominally directed against the black art, for the primary function of paganism was to foretell future events in this world, and hence its connexion with divination and its punishment as magic.

Persecutions of his successors.

Necessity of learning to the bishops.

But the persecution, though directed at paganism, struck also at what remained of philosophy. A great party had attained to power under circumstances which compelled it to enforce the principle on which it was originally founded. That principle was the exaction of unhesitating belief, which, though it will answer very well for the humbler and more numerous class of men, is unsuited for those of a higher intellectual grade. The policy of Constantine had opened a career in the state, through the Church, for men of the lowest rank. Many of such had already attained to the highest dignities. A burning zeal rather than the possession of profound learning animated them. But eminent position once attained, none stood more in need of the appearance of wisdom. Under such circumstances, they were tempted to set up their own notions as final and unimpeachable truth, and to denounce as magic, or the sinful pursuit of vain trifling, all the learning that stood in the way. In this the hand of the civil power assisted. It was intended to cut off every philosopher. Every manuscript that could be seized was forthwith burned. Throughout the East, men in terror destroyed their libraries, for fear that some unfortunate sentence contained in any of the books should involve them and their families in destruction. The universal opinion was that it was right to compel men to believe what the majority of society had now accepted as the truth, and, if they refused, it was right to punish them. No one in the dominating party was heard to raise his voice in behalf of intellectual liberty. The mystery of things above reason was held to be the very cause that they should be accepted by Faith; a singular merit was supposed to appertain to that mental condition in which belief precedes understanding.

Growth of bigotry and superstition.

The death-blow to paganism was given by the Emperor Theodosius, a Spaniard, who, from the services he rendered in this particular, has been rewarded with the title of "The Great." From making the practice of magic and the inspection of the entrails of animals capital offences, he proceeded to prohibit sacrifices, A.D. 391, and even the entering of temples. He alienated the revenues of many temples, confiscated the estates of others, some he demolished. The vestal virgins he dismissed, and any house profaned by incense he declared forfeited to the imperial exchequer. When once the property of a religious establishment has been irrevocably taken away, it is needless to declare its worship a capital crime.

Fanaticism of Theodosius.

But not only did the government thus constitute itself a thorough auxiliary of the new religion; it also tried to secure it from its own dissensions. Apostates were deprived of the right of bequeathing their own property. Inquisitors of faith were established; they were at once spies and judges, the prototypes of the most fearful tribunal of modern times. Theodosius, to whom the carrying into effect of these measures was due, found it, however, more expedient for himself to institute living emblems of his personal faith than to rely on any ambiguous creed. He therefore sentenced all those to be deprived of civil rights, and to be driven into exile, who did not accord with the belief of Damasus, the Bishop of Rome, and Peter, the Bishop of Alexandria. Those who presumed to celebrate Easter on the same day as the Jews he condemned to death. "We will," says he, in his edict, "that all who embrace this creed be called catholic Christians"—the rest are heretics.

Responsibility of the clergy in these events.

Impartial history is obliged to impute the origin of these tyrannical and scandalous acts of the civil power to the influence of the clergy, and to hold them responsible for the crimes. The guilt of impure, unscrupulous women, eunuchs, parasites, violent soldiers in possession of absolute power, lies at their door. Yet human nature can never, in any condition of affairs, be altogether debased. Though the system under which men were living pushed them forward to these iniquities, the individual sense of right and wrong sometimes vindicated itself. In these pages we shall again and again meet this personal revolt against the indefensible consequences of system. It was thus that there were bishops who openly intervened between the victim and his oppressor, who took the treasures of the Church to redeem slaves from captivity. For this a future age will perhaps excuse Ambrose, the Archbishop of Milan, the impostures he practised, remembering that, face to face, he held Theodosius the Great to accountability for the massacre of seven thousand persons, whom, in a fit of vengeance, he had murdered in the circus of Thessalonica, A.D. 390, and inexorably compelled the imperial culprit, to whom he and all his party were under such obligations, to atone for his crime by such

Massacre at Thessalonica.

penance as may be exacted in this world, teaching his sovereign "that though he was of the Church and in the Church, he was not above the Church;" that brute force must give way to intellect, and that even the meanest human being has rights in the sight of God.

Political events had thus taken a course disastrous to human knowledge. A necessity had arisen that they to whom circumstances had given the control of public faith should also have the control of public knowledge. The moral condition of the world had thus come into antagonism with scientific progress. As had been the case many ages before in India, the sacred writings were asserted to contain whatever was necessary or useful for man to know. Questions in astronomy, geography, chronology, history, or any other branch which had hitherto occupied or amused the human mind, were now to be referred to a new tribunal for solution, and there remained nothing to be done by the philosopher. A revelation of science is incompatible with any farther advance; it admits no employment save that of the humble commentator.

Introduction of Patristicism.

The early ecclesiastical writers, or Fathers, as they are often called, came thus to be considered not only as surpassing all other men in piety, but also as excelling them in wisdom. Their dictum was looked upon as final. This eminent position they held for many centuries; indeed, it was not until near the period of the Reformation that they were deposed. The great critics who appeared at that time, by submitting the Patristic works to a higher analysis, comparing them with one another and showing their mutual contradictions, brought them all to their proper level. The habit of even so much as quoting them went out of use, when it was perceived that not one of these writers could present the necessary credentials to entitle him to speak with authority on any scientific fact. Many of them had not scrupled to express their contempt of the things they thus presumed to judge. Thus Eusebius says: "It is not through ignorance of the things admired by philosophers, but through contempt of such useless labour, that we think so little of these matters, turning our souls to the exercise

Apology of the fathers for Patristicism.

of better things." In such a spirit Lactantius holds the whole of philosophy to be "empty and false." Speaking in reference to the heretical doctrine of the globular form of the earth, he says: "Is it possible that men can be so absurd as to believe that the crops and the trees on the other side of the earth hang downward, and that men have their feet higher than their heads? If you ask them how they defend these monstrosities? how things do not fall away from the earth on that side? they reply that the nature of things is such, that heavy bodies tend toward the centre like the spokes of a wheel, while light bodies, as clouds, smoke, fire, tend from the centre to the heavens on all sides. Now I am really at a loss what to say of those who, when they have once gone wrong, steadily persevere in their folly, and defend one absurd opinion by another." On the question of the antipodes, St. Augustine asserts that "it is impossible there should be inhabitants on the opposite side of the earth, since no such race is recorded by Scripture among the descendants of Adam."

The doctrines of Patristicism.

Patristicism, or the science of the Fathers, was thus essentially founded on the principle that the Scriptures contain all knowledge permitted to man. It followed, therefore, that natural phenomena may be interpreted by the aid of texts, and that all philosophical doctrines must be moulded to the pattern of orthodoxy. It asserted that God made the world out of nothing, since to admit the eternity of matter leads to Manichæism. It taught that the earth is a plane, and the sky a vault above it, in which the stars are fixed, and the sun, moon, and planets perform their motions, rising and setting; that these bodies are altogether of a subordinate nature, their use being to give light to man; that still higher and beyond the vault of the sky is heaven, the abode of God and the angelic hosts; that in six days the earth, and all that it contains, were made; that it was overwhelmed by a universal deluge, which destroyed all living things save those preserved in the ark, the waters being subsequently dried up by the wind; that man is the moral centre of the world; for him all things were created and are sustained; that, so far as his ever having shown any tendency to improvement, he has fallen both in wisdom and worth, the first man, before his sin, having been perfect in body and soul: hence Patristicism ever looked backward, never forward; that through that sin death came into the world; not even any animal had died previously, but all had been immortal. It utterly rejected the idea of the government of the world by law, asserting the perpetual interference of an instant Providence on all occasions, not excepting the most trifling. It resorted to spiritual influences in the production of natural effects, assigning to angels the duty of moving the stars, carrying up water from the sea to form rain, and managing eclipses. It affirmed that man had existed but a few centuries upon earth, and that he could continue only a little longer, for that the world itself might every moment be expected to be burned up by fire. It deduced all the families of the earth from one primitive pair, and made them all morally responsible for the sin committed by that pair. It rejected the doctrine that man can modify his own organism as absolutely irreligious, the physician being little better than an atheist, but it affirmed that cures may be effected by the intercession of saints, at the shrines of holy men, and by relics. It altogether repudiated the improvement of man's physical state; to increase his power or comfort was to attempt to attain what Providence denied; philosophical investigation was an unlawful prying into things that God had designed to conceal. It declined the logic of the Greeks, substituting miracle-proof for it, the demonstration of an assertion being supposed to be given by a surprising illustration of something else.

A wild astronomy had thus supplanted the astronomy of Hipparchus; the miserable fictions of Eusebius had subverted the chronology of Manetho and Eratosthenes; the geometry of Euclid and Apollonius was held to be of no use; the geography of Ptolemy a blunder; the great mechanical inventions of Archimedes incomparably surpassed by the miracles worked at the shrines of a hundred saints.

Of such a mixture of truth and of folly was Patristicism composed. Ignorance in power had found it necessary to have a false and unprogressive science, forgetting that sooner or later the time must arrive when it would be impossible to maintain stationary ideas in a world of which the affairs are ever advancing. A failure to include in the system thus imposed upon men any provision for intellectual progress was the great and fatal mistake of those times. Each passing century brought its incompatibilities. A strain upon the working of the system soon occurred, and perpetually increased in force. It became apparent that, in the end, the imposition would be altogether unable to hold together. On a futnre page we shall see what were the circumstances under which it at last broke down.

Intrinsic weakness of the Patristic system.

The wonder-worker who prepares to exhibit his phantasmagoria upon the wall, knows well how much it adds to the delusion to have all lights extinguished save that which is in his own dark lantern. I have now to relate how the last flickering rays of Greek learning were put out; how Patristicism, aided by her companion Bigotry, attempted to lay the foundations of her influence in security.

It commences by extinguishing Greek science.

In the reign of Theodosius the Great, the pagan religion and pagan knowledge were together destroyed. This emperor was restrained by no doubts, for he was very ignorant and, it must be admitted, was equally sincere and severe. Among his early measures we find an order that if any of the governors of Egypt so much as entered a temple he should be fined fifteen pounds of gold. He followed this by the destruction of the temples of Syria. At this period the Archbishopric of Alexandria was held by one Theophilus, a bold, bad man, who had once been a monk of Nitria. It was about A.D. 390. The Trinitarian conflict was at the time composed, one party having got the better of the other. To the monks and rabble of Alexandria the temple of Serapis and its library were doubly hateful, partly because of the Pantheistic opposition it shadowed forth against the prevailing doctrine, and partly because within its walls sorcery, magic, and other dealings with the devil had for ages been going on. We have related how Ptolemy Philadelphus commenced the great library in the aristocratic quarter of the city named

Acts of the Emperor Theodosius.

Alexandrian libraries.

Bruchion, and added various scientific establishments to it. Incited by this example, Eumenes, King of Pergamus, established out of rivalry a similar library in his metropolis. With the intention of preventing him from excelling that of Egypt, Ptolemy Epiphanes prohibited the exportation of papyrus, whereupon Eumenes invented the art of making parchment. The second great Alexandrian library was that established by Ptolemy Physcon at the Serapion, in the adjoining quarter of the town. The library in the Bruchion, which was estimated to contain 400,000 volumes, was accidentally, or, as it has been said, purposely burned during the siege of the city by Julius Cæsar, but that in the Serapion escaped. To make amends for this great catastrophe, Marc Antony presented to Cleopatra the rival library, brought for that purpose from Pergamus. It consisted of 200,000 volumes. It was with the library in the Bruchion that the Museum was originally connected; but after its conflagration, the remains of the various surviving establishments were transferred to the Serapion, which therefore was, at the period of which we are speaking, the greatest depository of knowledge in the world.

Library of Pergamus transferred to Egypt.

The pagan Roman emperors had not been unmindful of the great trust they had thus inherited from the Ptolemies. The temple of Serapis was universally admitted to be the noblest religious structure in the world, unless perhaps the patriotic Roman excepted that of the Capitoline Jupiter. It was approached by a vast flight of steps; was adorned with many rows of columns; and in its quadrangular portico—a matchless work of skill—were placed most exquisite statues. On the sculptured walls of its chambers, and upon ceilings, were paintings of unapproachable excellence. Of the value of these works of art the Greeks were no incompetent judges.

The temple of Serapis.

The Serapion, with these its precious contents, perpetually gave umbrage to the Archbishop Theophilus and his party. To them it was a reproach and an insult. Its many buildings were devoted to unknown, and therefore unholy uses. In its vaults and silent chambers the populace believed that the most abominable mysteries were carried on. There were magical brazen circles and sun-dials for fortune-telling in its porch; every one said that they had once belonged to Pharaoh or the conjurors who strove with Moses. Alas! no one of the ferocious bigots knew that with these Eratosthenes had in the old times measured the size of the earth, and Timocharis had determined the motions of the planet Venus. The temple, with its pure white marble walls, and endless columns projected against a blue and cloudless Egyptian sky, was to them a whited sepulchre full of rottenness within. In the very sanctuary of the god it was said that the priests had been known to delude the wealthiest and most beautiful Alexandrian women, who fancied that they were honoured by the raptures of the god. To this temple, so well worthy of their indignation, Theophilus directed the attention of his people. It happened that the Emperor Constantius had formerly given to the Church the site of an ancient temple of Osiris, and, in digging the foundation for the new edifice, the obscene symbols used in that worship chanced to be found. With more zeal than modesty, Theophilus exhibited them to the derision of the rabble in the market-place. The old Egyptian pagan party rose to avenge the insult. A riot ensued, one Olympius, a philosopher, being the leader. Their head-quarters were in the massive building of the Serapion, from which issuing forth they seized whatever Christians they could, compelled them to offer sacrifice, and then killed them on the altar. The dispute was referred to the emperor, in the meantime the pagans maintaining themselves in the temple-fortress. In the dead of night, Olympius, it is said, was awe-stricken by the sound of a clear voice chanting among the arches and pillars the Christian Alleluia. Either accepting, like a heathen, the omen, or fearing a secret assassin, he escaped from the temple and fled for his life. On the arrival of the rescript of Theodosius the pagans laid down their arms, little expecting the orders of the emperor. He enjoined that the building should forthwith be destroyed, intrusting the task to the swift hands of Theophilus. His work was commenced by the pillage and dispersal of the library. He entered the

Quarrel between the Christians and pagans in Alexandria.

Theodosius orders the Serapion to be destroyed.

sanctuary of the god—that sanctuary which was the visible sign of the Pantheism of the East, the memento of the alliance between hoary primeval Egypt and free-thinking Greece, the relic of the statesmanship of Alexander's captains. In gloomy silence the image of Serapis confronted its assailants. It is in such a moment that the value of a religion is tried; the god who cannot defend himself is a convicted sham. Theophilus, undaunted, commands a veteran to strike the image with his battle-axe. The helpless statue offers no resistance. Another blow rolls the head of the idol on the floor. It is said that a colony of frightened rats ran forth from its interior. The kingcraft, and priestcraft, and solemn swindle of seven hundred years are exploded in a shout of laughter; the god is broken to pieces, his members dragged through the streets. The recesses of the Serapion are explored. Posterity is edified by discoveries of frauds by which the priests maintain their power. Among other wonders, a car with four horses is seen suspended near the ceiling by means of a magnet laid on the roof, which being removed by the hand of a Christian, the imposture fell to the pavement. The historian of these events, noticing the physical impossibility of such things, has wisely said that it is more easy to invent a fictitious story than to support a practical fraud. But the gold and silver contained in the temple were carefully collected, the baser articles being broken in pieces or cast into the fire. Nor did the holy zeal of Theophilus rest until the structure was demolished to its very foundations—a work of no little labour—and a church erected in the precincts. It must, however, have been the temple more particularly which experienced this devastation. The building in which the library had been contained must have escaped, for, twenty years subsequently, Orosius expressly states that he saw the empty cases or shelves. The fanatic Theophilus pushed forward his victory. The temple at Canopus next fell before him, and a general attack was made on all similar edifices in Egypt. Speaking of the monks and of the worship of relics, Eunapius says: "Whoever wore a black dress was invested with tyrannical power;

Statue of Serapis is destroyed.

Persecutions of Theophilus.

philosophy and piety to the gods were compelled to retire into secret places, and to dwell in contented poverty and dignified meanness of appearance. The temples were turned into tombs for the adoration of the bones of the basest and most depraved of men, who had suffered the penalty of the law, and whom they made their gods."

Such was the end of the Serapion. Its destruction stands forth a token to all ages of the state of the times.

In a few years after this memorable event the Archbishop Theophilus had gone to his account. His throne was occupied by his nephew, St. Cyril, who had been expressly prepared for that holy and responsible office by a residence of five years among the monks of Nitria. He had been presented to the fastidious Alexandrians with due precautions, and by them acknowledged to be an effective and fashionable preacher. His pagan opponents, however, asserted that the clapping of hands and encores bestowed on the more elaborate passages of his sermons were performed by persons duly arranged in the congregation, and paid for their trouble. If doubt remains as to his intellectual endowments, there can be none respecting the qualities of his heart. The three parties into which the population of the city was divided —Christian, Heathen, and Jewish—kept up a perpetual disorder by their disputes. Of the last it is said that the number was not less than forty thousand. The episcopate itself had become much less a religious than an important civil office, exercising a direct municipal control through the Parabolani, which, under the disguise of city missionaries, whose duty it was to seek out the sick and destitute, constituted in reality a constabulary force, or rather actually a militia. The unscrupulous manner in which Cyril made use of this force, diverting it from its ostensible purpose, is indicated by the fact that the emperor was obliged eventually to take the appointments to it out of the archbishop's hands, and reduce the number to five or six hundred. Some local circumstances had increased the animosity between the Jews and the Christians, and riots had taken place between them in the theatre. These were followed by more serious conflicts in the streets; and the

St. Cyril.

Determines on supremacy in Alexandria.

Riots in that city.

Jews, for the moment having the advantage over their antagonists, outraged and massacred them. It was, however, but for a moment; for, the Christians arousing themselves under the inspirations of Cyril, a mob sacked the synagogues, pillaged the houses of the Jews, and endeavoured to expel those offenders out of the city. The prefect Orestes was compelled to interfere to stop the riot; but the archbishop was not so easily disposed of. His old associates, the Nitrian monks, now justified the prophetic forecast of Theophilus. Five hundred of those fanatics swarmed into the town from the desert. The prefect himself was assaulted, and wounded in the head by a stone thrown by Ammonius, one of them. The more respectable citizens, alarmed at the turn things were taking, interfered, and Ammonius, being seized, suffered death at the hands of the lictor. Cyril, undismayed, caused his body to be transported to the Cæsareum, laid there in state, and buried with unusual honours. He directed that the name of the fallen zealot should be changed from Ammonius to Thaumasius, or "the Wonderful," and the holy martyr received the honours of canonization.

In these troubles there can be no doubt that the pagans sympathized with the Jews, and therefore drew upon themselves the vengeance of Cyril. Among the cultivators of Platonic philosophy whom the times had spared, there was a beautiful young woman, Hypatia, the daughter of Theon the mathematician, who not only distinguished herself by her expositions of the Neo-Platonic and Peripatetic doctrines, but was also honoured for the ability with which she commented on the writings of Apollonius and other geometers. Every day before her door stood a long train of chariots; her lecture-room was crowded with the wealth and fashion of Alexandria. Her aristocratic audiences were more than a rival to those attending upon the preaching of the archbishop, and perhaps contemptuous comparisons were instituted between the philosophical lectures of Hypatia and the incomprehensible sermons of Cyril. But if the archbishop had not philosophy, he had what on such occasions is more valuable—power. It was not to be borne that a heathen sorceress should thus divide such a metropolis

Hypatia.

with a prelate; it was not to be borne that the rich, and noble, and young should thus be carried off by the black arts of a diabolical enchantress. Alexandria was too fair a prize to be lightly surrendered. It could vie with Constantinople itself. Into its streets, from the yellow sand-hills of the desert, long trains of camels and countless boats brought the abundant harvests of the Nile. A ship-canal connected the harbour of Eunostos with Lake Mareotis. The harbour was a forest of masts. Seaward, looking over the blue Mediterranean, was the great lighthouse, the Pharos, counted as one of the wonders of the world; and to protect the shipping from the north wind there was a mole three quarters of a mile in length, with its drawbridges, a marvel of the skill of the Macedonian engineers. Two great streets crossed each other at right angles—one was three, the other one mile long. In the square where they intersected stood the mausoleum in which rested the body of Alexander. The city was full of noble edifices—the palace, the exchange, the Cæsareum, the halls of justice. Among the temples, those of Pan and Neptune were conspicuous. The visitor passed countless theatres, churches, temples, synagogues. There was a time before Theophilus when the Serapion might have been approached on one side by a slope for carriages, on the other by a flight of a hundred marble steps. On these stood the grand portico with its columns, its chequered corridor leading round a roofless hall, the adjoining porches of which contained the library, and from the midst of its area arose a lofty pillar visible afar off at sea. On one side of the town were the royal docks, on the other the Hippodrome, and on appropriate sites the Necropolis, the market-places, the gymnasium, its stoa being a stadium long; the amphitheatre, groves, gardens, fountains, obelisks, and countless public buildings with gilded roofs glittering in the sun. Here might be seen the wealthy Christian ladies walking in the streets, their dresses embroidered with Scripture parables, the Gospels hanging from their necks by a golden chain, Maltese dogs with jewelled collars frisking round them, and slaves with parasols and fans trooping along. There might be seen the ever-trading, ever-thriving Jew, fresh from the

The city of Alexandria.

wharves, or busy negotiating his loans. But, worst of all, the chariots with giddy or thoughtful pagans hastening to the academy of Hypatia, to hear those questions discussed which have never yet been answered, "Where am I?" "What am I?" "What can I know?"—to hear discourses on antenatal existence, or, as the vulgar asserted, to find out the future by the aid of the black art, soothsaying by Chaldee talismans engraved on precious stones, by incantations with a glass and water, by moonshine on the walls, by the magic mirror, the reflection of a sapphire, a sieve, or cymbals; fortune-telling by the veins of the hand, or consultations with the stars.

Cyril at length determined to remove this great reproach, and overturn what now appeared to be the only obstacle in his way to uncontrolled authority in the city. We are reaching one of those moments in which great general principles embody themselves in individuals. It is Greek philosophy under the appropriate form of Hypatia; ecclesiastical ambition under that of Cyril.

Murder of Hypatia by Cyril.

Their destinies are about to be fulfilled. As Hypatia comes forth to her academy, she is assaulted by Cyril's mob—an Alexandrian mob of many monks. Amid the fearful yelling of these bare-legged and black-cowled fiends she is dragged from her chariot, and in the public street stripped naked. In her mortal terror she is haled into an adjacent church, and in that sacred edifice is killed by the club of Peter the Reader. It is not always in the power of him who has stirred up the worst passions of a fanatical mob to stop their excesses when his purpose is accomplished. With the blow given by Peter the aim of Cyril was reached, but his merciless adherents had not glutted their vengeance. They outraged the naked corpse, dismembered it, and incredible to be said, finished their infernal crime by scraping the flesh from the bones with oyster-shells, and casting the remnants into the fire. Though in his privacy St. Cyril and his friends might laugh at the end of his antagonist, his memory must bear the weight of the righteous indignation of posterity.

Thus, in the 414th year of our era, the position of philosophy in the intellectual metropolis of the world was determined; henceforth science must sink into obscurity and subordination. Its public existence will no longer be tolerated. Indeed, it may be said that from this period for some centuries it altogether disappeared. The leaden mace of bigotry had struck and shivered the exquisitely tempered steel of Greek philosophy. Cyril's acts passed unquestioned. It was now ascertained that throughout the Roman world there must be no more liberty of thought. It had been said that these events prove Greek philosophy to have been a sham, and, like other shams, it was driven out of the world when detected, and that it could not withstand the truth. Such assertions might answer their purposes very well, so long as the victors maintained their power in Alexandria, but they manifestly are of inconvenient application after the Saracens had captured the city. However this may be, an intellectual stagnation settled upon the place, an invisible atmosphere of oppression, ready to crush down, morally and physically, whatever provoked its weight. And so for the next two dreary and weary centuries things remained, until oppression and force were ended by a foreign invader. It was well for the world that the Arabian conquerors avowed their true argument, the scimitar, and made no pretensions to superhuman wisdom. They were thus left free to pursue knowledge without involving themselves in theological contradictions, and were able to make Egypt once more illustrious among the nations of the earth—to snatch it from the hideous fanaticism, ignorance, and barbarism into which it had been plunged. On the shore of the Red Sea once more a degree of the earth's surface was to be measured, and her size ascertained—but by a Mohammedan astronomer. In Alexandria the memory of the illustrious old times was to be recalled by the discovery of the motion of the sun's apogee by Albategnius, and the third inequality of the moon, the variation, by Aboul Wefa; to be discovered six centuries later in Europe by Tycho Brahe. The canal of the Pharaohs from the Nile to the Red Sea, cleared out by the Ptolemies in former ages, was to be cleared from its sand again. The glad desert listened once more to the cheerful cry of the merchant camel-driver instead of the midnight prayer of the monk.

Suppression of Alexandrian science.

CHAPTER XI.

PREMATURE END OF THE AGE OF FAITH IN THE EAST.

THE THREE ATTACKS, VANDAL, PERSIAN, ARAB.

THE VANDAL ATTACK *leads to the Loss of Africa.—Recovery of that Province by Justinian after great Calamities.*

THE PERSIAN ATTACK *leads to the Loss of Syria and Fall of Jerusalem.—The true Cross carried away as a Trophy.—Moral Impression of these Attacks.*

THE ARAB ATTACK.—*Birth, Mission, and Doctrines of Mohammed.—Rapid Spread of his Faith in Asia and Africa.—Fall of Jerusalem.—Dreadful Losses of Christianity to Mohammedanism.—The Arabs become a learned Nation.*

Review of the Koran.—Reflexions on the Loss of Asia and Africa by Christendom.

Three attacks made upon the Byzantine system.

I HAVE now to describe the end of the age of Faith in the East. The Byzantine system, out of which it had issued, was destroyed by three attacks: 1st, by the Vandal invasion of Africa; 2nd, by the military operations of Chosroes, the Persian king; 3rd, by Mohammedanism.

Of these three attacks, the Vandal may be said, in a military sense, to have been successfully closed by the victories of Justinian; but, politically, the cost of those victories was the depopulation and ruin of the empire, particularly in the south and west. The second, the Persian attack, though brilliantly resisted in its later years by the Emperor Heraclius, left, throughout the East, a profound moral impression, which proved final and fatal in the Mohammedan attack.

No heresy has ever produced such important political results as that of Arius. While it was yet a vital doctrine, it led to the infliction of unspeakable calamities on the empire, and, though long ago forgotten, has blasted permanently some of the fairest portions of the globe. When Count Boniface, incited by the intrigues of the patrician Ætius, invited Genseric, the King of the Vandals, into Africa, that barbarian found in the discontented sectaries his most effectual aid. In vain would he otherwise have attempted the conquest of the country with the 50,000 men he landed from Spain, A. D. 429. Three hundred Donatist bishops, and many thousand priests, driven to despair by the persecutions inflicted by the emperor, carrying with them that large portion of the population who were Arian, were ready to look upon him as a deliveror, and therefore to afford him support. The result to the empire was the loss of Africa.

The Vandal attack.

Conquest of Africa.

It was nothing more than might have been expected that Justinian, when he found himself firmly seated on the throne of Constantinople, should make an attempt to retrieve these disasters. The principles which led him to his scheme of legislation; to the promotion of manufacturing interests by the fabrication of silk; to the reopening of the ancient routes to India, so as to avoid transit through the Persian dominions; to his attempt at securing the carrying trade of Europe for the Greeks, also suggested the recovery of Africa. To this important step he was urged by the Catholic clergy. In a sinister but suitable manner, his reign was illustrated by his closing the schools of philosophy at Athens, ostensibly because of their affiliation to paganism, but in reality on account of his detestation of the doctrines of Aristotle and Plato; by the abolition of the consulate of Rome; by the extinction of the Roman senate, A.D. 552; by the capture and recapture five times of the Eternal City. The vanishing of the Roman race was thus marked by an extinction of the instruments of ancient philosophy and power.

The reign of Justinian.

The indignation of the Catholics was doubtless justly provoked by the atrocities practised in the Arian behalf by the Vandal kings of Africa, who, among other cruelties, had attempted to silence some bishops by cutting out their tongues. To carry out Justinian's intention of the recovery of Africa, his general Belisarius

His reconquest of Africa.

sailed at midsummer, A.D. 533, and in November he had completed the reconquest of the country.

Dreadful calamities produced by him.

This was speedy work, but it was followed by fearful calamities; for in this, and the Italian wars of Justinian, likewise undertaken at the instance of the orthodox clergy, the human race visibly diminished. It is affirmed that in the African campaign five millions of the people of that country were consumed; that during the twenty years of the Gothic War Italy lost fifteen millions; and that the wars, famines, and pestilences of the reign of Justinian diminished the human species by the almost incredible number of one hundred millions.

The Persian attack.

It is therefore not at all surprising that in such a deplorable condition men longed for a deliverer, in their despair totally regardless who he might be or from what quarter he might come. Ecclesiastical partisanship had done its work. When Chosroes II., the Persian monarch, A.D. 611, commenced his attack, the persecuted sectaries of Asia Minor, Syria, and Egypt followed the example of the African Arians in the Vandal invasion, and betrayed the empire. The revenge of an oppressed heretic is never scrupulous about its means of gratification. As might have been expected, the cities of Asia fell before the Persians. They took Jerusalem by assault, and with it the cross of Christ; ninety thousand Christians were massacred; and in its very birthplace Christianity was displaced by Magianism. The shock which religious men received through this dreadful event can hardly now be realized. The imposture of Constantine bore a bitter fruit; the sacred wood which had filled the world with its miracles was detected to be a helpless counterfeit, borne off in triumph by deriding blasphemers. All confidence in the apostolic powers of the Asiatic bishops was lost; not one of them could work a wonder for his own salvation in the dire extremity. The invaders overran Egypt as far as Ethiopia; it seemed as if the days of Cambyses had come back again. The Archbishop of Alexandria found it safer to flee to Cyprus than to defend himself by spiritual artifices or to rely on prayer. The

Fall and pillage of Jerusalem.

Triumphs of Chosroes.

Mediterranean shore to Tripoli was subdued. For ten years the Persian standards were displayed in view of Constantinople. At one time Heraclius had determined to abandon that city, and make Carthage the metropolis of the empire. His intention was defeated by the combination of the patriarch, who dreaded the loss of his position; of the aristocracy, who foresaw their own ruin; and of the people, who would thus be deprived of their largesses and shows. Africa was more truly Roman than any other of the provinces; it was there that Latin was last used. But when the vengeance of the heretical sects was satisfied, they found that they had only changed the tyrant without escaping the tyranny. The magnitude of their treason was demonstrated by the facility with which Heraclius expelled the Persians as soon as they chose to assist him.

The moral impression of these events.

In vain, after these successes, what was passed off as the true cross was restored again to Jerusalem—the charm was broken. The Magian fire had burnt the sepulchre of Christ, and the churches of Constantine and Helena; the costly gifts of the piety of three centuries were gone into the possession of the Persian and the Jew. Never again was it possible that faith could be restored. They who had devoutly expected that the earth would open, the lightning descend, or sudden death arrest the sacrilegious invader of the holy places, and had seen that nothing of the kind ensued, dropped at once into dismal disbelief. Asia and Africa were already morally lost. The scimitar of the Arabian soon cut the remaining tie.

Birth of Mohammed.

Four years after the death of Justinian, A.D. 569, was born at Mecca, in Arabia, the man who, of all men, has exercised the greatest influence upon the human race—Mohammed, by Europeans surnamed "the Impostor." He raised his own nation from Fetichism, the adoration of a meteoric stone, and from the basest idol-worship; he preached a monotheism which quickly scattered to the winds the empty disputes of the Arians and Catholics, and irrevocably wrenched from Christianity more than half, and that by far the best half of her possessions, since it included the Holy Land, the birthplace of our faith, and Africa, which had imparted to it its Latin form. That continent, and a very large part of Asia, after the lapse of more than a thousand years, still remain permanently attached to the Arabian doctrine. With the utmost difficulty, and as if by miracle, Europe itself escaped.

Mohammed possessed that combination of qualities which more than once has decided the fate of empires. A preaching soldier, he was eloquent in the pulpit, valiant in the field. His theology was simple: "There is but one God." The effeminate Syrian, lost in Monothelite and Monophysite mysteries; the Athanasian and Arian, destined to disappear before his breath, might readily anticipate what he meant. Asserting that everlasting truth, he did not engage in vain metaphysics, but applied himself to improving the social condition of his people by regulations respecting personal cleanliness, sobriety, fasting, prayer. Above all other works he esteemed almsgiving and charity. With a liberality to which the world had of late become a stranger, he admitted the salvation of men of any form of faith provided they were virtuous. To the declaration that there is but one God, he added, "and Mohammed is his Prophet." Whoever desires to know whether the event of things answered to the boldness of such an announcement, will do well to examine a map of the world in our own times. He will find the marks of something more than an imposture. To be the religious head of many empires, to guide the daily life of one-third of the human race, may perhaps justify the title of a messenger of God.

His preaching,

and title to apostleship.

Like many of the Christian monks, Mohammed retired to the solitude of the desert, and, devoting himself to meditation, fasting, and prayer, became the victim of cerebral disorder. He was visited by supernatural appearances, mysterious voices accosting him as the Prophet of God: even the stones and trees joined in the whispering. He himself suspected the true nature of his malady, and to his wife Chadizah he expressed a dread that he was becoming insane. It is related that as they sat alone, a shadow entered the room. "Dost thou see aught?" said Chadizah, who, after the manner of Arabian matrons, wore her veil. "I do," said the prophet.

His delusions.

Whereupon she uncovered her face and said, "Dost thou see it now?" "I do not." "Glad tidings to thee, O Mohammed!" exclaimed Chadizah: "it is an angel, for he has respected my unveiled face; an evil spirit would not." As his disease advanced, these spectral illusions became more frequent; from one of them he received the divine commission. "I," said his wife, "will be thy first believer;" and they knelt down in prayer together. Since that day nine thousand millions of human beings have acknowledged him to be a prophet of God.

Though, in the earlier part of his career, Mohammed exhibited a spirit of forbearance toward the Christians, it was not possible but that bitter animosity should arise, as the sphere of his influence extended. He appears to have been unable to form any other idea of the Trinity than that of three distinct gods; and the worship of the Virgin Mary, recently introduced, could not fail to come into irreconcilable conflict with his doctrine of the unity of God. To his condemnation of those Jews who taught that Ezra was the Son of God, he soon added bitter denunciations of the Oriental churches because of their idolatrous practices. The Koran is full of such rebukes: "Verily, Christ Jesus, the Son of Mary, is the apostle of God." "Believe, therefore, in God and his apostles, and say not that there are three gods. Forbear this; it will be better for you. God is but one God. Far be it from Him that he should have a son." "In the last day, God shall say unto Jesus, O Jesus, son of Mary! hast thou ever said to men, Take me and my mother for two gods beside God? He shall say, Praise be unto thee, it is not for me to say that which I ought not." Mohammed disdained all metaphysical speculations respecting the nature of the Deity, or of the origin and existence of sin, topics which had hitherto exercised the ingenuity of the East. He cast aside the doctrine of the superlative value of chastity, asserting that marriage is the natural state of man. To asceticism he opposed polygamy, permitting the practice of it in this life and promising the most voluptuous means for its enjoyment in Paradise hereafter, especially to those who had gained the crowns of martyrdom or of victory.

His gradual antagonism to Christianity.

Institution of polygamy.

Too often, in this world, success is the criterion of right. The Mohammedan appeals to the splendour and rapidity of his career as a proof of the divine mission of his apostle. It may, however, be permitted to a philosopher, who desires to speak of the faith of so large a portion of the human race with profound respect, to examine what were some of the secondary causes which led to so great a political result. From its most glorious seats Christianity was for ever expelled: from Palestine, the scene of its most sacred recollections; from Asia Minor, that of its first churches; from Egypt, whence issued the great doctrine of Trinitarian orthodoxy; from Carthage, who imposed her belief on Europe.

Results of his life.

It is altogether a misconception that the Arabian progress was due to the sword alone. The sword may change an acknowledged national creed, but it cannot affect the consciences of men. Profound though its argument is, something far more profound was demanded before Mohammedanism pervaded the domestic life of Asia and Africa, before Arabic became the language of so many different nations.

Causes of his success.

The explanation of this political phenomenon is to be found in the social condition of the conquered countries. The influences of religion in them had long ago ceased; it had become supplanted by theology—a theology so incomprehensible that even the wonderful capabilities of the Greek language were scarcely enough to meet its subtle demands; the Latin and the barbarian dialects were out of the question. How was it possible that unlettered men, who with difficulty can be made to apprehend obvious things, should understand such mysteries? Yet they were taught that on those doctrines the salvation or damnation of the human race depended. They saw that the clergy had abandoned the guidance of the individual life of their flocks; that personal virtue or vice were no longer considered; that sin was not measured by evil works but by the degrees of heresy. They saw that the ecclesiastical chiefs of Rome, Constantinople, and Alexandria were engaged in a desperate struggle for supremacy, carrying out their purposes by weapons and in ways revolting to the conscience of man. What an example when bishops were concerned in assassinations, poisonings, adulteries, blindings, riots, treasons, civil war; when patriarchs and primates were excommunicating and anathematizing one another in their rivalries for earthly power, bribing eunuchs with gold, and courtesans and royal females with concessions of episcopal love, and influencing the decisions of councils asserted to speak with the voice of God by those base intrigues and sharp practices resorted to by demagogues in their packed assemblies! Among legions of monks, who carried terror into the imperial armies and riot into the great cities, arose hideous clamours for theological dogmas, but never a voice for intellectual liberty or the outraged rights of man. In such a state of things, what else could be the result than disgust or indifference? Certainly men could not be expected, if a time of necessity arose, to give help to a system that had lost all hold on their hearts.

Civil weakness produced by ecclesiastical demoralization.

When, therefore, in the midst of the wrangling of sects, in the incomprehensible jargon of Arians, Nestorians, Eutychians, Monothelites, Monophysites, Mariolatrists, and an anarchy of countless disputants, there sounded through the world, not the miserable voice of the intriguing majority of a council, but the dread battle-cry, "There is but one God," enforced by the tempest of Saracen armies, is it surprising that the hubbub was hushed? Is it surprising that all Asia and Africa fell away? In better times patriotism is too often made subordinate to religion; in those times it was altogether dead.

Scarcely was Mohammed buried when his religion manifested its inevitable destiny of overpassing the bounds of Arabia. The prophet himself had declared war against the Roman empire, and, at the head of 30,000 men, advanced toward Damascus, but his purpose was frustrated by ill health. His successor Abu-Bekr, the first khalif, attacked both the Romans and the Persians. The invasion of Egypt occurred A.D. 638, the Arabs being invited by the Copts. In a few months the Mohammedan general Amrou wrote to his master, the khalif, "I have taken Alexandria, the great city of the West." Treason had done its work, and Egypt was thoroughly subjugated. To complete the conquest of Christian Africa, many attacks

Conquest of Africa.

were nevertheless required. Abdallah penetrated nine hundred miles to Tripoli, but returned. Nothing more was done for twenty years, because of the disputes that arose about the succession to the khalifate. Then Moawiyah sent his lieutenant, Akbah, who forced his way to the Atlantic, but was unable to hold the long line of country permanently. Again operations were undertaken by Abdalmalek, the sixth of the Ommiade dynasty, A.D. 698; his lieutenant, Hassan, took Carthage by storm and destroyed it, the conquest being at last thoroughly completed by Musa, who enjoyed the double reputation of a brave soldier and an eloquent preacher. And thus this region, distinguished by its theological acumen, to which modern Europe owes so much, was for ever silenced by the scimitar. It ceased to preach and was taught to pray.

In this political result—the Arabian conquest of Africa—there can be no doubt that the same element which exercised in the Vandal invasion so disastrous an effect, came again into operation. But, if treason introduced the enemy, polygamy secured the conquest. In Egypt the Greek population was orthodox, the natives were Jacobites, more willing to accept the Monotheism of Arabia than to bear the tyranny of the orthodox. The Arabs, carrying out their policy of ruining an old metropolis and erecting a new one, dismantled Alexandria; and thus the patriarchate of that city ceased to have any farther political existence in the Christian system, which for so many ages had been disturbed by its intrigues and violence. The irresistible effect of polygamy in consolidating the new order of things soon became apparent. In little more than a single generation all the children of the north of Africa were speaking Arabic.

Conquest of Syria and Persia.

During the khalifates of Abu-Bekr and Omar, and within twelve years after the death of Mohammed, the Arabians had reduced thirty-six thousand cities, towns, and castles in Persia, Syria, Africa, and had destroyed four thousand churches, replacing them with fourteen hundred mosques. In a few years they had extended their rule a thousand miles east and west. In Syria, as in Africa, their early successes were promoted in the most effectual manner by treachery. Damascus was taken after a siege of a year. At the battle of Aiznadin, A.D. 633, Kalid, "the Sword of God," defeated the army of Heraclius, the Romans losing fifty thousand men; and this was soon followed by the fall of the great cities Jerusalem, Antioch, Aleppo, Tyre, Tripoli. On a red camel, which carried a bag of corn and one of dates, a wooden dish, and a leather water-bottle, the Khalif Omar came from Medina to take formal possession of Jerusalem. He entered the Holy City riding by the side of the Christian patriarch Sophronius, whose capitulation showed that his confidence in God was completely lost. The successor of Mohammed and the Roman emperor both correctly judged how important in the eyes of the nations was the possession of Jerusalem. A belief that it would be a proof of the authenticity of Mohammedanism led Omar to order the Saracen troops to take it at any cost.

The fall of Jerusalem.

The conquest of Syria and the seizure of the Mediterranean ports gave to the Arabs the command of the sea. They soon took Rhodes and Cyprus. The battle of Cadesia and sack of Ctesiphon, the metropolis of Persia, decided the fate of that kingdom. Syria was thus completely reduced under Omar, the second khalif; Persia under Othman, the third.

If it be true that the Arabs burned the library of Alexandria, there was at that time danger that their fanaticism would lend itself to the Byzantine system; but it was only for a moment that the khalifs fell into this evil policy. They very soon became distinguished patrons of learning. It has been said that they overran the domains of science as quickly as they overran the realms of their neighbours. It became customary for the first dignities of the state to be held by men distinguished for their erudition. Some of the maxims current show how much literature was esteemed. "The ink of the doctor is equally valuable with the blood of the martyr." "Paradise is as much for him who has rightly used the pen as for him who has fallen by the sword." "The world is sustained by four things only: the learning of the wise, the justice of the great, the prayers of the good, and the valour of the brave." Within twenty-five years after the death of Mohammed, under Ali, the fourth khalif,

The Arabs become a learned nation.

the patronage of learning had become a settled principle of the Mohammedan system. Under the khalifs of Bagdad this principle was thoroughly carried out. The cultivators of mathematics, astronomy, medicine, and general literature abounded in the court of Almansor, who invited all philosophers, offering them his protection, whatever their religious opinions might be. His successor, Alraschid, is said never to have travelled without a retinue of a hundred learned men. This great sovereign issued an edict that no mosque should be built unless there was a school attached to it. It was he who confided the superintendence of his schools to the Nestorian Masué. His successor, Almaimon, was brought up among Greek and Persian mathematicians, philosophers, and physicians. They continued his associates all his life. By these sovereigns the establishment of libraries was incessantly prosecuted, and the collection and copying of manuscripts properly organized. In all the great cities schools abounded; in Alexandria there were not less than twenty. As might be expected, this could not take place without exciting the indignation of the old fanatical party, who not only remonstrated with Almaimon, but threatened him with the vengeance of God for thus disturbing the faith of the people. However, what had thus been commenced as a matter of profound policy soon grew into a habit, and it was observed that whenever an emir managed to make himself independent, he forthwith opened academies.

Rapidity of their intellectual development.

The Arabs furnish a striking illustration of the successive phases of national life. They first come before us as fetich worshippers, having their age of credulity, their object of superstition being the black stone in the temple at Mecca. They pass through an age of inquiry, rendering possible the advent of Mohammed. Then follows their age of faith, the blind fanaticism of which quickly led them to overspread all adjoining countries; and at last comes their period of maturity, their age of reason. The striking feature of their movement is the quickness with which they passed through these successive phases, and the intensity of their national life.

This singular rapidity of national life was favoured by

very obvious circumstances. The long and desolating wars between Heraclius and Chosroes had altogether destroyed the mercantile relations of the Roman and Persian empires, and had thrown the entire Oriental and African trade into the hands of the Arabs. As a merchant Mohammed himself makes his first appearance. The first we hear in his history are the journeys he has made as the factor of the wealthy Chadizah. In these expeditions with the caravans to Damascus and other Syrian cities, he was brought in contact with Jews and men of business, who, from the nature of their pursuits, were of more enlarged views than mere Arab chieftains or the petty tradesmen of Arab towns. Through such agency the first impetus was given. As to the rapid success, its causes are in like manner so plain as to take away all surprise. It is no wonder that in fifty years, as Abderrahman wrote to the khalif, not only had the tribute from the entire north of Africa ceased, through the population having become altogether Mohammedan, but that the Moors boasted an Arab descent as their greatest glory. For, besides the sectarian animosities on which I have dwelt as facilitating the first conquest of the Christians, and the dreadful shock that had been given by the capture of the Holy City, Jerusalem, the insulting and burning the sepulchre of our Saviour, and the carrying away of his cross as a trophy by the Persians, there were other very powerful causes. For many years the taxation imposed by the Emperors of Constantinople on their subjects in Asia and Africa had been not only excessive and extortionate, but likewise complicated. This the khalifs replaced by a simple well-defined tribute of far less amount. Thus, in the case of Cyprus, the sum paid to the khalif was only half of what it had been to the emperor; and, indeed, the lower orders were never made to feel the bitterness of conquest; the blows fell on the ecclesiastics, not on the population, and between them there was but little sympathy. In the eyes of the ignorant nations the prestige of the patriarchs and bishops was utterly destroyed by their detected helplessness to prevent the capture and insult of the sacred places. On the payment of a trifling sum the conqueror guaranteed to the Christian and the

Causes of the spread of Mohammedanism.

Jew absolute security for their worship. An equivalent was given for a price. Religious freedom was bought with money. Numerous instances might be given of the scrupulous integrity with which the Arab commanders complied with their part of the contract. The example set by Omar on the steps of the Church of the Resurrection was followed by Moawiyah, who actually rebuilt the church of Edessa for his Christian subjects; and by Abdulmalek, who, when he had commenced converting that of Damascus into a mosque, forthwith desisted on finding that the Christians were entitled to it by the terms of the capitulation. If these things were done in the first fervour of victory, the principles on which they depended were all the more powerful after the Arabs had become tinctured with Nestorian and Jewish influences, and were a learned nation. It is related of Ali, the son-in-law of Mohammed, and the fourth successor in the khalifate, that he gave himself up to letters. Among his sayings are recorded such as these: "Eminence in science is the highest of honours;" "He dies not who gives life to learning;" "The greatest ornament of a man is erudition." When the sovereign felt and expressed such sentiments, it was impossible but that a liberal policy should prevail.

Besides these there were other incentives not less powerful. To one whose faith sat lightly upon him, or who valued it less than the tribute to be paid, it only required the repetition of a short sentence acknowledging the unity of God and the divine mission of the prophet, and he forthwith became, though a captive or a slave, the equal and friend of his conqueror. Doubtless many thousands were under these circumstances carried away. As respects the female sex, the Arab system was very far from being oppressive; some have even asserted that "the Christian women found in the seraglios a delightful retreat." But above all, polygamy acted most effectually in consolidating the conquests; the large families that were raised—some are mentioned of more than one hundred and eighty children—compressed into the course of a few years events that would otherwise have taken many generations for their accomplishment. These children gloried in their Arab descent, and, being taught to speak the language of their conquering fathers, became to all intents and purposes Arabs. This diffusion of the language was sometimes expedited by the edicts of the khalifs; thus Alwalid I. prohibited the use of Greek, directing Arabic to be employed in its stead.

If thus without difficulty we recognise the causes which led to the rapid diffusion of Arab power, we also without difficulty recognise those which led to its check and eventual dissolution. Arab conquest implied, from the scale on which it was pursued, the forthgoing of the whole nation. It could only be accomplished, and in a temporary manner sustained, by an excessive and incessant drain of the native Arab population. That immobility, or, at best, that slow progress the nation had for so many ages displayed, was at an end, society was moved to its foundations, a fanatical delirium possessed it, the greatest and boldest enterprises were entered upon without hesitation, the wildest hopes or passions of men might be speedily gratified, wealth and beauty were the tangible rewards of valour in this life, to say nothing of Paradise in the next. But such an outrush of a nation in all directions implied the quick growth of diverse interests and opposing policies. The necessary consequence of the Arab system was subdivision and breaking up. The circumstances of its growth rendered it certain that a decomposition would take place in the political, and not, as was the case of the ecclesiastical Roman system, in the theological direction. All this is illustrated both in the earlier and later Saracenic history.

Causes of the arrest of Mohammedanism.

Necessary disintegration of the Arabian system

War makes a people run through its phases of existence fast. It would have taken the Arabs many thousand years to have advanced intellectually as far as they did in a single century, had they, as a nation, remained in profound peace. They did not merely shake off that dead weight which clogs the movement of a nation—its inert mass of common people; they converted that mass into a living force. National progress is the sum of individual progress; national immobility the result of individual quiescence. Arabian life was run through with rapidity, because an unrestrained career was

Effect on the low Arab class.

opened to every man; and yet, quick as the movement was, it manifested all those unavoidable phases through which, whether its motion be swift or slow, humanity must unavoidably pass.

Review of the Koran.

Arabian influence, thus imposing itself on Africa and Asia by military successes, and threatening even Constantinople, rested essentially on an intellectual basis, the value of which it is needful for us to consider. The Koran, which is that basis, has exercised a great control over the destinies of mankind, and still serves as a rule of life to a very large portion of our race. Considering the asserted origin of this book—indirectly from God himself—we might justly expect that it would bear to be tried by any standard that man can apply, and vindicate its truth and excellence in the ordeal of human criticism. In our estimate of it we must constantly bear in mind that it does not profess to be successive revelations made at intervals of ages and on various occasions, but a complete production delivered to one man. We ought, therefore, to look for universality, completeness, perfection. We might expect that it would present us with just views of the nature and position of this world in which we live, and that, whether dealing with the spiritual or the material, it would put to shame the most celebrated productions of human genius, as the magnificent mechanism of the heavens and the beautiful living forms of the earth are superior to the vain contrivances of man. Far in advance of all that has been written by the sages of India, or the philosophers of Greece, on points connected with the origin, nature, and destiny of the universe, its dignity of conception and excellence of expression should be in harmony with the greatness of the subject with which it is concerned.

Its asserted homogeneousness and completeness.

The characters it ought, therefore, to have presented.

We might expect that it should propound with authority. and definitively settle those all-important problems which have exercised the mental powers of the ablest men of Asia and Europe for so many centuries, and which are at the foundation of all faith and all philosophy; that it should distinctly tell us in unmistakable language what is God, what is the world, what is the soul, and whether man has any criterion of truth; that it should explain to us how evil can exist in a world the Maker of which is omnipotent and altogether good; that it should reveal to us in what the affairs of men are fixed by Destiny, in what by free-will; that it should teach us whence we came, what is the object of our continuing here, what is to become of us hereafter. And, since a written work claiming a divine origin must necessarily accredit itself even to those most reluctant to receive it, its internal evidences becoming stronger and not weaker with the strictness of the examination to which they are submitted, it ought to deal with those things that may be demonstrated by the increasing knowledge and genius of man, anticipating therein his conclusions. Such a work, noble as may be its origin, must not refuse, but court the test of natural philosophy, regarding it not as an antagonist, but as its best support. As years pass on, and human science becomes more exact and more comprehensive, its conclusions must be found in unison therewith. When occasion arises, it should furnish us at least the foreshadowings of the great truths discovered by astronomy and geology, not offering for them the wild fictions of earlier ages, inventions of the infancy of man. It should tell us how suns and worlds are distributed in infinite space, and how, in their successions, they come forth in limitless time. It should say how far the dominion of God is carried out by law, and what is the point at which it is his pleasure to resort to his own good providence or his arbitrary will. How grand the description of this magnificent universe written by the Omnipotent hand! Of man it should set forth his relations to other living beings, his place among them, his privileges, and responsibilities. It should not leave him to grope his way through the vestiges of Greek philosophy, and to miss the truth at last; but it should teach him wherein true knowledge consists, anticipating the physical science, physical power, and physical well-being of our own times, nay, even unfolding for our benefit things that we are still ignorant of. The discussion of subjects, so many and so high, is not outside the scope of a work of such pretensions. Its manner of dealing with them is the only criterion it can offer of its authenticity to succeeding times.

Tried by such a standard, the Koran altogether fails. In its philosophy it is incomparably inferior to the writings of Chakia Mouni, the founder of Buddhism; in its science it is absolutely worthless. On speculative or doubtful things it is copious enough; but in the exact, where a test can be applied to it, it totally fails. Its astronomy, cosmogony, physiology, are so puerile as to invite our mirth if the occasion did not forbid. They belong to the old times of the world, the morning of human knowledge. The earth is firmly balanced in its seat by the weight of the mountains; the sky is supported over it like a dome, and we are instructed in the wisdom and power of God by being told to find a crack in it if we can. Ranged in stories, seven in number, are the heavens, the highest being the habitation of God, whose throne—for the Koran does not reject Assyrian ideas—is sustained by winged animal forms. The shooting-stars are pieces of red-hot stone thrown by angels at impure spirits when they approach too closely. Of God the Koran is full of praise, setting forth, often in not unworthy imagery, his majesty. Though it bitterly denounces those who give him any equals, and assures them that their sin will never be forgiven; that in the judgment-day they must answer the fearful question, "Where are my companions about whom ye disputed?" though it inculcates an absolute dependence on the mercy of God, and denounces as criminals all those who make a merchandise of religion, its ideas of the Deity are altogether anthropomorphic. He is only a gigantic man living in a paradise. In this respect, though exceptional passages might be cited, the reader rises from a perusal of the 114 chapters of the Koran with a final impression that they have given him low and unworthy thoughts; nor is it surprising that one of the Mohammedan sects reads it in such a way as to find no difficulty in asserting that, "from the crown of the head to the breast God is hollow, and from the breast downward he is solid; that he has curled black hair, and roars like a lion at every watch of the night." The unity asserted by Mohammed is a unity in special contradistinction to the Trinity of the Christians, and the doctrine of a divine generation. Our Saviour is never called the Son of God,

Defects of the Koran.

Its God.

but always the son of Mary. Throughout there is a perpetual acceptance of the delusion of the human destiny of the universe. As to man, Mohammed is diffuse enough respecting a future state, speaking with clearness of a resurrection, the judgment-day, Paradise, the torment of hell, the worm that never dies, the pains that never end; but, with all this precise description of the future, there are many errors as to the past. If modesty did not render it unsuitable to speak of such topics here, it might be shown how feeble is his physiology when he has occasion to allude to the origin or generation of man. He is hardly advanced beyond the ideas of Thales. One who is so untrustworthy a guide as to things that are past, cannot be very trustworthy as to events that are to come.

Its views of man.

Of the literary execution of his work, it is, perhaps, scarcely possible to judge fairly from a translation. It is said to be the oldest prose composition among the Arabs, by whom Mohammed's boast of the unapproachable excellence of his work is almost universally sustained; but it must not be concealed that there have been among them very learned men who have held it in light esteem. Its most celebrated passages, as those on the nature of God, in Chapters II., XXIV., will bear no comparison with parallel ones in the Psalms and Book of Job. In the narrative style, the story of Joseph, in Chapter XII., compared with the same incidents related in Genesis, shows a like inferiority. Mohammed also adulterates his work with many Christian legends, derived probably from the apocryphal gospel of St. Barnabas; he mixes with many of his own inventions the scripture account of the temptation of Adam, the Deluge, Jonah and the whale, enriching the whole with stories like the later Night Entertainments of his country, the seven sleepers, Gog and Magog, and all the wonders of genii, sorcery, and charms.

Its literary inferiority compared with the Bible.

An impartial reader of the Koran may doubtless be surprised that so feeble a production should serve its purpose so well. But the theory of religion is one thing, the practice another. The Koran abounds in excellent moral suggestions and precepts; its composition is so fragmentary that we cannot turn to a

Causes of its surprising influence.

single page without finding maxims of which all men must approve. This fragmentary construction yields texts, and mottoes, and rules complete in themselves, suitable for common men in any of the incidents of life. There is a perpetual insisting on the necessity of prayer, an inculcation of mercy, almsgiving, justice, fasting, pilgrimage, and other good works; institutions respecting conduct, both social and domestic, debts, witnesses, marriage, children, wine, and the like; above all, a constant stimulation to do battle with the infidel and blasphemer. For life as it passes in Asia, there is hardly a condition in which passages from the Koran cannot be recalled suitable for instruction, admonition, consolation, encouragement. To the Asiatic and to the African, such devotional fragments are of far more use than any sustained theological doctrine. The mental constitution of Mohammed did not enable him to handle important philosophical questions with the well-balanced ability of the great Greek and Indian writers, but he has never been surpassed in adaptation to the spiritual wants of humble life, making even his fearful fatalism administer thereto. A pitiless destiny is awaiting us; yet the prophet is uncertain what it may be. "Unto every nation a fixed time is decreed. Death will overtake us even in lofty towers, but God only knoweth the place in which a man shall die." After many an admonition of the resurrection and the judgment-day, many a promise of Paradise and threat of hell, he plaintively confesses, "I do not know what will be done with you or me hereafter."

Its true nature.

The Koran thus betrays a human, and not a very noble intellectual origin. It does not, however, follow that its author was, as is so often asserted, a mere impostor. He reiterates again and again, I am nothing more than a public preacher. He defends, not always without acerbity, his work from those who, even in his own life, stigmatized it as a confused heap of dreams, or, what is worse, a forgery. He is not the only man who has supposed himself to be the subject of supernatural and divine communications, for this is a condition of disease to which any one, by fasting and mental anxiety, may be reduced.

In what I have thus said respecting a work held by so

many millions of men as a revelation from God, I have endeavoured to speak with respect, and yet with freedom, constantly bearing in mind how deeply to this book Asia and Africa are indebted for daily guidance, how deeply Europe and America for the light of science.

As might be expected, the doctrines of the Koran have received many fictitious additions and sectarian interpretations in the course of ages. In the popular superstition angels and genii largely figure. The latter, being of a grosser fabric, eat, drink, propagate their kind, are of two sorts, good and bad, and existed long before men, having occupied the earth before Adam. Immediately after death, two greenish, livid angels, Monkir and Nekkar, examine every corpse as to its faith in God and Mohammed; but the soul, having been separated from the body by the angel of death, enters upon an intermediate state, awaiting the resurrection. There is, however, much diversity of opinion as to its precise disposal before the judgment-day: some think that it hovers near the grave; some, that it sinks into the well Zemzem; some, that it retires into the trumpet of the Angel of the Resurrection; the difficulty apparently being that any final disposal before the day of judgment would be anticipatory of that great event, if, indeed, it would not render it needless. As to the resurrection, some believe it to be merely spiritual, others corporeal; the latter asserting that the os coccygis, or last bone of the spinal column, will serve, as it were, as a germ, and that, vivified by a rain of forty days, the body will sprout from it. Among the signs of the approaching resurrection will be the rising of the sun in the West. It will be ushered in by three blasts of a trumpet: the first, known as the blast of consternation, will shake the earth to its centre, and extinguish the sun and stars; the second, the blast of extermination, will annihilate all material things except Paradise, hell, and the throne of God. Forty years subsequently, the angel Israfil will sound the blast of resurrection. From his trumpet there will be blown forth the countless myriads of souls who have taken refuge therein or lain concealed. The day of judgment has now come. The Koran contradicts itself as to the length of this day; in one place

Popular Mohammedanism.

making it a thousand, in another fifty thousand years. Most Mohammedans incline to adopt the longer period, since angels, genii, men, and animals have to be tried. As to men, they will rise in their natural state, but naked; white winged camels, with saddles of gold, awaiting the saved. When the partition is made, the wicked will be oppressed with an intolerable heat, caused by the sun, which, having been called into existence again, will approach within a mile, provoking a sweat to issue from them, and this, according to their demerits, will immerse them from the ankles to the mouth; but the righteous will be screened by the shadow of the throne of God. The judge will be seated in the clouds, the books open before him, and everything in its turn called on to account for its deeds. For greater dispatch, the angel Gabriel will hold forth his balance, one scale of which hangs over Paradise and one over hell. In these all works are weighed. As soon as the sentence is delivered, the assembly, in a long file, will pass over the bridge Al-Sirat. It is as sharp as the edge of a sword, and laid over the mouth of hell. Mohammed and his followers will successfully pass the perilous ordeal; but the sinners, giddy with terror, will drop into the place of torment. The blessed will receive their first taste of happiness at a pond which is supplied by silver pipes from the river Al-Cawthor. The soil of Paradise is of musk. Its rivers tranquilly flow over pebbles of rubies and emeralds. From tents of hollow pearls, the Houris, or girls of Paradise, will come forth, attended by troops of beautiful boys. Each Saint will have eighty thousand servants and seventy-two girls. To these, some of the more merciful Mussulmans add the wives they have had upon earth; but the grimly orthodox assert that hell is already nearly filled with women. How can it be otherwise since they are not permitted to pray in a mosque upon earth? I have not space to describe the silk brocades, the green clothing, the soft carpets, the banquets, the perpetual music and songs. From the glorified body all impurities will escape, not as they did during life, but in a fragrant perspiration of camphor and musk. No one will complain I am weary; no one will say I am sick.

From the contradictions, puerilities, and impossibilities

indicated in the preceding paragraphs, it may be anticipated that the faith of Mohammed has been broken into many sects. Of such it is said that not less than seventy-three may be numbered. Some, as the Sonnites, are guided by traditions; some occupy themselves with philosophical difficulties, the existence of evil in the world, the attributes of God, absolute predestination and eternal damnation, the invisibility and non-corporeality of God, his capability of local motion: these and other such topics furnish abundant opportunity for sectarian dispute. As if to show how the essential principles of the Koran may be departed from by those who still profess to be guided by it, there are, among the Shiites, those who believe that Ali was an incarnation of God; that he was in existence before the creation of things; that he never died, but ascended to heaven, and will return again in the clouds to judge the world. But the great Mohammedan philosophers, simply accepting the doctrine of the Oneness of God as the only thing of which man can be certain, look upon all the rest as idle fables, having, however, this political use, that they furnish contention, and therefore occupation to disputatious sectarians, and consolation to illiterate minds.

The Mohammedan sects.

Thus settled on the north of Africa the lurid phantom of the Arabian crescent, one horn reaching to the Bosphorus and one pointing beyond the Pyrenees. For a while it seemed that the portentous meteor would increase to the full, and that all Europe would be enveloped. Christianity had lost for ever the most interesting countries over which her influence had once spread, Africa, Egypt, Syria, the Holy Land, Asia Minor, Spain. She was destined, in the end, to lose in the same manner the metropolis of the East. In exchange for these ancient and illustrious regions, she fell back on Gaul, Germany, Britain, Scandinavia. In those savage countries, what were there to be offered as substitutes for the great capitals, illustrious in ecclesiastical history, for ever illustrious in the records of the human race—Carthage, Alexandria, Jerusalem, Antioch, Constantinople? It was an evil exchange. The labours, intellectual

Effect of Mohammedanism on Christianity.

and physical, of which those cities had once been the scene; the preaching, and penances, and prayers so lavishly expended in them, had not produced the anticipated, the asserted result. In theology and morality the people had pursued a descending course. Patriotism was extinct. They surrendered the state to preserve their sect; their treason was rewarded by subjugation.

Reflexions on the course of historic events.

From these melancholy events we may learn that the principles on which the moral world is governed are analogous to those which obtain in the physical. It is not by incessant divine interpositions, which produce breaches in the continuity of historic action; it is not by miracles and prodigies that the course of events is determined; but affairs follow each other in the relation of cause and effect. The maximum development of early Christianity coincided with the boundaries of the Roman empire; the ecclesiastical condition depended on the political, and, indeed, was its direct consequence and issue. The loss of Africa and Asia was, in like manner, connected with the Arabian movement, though it would have been easy to prevent that catastrophe, and to preserve those continents to the faith by the smallest of those innumerable miracles of which Church history is full, and which were often performed on unimportant and obscure occasions. But not even one such miracle was vouchsafed, though an angel might have worthily descended. I know of no event in the history of our race on which a thoughtful man may more profitably meditate than on this loss of Africa and Asia. It may remove from his mind many erroneous ideas, and lead him to take a more elevated, a more philosophical, and, therefore, more correct view of the course of earthly affairs.

CHAPTER XII.

THE AGE OF FAITH IN THE WEST.

The Age of Faith in the West is marked by Paganism.—The Arabian military Attacks produce the Isolation and permit the Independence of the Bishop of Rome.

GREGORY THE GREAT *organizes the Ideas of his Age, materializes Faith, allies it to Art, rejects Science, and creates the Italian Form of Religion.*

An Alliance of the Papacy with France diffuses that Form.—Political History of the Agreement and Conspiracy of the Frankish Kings and the Pope.—The resulting Consolidation of the new Dynasty in France, and Diffusion of Roman Ideas.—Conversion of Europe.

The Value of the Italian Form of Religion determined from the papal Biography.

FROM the Age of Faith in the East, I have now to turn to the Age of Faith in the West. The former, as we have seen, ended prematurely, through a metamorphosis of the populations by military operations, conquests, polygamy; the latter, under more favourable circumstances, gradually completed its predestined phases, and, after the lapse of many centuries, passed into the Age of Reason.

The Age of Faith in the West.

If so many recollections of profound interest cluster round Jerusalem, "the Holy City" of the East, many scarcely inferior are connected with Rome, "the Eternal City" of the West.

The Byzantine system, which, having originated in the policy of an ambitious soldier struggling for supreme power, and in the devices of ecclesiastics intolerant of any competitors, had spread itself all over the eastern and southern portions of the

Is essentially marked by the paganization of religion.

Roman empire, and with its hatred of human knowledge and degraded religious ideas and practices, had been adopted at last even in Italy. Not by the Romans, for they had ceased to exist, but by the medley of Goths and half-breeds, the occupants of that peninsula. Gregory the Great is the incarnation of the ideas of this debased population. That evil system, so carefully nurtured by Constantine and cherished by all the Oriental bishops, had been cut down by the axe of the Vandal, the Persian, the Arab, in its native seats, but the offshoot of it that had been planted in Rome developed spontaneously with unexpected luxuriance, and cast its dark shadow over Europe for many centuries. He who knew what Christianity had been in the apostolic days, might look with boundless surprise on what was now ingrafted upon it, and was passing under its name.

Effects of the loss of Africa on events in Italy.

In the last chapter we have seen how, through the Vandal invasion, Africa was lost to the empire—a dire calamity, for, of all the provinces, it had been the least expensive and the most productive; it yielded men, money, and, what was perhaps of more importance, corn for the use of Italy. A sudden stoppage of the customary supply rendered impossible the usual distributions in Rome, Ravenna, Milan. A famine fell upon Italy, bringing in its train an inevitable diminution of the population. To add to the misfortunes, Attila, the King of the Huns, or, as he called himself, "the Scourge of God," invaded the empire. The battle of Chalons, the convulsive death throe of the Roman empire, arrested his career, A.D. 451.

Fall and pillage of Rome.

Four years after this event, through intrigues in the imperial family, Genseric, the Vandal king, was invited from Africa to Rome, The atrocities which of old had been practised against Carthage under the auspices of the senate were now avenged. For fourteen days the Vandals sacked the city, perpetrating unheard-of cruelties. Their ships, brought into the Tiber, enabled them to accomplish their purpose of pillage far more effectually than would have been possible by any land expedition. The treasures of Rome, with multitudes of noble captives, were transported to Carthage. In twenty-one years after this time, A.D. 476, the Western Empire became extinct.

Thus the treachery of the African Arians not only brought the Vandals into the most important of all the provinces, so far as Italy was concerned; it also furnished an instrument for the ruin of Rome. But hardly had the Emperor Justinian reconquered Africa when he attempted the subjugation of the Goths now holding possession of Italy. His general, Belisarius, captured Rome, Dec. 10, A.D. 556. In the military operations ensuing with Vitiges, Italy was devastated, the population sank beneath the sword, pestilence, famine. In all directions the glorious remains of antiquity were destroyed; statues, as those of the Mole of Hadrian, were thrown upon the besiegers of Rome. These operations closed by the surrender of Vitiges to Belisarius at the capture of Ravenna.

Effects of the wars of Justinian.

But, as soon as the military compression was withdrawn, revolt broke out. Rome was retaken by the Goths; its walls were razed; for forty days it was deserted by its inhabitants, an emigration that in the end proved its ruin. Belisarius, who had been sent back by the emperor, reentered it, but was too weak to retain it. During four years Italy was ravaged by the Franks and the Goths. At last Justinian sent the eunuch Narses with a well-appointed army. The Ostrogothic monarchy was overthrown, and the emperor governed Italy by his exarchs at Ravenna.

But what was the cost of all this? We may reject the statement previously made, that Italy lost fifteen millions of inhabitants, on the ground that such computations were beyond the ability of the survivors, but, from the asserted number we may infer that there had been a horrible catastrophe. In other directions the relics of civilization were fast disappearing; the valley of the Danube had relapsed into a barbarous state; the African shore had become a wilderness; Italy a hideous desert; and the necessary consequence of the extermination of the native Italians by war, and their replacement by barbarous adventurers, was the falling of the sparse population of that peninsula into a

Debased ideas of the incoming Age of Faith.

lower psychical state. It was ready for the materialized religion that soon ensued. An indelible aspect was stamped on the incoming Age of Faith. The East and the West had equally displayed the imbecility of ecclesiastical rule. Of both, the Holy City had fallen; Jerusalem had been captured by the Persian and the Arab, Rome had been sacked by the Vandal and the Goth.

But, for the proper description of the course of affairs, I must retrace my steps a little. In the important political events coinciding with the death of Leo the Great, and the constitution of the kingdom of Italy by the barbarian Odoacer, A.D. 476–490, the bishops of Rome seem to have taken but little interest. Doubtless, on one side, they perceived the transitory nature of such incidents, and, on the other, clearly saw for themselves the road to lasting spiritual domination. The Christians everywhere had long expressed a total carelessness for the fate of old Rome; and in the midst of her ruins the popes were incessantly occupied in laying deep the foundations of their power. Though it mattered little to them who was the temporal ruler of Italy, they were vigilant and energetic in their relations with their great competitors, the bishops of Constantinople and Alexandria. It had become clear that Christendom must have a head; and that headship, once definitely settled, implied the eventual control over the temporal power. Of all objects of human ambition, that headship was best worth struggling for.

Steady progress of the papacy to supremacy.

Steadily pursuing every advantage as it arose, Rome inexorably insisted that her decisions should be carried out in Constantinople itself. This was the case especially in the affair of Acacius, the bishop of that city, who, having been admonished for his acts by Felix, the bishop of Rome, was finally excommunicated. A difficulty arose as to the manner in which the process should be served; but an adventurous monk fastened it to the robe of Acacius as he entered the church. Acacius, undismayed, proceeded with his services, and, pausing deliberately, ordered the name of Felix, the Bishop of Rome, to be struck from the roll of bishops in communion with the East. Constantinople and Rome thus mutually excommunicated one another. It is in reference to this affair that Pope Gelasius, addressing the emperor, says: "There are two powers which rule the world, the imperial and pontifical. You are the sovereign of the human race, but you bow your neck to those who preside over things divine. The priesthood is the greater of the two powers; it has to render an account in the last day for the acts of kings." This is not the language of a feeble ecclesiastic, but of a pontiff who understands his power.

Its attitude toward the emperor.

The conquest of Italy by Theodoric, the Ostrogoth, A.D. 493, gave to the bishops of Rome an Arian sovereign, and presented to the world the anomaly of a heretic appointing God's vicar upon earth. There was a contested election between two rival candidates, whose factions, emulating the example of the East, filled the city with murder. The Gothic monarch ordered that he who had most suffrages, and had been first consecrated, should be acknowleged. In this manner Symmachus became pope.

The Gothic conquest gives the pope an Arian master.

Hormisdas, who succeeded Symmachus, renewed the attempt to compel the Eastern emperor, Anastasius, to accept the degradation of Acacius and his party, and to enforce the assent of all his clergy thereto, but in vain. On the accession of Justin to the imperial throne, Rome at last carried her point; all her conditions were admitted; the schism was ended in the humiliation of the Bishop of Constantinople, it was said, through the orthodoxy of the emperor. But very soon began to appear unmistakable indications that for this religious victory a temporal equivalent had been given. Conspiracies were detected in Rome against Theodoric, the Gothic king; and rumours were whispered about that the arms of Constantinople would before long release Italy from the heretical yoke of the Arian. There can be no doubt that Theodoric detected the treason. It was an evil reward for his impartial equity. At once he disarmed the population of Rome. From being a merciful sovereign, he exhibited an awful vengeance. It was in these transactions that Boethius, the philosopher, and Symmachus, the senator, fell victims to his wrath. The pope John himself was

The emperor and pope conspire against him.

The Gothic king detects them.

thrown into prison, and there miserably died. In his remonstrances with Justin, the great barbarian monarch displays sentiments far above his times, yet they were the sentiments that had hitherto regulated his actions. "To pretend to a dominion over the conscience is to usurp the prerogative of God. By the nature of things, the power of sovereigns is confined to political government. They have no right of punishment but over those who disturb the public peace. The most dangerous heresy is that of a sovereign who separates himself from part of his subjects because they believe not according to his belief."

The conspiracy matures.

Theodoric had been but a few years dead—his soul was seen by an orthodox hermit carried by devils into the crater of the volcano of Lipari, which was considered to be the opening into hell—when the invasion of Italy by Justinian showed how well-founded his suspicions had been. Rome was, however, very far from receiving the advantages she had expected; the inconceivable wickedness of Constantinople was brought into Italy. Pope Sylverius, who was the son of Pope Hormisdas, was deposed by Theodora, the emperor's wife. This woman, once a common prostitute, sold the papacy to Vigilius for two hundred pounds of gold. Her accomplice, Antonina, the unprincipled wife of Belisarius, had Sylverius stripped of his robes and habited as a monk. He was subsequently banished to the old convict island of Pandataria, and there died. Vigilius embraced Eutychianism and, it was said, murdered one of his secretaries, and caused his sister's son to be beaten to death. He was made to feel what it is for a bishop to be in the hands of an emperor; to taste of the cup so often presented to prelates at Constantinople; to understand in what estimation his sovereign held the vicar of God upon earth. Compelled to go to that metropolis to embrace the theological views which Justinian had put forth, thrice he agreed to them, and thrice he recanted; he excommunicated the Patriarch of Constantinople, and was excommunicated by him. In his personal contests with the imperial officials, they dragged him by his feet from a sanctuary with so much violence that a part of the structure was pulled down upon him; they confined him in a dungeon and fed him on

Subjugation of the pope by the emperor.

bread and water. Eventually he died an outcast in Sicily. The immediate effect of the conquest of Italy was the reduction of the popes to the degraded condition of the patriarchs of Constantinople. Such were the bitter fruits of their treason to the Gothic king. The success of Justinian's invasion was due to the clergy; in the ruin they brought upon their country, and the relentless tyranny they drew upon themselves, they had their reward.

In the midst of this desolation and degradation the Age of Faith was gradually assuming distinctive lineaments in Italy. Paganization, which had been patronized as a matter of policy in the East, became a matter of necessity in the West. To a man like Gregory the Great, born in a position which enabled him to examine things from a very general point of view, it was clear that the psychical condition of the lower social stratum demanded concessions in accordance with its ideas. The belief of the thoughtful must be alloyed with the superstition of the populace.

The paganization of religion proceeds.

Accordingly, that was what actually occurred. For the clear understanding of these events I shall have to speak, 1st, of the acts of Pope Gregory the Great, by whom the ideas of the age were organized and clothed in a dress suited to the requirements of the times; 2d, of the relations which the papacy soon assumed with the kings of France, by which the work of Gregory was consolidated, upheld, and diffused all over Europe. It adds not a little to the interest of these things that the influences thus created have outlasted their original causes, and, after the lapse of more than a thousand years, though moss-covered and rotten, are a stumbling-block to the progress of nations.

Division of the subjects to be treated of.

Gregory the Great was the grandson of Pope Felix. His patrician parentage and conspicuous abilities had attracted in early life the attention of the Emperor Justin, by whom he was appointed prefect of Rome. Withdrawn by the Church from the splendours of secular life, he was sent, while yet a deacon, as nuncio to Constantinople. Discharging the duties that had been committed to him with singular ability and firmness, he

Gregory the Great.

resumed the monastic life on his return, with daily increasing reputation. Elected to the papacy by the clergy, the senate, and people of Rome, A.D. 590, with well dissembled resistance he implored the emperor to reject their choice, and, on being refused, escaped from the city hidden in a basket. It is related that the retreat in which he was concealed was discovered by a celestial hovering light that settled upon it, and revealed to the faithful their reluctant pope. This was during a time of pestilence and famine.

Once made supreme pontiff, this austere monk in an instant resumed the character he had displayed at Constantinople, and exhibited the qualities of a great statesman. He regulated the Roman liturgy, the calendar of festivals, the order of processions, the fashions of sacerdotal garments; he himself officiated in the canon of the mass, devised many solemn and pompous rites, and invented the chant known by his name. He established schools of music, administered the Church revenues with precision and justice, and set an example of almsgiving and charity; for such was the misery of the times that even Roman matrons had to accept the benevolence of the Church. He authorized the alienation of Church property for the redemption of slaves, laymen as well as ecclesiastics.

An insubordinate clergy and a dissolute populace quickly felt the hand that now held the reins. He sedulously watched the inferior pastors, dealing out justice to them, and punishing all who offended with rigorous severity. He compelled the Italian bishops to acknowledge him as their metropolitan. He extended his influence to Greece; prohibited simony in Gaul; received into the bosom of the Church Spain, now renouncing her Arianism; sent out missionaries to Britain, and converted the pagans of that country; extirpated heathenism from Sardinia; resisted John, the Patriarch of Constantinople, who had dared to take the title of universal bishop; exposed to the emperor the ruin occasioned by the pride, ambition, and wickedness of the clergy, and withstood him on the question of the law prohibiting soldiers from becoming monks. It was not in the nature of such a man to decline the regulation of political affairs; he nominated tribunes, and directed the operations of troops.

No one can shake off the system that has given him power; no one can free himself from the tincture of the times of which he is the representative. Though in so many respects Gregory was far in advance of his age, he was at once insincere and profoundly superstitious. With more than Byzantine hatred he detested human knowledge. His oft-expressed belief that the end of the world was at hand was perpetually contradicted by his acts, which were ceaselessly directed to the foundation of a future papal empire. Under him was sanctified that mythologic Christianity destined to become the religion of Europe for many subsequent centuries, and which adopted the adoration of the Virgin by images and pictures; the efficacy of the remains of martyrs and relics; stupendous miracles wrought at the shrines of saints; the perpetual interventions of angels and devils in sublunary affairs; the truth of legends far surpassing in romantic improbability the stories of Greek mythology; the localization of heaven a few miles above the air, and of hell in the bowels of the earth, with its portal in the crater of Lipari. Gregory himself was a sincere believer in miracles, ghosts, and the resurrection of many persons from the grave, but who, alas! had brought no tidings of the secret wonders of that land of deepest shade. He made these wild fancies the actual, the daily, the practical religion of Europe. Participating in the ecclesiastical hatred of human learning, and insisting on the maxim that "Ignorance is the mother of devotion," he expelled from Rome all mathematical studies, and burned the Palatine library founded by Augustus Cæsar. It was valuable for the many rare manuscripts it contained. He forbade the study of the classics, mutilated statues, and destroyed temples. He hated the very relics of classical genius; pursued with vindictive fanaticism the writings of Livy, against whom he was specially excited. It has truly been said that "he was as inveterate an enemy to learning as ever lived;" that "no lucid ray ever beamed on his superstitious soul." He boasted that his own works were written without regard to the rules of grammar, and censured the crime of a priest who had taught that subject.

His superstition.

He materializes religion.

His hatred of learning,

and expulsion of classical authors.

It was his aim to substitute for the heathen writings others which he thought less dangerous to orthodoxy; and so well did he succeed in rooting out of Italy her illustrious pagan authors, that when one of his successors, Paul I., sent to Pepin of France "what books he could find," they were "an antiphonal, a grammar, and the works of Dionysius the Areopagite." He was the very incarnation of the Byzantine principle of ignorance.

If thus the misfortunes that had fallen on Italy had given her a base population, whose wants could only be met by a paganized religion, the more fortunate classes all over the empire had long been tending in the same direction. Whoever will examine the progress of Christian society from the earlier ages, will find that there could be no other result than a repudiation of solid learning and an alliance with art. We have only to compare the poverty and plainness of the first disciples with the extravagance reached in a few generations. Cyprian complains of the covetousness, pride, luxury, and worldly-mindedness of Christians, even of the clergy and confessors. Some made no scruple to contract matrimony with heathens. Clement of Alexandria bitterly inveighs against "the vices of an opulent and luxurious Christian community—splendid dresses, gold and silver vessels, rich banquets, gilded litters and chariots, and private baths. The ladies kept Indian birds, Median peacocks, monkeys, and Maltese dogs, instead of maintaining widows and orphans; the men had multitudes of slaves." The dipping three times at baptism, the tasting of honey and milk, the oblations for the dead, the signing of the cross on the forehead on putting on the clothes or the shoes, or lighting a candle, which Tertullian imputes to tradition without the authority of Scripture, foreshadowed a thousand pagan observances soon to be introduced. As time passed on, so far from the state of things improving, it became worse. Not only among the frivolous class, but even among historic personages, there was a hankering after the ceremonies of the departed creed, a lingering attachment to the old rites, and, perhaps, a religious indifference to the new. To the age of Justinian these remarks strikingly apply. Boethius

Gradual preparation for the debasement of religion.

Corruption of Christianity.

was, at the best, only a pagan philosopher; Tribonian, the great lawyer, the author of the Justinian Code, was suspected of being an atheist.

In the East, the splendour of the episcopal establishments extorted admiration even from those who were familiar with the imperial court. The well-ordered trains of attendants and the magnificent banquets in the bishops' palaces are particularly praised. Extravagant views of the pre-eminent value of celibacy had long been held among the more devout, who conceded a reluctant admission even for marriage itself. "I praise the married state, but chiefly for this, that it provides virgins," had been the more than doubtful encomium of St. Jerome. Among the clergy, who under the force of this growing sentiment found it advisable to refrain from marriage, it had become customary, as we learn from the enactments and denunciations against the practice, to live with "sub-introduced women," as they were called. These passed as sisters of the priests, the correctness of whose taste was often exemplified by the remarkable beauty of their sinful partners. A law of Honorius put an end to this iniquity. The children arising from these associations do not appear to have occasioned any extraordinary scandal. At weddings it was still the custom to sing hymns to Venus. The cultivation of music at a very early period attracted the attention of many of the great ecclesiastics—Paul of Samosata, Arius, Chrysostom. In the first congregations probably all the worshippers joined in the hymns and psalmody. By degrees, however, more skilful performers had been introduced, and the chorus of the Greek tragedy made available under the form of antiphonal singing. The Ambrosian chant was eventually exchanged for the noble Roman chant of Gregory the Great, which has been truly characterised as the foundation of all that is grand and elevated in modern music.

Episcopal splendour and wickedness.

Paganisms of Christianity.

It allies itself to art.

With the devastation that Italy had suffered the Latin language was becoming extinct. But Roman literature had never been converted to Christianity. Of the best writers among the Fathers, not one was a Roman; all were provincials. The literary basis was the Hebrew

Scriptures and the New Testament, the poetical imagery being, for the most part, borrowed from the prophets. In historical compositions there was a want of fair dealing and truthfulness almost incredible to us; thus Eusebius naïvely avows that in his history he shall omit whatever might tend to the discredit of the Church, and magnify whatever might conduce to her glory. The same principle was carried out in numberless legends, many of them deliberate forgeries, the amazing credulity of the times yielding to them full credit, no matter how much they might outrage common sense. But what else was to be expected of generations who could believe that the tracks of Pharaoh's chariot-wheels were still impressed on the sands of the Red Sea, and could not be obliterated either by the winds or the waves? He who ventured to offend the public taste for these idle fables brought down upon himself the wrath of society, and was branded as an infidel. In the interpretation of the Scriptures, and, indeed, in all commentaries on authors of repute, there was a constant indulgence in fanciful mystification and the detection of concealed meanings, in the extracting of which an amusing degree of ingenuity and industry was often shown; but these hermeneutical writings, as well as the polemical, are tedious beyond endurance; with regard to the latter, the energy of their vindictive violence is not sufficient to redeem them from contempt.

and rejects learning.

The relation of the Church to the sister arts, painting and sculpture, was doubtless fairly indicated at a subsequent time by the second Council of Nicea, A.D. 787; their superstitious use had been resumed. Sculpture has, however, never forgotten the preference that was shown to her sister. To this day she is a pagan, emulating in this the example of the noblest of the sciences, Astronomy, who bears in mind the great insults she has received from the Church, and tolerates the name of no saint in the visible heavens; the new worlds she discovers are dedicated to Uranus, or Neptune, or other Olympian divinities. Among the ecclesiastics there had always been many, occasionally some of eminence, who set their faces against the connexion of worship with art; thus Tertullian of old had manifested his displeasure against Hermogenes,

Painting and sculpture.

on account of the two deadly sins into which he had fallen, painting and marriage; but Gnostic Christianity had approved, as Roman Christianity was now to approve, of their union. To the Gnostics we owe the earliest examples of our sacred images. The countenance of our Saviour, along with those of Pythagoras, Plato, Aristotle, appears on some of their engraved gems and seals. Among the earlier fathers—Justin Martyn and Tertullian—there was an impression that the personal appearance of our Lord was ungainly; that he was short of stature; and, at a later period Cyril says, mean of aspect "even beyond the ordinary race of men." But these unsuitable delineations were generally corrected in the fourth century, it being then recognised that God could not dwell in a humble form or low stature. The model eventually received was perhaps that described in the spurious epistle of Lentulus to the Roman senate: "He was a man of tall and well-proportioned form; his countenance severe and impressive, so as to move the beholders at once with love and awe. His hair was of an amber colour, reaching to his ears with no radiation, and standing up from his ears clustering and bright, and flowing down over his shoulders, parted on the top according to the fashion of the Nazarenes. The brow high and open; the complexion clear, with a delicate tinge of red; the aspect frank and pleasing; the nose and mouth finely formed; the beard thick, parted, and of the colour of the hair; the eyes blue, and exceedingly bright." Subsequently the oval countenance assumed an air of melancholy, which, though eminently suggestive, can hardly be considered as the type of manly beauty.

Adopts a typical model of the Saviour,

At first the cross was without any adornment; it next had a lamb at the foot; and eventually became the crucifix, sanctified with the form of the dying Saviour. Of the Virgin Mary, destined in later times to furnish so many beautiful types of female loveliness, the earliest representations are veiled. The Egyptian sculptors had thus depicted Isis; the first form of the Virgin and child was the counterpart of Isis and Horus. St. Augustine says her countenance was unknown; there appears, however, to have been a very early Christian tradition that in com-

and of the Virgin.

plexion she was a brunette. Adventurous artists by degrees removed the veil, and next to the mere countenance added a full-grown figure like that of a dignified Roman matron; then grouped her with the divine child, the wise men, and other suggestions of Scripture.

While thus the papacy was preparing for an alliance with art, it did not forget to avail itself of the vast advantages within its reach by interfering in domestic life—an interference which the social demoralization of the time more than ever permitted. A prodigious step in power was made by assuming the cognizance of marriage, and the determination of the numberless questions connected with it. Once having discovered the influence thus gained, the papacy never surrendered it; some of the most important events in later history have been determined by its action in this matter. Perhaps even a greater power accrued from its assumption of the cognizance of wills, and of questions respecting the testamentary disposal of property. Though in many respects, at the time we are now considering, the papacy had separated itself from morality, had become united to monachism, and was preparing for a future alliance with political influences and military power; though its indignation and censures were less against personal wickedness than heresy of opinion, toward which it was inexorable and remorseless, a good effect arose from these assumptions upon domestic life, particularly as regards the elevation of the female sex. The power thus arising was re-enforced by a continually-increasing rigour in the application of penitential punishments. As in the course of years the intellectual basis on which that power rested became more doubtful, and therefore more open to attack, the papacy became more sensitive and more exacting. Pushed on by the influence of the lower population, it fell into the depths of anthropomorphism, asserting for the Virgin and the saints such attributes as omniscience, omnipresence, omnipotence. Everywhere present, they could always listen to prayer, and, if necessary, control or arrest the course of Nature. As it was certain that such doctrines must in

Consolidation of papal power in the West.

Roman Church anthropomorphized,

and necessarily becoming intolerant.

the end be overthrown, the inevitable day was put off by an instant and vindictive repression of any want of conformity. Despotism in the State and despotism in the Church were upheld by despotism over thought.

From the acts of Pope Gregory the Great, and his organization of the ideas of his age, the paganization of religion in Italy and its alliance with art, I have now to turn to the second topic to which this chapter is devoted—the relations assumed by the papacy with the kings of France, by which the work of Gregory was consolidated and upheld, and diffused all over Europe.

Origin of the alliance of the papacy and France.

The armies of the Saracens had wrested from Christendom the western, southern, and eastern countries of the Mediterranean; their fleets dominated in that sea. Ecclesiastical policy had undergone a revolution. Carthage, Alexandria, Jerusalem, Antioch, had disappeared from the Christian system; their bishops had passed away. Alone, of the great episcopal seats, Constantinople and Rome were left. To all human appearance, their fall seemed to be only a question of time.

Military results of the Arabian wars.

The disputes of the Bishop of Rome with his African and Asiatic rivals had thus come to an untimely end. With them nothing more remained to be done; his communications with the emperor at Constantinople were at the sufferance of the Mohammedan navies. The imperial power was paralysed. The pope was forced by events into isolation; he converted it into independence.

Independence of the pope.

But independence! how was that to be asserted and maintained. In Italy itself the Lombards seemed to be firmly seated, but they were Arian heretics. Their presence and power were incompatible with his. Already, in a political sense, he was at their mercy.

One movement alone was open to him; and, whether he rightly understood his position or not, the stress of events forced him to make it. It was an alliance with the Franks, who had successfully resisted the Mohammedan power, and who were orthodox.

An ambitious Frank officer had resolved to deprive his sovereign of the crown if the pope would sanctify the deed.

They came to an understanding. The usurpation was consummated by the one and consecrated by the other. It was then the interest of the intrusive line of monarchs to magnify their Italian confederate. In the spread of Roman principles lay the consolidation of the new Frankish power. It became desirable to compel the ignorant German tribes to acknowledge in the pope the vicegerent of God, even though the sword must be applied to them for that purpose for thirty years.

Conditions of his alliance with the Franks.

The pope revolted against his Byzantine sovereign on the question of images; but that was a fictitious issue. He did not revolt against his new ally, who fell into the same heresy. He broke away from a weak and cruel master, and attached himself on terms of equality to a confederate. But from the first his eventual ascendancy was assured. The representative of a system which is immortal must finally gain supremacy over individuals and families, who must die.

Though we cannot undervalue the labours of the monks, who had already nominally brought many portions of Europe to Christianity, the passage of the centre of the Continent to its Age of Faith, was, in an enlarged political sense, the true issue of the empire of the Franks. The fiat of Charlemagne put a stamp upon it which it bears to this day. He converted an ecclesiastical fiction into a political fact.

The conversion of Europe.

To understand this important event, it is necessary to describe, 1st, the psychical state of Central Europe; 2nd, the position of the pontiff and his compact with the Franks. It is also necessary to determine the actual religious value of the system he represents, and this is best done through, 3rd, the biography of the popes.

Three points for consideration.

1st. As with the Arabs, so with the barbarians of Europe. They pass from their Age of Credulity to their Age of Faith without dwelling long in the intermediate state of Inquiry. An age of inquiry implies self-investigation, and the absence of an authoritative teacher. But the Arabs had had the Nestorians and the Jews, and to the Germans the lessons of

The psychical change of Europe.

the monk were impressively enforced by the convincing argument of the sword of Charlemagne.

The military invasions of the south by the barbarians were retaliated by missionary invasions of the north. The aim of the former was to conquer, that of their antagonists to convert, if antagonists those can be called who sought to turn them from their evil ways. The monk penetrated through their most gloomy forests unarmed and defenceless; he found his way alone to their fortresses. Nothing touches the heart of a savage so profoundly as the greatness of silent courage. Among the captives taken from the south in war were often high-born women of great beauty and purity of mind, and sometimes even bishops, who, true to their religious principles, did not fail to exert a happy and a holy influence on the tribes among whom their lot was cast. One after another the various nations submitted: the Vandals and Gepidæ in the fourth century; the Goths somewhat earlier; the Franks at the end of the fifth; the Alemanni and Lombards at the beginning of the sixth; the Bavarians, Hessians, and Thuringians in the seventh and eighth. Of these, all embraced the Arian form except the Franks, who were converted by the Catholic clergy. In truth, however, these nations were only Christianized upon the surface, their conversion being indicated by little more than their making the sign of the cross. In all these movements women exercised an extraordinary influence: thus Clotilda, the Queen of the Franks, brought over to the faith her husband Clovis. Bertha, the Queen of Kent, and Gisella, the Queen of Hungary, led the way in their respective countries; and under similar influences were converted the Duke of Poland and the Czar Jarislaus. To women Europe is thus greatly indebted, though the forms of religion at the first were nothing more than the creed and the Lord's prayer. It has been truly said that for these conversions three conditions were necessary—a devout female of the court, a national calamity, and a monk. As to the people, they seem to have followed the example of their rulers in blind subserviency, altogether careless as to what the required faith might be.

Labours and successes of the monks

Influence of devout women.

Conversion of Europe.

The conversion of the ruler is naïvely taken by historians as the conversion of the whole people. As might be expected, a faith so lightly assumed at the will or whim of the sovereign was often as lightly cast aside; thus the Swedes, Bohemians, and Hungarians relapsed into idolatry.

Conversion of England.

Among such apostasies it is interesting to recall that of the inhabitants of Britain, to whom Christianity was first introduced by the Roman legions, and who might boast in Constantine the Great, and his mother Helena, if they were really natives of that country, that they had exercised no little influence on the religion of the world. The biography of Pelagius shows with what acuteness theological doctrines were considered in those remote regions; but, after the decline of Roman affairs, this promising state of things was destroyed, and the clergy driven by the pagan invaders to the inacessible parts of Wales, Scotland, and Ireland. The sight of some English children exposed for sale in the slave-market at Rome suggested to Gregory the Great the attempt of re-converting the island. On his assuming the pontificate he commissioned the monk Augustine for that purpose; and after the usual exertion of female influence in the court of King Ethelbert by Bertha, his Frankish princess, and the usual vicissitudes of backsliding, the faith gradually won its way throughout the whole country. A little opposition occurred on the part of the ancient clergy, who retained in their fastnesses the traditions of the old times, particularly in regard to Easter. But this at length disappeared: an intercourse sprang up with Rome, and it became common for the clergy and wealthy nobles to visit that city.

Irish and British missionaries.

Displaying the same noble quality which in our own times characterises it, British Christianity did not fail to exert a proselytizing spirit. As, at the end of the sixth century, Columban, an Irish monk of Banchor, had gone forth as a missionary, passing through France, Switzerland, and beyond the confines of the ancient Roman empire, so about a century later Boniface, an Englishman of Devonshire, repaired to Germany, under a recommendation from the pope and Charles Martel, and laboured among the Hessians and Saxons, cutting down their sacred oaks, overturning their altars, erecting churches, founding bishoprics, and gaining at last, from the hands of the savages, the crown of martyrdom. In the affinity of their language to those of the countries to which they went, these missionaries from the West found a very great advantage.

It is the glory of Pope Formosus, the same whose body underwent a posthumous trial, that he converted the Bulgarians, a people who came from the banks of the Volga. The fact that this event was brought about by a picture representing the judgment-day shows on what trifling circumstances these successes turned. The Slavians were converted by Greek missionaries, and for them the monk Cyril invented an alphabet, as Ulphilas had done for the Goths. The predatory Normans, who plundered the churches in their forays, embraced Christianity on settling in Normandy, as the Goths, in like circumstances, had elsewhere done. The Scandinavians were converted by St. Anschar.

Thus, partly by the preaching of missionaries, partly by the example of monks, partly by the influence of females, partly by the sword of the Frankish sovereigns, partly by the great name of Rome, Europe was at last nominally converted. The so-called religious wars of Charlemagne, which lasted more than thirty years, and which were attended by the atrocities always incident to such undertakings, were doubtless as much, so far as he was concerned, of a political as of a theological nature. They were the embodiment of the understanding that had been made with Rome by Pepin. Charlemagne clearly comprehended the position and functions of the Church; he never suffered it to intrude unduly on the state. Regarding it as furnishing a bond for uniting not only the various nations and tribes of his empire, but even families and individuals together, he ever extended to it a wise and liberal protection. His mental condition prevented him from applying its doctrines to the regulation of his own life, which was often blemished by acts of violence and immorality. From the point of view he occupied, he doubtless was led to the conclusion that the maxims of religion are intended for the edification and comfort of those who occupy a humbler sphere, but that

Influence of Charlemagne on these events.

for a prince it is only necessary to maintain appropriate political relations with the Church. To him baptism was the sign, not of salvation, but of the subjugation of people; and the foundation of churches and monasteries, the institution af bishoprics, and increase of the clergy, a more trustworthy means of government than military establishments. A priest must necessarily lean on him for support, a lieutenant might revolt.

If thus Europe, by its conversion, received from Rome an immense benefit, it repaid the obligation at length by infusing into Latin Christianity what was sadly needed—a higher moral tone. Earnestness is the attribute of savage life. That divorce between morality and faith which the southern nations had experienced was not possible among these converts. If, by communicating many of their barbarous and pagan conceptions to the Latin faith, they gave it a tendency to develop itself in an idolatrous form, their influence was not one of unmitigated evil, for while they lowered the standard of public belief, they elevated that of private life. In truth, the contamination they imparted is often overrated. The infusion of paganism into religion was far more due to the people of the classical countries. The inhabitants of Italy and Greece were never really alienated from the idolatries of the old times. At the best, they were only Christianized on the surface. With many other mythological practices, they forced image-worship on the clergy. But Charlemagne, who, in this respect, may be looked upon as a true representative of Frankish and German sentiment, totally disapproved of that idolatry.

Reflex action of converted Europe.

2nd. From this consideration of the psychical revolution that had occurred in Central Europe, I turn to an investigation of the position of the papacy and its compact with the Franks.

The conspiracy of the papacy and the Franks.

Scarcely had the Arabs consolidated their conquest of Africa when they passed into Spain, and quickly, as will be related in a subsequent chapter, subjugating that country, prepared to overwhelm Europe. It was their ambition and their threat to preach the unity of God in Rome. They reached the centre of France, but were beaten in the great battle of Tours by

Position of the Franks and Saracens.

Charles Martel, the Duke of the Franks, A.D. 732. That battle fixed the religious destiny of Europe. The Saracens did not, however, give up their attempt. Three years afterward they returned into Provence, and Charles was himself repulsed. But by this time their power had expanded too extensively for consolidation. It was already giving unmistakable tokens of decomposition. Scarcely, indeed, had Musa, the conqueror of Spain, succeeded in his expedition, when he was arrested at the head of his army, and ordered to give an account of his doings at Damascus. It was the occurrence of such disputes among the Saracens in Spain that constituted the true check to their conquest of France. Charles Martel had permitted Chilperic II. and Thierry IV. to retain the title of king; but his foresight of approaching events seems to be indicated by the circumstance that after the death of the latter he abstained from appointing any successor. He died A.D. 741, leaving a memory detested by the Church of his own country on account of his having been obliged to appropriate from its property sufficient for the payment of his army. He had taken a tithe from the revenues of the churches and convents for that purpose. The ignorant clergy, alive only to their present temporal interests, and not appreciating the great salvation he had wrought out for them, could never forgive him. Their inconceivable greed could not bear to be taxed even in its own defence. "It is because Prince Charles," says the Council of Kiersi to one of his descendants, "was the first of all the kings and princes of the Franks who separated and dismembered the goods of the Church; it is for that sole cause that he is eternally damned. We know, indeed, that St. Eucherius, Bishop of Orleans, being in prayer, was carried up into the world of spirits, and that among the things which the Lord showed to him, he beheld Charles tormented in the lowest depths of hell. The angel who conducted him, being interrogated on this matter, answered him that, in the judgment to come, the soul and body of him who has taken, or who has divided the goods of the Church, shall be delivered over, even before the end of the world, to eternal torments by the sentence of the saints, who shall sit together with the Lord to judge him.

Relations of Charles Martel to the Church.

This act of sacrilege shall add to his own sins the accumulated sins of all those who thought that they had purchased their redemption by giving for the love of God their goods to holy places, to the lights of divine worship, and to the alms of the servants of Christ." This amusing but instructive quotation strikingly shows how quickly the semibarbarian Frankish clergy had caught the methods of Rome in the defence of temporal possessions.

The epoch of Pepin.

Pepin, the son of Charles Martel, introduces us to an epoch and a policy resembling in many respects that of Constantine the Great; for he saw that by an alliance with the Church it would be possible for him to displace his sovereign and attain to kingly power. A thorough understanding was entered upon between Pepin and the pope. Each had his needs. One wanted the crown of France, the other liberation from Constantinople and the Lombards. Pepin commenced by enriching the clergy with immense gifts, and assigning to the bishops seats in the assembly of the nation. In thus consolidating ecclesiastical power he occasioned a great social revolution, as was manifested by the introduction of the Latin and the disuse of the Frankic on those occasions, and by the transmuting of military reviews into theological assemblies. Meantime Pope Zachary, on his part, made ready to accomplish his engagement, the chaplain of Pepin being the intermedium of negotiation. On the demand being formally made, the pope decided that "he should be king who really possessed the royal power." Hereupon, in March, A.D. 752, Pepin caused himself to be raised by his soldiers on a buckler and proclaimed King of the Franks. To give solemnity to the event, he was anointed by the bishops with oil. The deposed king, Childeric III., was shut up in the convent of St. Omer. Next year Pope Stephen III., driven to extremity, applied to Pepin for assistance against the Lombards. It was during these transactions that he fell upon the device of enforcing his demand by a letter which he feigned had been written by St. Peter to the Franks. And now, visiting France, the pope, as an earnest of his friendship, and as the token of his completion of the contract, in the monastery of St. Denis, placed, with his own hands, the

His conspiracy with the pope.

diadem on Pepin's brow, and anointed him, his wife, and children, with "the holy oil," thereby reviving the Jewish system of creating kings by anointment, and imparting to his confederate "a divine right." Pepin now finally defeated the Lombards, and assigned a part of the conquered territory to the pope. Thus, by a successful soldier, two important events had been accomplished—a revolution in France, attended by a change of dynasty, and a revolution in Christendom—the Bishop of Rome had become a temporal sovereign. To the hilt of the sword of France the keys of St. Peter were henceforth so firmly bound that, though there have been great kings, and conquerors, and statesmen who have wielded that sword, not one to this day has been able, though many have desired, to wrench the encumbrance away.

Its results.

Charlemagne, on succeeding his father Pepin, thoroughly developed his policy. At the urgent entreaty of Pope Stephen III. he entered Italy, subjugated the Lombards, and united the crown of Lombardy to that of France. Upon the pagan Saxons burning the church of Deventer, he commenced a war with them which lasted thirty-three years, and ended in their compulsory Christianization. As the circle of his power extended, he everywhere founded churches and established bishoprics, enriching them with territorial possessions. To the petty sovereigns, as they successively succumbed, he permitted the title of counts. True to his own and his father's understanding with the pope, he invariably insisted on baptism as the sign of submission, punishing with appalling barbarity any resistance, as on the occasion of the revolt, A.D. 782, when, in cold blood, he beheaded in one day 4500 persons at Verden. Under such circumstances, it is not to be wondered at that clerical influence extended so fast; yet, rapid as was its development, the power of Charlemagne was more so.

The reign of Charlemagne.

In the church of St. Peter at Rome, on Christmas-day, A.D. 800, Pope Leo III., after the celebration of the holy mysteries, suddenly placed on the head of Charlemagne a diadem, amid the acclamations of the people, "Long life and victory to Charles, the most pious Augustus, crowned by God, the great and

He is crowned Emperor of the West.

pacific Emperor of the Romans." His head and body were anointed with the holy oil, and, as was done in the case of the Cæsars, the pontiff himself saluted or adored him. In the coronation oath Charlemagne promised to maintain the privileges of the Church.

The noble title of "Emperor of the West" was not inappropriate, for Charlemagne ruled in France, Spain, Italy, Germany, Hungary. An inferior dignity would not have been equal to his deserts. His princely munificence to St. Peter was worthy of the great occasion, and even in his minor acts he exhibited a just appreciation of his obligations to the apostle. He proceeded to make in his dominions such changes in the Church organization as the Italian policy required, substituting, for instance, the Gregorian for the Ambrosian chant, and, wherever his priests resisted, he took from them by force their antiphonaries. As an example to insubordinates he, at the request of the pope, burnt some of the singers along with their books.

and carries out his compact with the papacy.

The rapid growth of the power of Charlemagne, his overshadowing pre-eminence, and the subordinate position of the pope, who had really become his Italian lieutenant, are strikingly manifested by the event of image-worship in the West. On this, as we shall in another chapter see, the popes had revolted from their iconoclastic sovereigns of Constantinople. The second Council of Nicea had authorized image-worship, but the good sense of Charlemagne was superior to such idolatry. He openly expressed his disapproval, and even dictated a work against it—the Carolinian books. The pope was therefore placed in a singular dilemma, for not only had image-worship been restored at Constantinople, and the original cause of the dispute removed, but the new protector, Charlemagne, had himself embraced iconoclasm. However, it was not without reason that the pope at this time avoided the discussion, for a profitable sale of bones and relics, said to be those of saints, but in reality obtained from the catacombs of Rome, had arisen. To the barbarian people of the north these gloomy objects proved more acceptable than images of wood, and the traffic, though contemptible, was more honourable than

He declines image-worship,

but permits relic-worship.

the slave-trade in vassals and peasant children which had been carried on with Jews and Mohammedans. Like all the great statesmen of antiquity, who were unable to comprehend the possibility of a highly civilized society without the existence of slavery, Charlemagne accepted that unfortunate condition as a political necessity, and attempted to draw from it as much benefit as it was capable of yielding to the state. From certain classes of slaves he appointed, by a system of apprenticeship, those who should be devoted to the mechanical arts and to trade. It was, however, slavery and warfare which, during his own life, by making the possession of property among small proprietors an absolute disadvantage, prepared the way for that rapid dissolution of his empire so quickly occurring after his death.

His policy as respects slavery.

Yet, though Charlemagne thus accepted the existence of slavery as a necessary political evil, the evidences are not wanting that he was desirous to check its abuses wherever he could. When the Italian dukes accused Pope Adrian of selling his vassals as slaves to the Saracens, Charlemagne made inquiry into the matter, and, finding that transactions of the kind had occurred in the port of Civita Vecchia, though he did not choose to have so infamous a scandal made public, he ever afterwards withdrew his countenance from that pope. At that time a very extensive child slave-trade was carried on with the Saracens through the medium of the Jews, ecclesiastics as well as barons selling the children of their serfs.

The European slave-trade.

Though he never succeeded in learning how to write, no one appreciated better than Charlemagne the value of knowledge. He laboured assiduously for the elevation and enlightenment of his people. He collected together learned men; ordered his clergy to turn their attention to letters; established schools of religious music; built noble palaces, churches, bridges; transferred, for the adornment of his capital, Aix-la-Chapelle, statues from Italy; organized the professions and trades of his cities, and gave to his towns a police. Well might he be solicitous that his clergy should not only become more devout, but more learned. Very few of them knew how to read,

Improvements of the physical state of the people.

State of the clergy.

scarcely any to write. Of the first half of the eighth century, a period of great interest, since it includes the invasion of France by the Saracens, and their expulsion, there is nothing more than the most meagre annals; the clergy understood much better the use of the sword than that of the pen. The schools of Charlemagne proved a failure, not through any fault of his, but because the age had no demand for learning, and the Roman pontiffs and their clergy, as far as they troubled themselves with any opinion about the matter, thought that knowledge was of more harm than good.

Private life of Charlemagne.

The private life of Charlemagne was stained with great immoralities and crimes. He indulged in a polygamy scarcely inferior to that of the khalifs, solacing himself with not less than nine wives and many concubines. He sought to increase the circle of the former, or perhaps it should be said, considering the greatness of his statesmanship, to unite the Eastern and Western empires together by a marriage with the Empress Irene. This was that Irene who put out the eyes of her own son in the porphyry chamber at Constantinople. His fame extended into Asia. The Khalif Haroun al Raschid, A.D. 801, sent him from Bagdad the keys of our Saviour's sepulchre as a mark of esteem from the Commander of the Faithful to the greatest of Christian kings. However, there was doubtless as much policy as esteem in this, for the Asiatic khalifs perceived the advantage of a good understanding with the power that could control the emirs of Spain. Always bearing in mind his engagement with the papacy, that Roman Christianity should be enforced upon Europe wherever his influence could reach, he remorselessly carried into execution the penalty of death that he had awarded to the crimes of, 1, refusing baptism; 2, false pretence of baptism; 3, relapse to idolatry; 4, the murder of a priest or bishop; 5, human sacrifice; 6, eating meat in Lent. To the pagan German his sword was a grim, but a convincing missionary. To the last he observed a savage fidelity to his bond. He died A.D. 814.

His relations with the Saracens.

Such was the compact that had been established between the Church and the State. As might be expected, the succeeding transactions exhibit an alternate preponderance of one and of the other, and the degradation of both in the end. Scarcely was Charlemagne dead ere the imbecile character of his son and successor, Louis the Pious, gave the Church her opportunity. By the expulsion of his father's numerous concubines and mistresses, the scandals of the palace were revealed. I have not the opportunity to relate in detail how this monarch disgracefully humiliated himself before the Church; how, under his weak government, the slave-trade greatly increased; how every shore, and, indeed, every country that could be reached through a navigable river, was open to the ravages of pirates, the Northmen extending their maraudings even to the capture of great cities; how, in strong contrast with the social decomposition into which Europe was falling, Spain, under her Mohammedan rulers, was becoming rich, populous, and great; how, on the east, the Huns and Avars, ceasing their ravages, accepted Christianity, and, under their diversity of interests the nations that had been bound together by Charlemagne separated into two divisions—French and German—and civil wars between them ensued; how, through the folly of the clergy, who vainly looked for protection from relics instead of the sword, the Saracens ranged uncontrolled all over the south, and came within an hair's-breadth of capturing Rome itself; how France, at this time, had literally become a theocracy, the clergy absorbing everything that was worth having; how the pope, trembling at home, nevertheless maintained an external power by interfering with domestic life, as in the quarrel with King Lothaire II. and his wife; how Italy, France, and Germany became, as Africa and Syria had once been, full of miracles; how, through these means the Church getting the advantage, John VIII. thought it expedient to assert his right of disposing of the imperial crown in the case of Charles the Bald (the imperial supremacy that Charlemagne had obtained in reality implied the eventual supremacy of the pope); how an opportunity which occurred for reconstructing the empire of the West under Charles the Fat was thwarted by the imbecility of that sovereign, an imbecility so great that his nobles were obliged to depose him; how, thereupon,

Course of events after the death of Charlemagne

a number of new kingdoms arose, and Europe fell, by an inevitable necessity, into a political chaos; how, since there was thus no protecting government, each great landowner had to protect himself, and the rightfulness of private war became recognised; how, through this evil state, the strange consequence ensued of a great increase in the population, it becoming the interest of every lord to raise as many peasants as he could, offering his lands on personal service, the value of an estate being determined by the number of retainers it could furnish, and hence arose the feudal system; how the monarchical principle, once again getting the superiority, asserted its power in Germany in Henry the Fowler and his descendants, the three Othos; how, by these great monarchs, the subjection of Italy was accomplished, and the morality of the German clergy vindicated by their attempts at the reformation of the papacy, which fell to the last degree of degradation, becoming, in the end, an appanage of the Counts of Tusculum, and, shameful to be said, in some instances given by prostitutes to their paramours or illegitimates, in some, to mere boys of precociously dissolute life; before long, A.D. 1045, it was actually to be sold for money. We have now approached the close of a thousand years from the birth of Christ; the evil union of the Church and State, their rivalries, their intrigues, their quarrels, had produced an inevitable result, doing the same in the West that they had done in the East; disorganizing the political system, and ending in a universal social demoralization. The absorption of small properties into large estates steadily increased the number of slaves; where there had once been many free families, there was now found only a rich man. Even of this class the number diminished by the same process of absorption, until there were sparsely scattered here and there abbots and counts with enormous estates worked by herds of slaves, whose numbers, since sometimes one man possessed more than 20,000 of them, might deceive us, if we did not consider the vast surface over which they were spread. Examined in that way, the West of Europe proves to have been covered with forests, here and there dotted with a convent or a town. From those countries, once full of the splendid evidences

Social condition of Europe.

of Roman civilization, mankind was fast disappearing. There was no political cause, until at a later time, when the feudal system was developed, for calling men into existence. Whenever there was a partial peace, there was no occasion for the multiplication of men beyond the intention of extracting from them the largest possible revenue, a condition implying their destruction. Soon even the necessity for legislation ceased; events were left to take their own course. Through the influence of the monks the military spirit declined; a vile fetichism of factitious relics, which were working miracles in all directions, constituted the individual piety. Whoever died without bequeathing a part of his property to the Church, died without confession and the sacraments, and forfeited Christian burial. Trial by battle, and the ordeals of fire and boiling water, determined innocence or guilt in those accused of crimes. Between places at no great distance apart intercommunication ceased, or, at most, was carried on as in the times of the Trojan War, by the pedlar travelling with his packs.

In these deplorable days there was abundant reason to adopt the popular expectation that the end of all things was at hand, and that the year 1000 would witness the destruction of the world. Society was dissolving, the human race was disappearing, and with difficulty the melancholy ruins of ancient civilization could be traced. Such was the issue of the second attempt at the union of political and ecclesiastical power. In a former chapter we saw what it had been in the East, now we have found what it was in the West. Inaugurated in selfishness, it strengthens itself by violence, is perpetuated by ignorance, and yields as its inevitable result, social ruin.

Expected end of the world, A.D. 1000.

Effects of the union of Church and state.

And while things were thus going to wreck in the state, it was no better in the Church. The ill-omened union between them was bearing its only possible fruit, disgrace to both—a solemn warning to all future ages.

3d. This brings me to the third and remaining topic I proposed to consider in this chapter, to determine the actual religious value of the system in process of being forced upon Europe, using, for the purpose, that which must be admitted as the best test—the private lives of the popes.

Value of the new system estimated from the lives of the popes.

To some it might seem, considering the interests of religion alone, desirable to omit all biographical reference to the popes; but this cannot be done with justice to the subject. The essential principle of the papacy, that the Roman pontiff is the vicar of Christ upon earth, necessarily obtrudes his personal relations upon us. How shall we understand his faith unless we see it illustrated in his life? Indeed, the unhappy character of those relations was the inciting cause of the movements in Germany, France, and England, ending in the extinction of the papacy as an actual political power, movements to be understood only through a sufficient knowledge of the private lives and opinions of the popes. It is well, as far as possible, to abstain from burdening systems with the imperfections of individuals. In this case they are inseparably interwoven. The signal peculiarity of the papacy is that, though its history may be imposing, its biography is infamous. I shall, however, forbear to speak of it in this latter respect more than the occasion seems necessarily to require; shall pass in silence some of those cases which would profoundly shock my religious reader, and therefore restrict myself to the ages between the middle of the eighth and the middle of the eleventh centuries, excusing myself to the impartial critic by the apology that these were the ages with which I have been chiefly concerned in this chapter.

Apology for referring to the biography of the popes.

On the death of Pope Paul I., who had attained the pontificate A.D. 757, the Duke of Nepi compelled some bishops to consecrate Constantine, one of his brothers, as pope; but more legitimate electors subsequently, A.D. 768, choosing Stephen IV., the usurper and his adherents were severely punished; the eyes of Constantine were put out; the tongue of the Bishop Theodorus was amputated, and he was left in a dungeon to expire in the agonies of thirst. The nephews of Pope Adrian seized his successor, Pope Leo III., A.D. 795, in the street, and, forcing him into a neighbouring church, attempted to put out his eyes and cut out his tongue; at a later period, this pontiff trying to suppress a conspiracy to depose him, Rome became the scene of rebellion, murder, and conflagration. His successor, Stephen V., A.D. 816, was ignominiously driven from the city; his successor, Paschal

The popes from A.D 757.

I., was accused of blinding and murdering two ecclesiastics in the Lateran Palace; it was necessary that imperial commissioners should investigate the matter, but the pope died, after having exculpated himself by oath before thirty bishops. John VIII., A.D. 872, unable to resist the Mohammedans, was compelled to pay them tribute; the Bishop of Naples, maintaining a secret alliance with them, received his share of the plunder they collected. Him John excommunicated, nor would he give him absolution unless he would betray the chief Mohammedans and assassinate others himself. There was an ecclesiastical conspiracy to murder the pope; some of the treasures of the Church were seized; and the gate of St. Pancrazia was opened with false keys, to admit the Saracens into the city. Formosus, who had been engaged in these transactions, and excommunicated as a conspirator for the murder of John, was subsequently elected pope, A.D. 891; he was succeeded by Boniface VI., A.D. 896, who had been deposed from the diaconate, and again from the priesthood, for his immoral and lewd life. By Stephen VII., who followed, the dead body of Formosus was taken from the grave, clothed in the papal habiliments, propped up in a chair, tried before a council, and the preposterous and indecent scene completed by cutting off three of the fingers of the corpse and casting it into the Tiber; but Stephen himself was destined to exemplify how low the papacy had fallen: he was thrown into prison and strangled. In the course of five years, from A.D. 896 to A.D. 900, five popes were consecrated. Leo V., who succeeded in A.D. 904, was in less than two months thrown into prison by Christopher, one of his chaplains, who usurped his place, and who, in his turn, was shortly expelled from Rome by Sergius III., who, by the aid of a military force, seized the pontificate, A.D. 905. This man, according to the testimony of the times, lived in criminal intercourse with the celebrated prostitute Theodora, who, with her daughters Marozia and Theodora, also prostitutes, exercised an extraordinary control over him. The love of Theodora was also shared by John X.: she gave him first the archbishopric of Ravenna, and then translated him to Rome, A.D. 915, as pope. John was not unsuited to the times; he organized a confederacy which perhaps prevented Rome from being captured by the Saracens, and the world was astonished and edified by the appearance of this warlike pontiff at the head of his troops. By the love of Theodora, as was said, he had maintained himself in the papacy for fourteen years; by the intrigues and hatred of her daughter Marozia he was overthrown. She surprised him in the Lateran Palace; killed his brother Peter before his face; threw him into prison, where he soon died, smothered, as was asserted, with a pillow. After a short interval Marozia made her own son pope as John XI., A.D. 931. Many affirmed that Pope Sergius was his father, but she herself inclined to attribute him to her husband Alberic, whose brother Guido she subsequently married. Another of her sons, Alberic, so called from his supposed father, jealous of his brother John, cast him and their mother Marozia into prison. After a time Alberic's son was elected pope, A.D. 956; he assumed the title of John XII., the amorous Marozia thus having given a son and a grandson to the papacy. John was only nineteen years old when he thus became the head of Christendom. His reign was characterized by the most shocking immoralities, so that the Emperor Otho I. was compelled by the German clergy to interfere. A synod was summoned for his trial in the Church of St. Peter, before which it appeared that John had received bribes for the consecration of bishops, that he had ordained one who was but ten years old, and had performed that ceremony over another in a stable; he was charged with incest with one of his father's concubines, and with so many adulteries that the Lateran Palace had become a brothel; he put out the eyes of one ecclesiastic and castrated another, both dying in consequence of their injuries; he was given to drunkenness, gambling, and the invocation of Jupiter and Venus. When cited to appear before the council, he sent word that "he had gone out hunting;" and to the fathers who remonstrated with him, he threateningly remarked "that Judas, as well as the other disciples, received from his master the power of binding and loosing, but that as soon as he proved a traitor to the common cause, the only power he retained was that of binding his own neck." Hereupon he was deposed, and

Leo VIII. elected in his stead, A.D. 963; but subsequently getting the upper hand, he seized his antagonists, cut off the hand of one, the nose, finger, tongue of others. His life was eventually brought to an end by the vengeance of a man whose wife he had seduced.

After such details it is almost needless to allude to the annals of succeeding popes: to relate that John XIII. was strangled in prison; that Boniface VII. imprisoned Benedict VII., and killed him by starvation; that John XIV. was secretly put to death in the dungeons of the Castle of St. Angelo; that the corpse of Boniface was dragged by the populace through the streets. The sentiment of reverence for the sovereign pontiff, nay, even of respect, had become extinct in Rome; throughout Europe the clergy were so shocked at the state of things, that, in their indignation, they began to look with approbation on the intention of the Emperor Otho to take from the Italians their privilege of appointing the successor of St. Peter, and confine it to his own family. But his kinsman, Gregory V., whom he placed on the pontifical throne, was very soon compelled by the Romans to fly; his excommunications and religious thunders were turned into derision by them; they were too well acquainted with the true nature of those terrors; they were living behind the scenes. A terrible punishment awaited the Anti-pope John XVI. Otho returned into Italy, seized him, put out his eyes, cut off his nose and tongue, and sent him through the streets mounted on an ass, with his face to the tail, and a wine-bladder on his head. It seemed impossible that things could become worse; yet Rome had still to see Benedict IX., A.D. 1033, a boy of less than twelve years, raised to the apostolic throne. Of this pontiff, one of his successors, Victor III., declared that his life was so shameful, so foul, so execrable, that he shuddered to describe it. He ruled like a captain of banditti rather than a prelate. The people at last, unable to bear his adulteries, homicides, and abominations any longer, rose against him. In despair of maintaining his position, he put up the papacy to auction. It was bought by a presbyter named John, who became Gregory VI., A.D. 1045.

The papacy bought at auction A.D. 1045, by Gregory VI.

More than a thousand years had elapsed since the birth of our Saviour, and such was the condition of Rome. Well may the historian shut the annals of those times in disgust; well may the heart of the Christian sink within him at such a catalogue of hideous crimes. Well may he ask, Were these the vicegerents of God upon earth—these, who had truly reached that goal beyond which the last effort of human wickedness cannot pass?

Conclusion respecting this biography.

Not until several centuries after these events did public opinion come to the true and philosophical conclusion—the total rejection of the divine claims of the papacy. For a time the evils were attributed to the manner of the pontifical election, as if that could by any possibility influence the descent of a power which claimed to be supernatural and under the immediate care of God. The manner of election was this. The Roman ecclesiastics recommended a candidate to the College of Cardinals; their choice had to be ratified by the populace of Rome, and, after that, the emperor must give his approval. There were thus to be brought into agreement the machinations of the lower ecclesiastics, the intrigues of the cardinals, the clamours of the rabble of Rome, and the policy of the emperor. Such a system must inevitably break to pieces with its own incongruities. Though we may wonder that men failed to see that it was merely a human device, we cannot wonder that the emperors perceived the necessity of taking the appointments into their own hands, and that Gregory VII. was resolved to confine it to the College of Cardinals, to the exclusion of the emperor, the Roman people, and even of the rest of Christendom—an attempt in which he succeeded.

The philosophical conclusion at last attained.

The evils imputed to the nature of papal election.

No one can study the development of the Italian ecclesiastical power without discovering how completely it depended on human agency, too often on human passion and intrigues; how completely wanting it was of any mark of the Divine construction and care—the offspring of man, not of God, and therefore bearing upon it the lineaments of human passions, human virtues, and human sins.

Human origin of the papacy.

CHAPTER XIII.

DIGRESSION ON THE PASSAGE OF THE ARABIANS TO THEIR AGE OF REASON.

INFLUENCE OF MEDICAL IDEAS THROUGH THE NESTORIANS AND JEWS.

The intellectual Development of the Arabians is guided by the Nestorians and the Jews, and is in the Medical Direction.—The Basis of this Alliance is theological.
Antagonism of the Byzantine System to Scientific Medicine.—Suppression of the Asclepions.—Their Replacement by Miracle-cure.—The resulting Superstition and Ignorance.
Affiliation of the Arabians with the Nestorians and Jews.
1st. The Nestorians, their Persecutions, and the Diffusion of their Sectarian Ideas.—They inherit the old Greek Medicine.
Sub-digression on Greek Medicine.—The Asclepions.—Philosophical Importance of Hippocrates, who separates Medicine from Religion.—The School of Cnidos.—Its Suppression by Constantine.
Sub-digression on Egyptian Medicine.—It is founded on Anatomy and Physiology.—Dissections and Vivisections.—The Great Alexandrian Physicians.
2nd. The Jewish Physicians.—Their Emancipation from Superstition.—They found Colleges and promote Science and Letters.
The contemporary Tendency to Magic, Necromancy, the Black Art.—The Philosopher's Stone, Elixir of Life, etc.
The Arabs originate scientific Chemistry.—Discover the strong Acids, Phosphorus, etc.—Their geological Ideas.—Apply Chemistry to the Practice of Medicine.—Approach of the Conflict between the Saracenic material and the European supernatural System.

Importance of the influence of the Arabians.

THE military operations of the Arabians, described in Chapter XI., overthrew the Byzantine political system, prematurely closing the Age of Faith in the East; their intellectual procedure gave rise to an equally important result, being destined, in the end, to close the Age of Faith in the West.

The Saracens not only destroyed the Italian offshoot, they also impressed characteristic lineaments on the Age of Reason in Europe.

Events so important make it necessary for me to turn aside from the special description of European intellectual advancement, and offer a digression on the passage of the Arabians to their Age of Reason. It is impossible for us to understand their action in the great drama about to be performed unless we understand the character they had assumed.

Their intellectual progress.

In a few centuries the fanatics of Mohammed had altogether changed their appearance. Great philosophers, physicians, mathematicians, astronomers, alchemists, grammarians, had arisen among them. Letters and science, in all their various departments, were cultivated.

Their teachers were the Nestorians and Jews.

A nation stirred to its profoundest depths by warlike emigration, and therefore ready to make, as soon as it reaches a period of repose, a rapid intellectual advance, may owe the path in which it is about to pass to those who are in the position of pointing it out, or of officiating as teachers. The teachers of the Saracens were the Nestorians and the Jews.

Their scientific progress was through medicine.

It has been remarked that Arabian science emerged out of medicine, and that in its cultivation physicians took the lead, its beginnings being in the pursuit of alchemy. In this chapter I have to describe the origin of these facts, and therefore must consider the state of Greek and Egyptian medicine, and relate how, wherever the Byzantine system could reach, true medical philosophy was displaced by relic and shrine-curing; and how it was, that while European ideas were in all directions reposing on the unsubstantial basis of the supernatural, those of the Saracens were resting on the solid foundation of a material support.

When the Arabs conquered Egypt, their conduct was that of bigoted fanatics; it justified the accusation made by some against them, that they burned the Alexandrian library for the purpose of heating the baths. But scarcely were they settled in their new dominion when they exhibited an extraordinary change. At once they became lovers and zealous cultivators of learning.

The Arab power had extended in two directions, and had been submitted to two influences. In Asia it had been exposed to the Nestorians, in Africa to the Jews, both of whom had suffered persecution at the hands of the Byzantine government, apparently for the same opinion as that which had now established itself by the sword of Mohammed. The doctrine of the unity of God was their common point of contact. On this they could readily affiliate, and hold in common detestation the trinitarian power at Constantinople. He who is suffering the penalties of the law as a heretic, or who is pursued by judicial persecution as a misbeliever, will readily consort with others reputed to cherish similar infidelities. Brought into unison in Asia with the Nestorians, and in Africa with the Alexandrian Jews, the Arabians became enthusiastic admirers of learning.

Causes of their union with Nestorians and Jews.

Not that there was between the three parties thus coalescing a complete harmony of sentiment in the theological direction; for, though the Nestorians and the Jews were willing to accept one-half of the Arabian dogma, that there is but one God, they could not altogether commit themselves to the other, that Mohammed is his Prophet. Perhaps estrangement on this point might have arisen, but fortunately a remarkable circumstance opened the way for a complete understanding between them. Almost from the beginning the Nestorians had devoted themselves to the study of medicine, and had paid much attention to the structure and diseases of the body of man; the Jews had long produced distinguished physicians. These medical studies presented, therefore, a neutral ground on which the three parties could intellectually unite in harmony; and so thoroughly did the Arabians affiliate with these their teachers, that they acquired from them a characteristic mental physiognomy. Their physicians were their great philosophers; their medical colleges were their foci of learning. While the Byzantines obliterated science in theology, the Saracens illuminated it by medicine.

Medicine becomes their neutral ground.

When Constantine the Great and his successors, under ecclesiastical influence, had declared themselves the enemies of worldly learning, it became necessary for the clergy to assume the duty of seeing to the physical as well as the religious condition of the people. It was unsuited to the state of things that physicians, whose philosophical tendencies inclined them to the pagan party, should be any longer endured. Their education in the Asclepions imparted to them ideas in opposition to the new policy. An edict of Constantine suppressed those establishments, ample provision being, however, made for replacing them by others more agreeable to the genius of Christianity. Hospitals and benevolent organizations were founded in the chief cities, and richly endowed with money and lands. In these merciful undertakings the empress-mother, Helena, was distinguished, her example being followed by many high-born ladies. The heart of women, which is naturally open to the desolate and afflicted, soon gives active expression to its sympathies when it is sanctified by Christian faith. In this, its legitimate direction, Christianity could display its matchless benevolence and charities. Organizations were introduced upon the most extensive and varied scale; one had charge of foundlings, another of orphans, another of the poor. We have already alluded to the parabolani or visitors, and of the manner in which they were diverted from their original intent.

Byzantine suppression of medicine.

Substitution of public charities.

But, noble as were these charities, they laboured under an essential defect in having substituted for educated physicians well-meaning but unskilful ecclesiastics. The destruction of the Asclepions was not attended by any suitably extensive measures for insuring professional education. The sick who were placed in the benevolent institutions were, at the best, rather under the care of kind nurses than under the advice of physicians; and the consequences are seen in the gradually increasing credulity and imposture of succeeding ages, until, at length, there was an almost universal reliance on miraculous interventions. Fetiches, said to be the relics of saints, but no better than those of tropical

Gradual fall into miracle-cure.

Africa, were believed to cure every disorder. To the shrines of saints crowds repaired as they had at one time to the temples of Æsculapius. The worshippers remained, though the name of the divinity was changed.

Closing of the schools of medicine and philosophy.

Scarcely were the Asclepions closed, the schools of philosophy prohibited, the libraries dispersed or destroyed, learning branded as magic or punished as treason, philosophers driven into exile and as a class exterminated, when it became apparent that a void had been created which it was incumbent on the victors to fill. Among the great prelates, who was there to stand in the place of those men whose achievements had glorified the human race? Who was to succeed to Archimedes, Hipparchus, Euclid, Herophilus, Eratosthenes? who to Plato and Aristotle? The quackeries of miracle-cure, shrine-cure, relic-cure, were destined to eclipse the genius of Hippocrates, and nearly two thousand years to intervene between Archimedes and Newton, nearly seventeen hundred between Hipparchus and Kepler. A dismal interval of almost twenty centuries parts Hero, whose first steam-engine revolved in the Serapion, from James Watt, who has revolutionized the industry of the world. What a fearful blank! Yet not a blank, for it had its products—hundreds of patristic folios filled with obsolete speculation, oppressing the shelves of antique libraries, enveloped in dust, and awaiting the worm.

Its deplorable results.

Never was a more disastrous policy adopted than the Byzantine suppression of profane learning. It is scarcely possible now to realize the mental degradation produced when that system was at its height. Many of the noblest philosophical and scientific works of antiquity disappeared from the language in which they had been written, and were only recovered, for the use of later and better ages, from translations which the Saracens had made into Arabic. The insolent assumption of wisdom by those who held the sword crushed every intellectual aspiration. Yet, though triumphant for a time, this policy necessarily contained the seeds of its own ignominious destruction. A day must inevitably come when so grievous a wrong to the human race must be exposed, and execrated, and punished—a day in which the poems of Homer might once more be read, the immortal statues of the Greek sculptors find worshippers, and the demonstrations of Euclid a consenting intellect. But that unfortunate, that audacious policy of usurpation once entered upon, there was no going back. He who is infallible must needs be immutable. In its very nature the action implied compulsion, compulsion implied the possession of power, and the whole policy insured an explosion the moment that the means of compression should be weak.

Insecurity of the Byzantine system.

It is said that when the Saracens captured Alexandria, their victorious general sent to the khalif to know his pleasure respecting the library. The answer was in the spirit of the age. "If the books be confirmatory of the Koran, they are superfluous; if contradictory, they are pernicious. Let them be burnt." At this moment, to all human appearance, the Mohammedan autocrat was on the point of joining in the evil policy of the Byzantine sovereign. But fortunately it was but the impulse of a moment, rectified forthwith, and a noble course of action was soon pursued. The Arab incorporated into his literature the wisdom of those he had conquered. In thus conceding to knowledge a free and unembarrassed career, and, instead of repressing, encouraging to the utmost all kinds of learning did the Koran take any harm? It was a high statesmanship which, almost from the beginning of the impulse from Mecca, bound down to a narrow, easily comprehended, and easily expressed dogma the exacted belief, and in all other particulars let the human mind go free.

Bigotry of the first Saracens.

The nobler policy soon pursued.

In the preceding paragraphs I have criticized the course of events, condemning or applauding the actions and the actors as circumstances seem to require, herein following the usual course, which implies that men can control affairs, and that the agent is to be held responsible for his deed. We have, however, only to consider the course of our own lives to be satisfied to how limited an extent such is the case. We are, as we often say, the creatures of circumstances. In that expression there is a higher philosophy than might at first sight appear. Our actions are not the pure and unmingled results of our desires; they are the offspring of

The true causes of the preceding events.

many various and mixed conditions. In that which seems to be the most voluntary decision there enters much that is altogether involuntary—more, perhaps, than we generally suppose. And, in like manner, those who are imagined to have exercised an irresponsible and spontaneous influence in determining public policy, and thereby fixing the fate of nations, will be found, when we understand their position more correctly, to have been the creatures of circumstances altogether independent and irrespective of them—circumstances which they never created, of whose influence they only availed themselves. They were placed in a current which drifted them irresistibly along.

From this more accurate point of view we should therefore consider the course of these events, recognizing the principle that the affairs of men pass forward in a determinate way, expanding and unfolding themselves. And hence we see that the things of which we have spoken as though they were matters of choice were, in reality, forced upon their apparent authors by the necessity of the times. But, in truth, they should be considered as the presentations of a certain phase of life which nations in their onward course sooner or later assume. In the individual, how well we know that a sober moderation of action, an appropriate gravity of demeanour, belong to the mature period of life; a change from the wanton wilfulness of youth, which may be ushered in, or its beginning marked, by many accidental incidents: in one perhaps by domestic bereavements, in another by the loss of fortune, in a third by ill health. We are correct enough in imputing to such trials the change of character, but we never deceive ourselves by supposing that it would have failed to take place had those incidents not occurred. There runs an irresistible destiny in the midst of all these vicissitudes.

Succession of affairs determined by law.

We may therefore be satisfied that, whatever may have been the particular form of the events of which we have had occasion to speak, their order of succession was a matter of destiny, and altogether beyond the reach of any individual. We may condemn the Byzantine monarchs, or applaud the Arabian khalifs—

our blame and our praise must be set at their proper value. Europe was passing from its Age of Inquiry to its Age of Faith. In such a transition the predestined underlies the voluntary. There are analogies between the life of a nation and that of an individual, who, though he may be in one respect the maker of his own fortunes for happiness or for misery, for good or for evil, though he remains here or goes there, as his inclinations prompt, though he does this or abstains from that as he chooses, is nevertheless held fast by an inexorable fate—a fate which brought him into the world involuntarily so far as he was concerned, which presses him forward through a definite career, the stages of which are absolutely invariable—infancy, childhood, youth maturity, old age, with all their characteristic actions and passions, and which removes him from the scene at the appointed time, in most cases against his will. So also it is with nations; the voluntary is only the outward semblance, covering, but hardly hiding the predetermined. Over the events of life we may have control, but none whatever over the law of its progress. There is a geometry that applies to nations, an equation of their curve of advance. That no mortal man can touch.

Arabian science in its stage of sorcery.

We have now to examine in what manner the glimmering lamp of knowledge was sustained when it was all but ready to die out. By the Arabians it was handed down to us. The grotesque forms of some of those who took charge of it are not without interest. They exhibit a strange mixture of the Neoplatonist, the Pantheist, the Mohammedan, the Christian. In such untoward times, it was perhaps needful that the strongest passions of men should be excited and science stimulated by inquiries for methods of turning lead into gold, or of prolonging life indefinitely. We have now to deal with the philosopher's stone, the elixir vitæ, the powder of projection, magical mirrors, perpetual lamps, the transmutation of metals. In smoky caverns under ground, where the great work is stealthily carried on, the alchemist and his familiar are busy with their alembics, cucurbites, and pelicans, maintaining their fires for so many years that salamanders are asserted to be born in them.

Experimental science was thus restored, though under a very strange aspect, by the Arabians. Already it displayed its connexion with medicine—a connexion derived from the influence of the Nestorians and the Jews. It is necessary for us to consider briefly the relations of each, and of the Nestorians first.

In Chapter IX. we have related the rivalries of Cyril the Bishop of Alexandria, and Nestorius, the Bishop of Constantinople. The theological point of their quarrel was whether it is right to regard the Virgin Mary as the mother of God. To an Egyptian still tainted with ancient superstition, there was nothing shocking in such a doctrine. His was the country of Isis. St. Cyril, who is to be looked upon as a mere ecclesiastical demagogue, found his purposes answered by adopting it without any scruple. But in Greece there still remained traces of the old philosophy. A recollection of the ideas of Plato had not altogether died out. There were some by whom it was not possible for the Egyptian doctrine to be received. Such, perhaps, was Nestorius, whose sincerity was finally approved by an endurance of persecutions, by his sufferings, and his death. He and his followers, insisting on the plain inference of the last verse of the first chapter of St. Matthew, together with the fifty-fifth and fifty-sixth verses of the thirteenth of the same Gospel, could never be brought to an acknowledgment of the perpetual virginity of the new queen of heaven.

The Nestorians.

They deny the virginity of the queen of heaven.

We have described the issue of the Council of Ephesus: the Egyptian faction gained the victory, the aid of court females being called in, and Nestorius, being deposed from his office, was driven, with his friends into exile. The philosophical tendency of the vanquished was soon indicated by their actions. While their leader was tormented in an African oasis, many of them emigrated to the Euphrates, and founded the Chaldæan Church. Under its auspices the college at Edessa, with several connected schools, arose. In these were translated into Syriac many Greek and Latin works, as those of Aristotle and Pliny. It was the Nestorians who, in connexion with the Jews, founded the medical college of Djondesabour, and first instituted a system of academical honours which has descended to our times. It was the Nestorians who were not only permitted by the khalifs the free exercise of their religion, but even intrusted with the education of the children of the great Mohammedan families, a liberality in striking contrast to the fanaticism of Europe. The Khalif Alraschid went so far as even to place all his public schools under the superintendence of John Masué, one of that sect. Under the auspices of these learned men the Arabian academies were furnished with translations of Greek authors, and vast libraries were collected in Asia.

They begin to cultivate medicine.

The Arabs affiliate with them.

Through this connexion with the Arabs, Nestorian missionaries found means to disseminate their form of Christianity all over Asia, as far as Malabar and China. The successful intrigues of the Egyptian politicians at Ephesus had no influence in those remote countries, the Asiatic churches of the Nestorian and Jacobite persuasions outnumbering eventually all the European Christians of the Greek and Roman churches combined. In later times the papal government has made great exertions to bring about an understanding with them, but in vain.

Their great spread in the East,

The expulsion of this party from Constantinople was accomplished by the same persons and policy concerned in destroying philosophy in Alexandria. St. Cyril was the representative of an illiterate and unscrupulous faction that had come into the possession of power through intrigues with the females of the imperial court, and bribery of eunuchs and parasites. The same spirit that had murdered Hypatia tormented Nestorius to death. Of the contending parties, one was respectable and had a tincture of learning, the other ignorant, and not hesitating at the employment of brute force, deportation, assassination. Unfortunately for the world, the unscrupulous party carried the day.

and persecutions in the West.

By their descent, the Nestorians had become the depositaries of the old Greek medical science. Its great names they revered. They collected, with the utmost assiduity, whatever works

They inherit the old Greek medicine.

remained on medical topics, whether of a Greek or Alexandrian origin, from the writings of Hippocrates, called, with affectionate veneration by his successors, "The Divine Old Man," down to those of the Ptolemaic school.

Greek medicine arose in the temples of Æsculapius, whither the sick were in the habit of resorting for the assistance of the god. It does not appear that any fee was exacted for the celestial advice; but the gratitude of the patient was frequently displayed by optional gifts, and votive tablets presented to the temple, setting forth the circumstances of the case, were of value to those disposed to enter on medical studies. The Asclepions thus became both hospitals and schools. They exercised, from their position, a tendency to incorporate medical and ecclesiastical pursuits. At this time it was universally believed that every sickness was due to the anger of some offended god, and especially was this supposed to be the case in epidemics and plagues. Such a paralyzing notion was necessarily inconsistent with any attempt at the relief of communities by the exercise of sanitary measures. In our times it is still difficult to remove from the minds of the illiterate classes this ancient opinion, or to convince them that under such visitations we ought to help ourselves, and not expect relief by penance and supplications, unless we join therewith rigorous personal, domestic, municipal cleanliness, fresh air, and light. The theological doctrine of the nature of disease indicated its means of cure. For Hippocrates was reserved the great glory of destroying them both, replacing them by more practical and material ideas, and, from the votive tablets, traditions, and other sources, together with his own admirable observations, compiling a body of medicine. The necessary consequence of his great success was the separation of the pursuits of the physician from those of the priest. Not that so great a revolution, implying the diversion of profitable gains from the ancient channel, could have been accomplished without a struggle. We should reverence the memory of Hippocrates for the complete manner in which he effected that object.

Origin of Greek medicine—Asclepions.

Hippocrates destroys the theological theory of disease.

Of the works attributed to Hippocrates, many are doubtless the production of his family, his descendants, or his pupils. The inducements to literary forgery in the times of the Ptolemies, who paid very high prices for books of reputation, have been the cause of much difficulty among critics in determining such questions of authorship. The works indisputably written by Hippocrates display an extent of knowledge answering to the authority of his name; his vivid descriptions have never been excelled, if indeed they have ever been equalled. The Hippocratic face of the dying is still retained in our medical treatises in the original terms, without any improvement.

Writings of Hippocrates.

In his medical doctrine, Hippocrates starts with the postulate that the body is composed of the four elements. From these are formed the four cardinal humours. He thinks that the humours are liable to undergo change; that health consists in their right constitution and proper adjustment as to quantity; disease, in their impurities and inequalities; that the disordered humours undergo spontaneous changes or coction, a process requiring time, and hence the explanation of critical days and critical discharges. The primitive disturbance of the humours he attributed to a great variety of causes, chiefly to the influence of physical circumstances, such as heat, cold, air, water. Unlike his contemporaries, he did not impute all the afflictions of man to the anger of the gods. Along with those influences of an external kind, he studied the special peculiarities of the human system, how it is modified by climate and manner of life, exhibiting different predispositions at different seasons of the year. He believed that the innate heat of the body varies with the period of life, being greatest in infancy and least in old age, and that hence morbific agents affect us with greater or less facility at different times. For this reason it is that the physician should attend very closely to the condition of those in whom he is interested as respects their diet and exercise, for thereby he is able not only to regulate their general susceptibility, but also to exert a control over the course of their diseases.

His opinions.

Referring diseases in general to the condition or distribution of the humours, for he regards inflammation as the passing of blood into parts not previously containing it, he considers that so long as those liquids occupy the system in an unnatural or adulterated state, disease continues; but as they ferment or undergo coction, various characteristic symptoms appear, and, when their elaboration is completed, they are discharged by perspiration or other secretions, by alvine dejections, etc. But where such a general relief of the system is not accomplished, the peccant humours may be localized in some particular organ or special portion, and erysipelatous inflammation, mortification, or other such manifestations ensue. It is in aiding this elimination from the system that the physician may signally manifest his skill. His power is displayed much more at this epoch than by the control he can exert over the process of coction. Now may he invoke the virtues of the hellebores, the white and the black, now may he use elaterium The critical days which answer to the periods of the process of coction are to be watched with anxiety, and the correspondence of the state of the patient with the expected condition which he ought to show at those epochs ascertained. Hence the physician may be able to predict the probable course of the disease during the remainder of its career, and gather true notions as to the practice it would be best for him to pursue to aid Nature in her operations.

The character of his practice.

It thus appears that the practice of medicine in the hands of Hippocrates had reference rather to the course or career of disease than to its special nature. Nothing more than this masterly conception is wanted to impress us with his surprizing scientific power. He watches the manner in which the humours are undergoing their fermenting coction, the phenomena displayed in the critical days, the aspect and nature of the critical discharges. He does not attempt to check the process going on, but simply to assist the natural operation.

When we consider the period at which Hippocrates lived, B.C. 400, and the circumstances under which he had studied medicine, we cannot fail to admire the very great advance he made. His merit is conspicuous in rejecting the superstitious tendency of his times by teaching his disciples to impute a proper agency to physical causes. He altogether discarded the imaginary influences then in vogue. For the gods he substituted, with singular felicity, Impersonal Nature. It was the interest of those who were connected with the temples of Æsculapius to refer all the diseases of men to supernatural agency; their doctrine being that every affliction should be attributed to the anger of some offended god, and restoration to health most certainly procured by conciliating his power. So far, then, as such interests were concerned, any contradiction of those doctrines, any substitution of the material for the supernatural, must needs have met with reprehension. Yet such opposition seems in no respect to have weighed with this great physician, who developed his theory and pursued his practice without giving himself any concern in that respect. He bequeathed an example to all who succeeded him in his noble profession, and taught them not to hesitate in encountering the prejudices and passions of the present for the sake of the truth, and to trust for their reward in the just appreciation of a future age.

His doctrine is truly scientific.

With such remarks we may assert that the medical philosophy of Hippocrates is worthy of our highest admiration, since it exhibits the scientific conditions of deduction and induction. The theory itself is compact and clear; its lineaments are completely Grecian. It presents, to one who will contemplate it with due allowance for its times, the characteristic quick-sightedness, penetration, and power of the Greek mind, fully vindicating for its author the title which has been conferred upon him by his European successors—the Father of Medicine—and perhaps inducing us to excuse the enthusiastic assertion of Galen, that we ought to reverence the words of Hippocrates as the voice of God.

The school of Cnidos.

The Hippocratic school of Cos found a rival in the school of Cnidos, which offered not only a different view of the nature of disease, but also taught a different principle for its cure. The Cnidians paid more particular attention to the special symptoms in individual cases, and pursued a less active treatment, declining, whenever they could, a resort to drastic purgatives, venesection, or other energetic means. As might be expected, the professional activity of these schools called into existence many able men, and produced many excellent works: thus Philiston wrote on the regimen for persons in health; Diocles on hygiene and gymnastics; Praxagoras on the pulse, showing that it is a measure of the force of disease. The Asclepion of Cnidos continued until the time of Constantine, when it was destroyed along with many other pagan establishments. The union between the priesthood and the profession was gradually becoming less and less close; and, as the latter thus separated itself, divisions or departments arose in it, both as regards subjects, such as pharmacy, surgery, etc., and also as respects the position of its cultivators, some pursuing it as a liberal science, and some as a mere industrial occupation. In those times, as in our own, many who were not favoured with the gifts of fortune were constrained to fall into the latter ranks. Thus Aristotle, than whom few have ever exerted a greater intellectual influence upon humanity, after spending his patrimony in liberal pursuits, kept an apothecary's shop at Athens. Aristotle the druggist, behind his counter, selling medicines to chance customers, is Aristotle the great writer, whose dictum was final with the schoolmen of the Middle Ages. As a general thing, however, the medical professors were drawn from the philosophical class. Outside of these divisions, and though in all ages continually repudiated by the profession, yet continually hovering round it, was a host of impostors and quacks, as there will always be so long as there are weak-minded and shallow men to be deluded, and vain and silly women to believe.

Is destroyed by Constantine.

Classes of physicians.

When the Alexandrian Museum was originated by Ptolemy Philadelphus, its studies were arranged in four faculties—literature, mathematics, astronomy, medicine. These divisions are, however, to be understood comprehensively: thus, under the faculty of medicine were included such subjects as natural history. The physicians who received the first appointments were Cleombrotus, Herophilus, and Erasistratus; among the subordinate professors was Philo-Stephanus,

Egyptian medicine. The Museum.

who had charge of natural history, and was directed to write a book on Fishes. The elevated ideas of the founder cannot be better illustrated than by the manner in which he organized his medical school. It was upon the sure basis of anatomy. Herophilus and his colleagues were authorized to resort to the dissection of the dead, and to ascertain, by that only trustworthy method, the true structure of the human body. The strong hand of Ptolemy resolutely carried out his design, though in a country where popular sentiment was strongly opposed to such practices. To touch a corpse in Egypt was an abomination. Nor was it only this great man's intention to ascertain the human structure; he also took measures to discover the mode in which its functions are carried forward, the manner in which it works. To this end he authorized his anatomists to make vivisections both of animals, and also of criminals who had been condemned to death, herein finding for himself that royal road in physiology which Euclid once told him, at a dinner in the Museum, did not exist in geometry, and defending the act from moral criticism by the plea that, as the culprits had already forfeited their lives to the law, it was no injury to make them serviceable to the interests of humanity. Herophilus had been educated at Cos; his pathological views were those known as humouralism; his treatment active, after the manner of Hippocrates, upon whose works he wrote commentaries. His original investigations were numerous; they were embodied, with his peculiar views, in treatises on the practice of medicine; on obstetrics; on the eye; on the pulse, which he properly referred to contractions of the heart. He was aware of the existence of the lacteals, and their anatomical relation to the mesenteric glands. Erasistratus, his colleague, was a pupil of Theophrastus and Chrysippus: he, too, cultivated anatomy. He described the structure of the heart, its connexions with the arteries and veins, but fell into the mistake that the former vessels were for the conveyance of air, the latter for that of blood. He knew that there are two kinds of nerves, those of motion and those of sensation. He referred all fevers to

Philadelphus founds medicine on anatomy.

He authorizes dissection and human vivisection.

Physicians of the Alexandrian school.

inflammatory states, and in his practice differed from the received methods of Hippocrates by observing a less active treatment.

By these physicians the study of medicine in Alexandria was laid upon the solid foundation of anatomy. Besides them there were many other instructors in specialties; and, indeed, the temple of Serapis was used for a hospital, the sick being received into it, and persons studying medicine admitted for the purpose of familiarizing themselves with the appearance of disease, precisely as in similar institutions at the present time. Of course, under such circumstances, the departments of surgery and pharmacy received many improvements, and produced many able men. Among these improvements may be mentioned new operations for lithotomy, instruments for crushing calculi, for reducing dislocations, etc. The active commerce of Egypt afforded abundant opportunity for extending the materia medica by the introduction of a great many herbs and drugs.

Improvements in surgery and pharmacy.

The medical school of Alexandria, which was thus originally based upon dissection, in the course of time lost much of its scientific spirit. But the influence of the first teachers may be traced through many subsequent ages. Thus Galen divides the profession in his time into Herophilians and Erasistratians. Various sects had arisen in the course of events, as the Dogmatists, who asserted that diseases can only be treated correctly by the aid of a knowledge of the structure and functions, the action of drugs, and the changes induced in the affected parts; they insisted, therefore, upon the necessity of anatomy, physiology, therapeutics, and pathology. They claimed a descent from Hippocrates. Their antagonists, the Empirics, ridiculed such knowledge as fanciful or unattainable, and relied on experience alone. These subdivisions were not limited to sects; they may also be observed under the form of schools. Even Erasistratus himself, toward the close of his life, through some dispute or misunderstanding, appears to have left the Museum and established a school at Smyrna. The study of the various branches of medicine was also pursued by others out of the immediate ranks of the profession.

Decline of Alexandrian medicine.

Mithridates, king of Pontus, thus devoted himself to the examination of poisons and the discovery of antidotes.

What a fall from this scientific medicine to the miracle-cure which soon displaced it! What a descent from Hippocrates and the great Alexandrian physicians to the shrines of saints and the monks!

To the foregoing sketch of the state of Greek medicine in its day of glory, I must add an examination of the same science among the Jews subsequently to the second century; it is necessary for the proper understanding of the origin of Saracen learning.

The Jewish physicians.

In philosophy the Jews had been gradually emancipating themselves from the influence of ancient traditions; their advance in this direction is shown by the active manner in which they aided in the development of Neo-platonism. After the destruction of Jerusalem all Syria and Mesopotamia were full of Jewish schools; but the great philosophers, as well as the great merchants of the nation, were residents of Alexandria. Persecution and dispersion, if they served no other good purpose, weakened the grasp of the ecclesiastic. Perhaps, too, repeated disappointments in an expected coming of a national temporal Messiah had brought those who were now advanced in intellectual progress to a just appreciation of ancient traditions. In this mental emancipation their physicians took the lead. For long, while their pursuits were yet in infancy, a bitter animosity had been manifested toward them by the Levites, whose manner of healing was by prayer, expiatory sacrifice, and miracle; or, if they descended to less supernatural means, by an application of such remedies as are popular with the vulgar everywhere. Thus, to a person bitten by a mad dog, they would give the diaphragm of a dog to eat. As examples of a class of men soon to take no obscure share in directing human progress may be mentioned Hannina, A.D. 205, often spoken of by his successors as the earliest of Jewish physicians; Samuel, equally distinguished as an astronomer, accoucheur, and oculist, the inventor of a collyrium which bore his name; Rab, an anatomist, who wrote a treatise on the structure of the

Their emancipation from the supernatural.

body of man as ascertained by dissections, thereby attaining such celebrity that the people, after his death, used the earth of his grave as a medicine; Abba Oumna, whose study of insanity plainly shows that he gave a material interpretation to the national doctrine of possession by devils, and replaced that strange delusion by the scientific explanation of corporeal derangement. This honourable physician made it a rule never to take a fee from the poor, and never to make any difference in his assiduous attention between them and the rich. These men may be taken as a type of their successors to the seventh century, when the Oriental schools were broken up in consequence of the Arab military movements. In the Talmudic literature there are all the indications of a transitional state, so far as medicine is concerned; the supernatural seems to be passing into the physical, the ecclesiastical is mixed up with the exact: thus a rabbi may cure disease by the ecclesiastical operation of laying on of hands; but of febrile disturbances, an exact, though erroneous explanation is given, and paralysis of the hind legs of an animal is correctly referred to the pressure of a tumour on the spinal cord. Some of its aphorisms are not devoid of amusing significance: "Any disease, provided the bowels remain open; any kind of pain, provided the heart remain unaffected; any kind of uneasiness, provided the head be not attacked; all manner of evils, except it be a bad woman."

The Arabs affiliate with them.

At first, after the fall of the Alexandrian school, it was all that the Jewish physicians could do to preserve the learning that had descended to them. But when the tumult of Arabic conquest was over, we find them becoming the advisers of crowned heads, and exerting, by reason of their advantageous position, their liberal education, their enlarged views, a most important influence on the intellectual progress of humanity. Maser Djaivah, physician to the Khalif Moawiyah, was distinguished at once as a poet, a critic, a philosopher; Haroun, a physician of Alexandria, whose Pandects, a treatise unfortunately now lost, are said to have contained the first elaborate description of the small-pox and method of its treatment. Isaac Ben Emran wrote an original treatise on

Rise of Jewish physicians to influence.

poisons and their symptoms, and others followed his example. The Khalif Al Raschid, who maintained political relations with Charlemagne by means of Jewish envoys, set that monarch an example by which indeed he was not slow to profit, in actively patronising the medical college at Djondesabour, and founding a university at Bagdad. He prohibited any person from practising medicine until after a satisfactory examination before one of those faculties. In the East the theological theory of disease and of its cure was fast passing away. Of the school at Bagdad, Joshua ben Nun is said to have been the most celebrated professor, the school itself actively promoting the translation of Greek works into Arabic—not alone works of a professional, but also those of a general kind. In this manner the writings of Plato and Aristotle were secured; indeed, it is said that almost every day camels laden with volumes were entering the gates of Bagdad. To add to the supply, the Emperor Michael III. was compelled by treaty to furnish Greek books. The result of this intellectual movement could be no other than a diffusion of light. Schools arose in Bassora, Ispahan, Samarcand, Fez, Morocco, Sicily, Cordova, Seville, Granada.

They found medical colleges,

and promote science and literature.

Through the Nestorians and the Jews the Arabs thus became acquainted with the medical science of Greece and Alexandria; but to this was added other knowledge of a more sinister kind, derived from Persia, or perhaps remotely from Chaldee sources, the Nestorians having important Church establishments in Mesopotamia, and the Jews having been long familiar with that country; indeed, from thence their ancestors originally came. More than once its ideas had modified their national religion. This extraneous knowledge was of an astrological or magical nature, carried into practice by incantations, amulets, charms, and talismans. Its fundamental principle was that the planetary bodies exercise an influence over terrestrial things. As seven planets and seven metals were at that time known—the sun, the moon, Mars, Mercury, Jupiter, Venus, Saturn, being the planets of astrology—a due allotment was made. Gold

Intermingling of magic and sorcery.

Dedication of portions of matter and time to the supernatural.

was held sacred to the sun, silver to the moon, iron to Mars, etc. Even the portions of time were in like manner dedicated; the seven days of the week were respectively given to the seven planets of astrology. The names imposed on those days, and the order in which they occur, are obviously connected with the Ptolemaic hypothesis of astronomy, each of the planets having an hour assigned to it in its order of occurrence, and the planet ruling first the hour of each day giving its name to that day. Thus arranged, the week is a remarkable instance of the longevity of an institution adapted to the wants of man. It has survived through many changes of empire, has forced itself on the ecclesiastical system of Europe, which, unable to change its idolatrous aspect, has encouraged the vulgar error that it owes its authenticity to the Holy Scriptures, an error too plainly betrayed by the pagan names that the days bear, and also by their order of occurrence.

Origin of the week.

These notions of dedicating portions of matter or of time to the supernatural were derived from the doctrine of a universal spirit or soul of the world, extensively believed in throughout the East. It underlies, as we have seen in Chapter III., all Oriental theology, and is at once a very antique and not unphilosophical conception. Of this soul the spirit of man was by many supposed to be a particle like a spark given off from a flame. All other things, animate or inanimate, brutes, plants, stones, nay, even natural forms, rivers, mountains, cascades, grottoes, have each an indwelling and animating spirit.

Amulets and charms, therefore, did not derive their powers from the material substance of which they consisted, but from this indwelling spirit. In the case of man, his immaterial principle was believed to correspond to his personal bodily form. Of the two great sects into which the Jewish nation had been divided, the Pharisees accepted the Assyrian doctrine; but the Sadducees, who denied the existence of any such spirit, boasted that theirs was the old Mosaic faith, and denounced their antagonists as having been contaminated at the time of the Babylonian captivity, before which catastrophe, according to them, these doctrines were unheard of in Jerusalem. In Alexandria, among the leading men there were many adherents to these opinions. Thus Plotinus wrote a book on the association of dæmons with men, and his disciple Porphyry proved practically the possibility of such an alliance; for, repairing to the temple of Isis along with Plotinus and a certain Egyptian priest, the latter, to prove his supernatural power, offered to raise up the spirit of Plotinus himself in a visible form. A magical circle was drawn on the ground, surrounded with the customary astrological signs, the invocation commenced, the spirit appeared, and Plotinus stood face to face with his own soul. In this successful experiment it is needless to inquire how much the necromancer depended upon optical contrivances, and how much upon an alarmed imagination. But if thus the spirit of a living man could be called up, how much more likely the souls of the dead.

Alexandrian necromancy.

In reality, these wild doctrines were connected with Pantheism, which was secretly believed in everywhere; for, though, in a coarse mode of expression, a distinction seemed thus to be made between matter and spirit, or body and soul, it was held by the initiated that matter itself is a mere shadow of the spirit, and the body a delusive semblance of the soul.

These ideas originate in Pantheism.

In the eighth century, many natural facts of a surprising and unaccountable description, well calculated to make a profound impression upon those who witnessed them, had accumulated. They were such as are now familiar to chemists. Vessels tightly closed were burst open when tormented in the fire, apparently by some invisible agency; intangible vapours condensed into solids; from colourless liquids gaudy precipitates were suddenly called into existence; flames were disengaged without any adequate cause; explosions took place spontaneously. So much that was unexpected and unaccountable justified the title of "the occult science," "the black art." From being isolated marvels unconnected with one another, these facts had been united. The Chaldee notions of a soul of the world, and of indwelling spirits, had furnished a thread on which all these pearls, for such they proved to be, might be strung.

The black art.

With avidity—for there is ever a charm in the supernatural – did the Arabs receive from their Nestorian and Jewish medical instructors these mystical interpretations along with true knowledge. And far from resting satisfied with what their masters had thus delivered, they proceeded forthwith to improve and extend it for themselves. They submitted all kinds of substances to all kinds of operations, greatly improving the experimental process they had been taught. By exposing various bodies to the fire, they found it possible to extract from them more refined portions, which seemed to concentrate in themselves the qualities pertaining in a more diffuse way to the substances from which they had been drawn. These, since they were often invisible at their first disengagement, yet capable of bursting open the strongest vessels, and sometimes of disappearing in explosions and flames, they concluded must be the indwelling spirit or soul of the body, from which the fire had driven them forth. It was the Chaldee doctrine realized. Thus they obtained the spirit of wine, the spirit of salt, the spirit of nitre. We still retain in commerce these designations, though their significance is lost. When first introduced they had a strictly literal meaning. Alchemy, with its essences, quintessences, and spirits, was Pantheism materialized. God was seen to be in everything, in the abstract as well as the concrete, in numbers as well as realities.

The Arabians fall into these delusions,

Anticipating what will have hereafter to be considered in detail, I may here remark that it was not the Mohammedan alone who delivered himself up to these mystic delusions; Christendom was prepared for them also. In its opinion, the earth, the air, the sea, were full of invisible forms. With more faith than even by paganism itself was the supernatural power of the images of the gods accepted, only it was imputed to the influence of devils. The lunatic was troubled by a like possession. If a spring discharged its waters with a periodical gushing of carbonic acid gas, it was agitated by an angel; if an unfortunate descended into a pit and was suffocated by the mephitic air, it was by some dæmon who was secreted; if the miner's torch produced an explosion, it was owing to the wrath of some malignant spirit guarding a treasure,

and the Christians also.

and whose solitude had been disturbed. There was no end to the stories, duly authenticated by the best human testimony, of the occasional appearance of such spirits under visible forms; there was no grotto or cool thicket in which angels and genii had not been seen, no cavern without its dæmons. Though the names were not yet given, it was well understood that the air had its sylphs, the earth its gnomes, the fire its salamanders, the water its undines; to the day belonged its apparitions, to the night its fairies. The foul air of stagnant places assumed the visible form of dæmons of abominable aspect; the explosive gases of mines took on the shape of pale-faced, malicious dwarfs, with leathery ears hanging down to their shoulders, and garments of grey cloth. Philosophical conceptions can never be disentangled from social ideas; the thoughts of man will always gather a tincture from the intellectual medium in which he lives.

In Christendom, however, the chief application of these doctrines was to the relics of martyrs and saints. As with the amulets and talismans of Mesopotamia, these were regarded as possessing supernatural powers. They were a sure safeguard against evil spirits, and an unfailing relief in sickness.

A singular force was given to these mystic ideas by the peculiar direction they happened to take. As there are veins of water in the earth, and apertures through which the air can gain access, an analogy was inferred between its structure and that of an animal, leading to an inference of a similarity of functions. From this came the theory of the development of metals in its womb under the influence of the planets, the pregnant earth spontaneously producing gold and silver from baser things after a definite number of lunations. Already, however, in the doctrine of the transmutation of metals, it was perceived that to Nature the lapse of time is nothing—to man it is everything. To Nature, when she is transmuting a worthless into a better metal, what signify a thousand years? To man, half a century embraces the period of his intellectual activity. The aim of the cultivator of the sacred art should be to shorten the natural term; and, since we observe the influence of heat in hastening the ripening of

Transmutation of metals—Alchemy.

fruits, may we not reasonably expect that duly regulated degrees of fire will answer the purpose? by an exposure of base material in the furnace for a proper season, may we not anticipate the wished for event? The Emperor Caligula, who had formerly tried to make gold from orpiment by the force of fire, was only one of a thousand adepts pursuing a similar scheme. Some trusted to the addition of a material substance in aiding the fire to purge away the dross of the base body submitted to it. From this arose the doctrine of the powder of projection and the philosopher's stone.

Philosopher's stone.

This doctrine of the possibility of transmuting things into forms essentially different steadily made its way, leading, in the material direction, to alchemy, the art of making gold and silver out of baser metals, and in theology to transubstantiation. Transmutation and transubstantiation were twin sisters, destined for a world-wide celebrity; one became allied to the science of Mecca, the other to the theology of Rome.

Transmutation and transubstantiation.

While thus the Arabs joined in the pursuit of alchemy, their medical tendencies led them simultaneously to cultivate another ancient delusion, the discovery of a universal panacea or elixir which could cure all diseases and prolong life for ever. Mystical experimenters for centuries had been ransacking all nature, from the yellow flowers which are sacred to the sun, and gold his emblem and representative on earth, down to the vilest excrements of the human body. As to gold, there had been gathered round that metal many fictitious excellences in addition to its real values; it was believed that in some preparation of it would be found the elixir vitæ. This is the explanation of the unwearied attempts at making potable gold, for it was universally thought that if that metal could be obtained in a dissolved state, it would constitute the long-sought panacea. Nor did it seem impossible so to increase the power of water as to impart to it new virtues, and thereby enable it to accomplish the desired solution. Were there not natural waters of very different properties? were there not some that could fortify the memory, others destroy it; some re-enforce the

The elixir of life.

Potable gold.

spirits, some impart dulness, and some, which were highly prized, that could secure a return of love? It had been long known that both natural and artificial waters can permanently affect the health, and that instruments may be made to ascertain their qualities. Zosimus, the Panopolitan, had described in former times the operation of distillation, by which water may be purified; the Arabs called the apparatus for conducting that experiment an alembic. His treatise on the virtues and composition of waters was conveyed under the form of a dream, in which there flit before us fantastically white-haired priests sacrificing before the altar; cauldrons of boiling water, in which there are walking about men a span long; brazen-clad warriors in silence reading leaden books, and sphinxes with wings. In such incomprehensible fictions knowledge was purposely, and ignorance conveniently concealed.

Chemical waters.

The practical Arabs had not long been engaged in these fascinating but wild pursuits, when results of very great importance began to appear. In a scientific point of view, the discovery of the strong acids laid the true foundation of chemistry; in a political point of view, the invention of gunpowder revolutionized the world.

The Arabs originate scientific chemistry.

There were several explosive mixtures. Automatic fire was made from equal parts of sulphur, saltpetre, and sulphide of antimony, finely pulverized and mixed into a paste, with equal parts of juice of the black sycamore and liquid asphaltum, a little quicklime being added. It was directed to keep the material from the rays of the sun, which would set it on fire.

Gunpowder and fire-works.

Of liquid or Greek fire we have not a precise description, since the knowledge of it was kept at Constantinople as a state secret. There is reason, however, to believe that it contained sulphur and nitrate of potash mixed with naphtha. Of gunpowder, Marcus Græcus, whose date is probably to be referred to the close of the eighth century, gives the composition explicitly. He directs us to pulverize in a marble mortar one pound of sulphur, two of charcoal, and six of saltpetre. If some of this powder be tightly rammed in a long narrow tube closed at one end, and then set on fire, the tube will fly through the air: this is clearly the rocket. He says that thunder may be imitated by folding some of the powder in a cover and tying it up tightly: this is the cracker. It thus appears that fireworks preceded fire-arms. To the same author we are indebted for prescriptions for making the skin incombustible, so that we may handle fire without being burnt. These, doubtless, were received as explanations of the legends of the times, which related how miracle-workers had washed their hands in melted copper, and sat at their ease in flaming straw.

Incombustible men.

Among the Saracen names that might be mentioned as cultivators of alchemy, we may recall El-Rasi, Ebid Durr, Djafar or Geber, Toghragé, who wrote an alchemical poem, and Dschildegi, one of whose works bears the significant title of "The Lantern." The definition of alchemy by some of these authors is very striking: the science of the balance, the science of weight, the science of combustion.

Arabian chemists.

To one of these chemists, Djafar, our attention may for a moment be drawn. He lived toward the end of the eighth century, and is honoured by Rhases, Avicenna, and Kalid, the great Arabic physicians, as their master. His name is memorable in chemistry, since it marks an epoch in that science of equal importance to that of Priestley and Lavoisier. He is the first to describe nitric acid and aqua regia. Before him no stronger acid was known than concentrated vinegar. We cannot conceive of chemistry as not possessing acids. Roger Bacon speaks of him as the magister magistrorum. He has perfectly just notions of the nature of spirits or gases, as we call them; thus he says, "O son of the doctrine, when spirits fix themselves in bodies, they lose their form; in their nature they are no longer what they were. When you compel them to be disengaged again, this is what happens: either the spirit alone escapes with the air, and the body remains fixed in the alembic, or the spirit and body escape together at the same time." His doctrine respecting the nature of the metals, though erroneous, was not without a scientific value. A metal he considers to

Djafar discovers nitric acid and aqua regia,

and that oxidation increases weight.

be a compound of sulphur, mercury, and arsenic, and hence he infers that transmutation is possible by varying the proportion of those ingredients. He knows that a metal, when calcined, increases in weight, a discovery of the greatest importance, as eventually brought to bear in the destruction of the doctrine of Phlogiston of Stahl, and which has been imputed to Europeans of a much later time. He describes the operations of distillation, sublimation, filtration, various chemical apparatus, water-baths, sand-baths, cupels of bone-earth, of the use of which he gives a singularly clear description. A chemist reads with interest Djafar's antique method of obtaining nitric acid by distilling in a retort Cyprus vitriol, alum, and saltpetre. He sets forth its corrosive power, and shows how it may be made to dissolve even gold itself, by adding a portion of sal ammoniac. Djafar may thus be considered as having solved the grand alchemical problem of obtaining gold in a potable state. Of course, many trials must have been made on the influence of this solution on the animal system, respecting which such extravagant anticipations had been entertained. The disappointment that ensued was doubtless the reason that the records of these trials have not descended to us.

He solves the problem of potable gold.

With Djafar may be mentioned Rhazes, born A.D. 860, physician-in-chief to the great hospital at Bagdad. To him is due the first description of the preparation and properties of sulphuric acid. He obtained it, as the Nordhausen variety is still made, by the distillation of dried green vitriol. To him are also due the first indications of the preparation of absolute alcohol, by distilling spirit of wine from quick-lime. As a curious discovery made by the Saracens may be mentioned the experiment of Achild Bechil, who, by distilling together the extract of urine, clay, lime, and powdered charcoal, obtained an artificial carbuncle, which shone in the dark "like a good moon." This was phosphorus.

Rhazes discovers sulphuric acid.

Bechil discovers phosphorus.

And now there arose among Arabian physicians a correctness of thought and breadth of view altogether surprising. It might almost be supposed that the following lines were written by one of our own contemporaries;

they are, however, extracted from a chapter of Avicenna on the origin of mountains. This author was born in the tenth century. "Mountains may be due to two different causes. Either they are effects of upheavals of the crust of the earth, such as might occur during a violent earthquake, or they are the effect of water, which, cutting for itself a new route, has denuded the valleys, the strata being of different kinds, some soft, some hard. The winds and waters disintegrate the one, but leave the other intact. Most of the eminences of the earth have had this latter origin. It would require a long period of time for all such changes to be accomplished, during which the mountains themselves might be somewhat diminished in size. But that water has been the main cause of these effects is proved by the existence of fossil remains of aquatic and other animals on many mountains." Avicenna also explains the nature of petrifying or incrusting waters, and mentions ærolites, out of one of which a sword-blade was made, but he adds that the metal was too brittle to be of any use. A mere catalogue of some of the works of Avicenna will indicate the condition of Arabian attainment. 1. On the Utility and Advantage of Science; 2. Of Health and Remedies; 3. Canons of Physic; 4. On Astronomical Observations; 5. Mathematical Theorems; 6. On the Arabic Language and its Properties; 7. On the Origin of the Soul and Resurrection of the Body; 8. Demonstration of Collateral Lines on the Sphere; 9. An Abridgment of Euclid; 10. On Finity and Infinity; 11. On Physics and Metaphysics; 12. An Encyclopædia of Human Knowledge, in 20 vols., etc, etc. The perusal of such a catalogue is sufficient to excite profound attention when we remember the contemporaneous state of Europe.

Geological views of Avicenna.

His works indicate the attainment of the times.

The pursuit of the elixir made a well-marked impression upon Arab experimental science, confirming it in its medical application. At the foundation of this application lay the principle that it is possible to relieve the diseases of the human body by purely material means. As the science advanced it gradually shook off its fetichisms, the spiritual receding

Effect of the search for the elixir on practical medicine.

into insignificance, the material coming into bolder relief. Not, however, without great difficulty was a way forced for the great doctrine that the influence of substances on the constitution of man is altogether of a material kind, and not at all due to any indwelling or animating spirit; that it is of no kind of use to practise incantations over drugs, or to repeat prayers over the mortar in which medicines are being compounded, since the effect will be the same, whether this has been done or not; that there is no kind of efficacy in amulets, no virtue in charms; and that, though saint-relics may serve to excite the imagination of the ignorant, they are altogether beneath the attention of the philosopher.

Medical conflict between Europe and Africa.

It was this last sentiment which brought Europe and Africa into intellectual collision. The Saracen and Hebrew physicians had become thoroughly materialized. Throughout Christendom the practice of medicine was altogether supernatural. It was in the hands of ecclesiastics; and saint relics, shrines, and miracle-cures were a source of boundless profit. On a subsequent page I shall have to describe the circumstances of the conflict that ensued between material philosophy on one side, and supernatural jugglery on the other; to show how the Arab system gained the victory, and how, out of that victory, the industrial life of Europe arose. The Byzantine policy inaugurated in Constantinople and Alexandria was, happily for the world, in the end overthrown. To that future page I must postpone the great achievements of the Arabians in the fulness of their Age of Reason. When Europe was hardly more enlightened than Caffraria is now, the Saracens were cultivating and even creating science. Their triumphs in philosophy, mathematics, astronomy, chemistry, medicine, proved to be more glorious, more durable, and therefore more important than their military actions had been.

CHAPTER XIV.

THE AGE OF FAITH IN THE WEST—(*Continued*).

IMAGE-WORSHIP AND THE MONKS.

Origin of IMAGE-WORSHIP.—*Inutility of Images discovered in Asia and Africa during the Saracen Wars.—Rise of Iconoclasm.*

The Emperors prohibit Image-worship.—The Monks, aided by court Females, sustain it.—Victory of the latter.

Image-worship in the West sustained by the Popes.—Quarrel between the Emperor and the Pope.—The Pope, aided by the Monks, revolts and allies himself with the Franks.

THE MONKS.—*History of the Rise and Development of Monasticism.—Hermits and Cœnobites.—Spread of Monasticism from Egypt over Europe.—Monk Miracles and Legends.—Humanization of the monastic Establishments.—They materialize Religion, and impress their Ideas on Europe.*

THE Arabian influence, allying itself to philosophy, was henceforth productive of other than military results. To the loss of Africa and Asia was now added a disturbance impressed on Europe itself, ending in the decomposition of Christianity into two forms, Greek and Latin, and in three great political events—the emancipation of the popes from the emperors of Constantinople, the usurpation of power by a new dynasty in France, the reconstruction of the Roman empire in the West.

Influence of the Arabians.

The dispute respecting the worship of images led to those great events. The acts of the Mohammedan khalifs and of the iconoclastic or image-breaking emperors occasioned that dispute.

Nothing could be more deplorable than the condition of southern Europe when it first felt the intellectual influence of the Arabians. Its old Roman and Greek populations had altogether disappeared; the races of half-breeds and mongrels substituted for them were immersed in fetichism. An observance of certain ceremonials constituted a religious life. A chip of the true cross, some iron filings from the chain of St. Peter, a tooth or bone of a martyr, were held in adoration; the world was full of the stupendous miracles which these relics had performed. But especially were painted or graven images of holy personages supposed to be endowed with such powers. They had become objects of actual worship. The facility with which the Empress Helena, the mother of Constantine the Great, had given an aristocratic fashion to this idolatry, showed that the old pagan ideas had never really died out, and that the degenerated populations received with approval the religious conceptions of their great predecessors. The early Christian fathers believed that painting and sculpture were forbidden by the Scriptures, and that they were therefore wicked arts; and, though the second Council of Nicea asserted that the use of images had always been adopted by the Church, there are abundant facts to prove that the actual worship of them was not indulged in until the fourth century, when, on the occasion of its occurrence in Spain, it was condemned by the Council of Illiberis. During the fifth century the practice of introducing images into churches increased, and in the sixth it had become prevalent.

Worship of relics and images.

The common people, who had never been able to comprehend doctrinal mysteries, found their religious wants satisfied in turning to these effigies. With singular obtuseness, they believed that the saint is present in his image, though hundreds of the same kind were in existence, each having an equal and exclusive right to the spiritual presence. The doctrine of invocation of departed saints, which assumed prominence in the fifth century, was greatly strengthened by these graphic forms. Pagan idolatry had reappeared.

Its rapid spread in Christendom.

At first the simple cross was used as a substitute for the amulets and charms of remoter times; it constituted a fetich able to expel evil spirits, even Satan himself. This Being, who had become singularly debased from what he was in the noble Oriental fictions, was an imbecile and malicious though not a malignant spirit, affrighted not only at pieces of wood framed in the shape of a cross, but at the form of it made by the finger in the air. A subordinate dæmon was supposed to possess every individual at his birth, but he was cast out by baptism. When, in the course of time, the cross became a crucifix, offering a representation of the dying Redeemer, it might be supposed to have gathered increased virtue; and soon, in addition to that adorable form, were introduced images of the Virgin, the apostles, saints, and martyrs. The ancient times seemed to have come again, when these pictures were approached with genuflexions, luminaries, and incense. The doctrine of the more intelligent was that these were aids to devotion, and that, among people to whom the art of reading was unknown, they served the useful purpose of recalling sacred events in a kind of hieroglyphic manner. But among the vulgar, and monks, and women, they were believed to be endowed with supernatural power. Of some, the wounds could bleed; of others, the eyes could wink; of others, the limbs could be raised. In ancient times, the statues of Minerva could brandish spears, and those of Venus could weep.

Simple fetiches replaced by images.

Bleeding and winking images.

In truth, the populations of the Greek and Latin countries were no more than nominally converted and superficially Christianized. The old traditions and practices had never been forgotten. A tendency to idolatry seemed to be the necessary incident of the climate. Not without reason have the apologists of the clergy affirmed that image-worship was insisted on by the people, and that the Church had to admit ideas that she had never been able to eradicate. After seven hundred years of apostolic labour, it was found that the populace of Greece and Italy were apparently in their old state, and that actually nothing at all had been accomplished; the new-comers had passed into the track of their predecessors. It is often said that the restoration of image-worship was owing to the extinction of civilization by the Northern barbarians. But this is not true. In the blood of the German nations the taint of idolatry is but small. In

Idolatry never extinguished in Greece and Italy.

their own countries they gave it little encouragement, and, indeed, hastened quickly to its total rejection. The sin lay not with them, but with the Mediterranean people.

Nor are those barbarians to be held accountable for the so-called extinction of civilization in Italy. The true Roman race had prematurely died; it came to an untimely end in consequence of its dissolute, its violent life. Its civilization would have spontaneously died with it had no barbarian been present: and, if these intruders produced a baneful effect at first, they compensated for it in the end. As, when fresh coal is added to a fire that is burning low, a still further diminution will ensue, perhaps there may be a risk of entirely putting it out; but in due season, if all goes well, the new material will join in the contagious blaze. The savages of Europe, thrown into the decaying foci of Greek and Roman light, did perhaps for a time reduce the general heat; but, by degrees, it spread throughout their mass, and the bright flame of modern civilization was the result. Let those who lament the intrusion of these men into the classical countries, reflect upon the result which must otherwise have ensued—the last spark would soon have died out, and nothing but ashes have remained.

Influence of the barbarians.

Three causes gave rise to Iconoclasm, or the revolt against image-worship: 1st, the remonstrances and derision of the Mohammedans; 2nd, the good sense of a great sovereign, Leo the Isaurian, who had risen by his merit from obscurity, and had become the founder of a new dynasty at Constantinople; 3rd, the detected inability of these miracle-working idols and fetiches to protect their worshippers or themselves against an unbelieving enemy. Moreover, an impression was gradually making its way among the more intelligent classes that religion ought to free itself from such superstitions. So important were the consequences of Leo's actions, that some have been disposed to assign to his reign the first attempt at making policy depend on theology; and to this period, as I have elsewhere remarked, they therefore refer the commencement of the Byzantine empire. Through one hundred and twenty years, six emperors

Origin of Iconoclasm.

devoted themselves to this reformation. But it was premature. They were overpowered by the populace and the monks, by the bishops of Rome, and by a superstitious and wicked woman.

It had been a favourite argument against the pagans how little their gods could do for them when the hour of calamity came, when their statues and images were insulted and destroyed, and hence how vain was such worship, how imbecile such gods. When Africa and Asia, full of relics and crosses, pictures and images, fell before the Mohammedans, those conquerors retaliated the same logic with no little effect. There was hardly one of the fallen towns that had not some idol for its protector. Remembering the stern objurgations of the prophet against this deadly sin, prohibited at once by the commandment of God and repudiated by the reason of man, the Saracen khalifs had ordered all the Syrian images to be destroyed. Amid the derision of the Arab soldiery and the tears of the terror-stricken worshippers, these orders were remorselessly carried into effect, except in some cases where the temptation of an enormous ransom induced the avengers of the unity of God to swerve from their duty. Thus the piece of linen cloth on which it was feigned that our Saviour had impressed his countenance, and which was the palladium of Edessa, was carried off by the victors at the capture of that town, and subsequently sold to Constantinople at the profitable price of twelve thousand pounds of silver. This picture, and also some other celebrated ones, it was said, possessed the property of multiplying themselves by contact with other surfaces, as in modern times we multiply photographs. Such were the celebrated images "made without hands."

Inutility of miraculous images discovered in the Arab invasions.

Destruction and sale of idols by the Arabs.

It was currently asserted that the immediate origin of Iconoclasm was due to the Khalif Yezed, who had completed the destruction of the Syrian images, and to two Jews, who stimulated Leo the Isaurian to his task. However that may be, Leo published an edict, A.D. 726, prohibiting the worship of images. This was followed by another directing their destruction, and the whitewashing of the walls of churches

The emperor prohibits image-worship.

ornamented with them. Hereupon the clergy and the monks rebelled; the emperor was denounced as a Mohammedan and a Jew. He ordered that a statue of the Saviour in that part of the city called Chalcopratia should be removed, and a riot was the consequence. One of his officers mounted a ladder and struck the idol with an axe upon its face; it was an incident like that enacted centuries before in the temple of Serapis at Alexandria. The sacred image, which had often arrested the course of Nature and worked many miracles, was now found to be unable to protect or to avenge its own honour. A rabble of women interfered in its behalf; they threw down the ladder and killed the officer; nor was the riot ended until the troops were called in and a great massacre perpetrated.

The monks sustain it.

The monks spread the sedition in all parts of the empire; they even attempted to proclaim a new emperor. Leo was everywhere denounced as a Mohammedan infidel, an enemy of the Mother of God; but with inflexible resolution he persisted in his determination as long as he lived.

His son and successor, Constantine, pursued the same iconoclastic policy. From the circumstance of his accidently defiling the font at which he was being baptized, he had received the suggestive name of Copronymus. His subsequent career was asserted by the monks to have been foreshadowed by his sacrilegious beginnings. It was publicly asserted that he was an atheist. In truth, his biography, in many respects, proves that the higher classes in Constantinople were largely infected with infidelity. The patriarch deposed upon oath that Copronymus had made the most irreligious confessions to him, as that our Saviour, far from being the Son of God, was, in his opinion, a mere man, born of his mother in the common way. The truth of these accusations was perhaps, in a measure, sustained by the revenge that the emperor took on the patriarch for his indiscreet revelations. He seized him, put out his eyes, caused him to be led through the city mounted on an ass, with his face to the tail, and then, as if to show his unutterable contempt for all religion, with an exquisite malice, appointed him to his office again.

They accuse the emperor of atheism.

If such was the religious condition of the emperor, the higher clergy were but little better. A council was summoned by Constantine, A.D. 754, at Constantinople, which was attended by 388 bishops. It asserted for itself the position of the seventh general council. It unanimously decreed that all visible symbols of Christ, except in the Eucharist, are blasphemous or heretical; that image-worship is a corruption of Christianity and a renewed form of paganism; it directed all statues and paintings to be removed from the churches and destroyed, it degraded every ecclesiastic and excommunicated every layman who should be concerned in setting them up again. It concluded its labours with prayers for the emperor who had extirpated idolatry and given peace to the Church.

Council of Constantinople prohibits image-worship.

But this decision was by no means quietly received. The monks rose in an uproar; some raised a clamour in their caves, some from the tops of their pillars; one, in the church of St. Mammas, insulted the emperor to his face, denouncing him as a second apostate Julian. Nor could he deliver himself from them by the scourging, strangling, and drowning of individuals. In his wrath, Copronymus, plainly discerning that it was the monks on one side and the government on the other, determined to strike at the root of the evil, and to destroy monasticism itself. He drove the holy men out of their cells and cloisters; made the consecrated virgins marry; gave up the buildings for civil uses; burnt pictures, idols, and all kinds of relics; degraded the patriarch from his office, scourged him, shaved off his eyebrows, set him for public derision in the circus in a sleeveless shirt, and then beheaded him. Already he had consecrated a eunuch in his stead. Doubtless these atrocities strengthened the bishops of Rome in their resolve to seek a protector from such a master among the barbarian kings of the West.

Uproar among the monks.

The emperor retaliates.

Constantine Copronymus was succeeded by his son, Leo the Chazar, who, during a short reign of five years, continued the iconoclastic policy. On his death his wife Irene seized the government, ostensibly in behalf of her son. This woman,

Re-establishment of image-worship by Irene the murderess

pre-eminently wicked and superstitious beyond her times, undertook the restoration of images. She caused the patriarch to retire from his dignity, appointed one of her creatures, Tarasius, in his stead, and summoned another council. In this second Council of Nicea that of Constantinople was denounced as a synod of fools and atheists, the worship of images was pronounced agreeable to Scripture and reason, and in conformity to the usages and traditions of the Church.

Irene, saluted as the second Helena, and set forth by the monks as an exemplar of piety, thus accomplished the restoration of image-worship. In a few years this ambitious woman, refusing to surrender his rightful dignity to her son, caused him to be seized, and, in the porphyry chamber in which she had borne him, put out his eyes. Constantinople, long familiar with horrible crimes, was appalled at such an unnatural deed.

During the succeeding reigns to that of Leo the Armenian, matters remained without change; but that emperor resumed the policy of Leo the Isaurian. By an edict he prohibited image-worship, and banished the Patriarch of Constantinople, who had admonished him that the apostles had made images of the Saviour and the Virgin, and that there was at Rome a picture of the Transfiguration, painted by order of St. Peter. After the murder of Leo, his successor, Michael the Stammerer, showed no encouragement to either party. It was affirmed that he was given to profane jesting, was incredulous as to the resurrection of the dead, disbelieved the existence of the devil, was indifferent whether images were worshipped or not, and recommended the patriarch to bury the decrees of Constantinople and Nicea equally in oblivion. His successor and son, however, observed no such impartiality. To Saracenic tastes, shown by his building a palace like that of the khalif; to a devotion for poetry, exemplified by branding some of his own stanzas on his image-worshipping enemies; to the composition of music and its singing by himself as an amateur in the choir; to mechanical knowledge, displayed by hydraulic contrivances, musical instruments, organs, automatic singing-birds sitting in golden trees, he added

Resumption of Iconoclasm by the succeeding emperors.

Their Saracenic tastes.

an abomination of monks and a determined iconoclasm. Instead of merely whitewashing the walls of the churches, he adorned them with pictures of beasts and birds. Iconoclasm had now become a struggle between the emperors and the monks.

Final restoration of image-worship by the Empress Theodora.

Again, on the death of Theophilus, image-worship triumphed, and triumphed in the same manner as before. His widow, Theodora, alarmed by the monks for the safety of the soul of her husband, purchased absolution for him at the price of the restoration of images.

Such was the issue of Iconoclasm in the East. The monks proved stronger than the emperors, and, after a struggle of 120 years, the images were finally restored. In the West far more important consequences followed.

Image-worship in the West.

To image-worship Italy was devoutly attached. When the first edict of Leo was made known by the exarch, it produced a rebellion, of which Pope Gregory II. took advantage to suspend the tribute paid by Italy. In letters that he wrote to the emperor he defended the popular delusion, declaring that the first Christians had caused pictures to be made of our Lord, of his brother James, of Stephen, and all the martyrs, and had sent them throughout the world; the reason that God the Father had not been painted was that his countenance was not known. These letters display a most audacious presumption of the ignorance of the emperor respecting common Scripture incidents, and, as some have remarked, suggest a doubt of the pope's familiarity with the sacred volume. He points out the difference between the statues of antiquity, which are only the representations of phantoms, and the images of the Church, which have approved themselves, by numberless miracles, to be the genuine forms of the Saviour, his mother, and his saints. Referring to the statue of St. Peter, which the emperor had ordered to be broken to pieces, he declares that the Western nations regard that apostle as a god upon earth, and ominously threatens the vengeance of the pious barbarians if it should be destroyed. In this defence of images Gregory found an active coadjutor in a Syrian, John of Damascus, who

It is sustained by the pope,

had witnessed the rage of the khalifs against the images of his own country, and whose hand, having been cut off by those tyrants, had been miraculously rejoined to his body by an idol of the Virgin to which he prayed.

But Gregory was not alone in his policy, nor John of Damascus in his controversies. The King of the Lombards, Luitprand, also perceived the advantage of putting himself forth as the protector of images, and of appealing to the Italians, for their sake, to expel the Greeks from the country. The pope acted on the principle that heresy in a sovereign justifies withdrawal of allegiance, the Lombard that it excuses the seizure of possessions. Luitprand accordingly ventured on the capture of Ravenna. An immense booty, the accumulation of the emperors, the Gothic kings, and the exarchs, which was taken at the storming of the town, at once rewarded his piety, stimulated him to new enterprises of a like nature, and drew upon him the attention of his enemy the emperor, whom he had plundered, and of his confederate the pope, whom he had overreached.

and by the Lombard king.

This was the position of affairs. If the Lombards, who were Arians, and therefore heretics, should succeed in extending their sway all over Italy, the influence and prosperity of the papacy must come to an end; their action on the question of the images was altogether of an ephemeral and delusive kind, for all the northern nations preferred a simple worship like that of primitive times, and had never shown any attachment to the adoration of graven forms. If, on the other hand, the pope should continue his allegiance to Constantinople, he must be liable to the atrocious persecutions so often and so recently inflicted on the patriarchs of that city by their tyrannical master; and the breaking of that connexion in reality involved no surrender of any solid advantages, for the emperor was too weak to give protection from the Lombards. Already had been experienced a portentous difficulty in sending relief from Constantinople, on account of the naval superiority of the Saracens in the Mediterranean. For the taxes paid to the sovereign no real equivalent was received; but Rome, in ignominy, was obliged to submit,

Position of affairs at this time.

The Saracens dominate in the Mediterranean.

like an obscure provincial town, to the mandates of the Eastern court. Moreover, in her eyes, the emperor, by reason of his iconoclasm, was a heretic. But if alliance with the Lombards and allegiance to the Greeks were equally inexpedient, a third course was possible. A mayor of the palace of the Frankish kings had successfully led his armies against the Arabs from Spain, and had gained the great victory of Tours. If the Franks, under the influence of their climate or the genius of their race, had thus far shown no encouragement to images, in all other respects they were orthodox, for they had been converted by Catholic missionaries; their kings, it was true, were mere phantoms, but Charles Martel had proved himself a great soldier; he was, therefore, an ambitious man. There was Scripture authority for raising a subordinate to sovereign power; the prophets of Israel had thus, of old, with oil anointed kings. And if the sword of France was gently removed from the kingly hand that was too weak to hold it, and given to the hero who had already shown that he could smite terribly with it—if this were done by the authority of the pope, acting as the representative of God, how great the gain to the papacy! A thousand years might not be enough to separate the monarchy of France from the theocracy of Italy.

Causes of the alliance of the popes and the Franks.

The resistance which had sprung up to the imperial edict for the destruction of images determined the course of events. The pope rebelled, and attempts were made by the emperor to seize or assassinate him. A fear that the pontiff might be carried to Constantinople, and the preparations making to destroy the images in the churches, united all Italy. A council was held at Rome, which anathematized the Iconoclasts. In retaliation, the Sicilian and other estates of the Church were confiscated. Gregory III., who in the meantime succeeded to the papacy, continued the policy of his predecessor. The emperor was defied. A fleet, fitted out by him in support of the exarch, was lost in a storm. With this termination of the influence of Constantinople in Italy came the imminent danger that the pope must acknowledge the supremacy of the Lombards. In his distress Gregory

Revolt of the pope from the emperor.

turned to Charles Martel. He sent him the keys of the sepulchre of St. Peter, and implored his assistance. The die was cast. Papal Rome revolted from her sovereign, and became indissolubly bound to the barbarian kingdoms. To France a new dynasty was given, to the pope temporal power, and to the west of Europe a fictitious Roman empire.

Alliance of the pope and the Franks.

The monks had thus overcome the image-breaking emperors, a result which proves them to have already become a formidable power in the state. It is necessary, for a proper understanding of the great events with which henceforth they were connected, to describe their origin and history.

The monks.

In the iconoclastic quarrel they are to be regarded as the representatives of the common people in contradistinction to the clergy; often, indeed, the representatives of the populace, infected with all its instincts of superstition and fanaticism. They are the upholders of miracle-cures, invocation of saints, worship of images, clamorous asserters of a unity of faith in the Church—a unity which they never practised, but which offered a convenient pretext for a bitter persecution of heresy and paganism, though they were more than half pagan themselves.

Their first position

It was their destiny to impress on the practical life of Europe that mixture of Christianity and heathenism engendered by political events in Italy and Greece. Yet, while they thus co-operated in great affairs, they themselves exhibited, in the most signal manner, the force of that law of continuous variation of opinion and habits to which all enduring communities of men must submit. Born of superstition, obscene in their early life, they end in luxury, refinement, learning. Theirs is a history to which we may profitably attend.

and subsequent improvement.

From very early times there had been in India zealots who, actuated by a desire of removing themselves from the temptations of society and preparing for another life, retired into solitary places. Such also were the Essenes among the Jews, and the Therapeutæ

The first hermits.

in Egypt. Pliny speaks of the blameless life of the former when he says, "They are the companions of palms;" nor does he hide his astonishment at an immortal society in which no one is ever born. Their example was not lost upon more devout Christians, particularly after the influence of Magianism began to be felt. Though it is sometimes said that the first of these hermits were Anthony and Paulus, they doubtless are to be regarded as only having rendered themselves more illustrious by their superior sanctity among a crowd of worthies who had preceded them or were their contemporaries. As early as the second and third centuries the practice of retirement had commenced among Christians; soon afterwards it had become common. The date of Hilarion is about A.D. 328, of Basil A.D. 360. Regarding prayer as the only occupation in which man may profitably engage, they gave no more attention to the body than the wants of nature absolutely demanded. A little dried fruit or bread for food, and water for drink, were sufficient for its support; occasionally a particle of salt might be added, but the use of warm water was looked upon as betraying a tendency to luxury. The incentives to many of their rules of life might excite a smile, if it were right to smile at the acts of earnest men. Some, like the innocent Essenes, who would do nothing whatever on the Sabbath, observed the day before as a fast, rigorously abstaining from food and drink, that nature might not force them into sin on the morrow. For some, it was not enough, by the passive means of abstinence, to refrain from fault or reduce the body to subjection, though starvation is the antidote for desire; the more active, and, perhaps, more effectual operation of periodical flagellations and bodily torture were added. Ingenuity was taxed to find new means of personal infliction. A hermit who never permitted himself to sleep more than an hour without being awakened endured torments not inferior to those of the modern fakir, who crosses his arms on the top of his head and keeps them there for years, until they are wasted to the bone, or suspends himself to a pole by means of a hook inserted in the flesh of his back.

Their self-denial.

Among the Oriental sects there are some who believe

that the Supreme Being is perpetually occupied in the contemplation of himself, and that the nearer man can approach to a state of total inaction the more will he resemble God. For many years the Indian sage never raises his eyes from his navel; absorbed in the profound contemplation of it, his perennial reverie is unbroken by any outward suggestions, the admiring by-standers administering, as chance offers, the little food and water that his wants require. Under the influence of such ideas, in the fifth century, St. Simeon Stylites, who in his youth had often been saved from suicide, by ascending a column he had built, sixty feet in height, and only one foot square at the top, departed as far as he could from earthly affairs, and approached more closely to heaven. On this elevated retreat, to which he was fastened by a chain, he endured, if we may believe the incredible story, for thirty years the summer's sun and the winter's frost. Afar off the passer-by was edified by seeing the motionless figure of the holy man with outstretched arms like a cross, projected against the sky, in his favourite attitude of prayer, or expressing his thankfulness for the many mercies of which he supposed himself to be the recipient by rapidly striking his forehead against his knees. Historians relate that a curious spectator counted twelve hundred and forty-four of these motions, and then abstained through fatigue from any farther tally, though the unwearied exhibition was still going on. This "most holy aerial martyr," as Evagrius calls him, attained at last his reward, and Mount Telenissa witnessed a vast procession of devout admirers accompanying to the grave his mortal remains.

Profound contemplation of God.

Aerial martyrs. Holy birds.

More commonly, however, the hermit declined the conspicuous notoriety of these "holy birds," as they were called by the profane, and, retiring to some cave in the desert, despised the comforts of life, and gave himself up to penance and prayer. Among men who had thus altogether exalted themselves above the wants of the flesh, there was no toleration for its lusts. The sinfulness of the marriage relation, and the pre-eminent value of chastity, followed from their principles. If it was objected to such practices that by their universal

The monks insist on celibacy.

adoption the human species would soon be extinguished, and no man would remain to offer praises to God, these zealots, remembering the temptations from which they had escaped, with truth replied that there would always be sinners enough in the world to avoid that disaster, and that out of their evil works good would be brought. St. Jerome offers us the pregnant reflection that, though it may be marriage that fills the earth, it is virginity that replenishes heaven.

If they were not recorded by many truthful authors, the extravagances of some of these enthusiasts would pass belief. Men and women ran naked upon all fours, associating themselves with the beasts of the field. In the spring season, when the grass is tender, the grazing hermits of Mesopotamia went forth to the plains, sharing with the cattle their filth, and their food. Of some, notwithstanding a weight of evidence, the stupendous biography must tax their admirers' credulity. It is affirmed that St. Ammon had never seen his own body uncovered; that an angel carried him on his back over a river which he was obliged to cross; that at his death he ascended to heaven through the skies, St. Anthony being an eye-witness of the event—St. Anthony, who was guided to the hermit Paulus by a centaur; that Didymus never spoke to a human being for ninety years.

Grazing hermits.

From the Jewish anchorites, who of old sought a retreat beneath the shade of the palms of Engaddi, who beguiled their weary hours in the chanting of psalms by the bitter waters of the Dead Sea; from the philosophic Hindu, who sought for happiness in bodily inaction and mental exercise, to these Christian solitaries, the stages of delusion are numerous and successive. It would not be difficult to present examples of each step in the career of debasement. To one who is acquainted with the working and accidents of the human brain, it will not be surprizing that an asylum for hermits who had become hopelessly insane was instituted at Jerusalem.

Insane hermits.

The biographies of these recluses, for ages a source of consolation to the faithful in their temptations, are not to be regarded as mere works of fiction, though they abound in supernatural occurrences, and are the forerunners of the dæmonology of the Middle Ages. The whole world was a scene of dæmoniac adventures, of miracles and wonders. So far from being mere impostures, they relate nothing more than may be witnessed at any time under similar conditions. In the brain of man, impressions of whatever he has seen or heard, of whatever has been made manifest to him by his other senses, nay, even the vestiges of his former thoughts, are stored up. These traces are most vivid at first, but, by degrees, they decline in force, though they probably never completely die out. During our waking hours, while we are perpetually receiving new impressions from things that surround us, such vestiges are overpowered, and cannot attract the attention of the mind. But in the period of sleep, when external influences cease, they present themselves to our regard, and the mind submitting to the delusion, groups them into the fantastic forms of dreams. By the use of opium and other drugs which can blunt our sensibility to passing events, these phantasms may be made to emerge. They also offer themselves in the delirium of fevers and in the hour of death.

Causes of hallucinations.

It is immaterial in what manner or by what agency our susceptibility to the impressions of surrounding objects is benumbed, whether by drugs, or sleep, or disease, as soon as their force is no greater than that of forms already registered in the brain, those forms will emerge before us, and dreams or apparitions are the result. So liable is the mind to practise deception on itself, that with the utmost difficulty it is aware of the delusion. No man can submit to long-continued and rigorous fasting without becoming the subject of these hallucinations; and the more he enfeebles his organs of sense, the more vivid is the exhibition, the more profound the deception. An ominous sentence may perhaps be incessantly whispered in his ear; to his fixed and fascinated eye some grotesque or abominable object may perpetually present itself. To the hermit, in the solitude of his cell, there doubtless often did appear, by the uncertain light of his lamp, obscene shadows of diabolical import; doubtless there was many an agony with fiends, many a struggle with monsters, satyrs, and imps, many an earnest, solemn, and manful controversy

Supernatural appearances.

with Satan himself, who sometimes came as an aged man, sometimes with a countenance of horrible intelligence, and sometimes as a female fearfully beautiful. St. Jerome, who, with the utmost difficulty, had succeeded in extinguishing all carnal desires, ingenuously confesses how sorely he was tried by this last device of the enemy, how nearly the ancient flames were rekindled. As to the reality of these apparitions, why should a hermit be led to suspect that they arose from the natural working of his own brain? Men never dream that they are dreaming. To him they were terrible realities; to us they should be the proofs of insanity, not of imposture.

If, in the prison discipline of modern times, it has been found that solitary confinement is a punishment too dreadful for the most hardened convict to bear, and that, if persisted in, it is liable to lead to insanity, how much more quickly must that unfortunate condition have been induced when the trials of religious distress and the physical enfeeblement arising from rigorous fastings and incessant watchings were added? To the dreadful ennui which precedes that state, one of the ancient monks pathetically alludes when he relates how often he went forth and returned to his cell, and gazed on the sun as if he hastened too slowly to his setting. And yet such fearful solitude is of but brief duration. Even though we flee to the desert we cannot be long alone. Cut off from social converse, the mind of man engenders companions for itself—companions like the gloom from which they have emerged. It was thus that to St. Anthony appeared the Spirit of Fornication, under the form of a lascivious negro boy; it was thus that multitudes of dæmons of horrible aspect cruelly beat him nearly to death, the brave old man defying them to the last, and telling them that he did not wish to be spared one of their blows; it was thus that in the night, with hideous laughter, they burst into his cell, under the form of lions, serpents, scorpions, asps, lizards, panthers, and wolves, each attacking him in his own way; thus that when, in his dire extremity, he lifted his eyes for help, the roof disappeared, and amid beams of light the Saviour looked down; thus it was with the enchanted silver dish that

Delusions created by the mind.

Satan gave him, which, being touched, vanished in smoke; thus with the gigantic bats and centaurs, and the two lions that helped him to scratch a grave for Paul.

The images that may thus emerge from the brain have been classed by physiologists among the phænomena of inverse vision, or cerebral sight. Elsewhere I have given a detailed investigation of their nature (Human Physiology, chap. xxi.), and, persuaded that they have played a far more important part in human affairs than is commonly supposed, have thus expressed myself: "Men in every part of the world, even among nations the most abject and barbarous, have an abiding faith not only in the existence of a spirit that animates us, but also in its immortality. Of these there are multitudes who have been shut out from all communion with civilized countries, who have never been enlightened by revelation, and who are mentally incapable of reasoning out for themselves arguments in support of those great truths. Under such circumstances, it is not very likely that the uncertainties of tradition, derived from remote ages, could be any guide to them, for traditions soon disappear except they be connected with the wants of daily life. Can there be, in a philosophical view, anything more interesting than the manner in which these defects have been provided for by implanting in the very organization of every man the means of constantly admonishing him of these facts—of recalling them with an unexpected vividness before even after they have become so faint as almost to die out? Let him be as debased and benighted a savage as he may, shut out from all communion with races whom Providence has placed in happier circumstances, he has still the same organization, and is liable to the same physiological incidents, as ourselves. Like us, he sees in his visions the fading forms of landscapes which are perhaps connected with some of his most grateful recollections, and what other conclusion can he possibly derive from these unreal pictures than that they are the foreshadowings of another land beyond that in which his lot is cast. Like us, he is revisited at intervals by the resemblances of those whom he has loved or hated while they were alive, nor can he ever be so brutalized as not to

Important religious results of cerebral sight.

A future world.

discern in such manifestations suggestions which to *him* are incontrovertible proofs of the existence and immortality of the soul. Even in the most refined social conditions we are never able to shake off the impressions of these occurrences, and are perpetually drawing from them the same conclusions that our uncivilized ancestors did. Our more elevated condition of life in no respect relieves us from the inevitable consequences of our own organization, any more than it relieves us from infirmities and disease. In these respects, all over the globe we are on an equality. Savage or civilized, we carry within us a mechanism intended to present to us mementoes of the most solemn facts with which we can be concerned, and the voice of history tells us that it has ever been true to its design. It wants only moments of repose or sickness, when the influence of external things is diminished, to come into full play, and these are precisely the moments when we are best prepared for the truths it is going to suggest. Such a mechanism is in keeping with the manner in which the course of nature is fulfilled, and bears in its very style the impress of invariability of action. It is no respecter of persons. It neither permits the haughtiest to be free from its monitions, nor leaves the humblest without the consolation of a knowledge of another life. Liable to no mischances, open to no opportunities of being tampered with by the designing or interested, requiring no extraneous human agency for its effect, but always present with each man wherever he may go, it marvellously extracts from vestiges of the impressions of the past overwhelming proofs of the reality of the future, and gathering its power from what would seem to be a most unlikely source, it insensibly leads us, no matter who or where we may be, to a profound belief in the immortal and imperishable, from phantoms that have scarcely made their appearance before they are ready to vanish away."

Immortality of the soul.

From such beginnings the monastic system of Europe arose—that system which presents us with learning in the place of ferocious ignorance, with overflowing charity to mankind in the place of malignant hatred of society. The portly abbot on his easy going palfrey, his hawk upon his fist, scarce looks like

Amelioration of monasticism.

the lineal descendant of the hermit starved into insanity. How wide the interval between the monk of the third and the monk of the thirteenth century—between the caverns of Thebais and majestic monasteries cherishing the relics of ancient learning, the hopes of modern philosophy—between the butler arranging his well-stocked larder, and the jug of cold water and crust of bread. A thousand years had turned starvation into luxury, and alas! if the spoilers of the Reformation are to be believed, had converted visions of loveliness into breathing and blushing realities, who exercised their charms with better effect than of old their phantom sisters had done.

Its final corruptions.

The successive stages to this end may be briefly described. Around the cell of some eremite like Anthony, who fixed his retreat on Mount Colzim, a number of humble imitators gathered, emulous of his austerities and of his piety. A similar sentiment impels them to observe stated hours of prayer. Necessity for supporting the body indicates some pursuit of idle industry, the plaiting of mats or making of baskets. So strong is the instinctive tendency of man to association, that even communities of madmen may organize. Hilarion is said to have been the first who established a monastic community. He went into the desert when he was only fifteen years old. Eremitism thus gave birth to Cœnobitism, and the evils of solitude were removed. Yet still there remained rigorous anchorites who renounced their associated brethren as these had renounced the world, and the monastery was surrounded by their circle of solitary cells—a Laura, it was called. In Egypt, the sandy deserts on each side of the rich valley of the river offered great facilities for such a mode of life: that of Nitria was full of monks, the climate being mild and the wants of man easily satisfied. It is said that there were at one time in that country of these religious recluses not fewer than seventy-six thousand males and twenty-seven thousand females. With countless other uncouth forms, under the hot sun of that climate they seemed to be spawned from the mud of the Nile. As soon as from some celebrated hermitage a monastery had formed, the associates submitted to the rules of brotherhood. Their meal, eaten

The modifications of eremitism.

Number of anchorites.

in silence, consisted of bread and water, oil, and a little salt. The bundle of papyrus which had served the monk for a seat by day, while he made his baskets or mats, served him for a pillow by night. Twice he was roused from his sleep by the sound of a horn to offer up his prayers. The culture of superstition was compelled by inexorable rules. A discipline of penalties, confinement, fasting, whipping, and, at a later period even mutilation, was inflexibly administered.

Spread of monasticism from Egypt.

From Egypt and Syria monachism spread like an epidemic. It was first introduced into Italy by Athanasius, assisted by some of the disciples of Anthony; but Jerome, whose abode was in Palestine, is celebrated for the multitude of converts he made to a life of retirement. Under his persuasion, many of the high-born ladies of Rome were led to the practice of monastic habits, as far as was possible, in secluded spots near that city, on the ruins of temples, and even in the Forum. Some were induced to retreat to the Holy Land, after bestowing their wealth for pious purposes. The silent monk insinuated himself into the privacy of families for the purpose of making proselytes by stealth. Soon there was not an unfrequented island in the Mediterranean, no desert shore, no gloomy valley, no forest, no glen, no volcanic crater, that did not witness exorbitant selfishness made the rule of life. There were multitudes of hermits on the desolate coasts of the Black Sea. They abounded from the freezing Tanais to the sultry Tabenné. In rigorous personal life and in supernatural power the West acknowledged no inferiority to the East; his admiring imitators challenged even the desert of Thebais to produce the equal of Martin of Tours. The solitary anchorite was soon supplanted by the cœnobitic establishment, the monastery. It became a fashion among the rich to give all that they had to these institutions for the salvation of their own souls. There was now no need of basket-making or the weaving of mats. The brotherhoods increased rapidly. Whoever wanted to escape from the barbarian invaders, or to avoid the hardships of serving in the imperial army—whoever had become discontented with his worldly affairs, or saw in those dark times no inducements in a home and family of his own, found in the monastery a sure retreat. The number of these religious houses eventually became very great. They were usually placed on the most charming and advantageous sites, their solidity and splendour illustrating the necessity of erecting durable habitations for societies that were immortal. It often fell out that the Church laid claim to the services of some distinguished monk. It was significantly observed that the road to ecclesiastical elevation lay through the monastery porch, and often ambition contentedly wore for a season the cowl, that it might seize more surely the mitre.

Increase of the religious houses.

Though the monastic system of the East included labour, it was greatly inferior to that of the West in that particular. The Oriental monk, at first making selfishness his rule of life, and his own salvation the grand object, though all the world else should perish, in his maturer period occupied his intellectual powers in refined disputations of theology. Too often he exhibited his physical strength in the furious riots he occasioned in the streets of the great cities. He was a fanatic and insubordinate. On the other hand, the Occidental monk showed far less disposition for engaging in the discussion of things above reason, and expended his strength in useful and honourable labour. Beneath his hand the wilderness became a garden. To a considerable extent this difference was due to physiological peculiarity, and yet it must not be concealed that the circumstances of life in the two cases were not without their effects. The old countries of the East, with their worn-out civilization and worn-out soil, offered no inducements comparable with the barbarous but young and fertile West, where to the ecclesiastic the most lovely and inviting lands were open. Both, however, coincided in this, that they regarded the affairs of life as presenting perpetual interpositions of a providential or rather supernatural kind—angels and devils being in continual conflict for the soul of every man, who might become the happy prize of the one or the miserable prey of the other. These spiritual powers were perpetually controlling the course of nature and giving rise to prodigies. The measure of holiness in a saint was the number of

Difference of the Eastern and Western monk.

miracles he had worked. Thus, in the life of St. Benedict, it is related that when his nurse Cyrilla let fall a stone sieve, her distress was changed into rejoicing by the prayer of the holy child, at which the broken parts came together and were made whole; that once on receiving his food in a basket, let down to his otherwise inaccessible cell, the devil vainly tried to vex him by breaking the rope; that once Satan, assuming the form of a blackbird, nearly blinded him by the flapping of his wings; that once, too, the same tempter appeared as a beautiful Roman girl, to whose fascinations, in his youth, St. Benedict had been sensible, and from which he now hardly escaped by rolling himself among thorns. Once, when his austere rules and severity excited the resentment of the monastery over which he was abbot, the brethren—for monks have been known to do such things—attempted to poison him, but the cup burst asunder as soon as he took it into his hands. When the priest Florentius, being wickedly disposed, attempted to perpetrate a like crime by means of an adulterated loaf, a raven carried away the deadly bread from the hand of St. Benedict. Instructed by the devil, the same Florentius drove from his neighbourhood the holy man, by turning into the garden of his monastery seven naked girls; but scarcely had the saint taken to flight, when the chamber in which his persecutor lived fell in and buried him beneath its ruins, though the rest of the house was uninjured. Under the guidance of two visible angels, who walked before him, St. Benedict continued his journey to Monte Casino, where he erected a noble monastery; but even here miracles did not cease; for Satan bewitched the stones, so that it was impossible for the masons to move them until they were released by powerful prayers. A boy, who had stolen from the monastery to visit his parents was not only struck dead by God for his offence, but the consecrated ground threw forth his body when they attempted to bury it; nor could it be made to rest until consecrated bread was laid upon it. Two garrulous nuns, who had been excommunicated by St. Benedict for their perverse prating, chanced to be buried in the church. On the next administration of the sacrament, when the

Legends of Western saints.

deacon commanded all those who did not communicate to depart, the corpses rose out of their graves and walked forth from the church.

The character of these miracles.

Volumes might be filled with such wonders, which edified the religious for centuries, exacting implicit belief, and being regarded as of equal authority with the miracles of the Holy Scriptures.

Rise and progress of monastic orders.

Though monastic life rested upon the principle of social abnegation, monasticism, in singular contradiction thereto, contained within itself the principle of organization. As early as A.D. 370, St. Basil, the Bishop of Cæsarea, incorporated the hermits and cœnobites of his diocese into one order, called after him the Basilian. One hundred and fifty years later, St. Benedict, under a milder rule, organised those who have passed under his name, and found for them occupation in suitable employments of manual and intellectual labour. In the ninth century, another Benedict revised the rule of the order, and made it more austere. Offshoots soon arose, as those of Clugni, A.D. 900; the Carthusians, A.D. 1084; the Cistercians, A.D. 1098. A favourite pursuit among them being literary labour, they introduced great improvements in the copying of manuscripts; and in their illumination and illustration are found the germs of the restoration of painting and the invention of cursive handwriting. St. Benedict enjoined his order to collect books. It has been happily observed that he forgot to say anything about their character, supposing that they must all be religious. The Augustinians were founded in the eleventh century. They professed, however, to be a restoration of the society founded ages before by St. Augustine.

The Benedictines.

The influence to which monasticism attained may be judged of from the boast of the Benedictines that "Pope John XXII., who died in 1334, after an exact inquiry, found that, since the first rise of the order, there had been of it 24 popes, near 200 cardinals, 7000 archbishops, 15,000 bishops, 15,000 abbots of renown, above 4000 saints, and upward of 37,000 monasteries. There have been likewise, of this order, 20 emperors and 10 empresses, 47 kings and above 50 queens, 20 sons of emperors, and 48 sons of kings; about 100 princesses, daughters of kings and emperors; besides dukes, marquises, earls, countesses, etc., innumerable. The order has produced a vast number of authors and other learned men. Their Rabanus set up the school of Germany. Their Alcuin founded the University of Paris. Their Dionysius Exiguus perfected ecclesiastical computation. Their Guido invented the scale of music; their Sylvester, the organ. They boasted to have produced Anselm, Ildefonsus, and the Venerable Bede."

We too often date the Christianization of a community from the conversion of its sovereign, but it is not in the nature of things that that should change the hearts of men. Of what avail is it if a barbarian chieftain drives a horde of his savages through the waters of a river by way of extemporaneous or speedy baptism? Such outward forms are of little moment. It was mainly by the monasteries that to the peasant class of Europe was pointed out the way of civilization. The devotions and charities; the austerities of the brethren; their abstemious meal; their meagre clothing, the cheapest of the country in which they lived; their shaven heads, or the cowl which shut out the sight of sinful objects; the long staff in their hands; their naked feet and legs; their passing forth on their journeys by twos, each a watch on his brother; the prohibitions against eating outside of the wall of the monastery, which had its own mill, its own bakehouse, and whatever was needed in an abstemious domestic economy; their silent hospitality to the wayfarer, who was refreshed in a separate apartment; the lands around their buildings turned from a wilderness into a garden, and, above all, labour exalted and ennobled by their holy hands, and celibacy, for ever, in the eye of the vulgar, a proof of separation from the world and a sacrifice to heaven—these were the things that arrested the attention of the barbarians of Europe, and led them on to civilization. In our own material age, the advocates of the monastery have plaintively asked, Where now shall we find an asylum for the sinner who is sick of the world—for the man of contemplation in his old age, or for the statesman who is tired of affairs? It was through the leisure procured by their wealth that the monasteries

Civilization of Europe by the monks.

produced so many cultivators of letters, and transmitted to us the literary relics of the old times. It was a fortunate day when the monk turned from the weaving of mats to the copying of manuscripts—a fortunate day when he began to compose those noble hymns and strains of music which will live for ever. From the "Dies Iræ" there rings forth grand poetry even in monkish Latin. The perpetual movements of the monastic orders gave life to the Church. The Protestant admits that to a resolute monk the Reformation was due.

Their later intellectual influence.

With these pre-eminent merits, the monastic institution had its evils. Through it was spread that dreadful materialization of religion which, for so many ages, debased sacred things; through it that worse than pagan apotheosis, which led to the adoration—for such it really was—of dead men; through it were sustained relics and lying miracles, a belief in falsehoods so prodigious as to disgrace the common sense of man. The apostles and martyrs of old were forgotten; nay, even the worship of God was forsaken for shrines that could cure all diseases, and relics that could raise the dead. Through it was developed that intense selfishness which hesitated at no sacrifice either of the present or the future, so far as this life is concerned, in order to insure personal happiness in the next--a selfishness which, in the delusion of the times, passed under the name of piety; and the degree of abasement from the dignity of a man was made the measure of the merit of a monk.

Their materialization of religion.

END OF VOL. I.

www.ingramcontent.com/pod-product-compliance
Lightning Source LLC
La Vergne TN
LVHW021130110826
845150LV00005B/988

* 9 7 8 1 4 2 5 5 5 0 1 6 5 *